Colonial
American
Poetry

Colonial American Poetry

Edited with Introductions by

Kenneth Silverman

HAFNER PUBLISHING CO.

NEW YORK and LONDON

1 9 6 8

For Sharon

The Text

I have followed a conservative editorial policy. As often as possible I have reproduced the earliest extant editions of the various poems included here, and in some instances have freshly transcribed the manuscripts. In a few cases, noted in the text, I have used modern editions. I have lowered superscript letters and abbreviations, and transformed consonantal *u*, vocalic *v*, initial double *f*, initial *VV*, and long *s* to *u*, *v*, *F*, *W*, and *s*. In only a very few places where the original texts showed clearcut typographical or scribal errors have I silently amended them. Otherwise I have tried to retain the original spelling and punctuation of the poems, and as nearly as possible their contemporary appearance.

Many of the poems call for a large number of footnotes, but for the sake of economy I have expanded allusions and defined obsolete or archaic words only when such information seemed absolutely necessary to make a passage intelligible. For the same reason I have not added a bibliography. The reader may profitably consult the ever-growing bibliographies of colonial studies in *PMLA, American Literature, The New England Quarterly, Seventeenth Century News,* and *Early American Literature Newsletter.*

I would like to thank Professor James Clifford of Columbia University and Robert Cross, President of Hunter College, for their helpful reading of the introductory essays. My thanks also go to Professor John Mulder, my colleague at New York University, for his rendering of Henricus Selijn's Latin poem, his revisions of the Dutch poems, and his translations of several Latin epigraphs. Finally, with long-anticipated pleasure, I enter my thanks to Professor Lewis Leary of Columbia University. Anyone writing on early American literature must be sensible of his rich and painstaking scholarship. But on top of it I owe him innumerable personal favors and some lasting inspirations. His generosity is inexhaustible.

K.S.

Acknowledgments

The editor thanks the following institutions, publishers, and copyright owners for permission to use poems reprinted in this anthology:

Harvard University Press—Samuel Torrey's elegy on William Tompson, in Kenneth B. Murdock, ed., *Handkerchiefs from Paul* (Cambridge, 1927).

Historical Society of Pennsylvania—Nicholas Scull's "The Junto."

Houghton Mifflin Company—*New-Englands Crisis;* epitaph on "Gulielmi Tompsoni"; elegy on John Winthrop, in Howard Judson Hall, ed., *Benjamin Tompson His Poems* (Boston, 1924).

Professor Harold S. Jantz and The American Antiquarian Society—Thomas Tillam's "Uppon the first sight of New-England"; anonymous elegy on Thomas Dudley; John Fiske's elegies on John Cotton, Thomas Hooker, Samuel Sharpe, and Anne Griffin; Daniel Henchman's elegy on William Phips; John James's "Of John Bunyans Life," in *The First Century of New England Verse* (Worcester, 1944).

Professor Thomas H. Johnson and the *New England Quarterly*—Edward Taylor's "Meditation 10"; "Meditation 40"; "Upon the Sweeping Flood," in "Some Edward Taylor Gleanings," *New England Quarterly, XVI* (1943).

Library Company of Philadelphia—Joseph Breintnal's "On the lately discover'd Wild Raspberries."

Princeton University Press and Thomas H. Johnson—Edward Taylor's "Prologue"; "Meditation 1"; "The Reflexion"; "Meditation 6"; "Meditation 29"; "Meditation 3"; "Meditation 82"; "Huswifery"; "Upon Wedlock"; "Meditation 56"; "An Address to the Soul," in Thomas H. Johnson, ed., *The Poetical Works of Edward Taylor* (Princeton, 1948), reprinted by permission of Princeton University Press.

Rhode Island Historical Society—John Saffin's "Epithalmium"; "From Virginia"; "Letter to his Dear Martha"; "Cankers touch fairest fruites"; "The Painters Premonition"; "on a Rogue"; "To . . . Hubbard"; "A lamentation"; "One presenting a rare Book"; "Consideratus Considerandus."

South Caroliniana Library of the University of South Carolina—"Description of Charles Town in 1769."

State of North Carolina Department of Archives and History—William Byrd's "Long has the Furious Priest."

University of North Carolina Library—William Byrd's "A Song"; "Upon a Sigh"; "Upon a Fart"; "A Poem upon Some Ladys," in the Southern Historical Collection.

Yale University Library *Gazette*—Edward Taylor's "Meditation 32."

Yale University Press—Edward Taylor's "Meditation 44"; "Meditation 66"; "Meditation 161A," in Donald E. Stanford, ed., *The Poems of Edward Taylor* (New Haven, 1960).

Special thanks are owing to the various copyright holders of Edward Taylor's poems, and in particular to Professor Donald E. Stanford of Louisiana State University, for allowing me to create a uniform text of the poems by using Professor Stanford's edition throughout.

CONTENTS

The Puritan Elegy

Edward Taylor

Later New England Verse

Verse of the Middle Colonies

The Rising Empire

Introduction

I readily admit that the Americans have no poets;
I cannot allow that they have no poetic ideas.

—ALEXIS DE TOCQUEVILLE,
Democracy in America

Is colonial verse English or American? Few colonial poets used diction any different from that of contemporary English writers. None tried new forms. Most were born in England. Yet the title of Anne Bradstreet's volume shows that from the beginning they were conscious of composing in a new world, one that demanded a Tenth Muse to define its unique contribution to human culture. And, as almost no English poets did, they often wrote about America.

The discovery and settlement of America struck the imagination of sensitive Europeans with the impact of a new physical system, or the first flight to a planet. It renewed and encouraged speculation on unlimited human possibility: "in the beginning," John Locke wrote, "all the world was America. . . ." [1] Much colonial verse, however derivative, however awkward, is pervaded by a poetic sense of the new world. That statement perhaps rests on a sentimental view of the 'poetic.' But this anthology is not designed to show off the literary virtues of colonial verse nor to expose its obvious shortcomings. More often than not, my choice of poems has been guided by the question, What did the settlers who cared enough to write about it think about America? Indeed, an anthology of colonial verse might be compiled presenting the poetry more favorably as poetry. Quite a few colonial poets wrote more skillfully than some included here, for instance William Livingston in "Philosophic Solitude." But they did not write about the place they knew. It could be said that their verse is more crude because it is more remote from their experience. It is certainly less American.

This anthology, then, is designed to disclose the subtle and often contrary feelings and assumptions about America which its earliest

1

settlers had. I would call the value of the poems not antiquarian, but historical. They reveal how workable that theoretical America which Locke compared to the beginnings of all the world, seemed to the people who first lived in the actual place. Are these poems American? Certainly in the seventeenth and most of the eighteenth centuries there was no national character, indeed no nation. Yet those colonists who delighted in supposing what the country should and might be, grew aware of a surrounding culture to which they could meaningfully refer; and their awareness changed English colonists into colonial Englishmen with strong local loyalties,[2] loyalties which by everywhere coloring their verse make it, if not American, not English either.

In the brief introductions I have tried to show what colonial poets thought about America by explicating the imagery in which they dramatized and entertained their thoughts. This imagery was partly invented from what they felt was missing in English life, and more largely borrowed from current conventions of English verse. To some extent the conventions determined their thoughts; but their thought and experience also changed the conventions. For example, the hope many colonists voiced that America would become "The Athens of Mankind" was based on the theory of the westward migration of the arts from the classical world to England. But the expression of this hope in any one poem is colored by local loyalties and provincial enthusiasms, and the image of thriving commercial Philadelphia as the Athens of Mankind has little in common with neoclassic ideals of the cultured life. Three such ideal descriptions of America appear widely in colonial verse: The Wilderness Zion, The Athens of Mankind, and The Rising Empire—America as a religious sanctuary, as a repository for the culture of the whole western world, as a wealthy imperial power.

Each projection of the ideal America implied its own politically and emotionally satisfying description of national origins. Insular British origins were incommensurate with the grandiose possible America of the 1770's, whose destiny was transcontinental and even imperial. Puritan settlers of the Wilderness Zion believed themselves and their mission descended, temperamentally at least, from the ancient Hebrews. As the Athens of Mankind, America was fulfilling a process begun in antiquity. As a Rising Empire, its past was diffuse, prehistoric, a kind of myth. The growth and substance of these ideals are too complex for this introduction, but they are described more fully in the subsequent essays. Proclamations of the Wilderness Zion were muted around 1700; the Athens of Mankind announced itself around 1730; the first fanfare for Imperial America was sounded in Freneau and Brackenridge's commencement poem of 1771. The dates are approximate and do not suggest the important regional variations: The Wilderness Zion was a New England ideal only; Pennsylvania poets thought Philadelphia would be The Athens of Mankind, but Southerners had their doubts about Charleston and Williamsburg.

This continuing interest in America gives the history of colonial verse an inner unity. Yet it disguises how freakish and obscure its development in fact was: how full of eccentric survivals; how free of dramatic events, dates, movements, literary groups or influential figures to signal important shifts; how baffling to even the vaguest classifications of literary history. Moses Coit Tyler's monumental study of colonial writing betrays by its lack of revealing categories of discussion the disunity of the subject itself. There existed isolated verse writers, who were not primarily verse writers anyway, writing at different times about unrelated things. Their verse presents its own problems. Criticism is left a little breathless by such a poem as appeared in the *American Magazine,* "Attempted from the Latin of an American Indian." Much of the verse—by one estimate, as much as four-fifths of it—is lost or unrecorded.[3] And much of what remains amounts to direct imitation without self-expression, or that primitivism one finds in other colonial arts: vision direct but crude, honest but graceless, moving but semi-literate, escaping by its primitivism any literary category whatsoever.

No dates are telling. A few, barely worth remembering, mark the founding of magazines, newspapers, and colleges. *The Maryland Gazette* made available the poems of Richard Lewis; the college of Philadelphia drew together under William Smith's guidance Thomas Godfrey, Nathaniel Evans, and Francis Hopkinson. The dates of some political events have literary consequence. In 1660 the Commonwealth was effectually ended. After that time, New England was less a religious than a commercial venture, a progress accompanied by a torrent of jeremiads in verse and prose. The next suggestive date is 1760: the coronation of George III; the publication of the Ossianic *Fragments of Ancient Poetry* (a sign of the new morbid subjectivity); and a sudden extraordinary interest in drama. (While before 1760 few plays were printed in America, in 1761 at least half the literary product of American presses consists of plays.)[4] To the same date gather the first American publication of Goldsmith (1768) and, of real importance, the noticeable stirrings of literary nationalism. By 1769, "Timothy Sobersides" tells readers of the *Pennsylvania Chronicle* his wish that "we shall no longer be so entirely beholden to the Mother Country, as we have hitherto been, for all the articles of *Poetical Haberdashery;* but that we may, at length, become able to furnish ourselves with a sufficiency of *sing-song,* the produce of our own *labour* and *Industry."*

Perhaps this political calendar is only imposed on the poetry by violence, having nothing to do with those growths and deaths of a style, which constitute the real periods of literary history. Yet the three versions of America that make up the inner unity of colonial verse arose not merely from changing conventions in English verse or from self-propelled flights of personal imagination. They were allied to actual social and political events in the colonies. It could be shown how rhetorical changes in the poetry parallel growing animosity toward England. The notion of America's prehistoric past, a commonplace of those writers who trumpeted the Rising Empire, certainly derived from the convention of timelessness in eighteenth-century English visionary odes; but it also served to assure the fuming colonists that they were one stock, and the stamp-taxers another.

Still, no single date or figure has any decisive importance. The lack of those institutions and events that commonly make up the literary life of a nation was partly due to the colonial literary situation. Although outlets for verse existed (by 1764, the year of the Sugar Act, twenty-three newspapers; thirty-eight by the time of Lexington and Concord),[5] and although they printed any kind of verse, from elegies and Pindaric odes to smutty fables, and although there was a great volume of verse produced in the colonies, there never was a literary class. In a century and a half of their existence, the colonies supported not one professional imaginative writer. An audience for poetry existed, but it was scattered about. Freight was expensive and risky; so books were published locally. A Philadelphian might as profitably seek readers in London as in Williamsburg—as the one professional writer America produced, James Ralph, did. He quit Philadelphia to become a Grub Street hack (and minor casualty of Pope's *Dunciad*), confirming the advice of another Philadelphian, Benjamin Rush, that "Men who are philosophers or poets, without other pursuits, had better end their days in an old country." [6] Besides, except for local subscriptions to whole volumes, no money was paid for verse; poets sometimes paid editors of periodicals to have their verse inserted.[7]

Then however much verse was written in the colonies, there was never, in any place, a literary atmosphere. Perhaps the testiest description of literary life in the colonies appears in the *Itinerarium* of Dr. Alexander Hamilton, organizer of the Annapolis Tuesday Club, who in 1744 travelled from Maryland to Maine and back for his health. He has been called "the first American to take a holiday";[8] but his dispirited

account leaves one imagining the grueling journey, the perilous backwoods, as no holiday. Hamilton can never find anyone to match his culture. At the Philadelphia Governour's Club he turns up members who
can chat about Cervantes; but his taste, his tone, is ever alien. At a New
York inn he meets a Major Spratt. Carbuncled, phthisticall Spratt, "half
seas over in Liquor," recited his own verses:

> "Gentlemen," said he, "pray take notise now, give good
> attention. It is perhaps the concisest, wittiest, prittiest, epigram
> or epitaph, call it what you will, that you ever heard. Shall I
> get you pen and ink to write it down? Perhaps you mayn't
> remember it else. It is highly worth your noting. Pray observe
> how it runs,—
>
>> Here lyes John Purcell;
>> And whether he be in heaven or in hell,
>> Never a one of us all can tell."

"This poet," Hamilton comments, "asked me very kindly how I did and
took me by the hand, tho I never had seen him in my life before." [9]
Where the literary atmosphere was not crude, as at Annapolis, it was
derivative. Otherwise there was no atmosphere. There was no criticism
to create and sharpen taste. There were no literary centers; no literary
clubs, except a few either frolicsome or over-refined, shallow or sterile.
There was no reading aristocracy except in the South, and that was not
a transplanted aristocracy but a local growth of the merchant class sharing merchant class ideals. So in a land urban one hundred years after its
settlement, poetry flourished only locally. No poem, no writer, ever
made a splash.

Naturally the writer's place was England. As late as 1766 Franklin
could ask the London printer Strahan to "treat" a friend "with the sight
of Samuel Johnson & a few more of your Authors." Americans when
they got to England, Franklin wrote, "have as much curiosity to see a
live author as Englishmen have to see a live ostrich, or Cherokee
Sachem." [10] English influence on colonial culture was very great. News
from the home country, literary excitement abroad, aroused envy and
imitation in local dilettantes already pained by limited awareness and
unglamorous lives. (Those same colonists did not, on the other hand,
like being patronized. The intention of much colonial writing, especially
of promotional verse, was to correct English misconceptions about America: to most Englishmen Americans meant Indians.) A few Englishmen
granted that cultured and even gifted writers existed in the colonies.

Critics in the *Grand Magazine of Universal Intelligence* approvingly reviewed the verse of James Sterling and Thomas Godfrey.[11] Richard Lewis attracted half a dozen favorable notices. But the English were far less impressed by the colonists than the colonists by them. Of the 105 poems printed in the *American Magazine and Historical Chronicle* between 1744-45, thirteen are from the English *Gentleman's Magazine* and sixty-six are from the *London Magazine*.[12] Few are beyond dispute American, and they sound English.

However, this statistical dependence of colonial verse on British is too general an account of English influence in America. American fashion rejected much of British. The Restoration affected only the colonial South. In New England there is scant trace of Wycherly or Congreve, of Fielding, of Gay, Sterne or Smollett. And, as Oldmixon and many writers since have commented, Americans were old-fashioned. American verse not only diverged from English; it fell behind. The cultural lag was a tangible phenomenon in America, where the metaphysical style lasted until 1729, the death of Edward Taylor, a whole century after the death of Taylor's model, George Herbert, and three years after the publication of Pope's *Poems*. Nor by any means did the colonists read English verse as 'part of their heritage' or know it 'in the blood.' They received it under conditions quite unlike those which had brought it into being, and it meant different things to them. Remarking on the popularity of Pope and other English poets in the colonies, Franklin wrote to Strahan that "We are a kind of Posterity in respect to them. We read their Works with perfect impartiality, being at too great distance to be bypassed by the Factions, Parties and Prejudices that prevail among you." [13] The colonist could judge English verse objectively because he had no personal stake in it; and it meant less to him because he had no very clear understanding of its topical allusions.

Thus the colonial poet used English diction and conventions, but had lost contact with the impulses that had demanded expression in those conventions. He was doubly damned when trying to express an unformed culture in which he had no deep roots and that provided him with no literary conventions of its own. He never found a proper voice. He was pulled between the sophisticated tone of cosmopolitan England, whose home affairs meant increasingly less to him, and the raw innocence of his subject, whose affairs meant increasingly more. Personally this bred in him, in Bernard Bailyn's words, "a rootlessness, an alienation either from the higher sources of culture or from the familiar local environment that had formed the personality." [14] As a poet his alienation dictated a certain incongruity between tone and matter. He had to handle alligators and swamps in the balanced couplet, capture the treacherous backwoods in the devices of conventional English pastoral. The Horatian Ode could not comfortably contain what America had to offer:

> —As thro' thy pleasing lawns I stray'd;
> While *Virtue,* like a blooming maid,
>   Employ'd my tho'ts on all her charms)
> From neighb'ring groves, with threat'ning eyes,
> A *Buffalo* of monstrous size,
> Rush'd sudden forth. . . . (James Sterling) [15]

The effect of this is not different from the effect produced when James Fenimore Cooper tried clothing his frontier roughs in Walter Scott's prose. Conditions in eighteenth-century America could not nourish the English ideal of the poet as a man educated, well read, travelled, accustomed to the best society. And the abstract language of much eighteenth-century English poetry resisted immediate naked experience:[16] how could it respond to those exotic marvels of the new world whose singularity writers made known in deliriously interminable catalogues of new concrete nouns. Eighteenth-century meter and diction bespoke a sense of harmony, of moral and philosophical certainty, that settlers on a raw frontier could hardly feel. The urbane voice narrating *The Rape of the Lock* could only be oppressed by American conditions. Here that voice lost its personal authority; it was a mannerism. The jarring effect of much eighteenth-century colonial verse, the reader's sense that the poet has not responded appropriately to the occasion, is the upshot of training a refined and chaste diction on the affairs of unformed towns and wilderness outposts.[17]

This incongruity of tone and matter, this confusion of voice, had one very important consequence. The diction and conventions colonial poets used, both in the seventeenth and eighteenth centuries, after all expressed a certain vision of life, an expectation. But colonial poets had experiences for which their borrowed conventions did not prepare them. That they clung to this language while detailing experiences that were new, often forced them to show that their expectations were not being met and that their experience was not what they wanted it to be. If, like James Sterling, one comes to prize "pleasing lawns," what does he say when a monster buffalo comes running across the grass. What entitles colonial verse to serious consideration is just this lapse between language and experience. For it represents deeper incongruities between character and personality, propaganda and fulfillment, expectation and reality, that are characteristic of American literature as a whole.

What is American about colonial verse? It is the first instance in American literature of the stylization of national consciousness in terms of unfulfilled but meaningful promises. Like much later American writing, it exists to explain or else unconsciously embodies certain disappointments of American life. Michael Wigglesworth's panicked effort to understand why Zion had turned Sodom, and Richard Lewis' abashed sympathy for Southern planters starving amidst lush virgin land, raise the same questions that occupy American writers from James Fenimore Cooper to Allen Ginsberg. In those colonial poems dealing with America there is often a clash between the expected and the given, between the hoped-for Cathay bursting with all conceivable material goods and the Southern starving times that forced Englishmen to become cannibals; between the Utopia whose norm is Peace and the barbarian wilderness where Iroquois smashed infants against trees; between the theory of translation promising the inevitable Progress of Arts to America, and the fact that colonial America was barren of culture.

NOTES

[1] In Daniel Boorstin, *The Americans*: *The Colonial Experience* (New York, 1958), p. 97.

[2] On local loyalties in the formation of national character see James Morton Smith, ed., *Seventeenth Century America*: *Essays in Colonial History* (Chapel Hill, 1959), p. xv.

[3] Lawrence Wroth, *An American Bookshelf 1755* (Philadelphia, 1934), p. 4.

[4] I owe part of this chronology to Foster Damon, *Some Colonial Poets 1609-1760* (Providence, 1947). My own comments on the sudden outpouring of drama may be checked against Charles Evans, *American Bibliography*, 12 vols. (Chicago, 1903-1934).

[5] Arthur M. Schlesinger, *Prelude to Independence*: *The Newspaper War on Britain 1764-1776* (New York, 1958), p. 52.

[6] *The Letters of Benjamin Rush*, ed. L. H. Butterfield (Princeton, 1951), I, 550.

[7] Hennig Cohen, *The South-Carolina Gazette 1732-1775* (Columbia, S.C., 1953), p. 10.

[8] George Stuart Gordon, *Anglo-American Literary Relations* (London, 1942), p. 23.

[9] Alexander Hamilton, *Gentleman's Progress*: *The Itinerarium of Dr. Alexander Hamilton,* ed. Carl Bridenbaugh (Chapel Hill, 1948), p. 81.

[10] Benjamin Franklin, *Works,* ed. John Bigelow (New York, 1904), V, 130. William Byrd went to England five times, William Smith three. See William L. Sachse, *The Colonial American in Britain* (Madison, Wis., 1956).

[11] C. Lennart Carlson, "A Further Note on Thomas Godfrey in England," *American Literature*, IX (November 1937), 75.

[12] Tabulated in the unpublished Master's essay (Columbia, 1933) by Samuel H. Levine, "The Verse in *The American Magazine and Historical Chronicle* Sept. 1744-Aug. 1745," p. 28.

[13] Benjamin Franklin, *Works*, ed. Albert Henry Smyth (New York, 1905), II, 242.

[14] John Clive and Bernard Bailyn, "England's Cultural Provinces: Scotland and America," *William and Mary Quarterly*, 3d Ser., XI (1954), 213.

[15] I have thought it unnecessary to annotate quotations from poems included in the anthology. In all such cases the author or title or both are given in the text.

[16] See James Sutherland, *A Preface to Eighteenth Century Poetry* (Oxford, 1948), *passim*.

[17] Perhaps, as Clive and Bailyn suggest, the revealing comparison to be drawn is between America and Scotland, England's 'cultural provinces.' Boston, they point out, was more like Edinburgh than like London; and there is a suggestive similarity in social origins between the Scottish and American literatti. It might be argued, however, that Scottish poets need have experienced no such loss of voice. They had an established dialect tradition that was something apart from English verse.

Promotional Verse

A Grand-childe to earths Paradize is borne,
Well lim'd, well nerv'd, faire, rich, sweete, yet forlorne.

—WILLIAM MORRELL,
Nova Anglia (London, 1625).

The earliest verse from America was written to promote settlement. It told enticingly what the new world was like and counteracted criticism against it. However unadorned and crude, promotional literature was very popular. Thomas Harriot's *Brief Report,* the first English book on America, was reprinted seventeen times in twenty-five years. The appeals to prospective settlers varied by region, from decade to decade, and according to the audience addressed.[1] The promotional literature of Georgia, for instance, is alone in its appeal to philanthropic motives.

While in fact there probably were as many combinations of motives as emigrants, three appeals became especially popular: to virtú, piety, and prosperity. The poems in this section illustrate each of them, often more than one. As for virtú, "Newes from Virginia" praises settlement as an adventure for "brave Souldiers," "gallant worthy wights."

That refining element of virtú which lends politeness and grace is also guaranteed. The prospective emigrant can enhance his tone by comporting with the "eight hundred worthy men, / some Noble, all of fashion" who presumably dwell in the colony. Although some historians have minimized religion as a moving force in the migrations, many settlers professed a sacred purpose.[2] In the same poem, Virginia is being settled to "glorifie the Lord." And this pious motive dispels the odium of expatriation: New York's first poet, Jacob Steendam, asks "Is God not over all? the heavens ever wide?" Still more insistent is the appeal to wealth and prosperity. In America one can make out. All the promotional poems list the plants and animals comprising the new world's fabulous abundance. Here, Richard Rich promises, "he that wants shall have reliefe," and enjoy to satiety goods that are in England "dainty."

11

John Holme makes the same appeal for Pennsylvania: a man can earn money working with his hands, own a nice house and, a crucial point, land. England is too crowded. In America, land is superabundant and "each poor man may make some his own."

The lures of adventure, God, and wealth are no surprise, of course. But promotional verse made another pledge subtler than these and more inclusive. It beckoned to any kind of dissatisfaction. The ultimate promise of the poems is that in America the settler can start again, forget his troubles, and be happy. Jacob Steendam tells prospective New Netherlanders that as the indigent can find wealth, the wealthy can find peace of mind, the melancholy, joy. In Virginia, Richard Rich says, character is reformed: "Those men that *Vagrants* liv'd with us" become useful citizens. John Holme reports that Pennsylvanians have nothing to fear; no political or religious authorities oppress them, they live in pacific content "Whilst Europe broils in war." (The promise of peace is a continuing motif in colonial idealizations of America.) "Our care," Holme says, "is to keep innocent." That is a summary of promotional verse. In America life will be untroubled, an Eden, Steendam actually calls it, whose stores "thrive unguarded," requiring no nurture, where even dangerous animals have become extinct.

We cannot tell how trustingly readers took this. By peddling contentedness, the poets were promising what the country naturally could not, and did not, deliver. From the beginning there was built into the idea of America an unworkable expectation. One wonders whether the writers' repeated vow that "it is truth which I do tell," whether the defensive tone of much promotional verse, does not reflect contemporary gossip that wilderness America was less than Paradise. The wild and contradictory claims of these earliest writings from America forecast that sense of unfulfilled promise which is the main theme of colonial verse. In aspiring to appeal to everyone, in fetching adventurer and bourgeois alike, America had to offer both risk and safety, novelty and comfort. And in the desire to tell what they had seen of the new world, while at the same time alluring settlers, promotional writers made America lushly abundant and arid, treacherous and benign, "well nerv'd, faire, rich, sweete, yet forlorne."

NOTES

[1] In Elizabethan literature the motives are often presented as crass. The distress England felt over Spanish ascendency in the new world she often related to Spanish looting of American gold and silver. In this light America was often called Ind or the Western Ind. In *Tamburlaine* we hear: "Desire of gold, great

sir? / That's to be gotten in the Western Ind." The ideal of America as Ind accounts for the many images of mines in colonial verse. Promotional literature is discussed in Howard Mumford Jones, "The Colonial Impulse," *Proceedings of the American Philosophical Society,* XC (May 1946), 131-161, and in the same author's *O Strange New World* (New York, 1964), pp. 1-71. And see A. L. Rowse, *The Elizabethans and America* (New York, 1959).

[2] This was especially true of the Puritans, who tirelessly discussed their emigration. Kenneth Murdock has commented on how outstanding a feature of New England biographies is the patient attention they give to the migration, treating it "about as seriously as the details of . . . conversion." *Literature and Theology in Colonial New England* (Cambridge, 1949), p. 122. Nearly every one of the many panegyrical verses in Edward Johnson's *Wonder-working Providence* details its subject's motives for emigration.

Richard Rich
(fl. 1609-1610)

"Newes from Virginia"

TEXT: *Newes from* Virginia. *The lost Flocke* Triumphant.
(London, 1610).

*Of the happy arrivall of that famous & worthy knight Sir Thomas Gates
and well reputed and valiant Captaine Newport into England.*

> IT is no idle fabulous tale,
>   nor is it fayned newes:
> For *Truth* herselfe is heere arriv'd,
>   because you should not muse.
> With her, both Gates and *Newport*[1] come,
>   to tell *Report* doth lye:
> Which did devulge unto the world,
>   that they at Sea did dye.
>
> Tis true that Eleaven monthes and more,
>   these gallant worthy wights:
> Was in the Shippe (*Sea-venture* nam'd)
>   depriv'd *Virginia's* sight.
> And bravely did they glyde the maine,
>   till *Neptune* gan to frowne:
> As if a Courser prowdly backt,
>   would throwe his ryder downe.
>
> The Seas did rage, the windes did blowe,
>   distressed were they then:
> Their Ship did leake, her tacklings breake,
>   in daunger were her men.
> But heaven was Pylotte in this storme,
>   and to an Iland nere:
> *Bermoothawes*[2] call'd, conducted then,
>   which did abate their feare.

But yet these Worthies forced were,
    opprest with weather againe:
To runne their Ship betweene two Rockes,
    where she doth still remaine.
And then on shoare the Iland came,
    Inhabited by Hogges:
Some Foule and Tortoyses there were
    they onely had one Dogge

To kill these swyne, to yeild them food
    that little had to eate:
Their store was spent, and all things scant,
    alas they wanted meate.
A thousand hogges that dogge did kill,
    their hunger to sustaine:
And with such foode, did in that Ile
    two and forty weekes remaine.

And there two gallant Pynases,
    did build, of Seader-tree:
The brave *Deliverance* one was call'd,
    of seaventy Tonne was shee.
The other *Patience* had to name,
    her burthen thirty Tonne:
Two only of their men which there,
    pale death did overcome.

And for the losse of those two soules,
    which were accounted deere:
A Sonne and Daughter then was borne
    and were Baptized there.
The two and forty weekes being past,
    They hoyst Sayle and away:
Their Ships with hogs well freighted were,
    their harts with mickle joy.

And so unto *Virginia* came,
    where these brave Souldiers finde
The English-men opprest with greife
    and discontent in minde.
They seem'd distracted and forlorne,

for those two worthyes losse:
Yet at their home returne they joyd,
    among'st them some were crosse.

And in the mid'st of discontent,
    came noble *Delaware*:
He heard the greifes on either part,
    and sett them free from care.
He comforts them and cheeres their hearts,
    that they abound with joy:
He feedes them full and feedes their soules,
    with Gods word every day.

A discreet counsell he creates,
    of men of worthy fame:
That noble *Gates* leiftenant was
    the Admirall had to name.
The worthy Sir George *Somers* knight,
    and others of commaund:
Maister Georg *Pearcy* which is brother,
    unto *Northumberland*.

Sir Fardinando *Wayneman* knight
    and others of good fame:
That noble Lord, his company,
    which to *Virginia* came
And landed there: his number was
    One hundred Seaventy: then
Ad to the rest and they make full,
    foure hundred able men.

Where they unto their labour fall,
    as men that meane to thrive:
Let's pray that heaven may blesse them all
    and keep them long alive.
Those men that *Vagrants* liv'd with us,
    have there deserved well:
Their Governour writes in their praise,
    as divers Letters tel.

And to th' Adventurers thus he writes,
    be not dismayd at all:

For scandall cannot doe us wrong
    God will not let us fall.
Let England knowe our willingnesse,
    for that our worke is good,
Wee hope to plant a Nation,
    where none before hath stood.

To glorifie the Lord tis done,
    and to no other end:
He that would crosse so good a worke,
    to God can be no friend.
There is no feare of hunger here,
    for Corne much store here growes,
Much fish the gallant Rivers yeild,
    tis truth, without suppose.

Great store of Fowle, of Venison,
    of Grapes, and Mulberries,
Of Chesnuts, Walnuts, and such like,
    of fruits and Strawberries,
There is indeed no want at all:
    but some condiciond ill,
That wish the worke should not goe on,
    with words doe seeme to kill.

And for an instance of their store,
    the noble *Delaware,*
Hath for a present hither sent,
    to testifie his care,
In mannaging so good a worke,
    two gallant ships: by name
The *Blessing* and the *Hercules,*
    well fraught, and in the same

Two ships, are these commodities:
    Furres, Sturgeon, Caviare,
Blacke-walnut-tree, and some deale-boords,
    with such they laden are:
Some Pearle, some Wainscot and clapbords,
    with some Sassafras wood:
And Iron promist, for tis true,
    their Mynes are very good.

Then maugre scandall, false report,
	or any opposition
Th'adventurers doe thus devulge:
	to men of good condition:
That he that wants shall have reliefe,
	be he of honest minde:
Apparell, coyne, or any thing,
	to such they will be kinde.

To such as to *Virginia,*
	do purpose to repaire:
And when that they shall thither come,
	each man shall have his share.
Day wages for the Laborer,
	and for his more content,
A house and garden plot shall have,
	besides, t'is further ment

That every man shall have a part,
	and not thereof denaid:
Of generall profit, as if that he
	twelve pounds ten shillings paid,
And he that in Virginia,
	shall copper coyne receive,
For hyer or commodities,
	and will the country leave,

Upon delivery of such coyne,
	Unto the Governour:
Shall by exchange at his returne,
	be by their Treasurer
Paid him in London at first sight,
	no man shall cause to grieve:
For 'tis their generall will and wish
	That every man should live.

The number of Adventurers,
	that are for this Plantation:
Are full eight hundred worthy men,
	some Noble, all of fashion.
Good, discreete, their worke is good,

and as they have begun:
May Heaven assist them in their worke,
and thus our newes is done.

John Holme

(? -1701)

From
"A True Relation of the Flourishing State
of Pennsylvania."

TEXT: *Bulletin of the Historical Society of Pennsylvania*
(1845), pp. 161-180.

THE INTRODUCTION.

Good people all, who dwell far off or near,
And do desire the truth from hence to hear,
Mark well [the] things which to you I relate,
They will inform you of our happy state.
Tis now ten years, as many know full well,
Since I came into this good land to dwell,
And I have often travelled up and down,
And made my observations at each town.
The truth of matters I well understand,
And thereby know how to describe this land.
All those of you who hither do resort
Will find the truth of what I do report;
Nay, when you come, and have our country seen,
Then you will be like unto Sheba's Queen,
Who, when to Solomon she did resort,
To know the truth of what some did report,
She did confess that what she did behold
Was more by half than had been to her told.
Also, when I have finished my relation
In j[ust] commending of this brave plantation,
Those who [do] come from far this place to view,

May say I [did] not give it half its due;
I know there's many things which I omit—
There may be many more which I forget—
All which to add would make a book so large
The purchase of it would be too much charge;
My matter in short compass I will bring,
Observe it well, for now it doth begin.

THE LAND LARGE AND CHEAP.

This land is large and cheap, as is well known,
So that each poor man may make some his own,
Enjoy it whilst he lives, and at the end
Bestow it on his children or his friend.

GOODNESS OF THE SOIL.

The soil is good, as plainly doth appear,
What grows in England doth or may grow here;
Yea here are many things grow for our use
Which we know English ground will not produce.
Here's store of timber trees of the best sort,
Both for our use and also to transport;
Cedar, Beech, Maple, and Black Walnut fine
The Ash, Oak, Hickory, and sweet scented Pine;
With such abundance more, both great and small,
That scarcely any man can name them all.

[There follow verse paragraphs on gardens, local plants, animals, and
building.]

INHABITANTS.

If you desire to understand
Who first inhabited this land,
Twas Indians whose skins do look
As black as bacon dried in smoke.
They take no care, nor fear no want;
When they drink rum they sing and rant.

They lay but little up in store,
And when that's spent they seek for more.
The women they do plant and weed
Some Indian corn, to serve their need.
The men go out to hunt and fish.
And bring home food to fill their dish;
They furnish us with flesh and skins,
Of bucks and divers other things.
What clothes they wear are quickly made—
They do not help the tailors trade.
Like idle heathens they do live—
This short account of them I give.
Here's many Sweeds, some Finns and Dutch,
Whose trade with Indians was much,
Before the government of Penn,
But since, here are some other men
Who do not think it is unfair
To strike in with them for a share.
Here are some Germans up and down,
Besides the settlers of a town.
A town here is that's long and large,
All builded at the cost and charge
Of those stout Germans, who can work
As hard as slaves under the Turk,
Although here's no need of such toil,
We live in such a fertile soil.
Here are some Scots who think no shame
To own the country whence they came;
But I do think they have more wit
Than ever to return to it.
Here's Irish, French, some of all sorts,
Fast unto this good land resorts;
But greatest number came here when
The King granted Governer Penn
To be Chief Lord and Ruler here:
Then multitudes hither did steer,
And the most part of them indeed
Are English people, or Welsh breed.
The Welshmen mostly thrive amain,
They need not go to Wales again;
The richer sort bring store of stuff

Upon which they live well enough.
The poor man he soon understands
That he, by working with his hands,
Gets money faster here by much
Than he himself and two more such
Could do before he did come here,
So they on with pleasant cheer.

[Two verse paragraphs on Barbados and Bermuda follow.]

UPON THIS CONTINENT.

Upon this brave large continent,
Remote from us some do repent
That they at first settled not here;
But now this way some of them steer.
Carolina and New England,
As we may see and understand,
Are much in love with this good place,
And think it to be no disgrace
To leave their lands and come thus far
To dwell with us at Delawar.

IMPROVEMENTS.

Some drives on as if fully bent
To outdo all this continent;
And so they do I understand,
For they build houses and clear land
So fast as was not known before,
Since Christian men dwelt on this shore;
As such of New England knows well
Who do come here to buy and sell;
Great store of wheat and other grain
They fetch from us without disdain,
As they have done full nine year,
As is well known unto most here.

TOWNS.

The city where most people dwell,
Is PHILADELPHIA, known full well;
It is a famous place indeed
To be built here with so much speed.
This lovely city it doth stand
Upon a stately neck of land,
Between two rivers, deep and wide,
Where gallant ships may safely ride.
Our houses are comely and good,
Some few of them are built with wood,
But the most part are stone and brick,
Placed in order pretty thick.
Upon this river Delawar,
Extending in length very far,
Also in breadth every way,
Strangers do wonder, and some say
What means these Quakers thus to raise
These stately fabrics to their praise,
Since we well know and understand,
When they were in their native land,
They were in prison trodden down—
And can they now build such a town?
They wonder thus at what is past,
But what will they say of the last,
When all the buildings are quite done,
Which are intended and begun,
Here's many good houses in hand,
And many more, I understand,
Will be begun now with all speed,
To make a famous place indeed.
Here are more towns, but not so great,
Where many Welsh take up their seat,
And lives in love with much content,
That they came here do not repent.
Some towns and farms had settlement
Long time before Penn's government.
But since, they are improved much
By English, Scotchmen, Welsh and Dutch.

[There follow verse paragraphs on hops, pottery, brick, mines, isinglass, loadstone, linen, wool, saw-mills, and corn mills.]

THE LAWS.

If any finds fault with our laws,
As if in them there were some flaws,
Let all such know that our foundation
Is the laws o' th' English nation,
Some few added to serve this place,
Which can to us be no disgrace.
They being built upon God's law,
Are fit to keep bad men in awe:
I hope they do all good men please,
For under them we live at ease.
We have no proud Lord Bishops here,
Nor do we need their courts to fear;
Which [we] too well did understand
When we were in our native land,
Were such a cruel plague and pest
That for them we could seldom rest.
The priests, that persecuting crew,
Who craveth what is not their due,
In this place they can never thrive,
Because our laws allow no tithe;
Each man here freely serves his God
Free from the persecutor's rod.

OF OUR PRESERVATION FROM ENEMIES.

Some may think we in danger stand
Of enemies by sea and land,
And that we are such silly sheep
We take no care our goods to keep.
'Tis true there are some fighting men,
Who thus upbraid us now and then;
But I do say unto them this,
And wish them not to take't amiss—
Self-preservation we do seek

By all such means as we see meet;
Our care is to keep innocent,
That none within our government
Hurt any people, weak or strong,
To give them cause to seek our wrong.
Whilst we love and obey our God,
We [do] not dread the wicked's rod.
If we lose what is transitory,
God can give lasting things in glory;
And tho' by bloody hands we die,
Yet we may live eternally.
God hitherto preserved us, when
Distresses came on fighting men;
And so we hope he will do still.
Although we have no mind to kill
The creatures that are of our kind;
We are not of a bloody mind:
Yet know that we are men of reason,
And may resist at a fit season;
If from our rights they would thrust us,
For not fighting do not trust us.
I know some men lives on this shore—
Perhaps there may be many more—
Who think they break not God's command
When they resist, with a strong hand,
The greedy wolf who comes to rent,
As here you have a precedent.

[A verse narrative of a pirate raid follows, and sections on schools, Quakers, and precious stones.]

THE WORST OF PENNSYLVANIA.

But perhaps some men now will say,
Thy pen runs fast, I pray thee stay;
Thou givest this land a good report,
But before thither I resort
Let me now have as full relation
Of all that's bad in your plantation;
Let all the worst be open laid,

Of which as yet is nothing said.
My friend, wherever thou dost live,
This answer unto thee I give:
My business now is to remove
Some false reports, and to disprove
Those lying tongues, I understand,
Brought ill report on this good land.
However, notwithstanding I
Am willing thee to gratify,
For were I in the greatest haste,
Much time in this I need not waste;
The most and worst I can unfold,
Is some extremes of heat and cold,
Which now and then do change so quick
It almost makes some people sick,
Who do not of themselves take care,
Nor heed what clothing they do wear.
But such as are prudently wise
In meat, drink, clothes and exercise,
May have their health here full as well
As any place that I can tell.

CONCLUSION.

Poor people here stand not in fear
    The nuptial knot to tie,
The working hand in this good land
    Can never want supply.

If children dear increase each year,
    So doth our crops likewise,
Of stock and trade, such gain is made
    That none do want supplies.

Whoe'er thou art, take in good part
    These lines which I have penned,
It is true love which doth me move
    Them unto thee to send.

Some false reports hinders resorts
    Of those who would come here;

Therefore in love I would remove
 That which puts them in fear.

Here's many say they bless the day
 That they did see Penn's wood;
To cross the main back home again,
 They do not think it good.

But here they'll bide and safely hide
 Whilst Europe broils in war;
The fruit of the curse which may prove worse
 Than hath been yet by far.

For why should we, who quiet be,
 Return into the noise
Of fighting men, who now and then,
 Great multitudes destroys.

I bid farewell to all who dwell
 In England or elsewhere;
Wishing good speed when they indeed
 Set forward to come here.

Jacob Steendam

(1616-1671?)

"Spurring-Verses"

TEXT: Henry Cruse Murphy, *Jacob Steendam* (The Hague, 1861), pp. 54-59, emended by John Mulder.

You poor, who know not how your living to obtain;
You affluent, who seek in mind to be content;
Choose you New Netherland, which no one shall disdain;
Before your time and strength here fruitlessly are spent.
There have you other ends, your labor to incite;
Your work, will generous soils, with usury, requite.[1]

New Netherland's the flow'r, the noblest of all lands;
With richest blessings crowned, where milk and honey flow;
By the most High of All, with doubly lib'ral hands
Endowed; yea filled up full, with what may thrive and grow.
The air, the earth, the sea, each pregnant with its gift,
The needy, without trouble, from distress to lift.

The birds obscure the sky, so numerous in their flight;
The animals roam wild, and flatten down the ground;
The fish swarm in the waters, and exclude the light;[2]
The oysters there, than which none better can be found,
Are piled up, heap on heap, till islands they attain;
And vegetation clothes the forest, mead and plain.

You have a portion there which costs not pains or gold:
But if you labor give, then shall you also share
(With trust in Him who you from want does there uphold)
A rich reward, in time, for all your toil and care.
In cattle grain and fruit, and every other thing;
Whereby you always have great cause His praise to sing.

What see you in your houses, towns and Fatherland?
Is God not over all? the heavens ever wide?
His blessings deck the earth,—like bursting veins expand
In floods of treasures o'er, wherever you abide;
Which neither are to monarchies nor duke-doms bound,
They are as well in one, as other country found.

But there, a living view does always meet your eye,
Of Eden, and the promised land of Jacob's seed;
Who would not, then, in such a formed community,
Desire to be a freeman; and the rights decreed,
To each and every one, by Amstel's[3] burgher Lords,
T'enjoy? and treat with honor what their rule awards?[4]

Communities the groundwork are of every state;
They first the hamlet, village and the city make;
From whence proceeds the commonwealth; whose members, great
Become, an intérest in the common welfare take.[5]
'T is no Utopia; it rests on principles,
Which, for true liberty, prescribes you settled rules.

You will not aliens, in those far lands appear;
As formerly, in Egypt, e'en was Israel.
Nor have you slavery nor tyranny to fear,
Since Joseph's eyes do see, and on the compass fall.
The civic Fathers who on th' Y,[6] perform their labors,
Are your protectors; and your countrymen are neighbors.

New Netherland's South River,—second Amazon,
For you a pleasure garden on its banks concedes.
Choose you the Swanendael, where Osset had his throne,
Or any other spot your avocation needs.
You have the choice of all; and you're left free to choose;
Keep the conditions well, and you have naught to lose.

Discard the base report, unworthy of your ear;
'Tis forged by ignorance and hate and jealous spite,
By those who are its authors, to bedim this fair
Bright morning sun before the laughing noonday light.
An accident may hinder, but not change the plan,
Whose gloss, take that away, you then may fairly scan.

'T was but an accident, which gives them stuff to slight
That land, which, *as I know,* no proper rival has;
In order from your purpose they may you affright,
Who there desire to live, before you thither pass.
'T is groundless, ev'ry one may easily perceive.
Who now neglects the chance, great treasures does he leave.

Puritan Verse

Uppon the first sight of New-England

June 29 1638

hayle holy-land wherein our holy lord
hath planted his most true and holy word
hayle happye people who have dispossest
your selves of friends, and meanes, to find some rest
for your poore wearied soules, opprest of late
for Jesus-sake, with Envye, spight, and hate
to yow that blessed promise truly's given
of sure reward, which you'l receve in heaven
methinks I heare the Lambe of God thus speake
Come my deare little flocke, who for my sake
have lefte your Country, dearest friends, and goods
and hazarded your lives o'th raginge floods
Posses this Country; free from all anoye
heare I'le bee with yow, heare yow shall Inioye
my sabbaths, sacraments, my minestrye
and ordinances in their puritye
but yet beware of Sathans wylye baites
hee lurkes amongs yow, Cunningly hee waites
to Catch yow from mee; live not then secure
but fight 'gainst sinne, and let your lives be pure
prepare to heare your sentence thus expressed
Come yee my servants of my father Blessed

—THOMAS TILLAM
(16?-after 1668)

Two common explanations for the aesthetic failings of Puritan verse
are that its writers, inhibited by their piety, regarded poetry as an ornament, as mere heightened prose; and that the wilderness was an un-

31

favorable environment for poetry. These arguments have been applied
to colonial verse as a whole. Yet the first is false, the second dubious.
The Puritans thought of poetry as a superior form of discourse, mainly
because of its importance in the Old Testament. Although William Bradford damned as lascivious the verse tacked on Thomas Morton's may-
pole, the Plymouth leader wrote two long pious poems of his own.[1] Nor
had religious conservatism among Puritan writers any bearing on literary
merit. The best Puritan poet, Edward Taylor, was of the orthodox
orthodox. Besides, many New England poets were not ministers: John
Saffin was a merchant, Anne Bradstreet a housewife, Edward Johnson
a soldier. And it is clear from John Rogers' introductory poem to Anne
Bradstreet's works, that by Puritans themselves she was appreciated as a
secular poet, and as a secular poet praised.

To the second, dubious view one should say flatly, the sources of
creation are unpredictable. An atmosphere that stifles one writer releases
another's energies. To stimulate his imagination Schiller needed a
drawerful of rotten apples; Hart Crane played rumba records; Cervantes
and Boethius wrote in dungeons. And again, the outstanding imaginative
writer of the colonial period, Edward Taylor, wrote at Westfield, a
frontier village more exposed and primitive than seventeenth-century
Boston or Salem. Cities, proliferating in the eighteenth century, did
nothing to improve the quality of colonial verse. Eighteenth-century
Charleston, the wealthiest city, and eighteenth-century Philadelphia, the
most intellectual, produced nothing as good as the sacramental poems
of the Westfield minister. And despite the wilderness, Puritans were
never cut off from English poetry. Anne Bradstreet labels herself a
countryman of Sir Philip Sidney's and comments that the same blood
runs in their veins. New Englanders read Sidney, Spenser, Drayton,
DuBartas, Marlowe and Jonson.[2] Cotton Mather owned a first Folio
Shakespeare,[3] and at least six copies of *Paradise Lost* landed in New
England before 1700. Roger Williams became a personal friend of
Milton, and Milton corresponded with John Winthrop Jr. Anne Hutchinson was Dryden's second cousin.[4] The Puritans knew English verse of
the period, especially George Herbert's, which they loved to quote;
Francis Quarles contributed translations for the *Bay Psalm Book*. And it
might be added that only by accident are the poems of Sir Philip Sidney
and of John Donne missing from this anthology; both of them seriously
considered emigration.[5] The wilderness will not account for what the
poems lack.

Puritan Literary Theory

While the wilderness and the observances of Puritanism did not repress poetry, the Puritans never aggressively formulated a literary theory. They casually accepted current literary ideas and casually modified them when they pleased. They never rebelled, in fact, against the standard critical theory of their time. One often cannot distinguish Anglican from Puritan theory or practice.[6]

Despite much talk about The Plain Style, both by Puritans and later writers, one finds many modes of Puritan verse. The term "plain style" obscures fundamental differences between say the esoteric doctrinal poetry of Edward Taylor and the bourgeois moralising of Michael Wigglesworth, or between Anne Bradstreet and Cotton Mather. What was *the* plain style is difficult to determine. It varied according to the subject and the audience addressed, different writers intended different things by it, not all writers took it seriously, few took it as a program. Generally the Puritans meant their prose and verse to be easily understood by anyone. They believed God's word and wanted to make it universally available. The three characteristics of the plain style most often invoked are brevity, spirituality, and perspicuity. The most common argument for using the style is regard for the comprehension of the least gifted hearer. A more particular argument is that simple and familiar verse can combat on its own grounds the corruptive effects of contemporary popular ballads. Cotton Mather in 1713 lamented how

> . . . the Minds and Manners of many People about the Countrey are much corrupted, by foolish Songs and Ballads, which the Hawkers and Pedlars carry into all parts of the Countrey. By way of Antidote, I would procure poetical Composures full of Piety, and such as may have a Tendency to advance Truth and Goodness, to be published, and scattered to all Corners of the Land.[7]

This plan to compete with ballads and romances may explain the Puritans' frequent choice, even in their most pious works, of ballad meter, the meter of Michael Wigglesworth's *Day of Doom*. Since much Puritan didactic poetry, such as John Wilson's *A Song of Deliverance,* was aimed at children, a plain style had the obvious advantage of lightening instruction. Puritans learned from Deuteronomy that God told Moses to "write ye this song for you and teach thou it the children of Israel." Wilson began his poem with the paraphrase, "Now therefore write you, for your selves, this Song / Which thou mayst teach the Isralytish fry." [8] The "fry" were nourished best on plain fare.

In addition to the restraints imposed by the writer's regard for the intelligence of his audience, Puritan distrust of Enthusiasm, Imagination, and Rhetoric had a sobering effect on style. Most Puritan versifiers expressly loathed the classical muses because of their association with heathen gods. Wigglesworth prayed to Christ:

> *Thee, thee* alone I'le invocate
> For I do much abominate
> To call the *Muses* to mine aid.

The Imagination, most Puritans felt, presents to the mind things as they are not in nature, and can pervert the will.[9] Roger Williams tied Puritan distrust for imagination to the theory of the plain style, insisting by a new world example that truth reveals itself unveiled to the mind:

> *Truth is a Native, naked Beauty; but*
> *Lying Inventions are but Indian Paints,*

The best style is that which allows its subject its own terms. Thus while literate Puritans delighted in rhetorical displays, it was with some uneasiness that rhetoric might be used to dazzle merely. By Ramist logic they deduced the superiority of tropes to figures, similes and examples to metaphors and conceits. Ingenious conceits seemed inducements to skip the sense; examples were ornaments that left the sense untransformed.[10] Deeply suspicious of any form of impersonation, most Puritans associated a plain sober style with truth, a figured heightened style with fraud. As in their sermons, in their verse they struck a bargain between figured and naked speech by deploying homely similes. Edward Taylor's "Huswifery," poem and image, is the essential Puritan way of conveying ideas. Far from arbitrary, its mingling of the homely and esoteric expresses the total Puritan effort to return the church to apostolic simplicity by ridding it of symbols and ceremony, without yielding the mysteries that made it vivid and persuasive.

The plain style, then, was not to be mistaken for simple-mindedness or drabness. Cotton Mather, whose own excursions into baroque prose show how casually the theory was entertained, commended the schoolmaster Nathanael Collins' style, because while plain it was profound, "Suited unto the *leather Dublet's* Wants" but so deep that *"Elephants / Might take Content"* in it.[11] The leather doublet implies the sort of audience the plain style was meant for, tough active people unmoved by swank. But Mather's figure of the elephant implies that no one felt offended by an exotic touch. When approving the didactic utility of verse, Puritans often cited George Herbert's dictum that "A Verse may find him who a Sermon flies": and they often added, as did Jonathan

Mitchell in his prefatory poem to *The Day of Doom,* that "Truth in Sugar roll'd may taste the sweeter." Similarly anxious to delight as well as teach, John Saffin wrote that verse should be "Significant, plaine, yet Ellegant," and he complimented Benjamin Colman because his "Towering Phansey Flys above the Common pitch of the Capacity of Ordinary Readers" and because his language is "suitable to the nature and Eminence of the Theme. . . ." [12] So while accounting for the capacity of the common reader, theorists of the plain style often left room for the "Eminence of the Theme," and in practice poets worked with whatever ornaments and conceits attracted them. Many rhetorical devices they used with abandon, particularly anastomasia and anagram. Anastomasia, the identification of character traits with historical figures, by which a wise man is a Cato, fitted their penchant for manipulating historical parallels. Anagrams of course had scriptural authority.[13] Sometimes they viewed the anagram as a wonderfully compressed statement of vast issues. Cotton Mather delighted in how the anagrams of John Wilson produced "Out of meer *Nothings,* by *Creating Art* / Whole *Worlds* of Counsil. . . ." [14] But far more often the anagram in Puritan verse is an opening flourish indulged for its own sake. Wilson, the chief anagram writer of New England, introduces his poem on Thomas Shepard with the anagram "ô a map's thresh'd"; but instantly he drops the figure and launches a long unrelated discussion of infant baptism.[15]

The ideal of the plain style, like the idea of salvation, like much else in Puritan life, was contradictory and to later readers but not to Puritans, tantalizing. Actually, in explaining why they wrote poetry, Puritans were not likely to be solemn. Nathaniel Ward confessed that he wrote verse because "the flatuousnesse of our diet" brings on "sudden raptures." [16] Theoretically directed at the meanest intelligence, in practice the plain style could be anything at all: intelligence varied according to the audience addressed, certain subjects seemed to demand decorative treatment, and no one minded a little high.

The Concerns of Puritan Verse

The mind that so often, if so informally, focussed on an ideal of plain style, chose for Puritan verse a definitive set of themes. Granted much of that verse is crude: syntax twisted, images repellent, verse unmelodious. What is best about it, even the crudest, is contempt for borrowed feelings and freedom from cant. Read as underived human expression, as utterance, it is very often moving. And the most original poems have the eloquence of intense people who seldom found the world boring and sometime saw eternity in a shower. The occasions that prompted Puritan verse were uncommonly solemn, since each event, toothache or earthquake, bespoke God's intercession in human affairs. Nearly every Puritan poem is meant to narrate a moment in the unfolding history of God's will, often gaining its force from the writer's sense of partaking in a revolutionary historic mission fathered by that will. In the same way as the Old Testament, every Puritan poem is epic.

Some few occasions Puritans specially favored. Natural disasters seemed unmistakable signs of God's disposition. Many poems concern earthquakes and storms, although nature as experience, as sensation, is rarely the subject of Puritan verse, except in the Almanacs. Versed history and biography likewise enabled the poets to set down what they knew of God's design. And in hundreds of panegyrics they drew pictures of ideal Puritans, models of conduct for their society. The dozens of variously addressed panegyrics in Edward Johnson's *Wonder-working Providence* are all portraits of the same, ideal minister. Indeed they are theoretical discussions of leadership, of the conduct suitable to governors and ministers. This element of panegyric, which amounts to a codification of conduct, is omnipresent in Puritan verse.[17] It strives to encourage the continuation of the divine plantation and build confidence in the Puritan ranks by exalting living embodiments of ideal Puritan virtues. (One major shift in Puritan verse occurs in the 1660's, when the social function of poetry becomes the destruction of confidence.) Lastly, as gestures of friendship, Puritans wrote many dedicatory poems to other works, particularly sermons.

Next to God, the chief domain of Puritan poetry, and the chief source of all its imagery, is the family. Puritans conceived of the world, the state, the colony and the church made up not of individuals, but of families historically descended from the families of Abraham. So descended, the family was an institution particularly close to God, an instrument of messianic reform; and the tenderness Puritan writers invested in descriptions of domestic life ought to correct any received generalities about Puritan harshness. However cruel to heresy and intolerant of difference, Puritans lived in the belief that, according to Benjamin Wadsworth, God Himself "required Husbands and Wives, to have and manifest very great affection, love and kindness to one another."[18] Imagery of domestic life pervades everything Puritans wrote about the world and should enter our interpretations of their thought. Anne Bradstreet's "The Four Seasons" presents the four humours as sisters, the four elements as their mother, the four ages of man as grandchildren. The Flesh and Spirit in her dialogue are two ingratiating, mildly jealous sisters. She habitually personifies religious and other values as family relations. The values are brought home, dramatized. And in her secular verses on husband and children, the religious consciousness has deepened the love of home and denied it sentimentality by specifying its value. The other leading domestic poet, John Saffin, Speaker of the Massachusetts House and one of the Governor's Council, similarly refers all values to domestic experience, making home life a metaphor for experience itself.

Perhaps the affection Puritans attached to their homes made it inevitable that the local scene should occupy much of their verse. However that may be, it is a fact that Puritans concerned themselves not only with God, but, at great length, with America. The Puritans' favorite analogy to their experience in the new world was drawn from ancient Jewish history. They called their plantation the Wilderness Zion or Christian Israel or Israel in America. In their religion they professed themselves akin to the ancient Jews and desired, as Paul had said, to be grafted onto the stem of Judah, to rediscover that special intimacy with the Divine once granted the Beloved Jews. Thus they named their sons Samuel and called their towns Canaan and Salem. "Abraham, Isaac and Jacob," Thomas Hutchinson said, have as good right to be called saints as "Peter, James and John." [19] (One Puritan named his dog Moreover according to the text, "Moreover, the dog came and lapped up the water.") Puritans felt that history, during their lifetime, had completed a cycle. Like the Jews, they had fled into the wilderness; they too were wanderers, and persecuted; they were Chosen.[20] Members of the colony were identified as Jews: John Winthrop was Joshua, Anne Hutchinson Jezebel. Through their theory of typology they made circumcision the type of baptism, David the type of Christ, and Zion the type of wilderness America.[21] Because, as John Wilson wrote, what is in the Bible "to Israll committed, / Hath a more large and general extent, / And to our present times may well be fitted," [22] the pedagogue Charles Morton could compose two Biblical verse epics, *Exodus* and *The Ark,* in which he disguised New England events in Biblical scenes. So for Puritans in America, James I was Pharoah, the Atlantic was the Red Sea, England Egypt.

The image of Christian Israel underlies all Puritan expectations for the new world. Unlike Elizabethan voyagers, who often picture primitive America as a wealthy Cathay, Puritans conceived it as a desert which only their migration and God's goodness had fructified. Here Paradise was to be born anew on earth. In idealizing America, Puritans stressed how their holy mission prepared for God's Seat by converting an infernal wilderness into Zion. Contrary to the writers of promotional verse who described the new world's unlimited abundance, Michael Wigglesworth saw pre-Puritan America as "The dark and dismal western woods / (The Devils den whilere)." The land became bountiful only after the settlement, when for the Puritans' "dear sake" God turned "a howling wildernes" into a "fruitfull paradeis." America was particularly blessed in another way. While Europe roiled in war, America would enjoy peace. For Wigglesworth's God the Puritans were people "with whom I made a Covenant of peace." The Covenant of Peace is a key doctrine of American Puritanism, equally important as the much discussed social and religious covenants. In Europe, men lay "weltring in their gore." But the Puritans, Wigglesworth continues, "only we, enjoyd such peace / As none enjoyd before." In America, God infused all nature with peace, making the treacherous benign:

> The Lord had made (such was his grace)
>   For us a Covenant
> Both with the men, and with the beasts,
>   That in this desert haunt:
> So that through places wilde and waste
>   A single man, disarm'd,
> Might journey many hundred miles,
>   And not at all be harm'd.

The Puritan ideal of a life freed from peril is only a more direct statement of the subtler promises of the promotional verse. Naturally, what with frequent Indian raids and a harsh climate, such an ideal often was frustrated. The distance between the hope for peace in America and the facts of frontier existence is a keynote of Puritan verse.

Never in the history of American Puritanism was the ideal so severely tested as in the 1660's and 70's, when ministers and poets alike turned abruptly, with scorching self-denunciation, to the urgent problem of New England's degeneration.[23] They saw themselves punished for spiritual backsliding by a withdrawal of the Covenant of Peace, and counted up the consequences by increases in crime, disease, and frontier violence. Many Puritans, and many later historians, chose to explain the relaxation of the original messianic purpose theoretically, by doctrinal confusions and inner philosophical contradictions. But these were probably only the byproduct of social changes.[24] A new society was building in Massachusetts and crowding Puritanism out. The ideal Puritan colony could only be maintained in a small city-state; but Americans soon began fore-

casting a continental destiny, if not an Empire. Increased commerce
made New Englanders wealthy and worldly and brought to their ports
cussing, dissolute sailors. (Perhaps to the meager list of significant dates
in colonial history, one should add 1672, when Alice Thomas opened
Boston's first whore house.) The three most outraged responses in verse
to the social upheaval were Edward Johnson's "Of the wonder-working
providences of Christ," Michael Wigglesworth's "God's Controversy
with New-England," and Benjamin Tompson's "New-Englands Crisis."

The differences between Johnson's "briefe description" and his later
"wonder-working providences" indicate what happened to the Puritan
ideal during thirty years in the new world. The theocracy became vul-
nerable; the 'city on the hill,' many Puritans felt, looked every day more
like The Cities of the Plain. "Lord, stay thy hand," Johnson prays, "thy
Jacobs number's small." The poetry of the Sixties and Seventies is
plagued by this sense of exposure. The assured air of historic mission is
gone, Puritans find that the rash world has popped their splendid bubble.
In the earlier poem Johnson boasts of the soil's bounty and the land's
peace. But in the "wonder-working providences," locusts and caterpillars
devour crops; fire, political dissension, and inflation bring ruin; pride in
apparel, disrespect for authority, delight in *"new fangled doctrines"* breed
chaos: the people of New England *"stand at a stay, as if the Lord had
no farther work for his people to do"* and the *"chief end of our coming
hither is forgotten."* Johnson's later poem is both the *mea culpa* of a
personal spiritual crisis and an unblinking, nauseated registry of New
England waywardness: the catalogues alternate between defects of character and communal disasters. Of course the two are one. The personal
fate of Saints and the fate of the community were never for the Puritans
different. Wigglesworth also measures the decline in both communal and
personal degrees. "God's Controversy with New-England," significantly
"written in the time of the great drought Anno 1662," indicts personal
malaise:

> For burning zeal luke-warm Indifferency,
> For flaming love, key-cold Dead-heartedness.

But there is also large-scale drought, fire, and illness. God's Covenant of
Peace, his promise to rid the new world of violence, disease, and death,
has been broken:

> New-England, where for many yeers
> You scarcely heard a cough,
> And where Physicians had no work,
> Now finds them work enough.

Wigglesworth explains that God resists venting his full wrath only because some few New Englanders still follow His way. For it is not so much external social pressure as the Puritans' own sinfulness that sped the decline: "This hast thou brought upon thy self / By pride & wantonness." Unlike Wigglesworth, Benjamin Tompson lays the fall to increasing contact with the outer world. "The renowned poet of New England" (as his gravestone calls him) juxtaposes New England of the late 1660's not against the Puritans' grand theoretical purpose but against the actual life of New England in 1630. On this scale, it is a slip from rugged and satisfying primitive times into decadence. In *"Plain Dealings Reign"* men ate out of clam shells but were untroubled. Love of gold introduced foppish dress and mannered conduct; hunger for the world brought war.

Puritan Verse as American

"New-Englands Crisis" and the verse jeremiads of the Sixties, despite the former's indebtedness to Quarles and Dryden, seem distinctively American poems, the first in that tradition of verse and fiction bemoaning a loss of innocence and promise. There are no English works of the period wholly like them.

Not only by its themes was colonial verse growing apart from contemporary English verse. In 1703 one writer defended her poems by reminding the reader that if he "take Notice of their *Plainness,* Let him Consider, That they were *Plain Folks* for whose Benefit they were at first intended." [25] The nebulous ideal of a plain style appears and reappears over the whole course of colonial verse. One feels challenged to show how its lingering stimulated (or, perhaps, responded to) the need in America to "domesticate culture," as Emerson said, to deal with ideas in the language of the firkin and pan. The theory of the plain style gave poetry a novel social function. Designed to appeal universally and to no coterie, it insinuates the standard, two centuries later, of Whitman: that the test of a poet is his acceptance by the common man. The part of colonial verse which is poetry for the common man (it includes most of the verse of the Revolution) typifies a way of thinking about literature that seems, despite countless European and English ventures into a middle style, uniquely American. Its problem has been more than how to reach the intelligence of the least gifted hearer. During the Revolution it was how to organize in the expectation of power Quakers, Southern planters, and Yankee merchants and, later, how to be so public as to embrace the most diverse social and ethnic groups. The continued interest in a plain style seems the result in the arts of that new concept of knowledge Daniel Boorstin calls an outstanding revolution of the colonial period—trust and faith in the public mind.

More tangible differences divide American Puritan verse of the period from English. Occasionally if never consistently, poets found imagery in the sensations of the new world. The Puritan view of nature as a portent took a special slant from the novel and sometimes hellish sights of America—the wilderness, the New England winter, and the Indians, those "Monsters," Tompson called them, "shapt and fac'd like men." Roger Williams made Indian nakedness a complex image of the Puritan endeavor to strip the church of decoration and ceremony, and found in the wilderness itself a medieval *moralitas,* with its "cleere resemblance of the world, where greedie and furious men persecute and devoure the harmlesse and innocent as the wilde beasts pursue and devoure the Hinds and Roes." Tompson himself discovered in the wilderness new epic subjects and by drawing mythological parallels related them to the literary traditions of Europe: the Indians' hair is like Medusa's; their clubs remind him of a Vulcan, clobbering New England's brain; they move slyly, like Aeneas in his magic cloak. Many poets made the dark New England forest a grim symbol of that classic moment of Puritan psychology, the silent night. That fear of spiritual nullity and expectation of God's wrath which Anne Bradstreet called a "silent night," the "fittest time for moan," which was to Edward Johnson a "silent night true Register of moans," found a natural expression in the image of the gloomy forest settlement terrorized at midnight by Indian attacks and fires.

Not much of the Puritans' local imagery would have moved an English audience. To appreciate how unlike English verse colonial verse was becoming one must add that while developing a fund of native imagery American Puritans were also failing to respond to changes in English style, largely by reason of distance from the home country and because of the cultural lag. English verse of the early seventeenth century was being written in New England of the early eighteenth century and accommodating local issues that had no counterparts in England. Even the Puritans' language had a dated air, and had become ingrained with local reference, reference not only to the local scene but also to the local literature. One finds allusions to Johnson's *Wonder-working Providence* in "God's Controversy with New-England" and in many later works by Cotton Mather. Urian Oakes's elegy on Thomas Shepard is quoted and echoed in a dozen later elegies. Benjamin Tompson bases a passage of "New-Englands Crisis" on Edward Johnson's description of the Indians' reaction to the first Europeans, and in his ode "To Lord Bellamont" in-

vokes the Simple Cobbler of Aggawam sixty years earlier. Anne Bradstreet's tone was consciously recaptured a century later by a woman poet
of Connecticut, Martha Brewster. Many writers caught up the rhythms
and syntax of their own *Bay Psalm Book,* for instance Anne Bradstreet
herself:

> My pleasant things in ashes lye,
> And them behold no more shall I.

Few of these allusions and imitations would have struck a contemporary
English reader. They betray a tenuous but real literary continuity, a
turning, ever more enthusiastic, toward the regional culture for meaningful language and imagery.

   Although the Puritan elegy is treated separately in the next section,
this brief assay of Puritan verse has had to omit much. A number of
interesting poets, excluded here, deserve analysis. There is the minister
John Danforth, in whose verse many forceful images and conceits are
spent in vastnesses of prosy abstract moralising. There is the soldier
Philip Walker, whose brief warmongering epic "Captan Perse and his
coragios Company" gives probably the blackest account of the Indians
in New England literature, and has the added interest by its bizarre
phonetic spelling of being New England's *Orrmulum,* a guide to colonial
speech. One would like to demonstrate more conclusively how American
Puritan verse differs from English poetry, more complexly what theory
of expression lies behind it. Faced with a body of work that has a major
symbolic value as representing the culture of the founders of America,
and perhaps a direct relation to what poetry in America became, but
that in addition is often mediocre, enough may be too much. The poems
included here show the Puritan inspired by his God and his hearth, faced
a few years later by the wrath of one and threats to the other: by the
loss of promise. The Wilderness Zion was over before it started. Almost
the first thing Puritans did when they got here was complain that America was not what it used to be.

NOTES

   [1] Charles M. Andrews points out that the Pilgrims objected to Morton "not so
much for his revelries as for his rivalries in dealing with the Indians . . . and
competing with themselves successfully in the fur trade." *The Colonial Period of
American History* (New Haven, 1934), I, 362. Bradford's poems are reprinted in
Proceedings of the Massachusetts Historical Society, 1st Ser., XI, and *Collections
of the Massachusetts Historical Society,* 3d Ser., VII.

   [2] Randall Stewart, "Puritan Literature and the Flowering of New England,"
William and Mary Quarterly, 3d Ser., III (July 1946), 324.

[3] And William Byrd probably owned a fourth Folio. See Edwin Willoughby, "The Reading of Shakespeare in Colonial America," *Papers of the Bibliographical Society of America,* XXXI (1937), 48-49.

[4] Thomas Goddard Wright, *Literary Culture in Early New England 1620-1730* (New Haven, 1920), p. 70.

[5] A. L. Rowse, *The Elizabethans and America* (New York, 1959), p. 247.

[6] My discussion of the plain style owes much to Lawrence A. Sasek, *The Literary Temper of the English Puritans* (Baton Rouge, 1961). The emphasis on the Puritans' freedom with the theory, however, is my own.

[7] *Diary of Cotton Mather,* ed. Worthington Chauncey Ford (repr. New York, n.d.), II, 242. Franklin, who practiced much of what he preached against in Mather, felt the same way. In his "Apology for Printers" in the *Pennsylvania Gazette* (June 10, 1731) Franklin complained that "I have known a very numerous Impression of *Robin Hood's Songs* go off in this Province at 2s. per Book, when a small Quantity of *David's Psalms* (an excellent Version) have lain upon my Hands above twice the Time."

[8] John Wilson, *A Song of Deliverance,* in Kenneth Murdock, ed., *Handkerchiefs from Paul* (Cambridge, 1927), p. 27.

[9] Perry Miller, *The New England Mind: The Seventeenth Century* (Cambridge, 1954), p. 258. According to Thomas Hooker, the imagination was a "forge of villany . . . the Warehouse of wickedness, the Magazine of al mischief and iniquity." *Ibid.*

[10] *Ibid.,* Ch. XI *passim.* And see Walter J. Ong, *Ramus: Method and the Decay of Dialogue* (Cambridge, 1958).

[11] Cotton Mather, "An Elegy on . . . Mr. Nathanael Collins," repr. in *Early American Poetry* (Boston, 1896), III, 11.

[12] *John Saffin His Book (1665-1708),* ed. Caroline Hazard (New York, 1928), pp. 2, 170.

[13] Cotton Mather remarked that in writing anagrams the Puritans were justified by the Bible, and called upon "the *Temurah,* or *Mutation,* with which the *Jews* do Criticise upon the Oracles of the *Old* Testament. *There,* they say, you'll find the *Anagram* of our *First Fathers* Name *Ha Adam,* to express *Adamah,* the name of the . . . *Earth,* whence he had his Original." Quoted in Murdock, p. iv.

[14] Cotton Mather, *Johannes in Eremo* (Boston, 1695), n.p.

[15] John Wilson, "Thomas SHEPARD," in Shepard's *The Church-Membership of Children* (Cambridge, 1663), n.p.

[16] Nathaniel Ward, *The Simple Cobler of Aggawam in America* (repr. Boston, 1843), p. 90. The conclusion of Ward's book is one of the fullest Puritan treatises on style, and certainly the most delightful. Ward argues for suiting manner to matter: "To speak to light heads with heavy words, were to break their necks: to cloathe Summer matter, with Winter Rugge, would make the Reader sweat. It is musick to me, to heare every Ditty speak its spirit in its apt tune: every breast, to sing its proper part, and every creature, to expresse it self in its naturall note: should I heare a Mouse roare like a Beare, a Cat lowgh like an Oxe, or a Horse whistle like a Red-breast, it would scare—mee."

[17] Puritans always qualified their panegyrics by noting that any praise given to anything is ultimately praise of God, source of all. As Johnson says in his *Wonder-working Providence,*

> What courage was in *Winthrope,* it was thine;
> *Shepheards'* sweet Sermons from thy blessing came,

There is ever in Puritan panegyric a curious backtracking, a deliberate effort by the poet to show his consciousness that, whatever on earth he praise, the praise is God's. On Cotton, Johnson writes:

> Then praise I Man, no, Christ this Man doth make.

And Urian Oakes says that disease, "(like *High-way-men*)" did

> . . . rob dear *Shepard* of his life (Ah!) then,
> When he was on the Road, where Duty lay.
> Forbear, bold Pen! 'twas God that took him thus.

Austin Warren notes the "rigid view not only that we should have no 'personal friends' but that any spontaneous preferences among God's creatures deprive God of the total loyalty which should be His." *The New England Conscience* (Ann Arbor, 1966), p. 68 and *passim*.

[18] In Edmund S. Morgan, *The Puritan Family* (Boston, 1944), p. 12. My remarks on Puritan domesticity are guided by Morgan's monograph. He goes so far as to attribute to this "tribalism" the downfall of New England Puritanism: grace could be inherited, the argument runs, one had no longer to earn his salvation. Indeed, the doctrinal battles over infant baptism caught up all the latent concrete social and political difficulties of the 1660's. Kenneth Murdock has also spoken accurately of "those domestic dramas in which the Puritan felt himself closest to the inscrutable power of God." *Handkerchiefs,* p. xix.

[19] Thomas Hutchinson, *History of Massachusetts,* in Edmund Clarence Stedman and Ellen Mackay Hutchinson, eds., *A Library of American Literature* (New York, 1891), III, 56.

[20] In the mother country Waldensians and Hussites likened their revolt to the Maccabean uprising, and William Crashaw in a sermon of 1609 announced: "The Israelites had a *commandement* to dwell in *Canaan,* we have *leave* to dwell in *Virginea*." See Louis Israel Newman, *Jewish Influence on Christian Reform Movements* (New York, 1925). Cowley had written a Vergilian epic of David. In his *Discoveries,* Ben Jonson noted how the Jews received poetry from heaven, gave it to the Greeks, who gave it to the Romans.

[21] Benjamin Colman, for one, says that circumcision "was (as *Baptism* now is) a Sacrament of *Initiation* into the Covenant of Grace." "A Discourse held in the College Hall" (Boston, 1722), p. 14. And Samuel Willard: "by a frequent scripture *Metonymie, Christ the Antitype* is called by the name of *David the Type*." *The Fountain Opened* (Boston, 1700), p. 44.

[22] Murdock, p. 28.

[23] Perry Miller called these jeremiads "the first American literary form" since only this "concentration of emotion upon the destiny of a group . . . could draw out the energy and imagination of the Americanized Puritan artist." *Colony to Province,* p. 33. The designation, I think, ought to go to the Puritan elegy, for the same reasons Miller gave and because New England writers themselves considered the elegy a unique local product.

[24] The view of H. Richard Niebuhr, *The Social Sources of Denominationalism* (New York, 1929), *passim*. Cf. Peter Gay, *A Loss of Mastery: Puritan Historians in Colonial America* (Berkeley, 1966), which demonstrates how determinedly Puritans held on to the orthodoxy in the face of these changes (reviving the oversimplified idea of a 'Glacial Age' of American Puritanism.)

[25] Mary French, *Good Fetch'd out of Evil* (n.pl., 1703), p. 22. She adds that Christ "chose" for his mother not "an Empress or a Queen" but a woman "of Low Degree and Mean." For the persistence of the theory see Jane Dunlap, *Poems* (Boston, 1771):

> No eloquence does in these lines,
> I'm very sure appear
> But sacred truths will always shine,
> Tho' in the lowest sphere. (p. 19)

Or, as the Bay psalmists said a century earlier, "Gods Altar needs not our pollishings."

Edward Johnson
(1598-1672)

"A briefe description of the Land,
Birds, Trees, and Fruits"

TEXT: *Good news from NEW ENGLAND* (London, 1648), pp. 7-9.

UNlevel'd lies this land new found with hills and vallies low,
With many mixtures of such mold where fruits do firtile grow.
Well watered with the pleasant springs that from the hills arise,
The waters run with warbling tunes, with stones that in them lies.
To welcome weary travellers, resting unneath the shade,
Of lofty banks, where lowly boughs, for them fresh harbour made.
The lesser Rivelets rent themselves into a wider way,
Where scouring torrents furious fall, through rocks their streames
    doe stray.

SPRING.

AT end of *March* begins the Spring, by *Sols* new elivation,
Stealing away the earths white robe, dropping with sweats vexation.
The Codfish, Holybut, & Basse, do sport the rivers in,
And Allewifes with their crowding sholes, in every creek do swim.
Leaving their spawn in ponds to thrive 'mongst Pikes devouring
    jawes.
That swallow Trowts, Tench, Roach and Breme into their greedy
    mawes.

Pirch, Shad, and Eeles, there plenty fill the panyard and the pan,
Smelts, Lobsters, Crab-fish, pranes and shrimps, with cockles
     mussels clams.
Plenty of oysters overgrow the flowed lands so thick,
That thousand loads to lime are turn'd, to lay fast stone and brick.
The Cormorants with greedy gut full fast the fishes follow,
And Eagles with their piercing sight look through the waters
     shallow.
Ducks, Hens, and Pheasants often row upon the waters brim,
With plenty of their fellow fowles to welcome in the Spring.
Devouring fires burning black the earths old rusty hew,
Like torch-bearers in gloomy night, their flames with wind
     sore flew.
Like Phoenix rare, from ashes old, of grasse, doth grasse arise,
The earth casts off her mourning coate, gay clad like bride to eyes.
With herbs and divers precious plants for physicks operation,
Diversity of fragrant flowers for sences recreation.

SOMMER.

BEspread with Roses Sommer 'gins take place with hasty speed,
    Whose parching heate Strawberries coole doth moderation breed.
Ayre darkening sholes of pigeons picke their berries sweet and
    good,
    The lovely Cherries birds entice, to feast themselves in woods.
The Turkies, Partridge, Heath-hens and their young ones tracing
    passe,
    The woods and meadowes, Achorns eat, and hoppers in the
    grasse.
Like *Virgils* knat musketo flies with buzzy humming dare
    Assault the stoutest with long trunke, both blood and blisters
    reare.
When little lineaments the Sun, or winde doth feeble make
    Yea cooling dewes their swarms allay, and strength of stinging
    slake.
The little hum-birds sucking sweet, from flowers draw their food,
    Humilities in sommer-time only find livelihood.

AUTUMNE.

GOod wholsome and delightfull food, variety & store,

The Husband-man rejoycing keeps, with fruit the earths wombe
    boare.
Peas plenty, Barley, Oats and wheat, Rye richly stocking stands,
    Such store the plough-man late hath found, that they feed
        forreign lands.
Cucumbers, mellons, apples, peares, and plums do flourish faire,
    Yea what delight and profit would, they still are adding there.
Sixe sorts of Oakes the land affords, Walnuts doe differ so,
    That divers shapes their fruit retains, and food that in them grow.
Roots are not wanting, wild and tame, in gardens they encrease,
    Ground nuts, ground beans, not gathered till, warmth doth
        the earth release.
Grapes wanting vintage, common grow, fit for the travellers hand,
    With food from berries multitude, that grow throughout the land.

WINTER.

SHarpe, sudden, yet with lightsome looks doth winter cold come in,
    With thicke, large Coat doth cloath the earth, both soft,
        smooth, white and trim.
The large tempestuous surges are bound in with frozen band,
    Where ship did anker, men doe walke, and carts as on the land.
The Geese flye prating night and day, to tell the approaching
        season,
    Brought downe by gun-shot from their flight unto the Indians
        geson.
The tumbling beares intrapped are, 'mongst houses sudden enter,
    O'rethrowne by eager hunters, who pursue them in this venter.
The tripping Deer with length of leaps, do burst through frozen
        snow,
    Hunters pursue with bracket shooes, at length they weary grow.
Then down the dogs them sudden draw, expos'd to hunters
        pleasure,
    Their flesh well welcome, and their skins, are chiefe of
        Indian treasure.
Whole kennels of devouring wolves both Deer and Swine destroy,
    Yet scar'd by weakest children, they them the lesse annoy.
The Suns bright presence most dayes doth cheere man and beast
        with joy,
    With hope of pleasant springs approach to free from colds annoy.
With mineralls the earth is fraught, though Alcumists are wanting,

Which makes current mettle priz'd 'mongst Merchants daily
    scanting.

"Of the wonder-working providences of Christ, wrought
    for his people among our English Nation, both in
      our Native country, and also in *N.E.,* which
        should stir us up to mourn for all our
          miscarriages much the more."

TEXT: *Wonder-working Providence of Sions Saviour, in* New England
    (London, 1654), pp. 218-223.

FRom silent night true Register of moans,
    From saddest soul consum'd in deepest sin,
[A] From heart quite rent with sighs and heavy groans,
    My wailing muse her woful work begins,
And to the world brings tunes of sad lament,
Sounding nought els but sorrows sad relent.

Sorry to see my sorrows cause augmented,
    And yet less sorrowful were my sorrows more,
[A] Grief that with grief, is not with grief prevented,
    Yet grief it is must ease my grieved sore;
So grief and sorrow, care but how to grieve,
For grief and sorrow must my cares relieve.

The wound fresh bleeding must be stanch'd with tears,
    Tears cannot come unless some grief proceed,
[A] Grief comes but slack, which doth increase my fears,
    Fear, lest for want of help I still shall bleed;
Do what I can to lengthen my lifes breath,
If Christ be wanting, I shall bleed to death.

Thou deepest searcher of each secret thought,
    Infuse in me thy all-affecting grace,
[A] So shall my work to good effect be brought,
    While I peruse my ugly sins a space,
Whose staining filth so spotted hath my soul,
That nought can wash, but tears of inward dole.

A *The consideration of the wonderful providence of Christ in plant-*
ing his N.E. Churches, and with the right hand of his power preserving,
protecting, favouring, and feeding them upon his tender knees: Together
with the ill requital of his all-infinite and undeserved mercies bestowed
upon us, hath caused many a soul to lament for the dishonor done to
his Name, and fear of his casting of this little handful of his, and the in-
sulting of the enemy, whose sorrow is set forth in these four first staffs
of verses.

How soon my soul hast thou the Lord forgot,
    [B] Who thee and thine through troublous Seas hath lead,
On earth thy parts should praise him, suddain rot,
    Why dost neglect his glorious Kingdom spread.
Thy eyes have seen the Mountains mov'd with's hand,
And sunk in Seas to make his Sion stand.

No wonder then thy works with Eastern wind
    [B] On Seas are broke, and thy best Seamen slain,
Sith, thou thy gain, and not Christs work dost mind,
    Lord stay thy hand, I see my works are vain.
Our ships they shall thy Gospel forth convey,
And not bring home strange errors here to stay.

Instead of home-oppression, they shall now
    Thy Saints abroad relieve, by Sea them send;
No riot shall our Merchantmen allow,
    Time in exchange walks, not in Taverns spend:
Godly grief and good purpose comes from thee,
Lord Christ command, and then to work go we.

B *The Rod of God toward us in our Maritine affairs manifested,*
not only to our own shipping, but strangers: as the Mary Rose *blown up*
in Charles River, and sunk in a moment, with about thirteen men slain
therein: As also one Capt. Chadwicks *Pinnace, and about four men*
slain therein, beside what hath been formerly said touching our own
shipping.

Oh thou my soul how weak's thy faith become,
    With scatter'd seed of man and beast, thou hast
Seen thy great God increase thy little sum,

C Towns close compact in desart land hath plac't:
In Wilderness thy table richly spread,
Thy poor therein hath satisfi'd with bread.

While firtil lands with hunger have been pined,
     C Thy harvest hath with heaps on heaps come in;
Oh mourn, that thou no more thy God should'st mind,
     His gentle rod to teach thee doth begin;
Then wonder not that swarms of Locust fly,
And that earths fruits for want of moysture die.

A countless crew of Caterpillers craul,
     To rob the earth of her green mantle quite;
Wolves only wont on lesser beasts to fall,
     C On great ones prey by day, and eke by night:
Thy houses are consum'd with much good store,
By fearful fires, which blustering winds blow o're.

Lord stay thy hand, and stop my earthly mind,
     Thy Word, not world, shall be our sole delight,
C Not Medow ground, but Christs rich pearl wee'l find,
     Thy Saints imbrace, and not large lands down plight.
Murmure no more will we at yearly pay,
To help uphold our Government each way;

Not strive who least, but who the most shall give,
     Rejoyce will we, our hearts inlarged are,
C Those wait on th'Altar, shall on Altar live,
     Nor shall our riches their good doctrine mar;
Our pride of parts in thought of clear discerning,
No longer shall disgrace their godly learning.

Our meaner sort that metamorphos'd are,
     With womens hair, in gold and garments gay,
C Whose wages large our Commonwealths work mar,
     Their pride they shall with moderation lay:
Cast off their cloaths, that men may know their rank,
And women that with outward deckings prank,

C *Of the Lords hand against our Land affairs, as is heretofore ex-*
pressed; and also in the suddain taking away many mens estates by fire,

*and chiefly by a most terrible fire which happened in Charles-Town, in
the depth of Winter, 1650. by a violent wind blown from one house to
another, to the consuming of the fairest houses in the Town: Under the
pretence of being unequally rated, many men murmure exceedingly, and
withdraw their shoulders from the support of Government, to the great
discouragement of those that govern, 1651. Pride and excess in apparrel
is frequent in these daies, when the Lord calls his people to humiliation
and humble acknowledgment of his great deliverances; and that which
is far worse, spiritual pride, to shew our selves to be somebody, often step
out of our ranks, and delight in new fangled doctrines.*

The worlds imbrace our longing lust for gain,
    D No longer shall us into corners draw,
Nor our large herds us from Gods house detain
    From fellowship of Saints, who learn thy Law:
Thy righteous Judgments Lord do make me tremble,
Nor word, nor rod, but deep in this dissemble.

Two Masters, Lord, we will professed serve;
    How can we Christ united be to thee,
D When from thy Law learn'd we so greatly swarve,
    With watry tears unclued we will be.
From creature-comforts, Christ thou art our stay,
Work will and deed in us we humbly pray.

D *An over-eager desire after the world hath so seized on the spirits
of many, that the chief end of our coming hither is forgotten; and notwithstanding all the powerful means used, we stand at a stay, as if the
Lord had no farther work for his people to do, but every bird to feather
his own nest.*

Oh thou, my soul, and every part in me
    Lament, the Lord his worthies from the earth
Takes to himself, and makes our earth to be
    [E] A mourning place left destitute of mirth;
Are these the daies wherein that Beast shall fall,
Lord leave us means, though thou be all in all.

What courage was in *Winthrope*, it was thine;
    Shepheards sweet Sermons from thy blessing came,
[E] Our heavenly *Hooker* thy grace did refine,

And godly *Burr* receiv'd from thee his frame:
Philips didst thou indue with Scripture light,
And *Huet* had his arguings strong and right.

Grave *Higginson* his heavenly truths from thee,
    [E] *Maveruck* was made an able help to thine;
What *Harver* had thou gavest, for's people free;
    Follow *Green* full of grace, to work thou didst assign:
Godly *Glover*[1] his rich gifts thou gavest,
Thus thou by means thy flocks from spoiling savest.

But Lord, why dost by death withdraw thy hand
    From us, these men and means are sever'd quite;
Stretch forth thy might, Lord Christ do thou command,
    Their doubled spirit on those left to light:
Forth of their graves call ten times ten again,
That thy dear flocks no damage may sustain.

Can I forget these means that thou hast used,
    To quicken up my drowsie drooping soul;
Lord I forget, and have the same abused,
    Which makes me now with grief their deaths condole,
And kĩss thy rod, laid on with bowels tender,
By death of mine, makes me their death remember.

Lord, stay thy hand, thy *Jacobs* number's small,
    Powre out thy wrath on Antichrists proud Thrones;
Here thy poor flocks that on thee daily call,
    Bottle their tears, and pity their sad groans.
Where shall we go Lord Christ? we turn to thee,
Heal our back-slidings, forward press shall we.

Not we, but all thy Saints the world throughout
    Shall on thee wait, thy wonders to behold;
Thou King of Saints, the Lord in battel stout
    Increase thy armies many thousand fold.
Oh Nations all, his anger seek to stay,
That doth create him armies every day.

    E *The Lords taking away by death many of his most eminent ser-*
vants from us, shewes, that either the Lord will raise up another people
to himself to do his work, or raise us up by his Rod to a more eager

pursuit of his work, even the planting of his Churches the world through-
out. The Lord converts and calls forth of their graves men to fight his
battels against the enemies of his truth.

Roger Williams
(c. 1603-1683)

"The observation generall from their eating, Etc."

TEXT: *A Key into the Language of America* (London, 1643),
   pp. 16-17.

It is a strange *truth,* that a man shall generally finde more free entertainment and refreshing amongst these *Barbarians,* then amongst thousands that call themselves *Christians.*

More particular.

1   *Course* bread *and* water's *most their fare;*
    O Englands *diet fine;*
   Thy cup *runs ore with plenteous store*
    Of wholesome beare *and* wine.

2   *Sometimes* God *gives them* Fish *or* Flesh,
    Yet they're content *without;*
   And what comes in, they part *to friends*
    and strangers *round about.*

3   *Gods* providence *is rich to his,*
    Let none distrustfull *be;*
   In wildernesse, *in great* distresse,
    These Ravens *have fed me.*

"From their Sleeping: The Observation generall."

TEXT: *A Key,* p. 21.

Sweet rest is not confind to soft Beds, for, not only God gives his
beloved sleep on hard lodgings: but also Nature and Custome gives

sound sleep to these Americans on the Earth, on a Boord or Mat. Yet how is *Europe* bound to God for better lodging, *Etc.*

More particular.

1. *God gives them sleep on Ground, on Straw,*
    on Sedgie[1] Mats or Boord:
When English softest Beds of Downe,
    sometimes no sleep affoord.

2. *I have knowne them leave their House and Mat*
    to lodge a Friend or stranger,
When Jewes and Christians oft have sent
    Christ Jesus *to the Manger.*

3. *'Fore day they invocate their Gods,*
    though Many, False and New:
O how should that God worshipt be,
    who is but One and True?

"The generall Observation *of the Beasts."*

TEXT: *A Key,* p. 107.

The Wildernesse is a cleere resemblance of the world, where greedie and furious men persecute and devoure the harmlesse and innocent as the wilde beasts pursue and devoure the Hinds and Roes.

More particular.

1. *The* Indians, *Wolves, yea, Dogs and Swine,*
I have knowne the Deere devoure,
Gods children are sweet prey to all;
But yet the end proves sowre.
2. *For though Gods children lose their lives,*
They shall not loose an haire;
But shall arise, and judge all those,
That now their Iudges are.
3. New-England's *wilde beasts are not fierce,*

As other wild beasts are:
Some men are not so fierce, and yet
From mildnesse are they farre.

"Generall Observations *of their Garments."*

TEXT: *A Key,* p. 113.

How deep are the purposes and Councells, of God? what should bee
the reason of this mighty difference of One mans children that all the
Sonnes of men on this side the way (in *Europe, Asia* and *Africa* should
have such plenteous clothing for Body for Soule! and the rest of *Adams*
sonnes and Daughters on the other side, or *America* (some thinke as
big as the other three,) should neither have nor desire clothing for their
naked Soules, or Bodies.

More particular.

O what a Tyrant's Custome long,
How doe men make a tush,
At what's in use, though ne're so fowle:
Without once shame or blush?

Many thousand proper Men and Women,
I have seen met in one place:
Almost all naked, yet not one,
Thought want of clothes disgrace.

Israell was naked, wearing cloathes!
The best clad English-man,
Not cloth'd with Christ, more naked is:
Then naked Indian.

"Generall Observations of their paintings."

TEXT: *A Key,* p. 184.

It hath been the foolish Custome of all barbarous Nations to paint
and figure their Faces and Bodies (as it hath been to our shame and
griefe, wee may remember it of some of our Fore-Fathers in this Nation.) How much then are we bound to our most holy Maker for so

much knowledge of himselfe revealed in so much Civility and Piety? and how should we also long and endeavour that *América* may partake of our mercy:

More particular.

Truth is a Native, naked Beauty; but
    Lying Inventions are but Indian Paints,
2 *Dissembling hearts their Beautie's but a Lye,*
Truth is the proper Beauty of Gods Saints.

Fowle are the Indians *Haire and painted Faces,*
    2 *More foule such Haire, such Face in* Israel.
England *so calls her selfe, yet there's*
    Absoloms *foule Haire and Face of* Jesabell.

Paints will not bide Christs washing Flames of fire,
    Fained Inventions will not bide such stormes:
O that we may prevent him, that betimes,
    Repentance Teares may wash of all such Formes.

Anne Bradstreet
(c. 1612-1672)

"THE PROLOGUE."

TEXT: *The Works of Anne Bradstreet,* ed. John Harvard Ellis (Charlestown, 1867), pp. 100-102.

1.

To sing of Wars, of Captains, and of Kings,
Of Cities founded, Common-wealths begun,
For my mean pen are too superiour things:
Or how they all, or each their dates have run
Let Poets and Historians set these forth,
My obscure Lines shall not so dim their worth.

2.

But when my wondring eyes and envious heart
Great *Bartas*[1] sugar'd lines, do but read o're
Fool I do grudg the Muses did not part
'Twixt him and me that overfluent store;
A *Bartas* can, do what a *Bartas* will
But simple I according to my skill.

3.

From school-boyes tongue no rhet'rick we expect
Nor yet a sweet Consort from broken strings,
Nor perfect beauty, where's a main defect:
My foolish, broken, blemish'd Muse so sings
And this to mend, alas, no Art is able,
'Cause nature, made it so irreparable.

4.

Nor can I, like that fluent sweet tongu'd Greek,
Who lisp'd at first, in future times speak plain
By Art he gladly found what he did seek
A full requital of his, striving pain
Art can do much, but this maxime's most sure
A weak or wounded brain admits no cure.

5.

I am obnoxious to each carping tongue
Who says my hand a needle better fits,
A Poets pen all scorn I should thus wrong,
For such despite they cast on Female wits:
If what I do prove well, it won't advance,
They'l say it's stoln, or else it was by chance.

6.

But sure the Antique Greeks were far more mild
Else of our Sexe, why feigned they those Nine
And poesy made, *Calliope's* own Child;

So 'mongst the rest they placed the Arts Divine,
But this weak knot, they will full soon untie,
The Greeks did nought, but play the fools & lye.

7.

Let Greeks be Greeks, and women what they are
Men have precedency and still excell,
It is but vain unjustly to wage warre;
Men can do best, and women know it well
Preheminence in all and each is yours;
Yet grant some small acknowledgement of ours.

8.

And oh ye high flown quills that soar the Skies,
And ever with your prey still catch your praise,
If e're you daigne these lowly lines your eyes
Give Thyme or Parsley wreath, I ask no bayes,
This mean and unrefined ure of mine
Will make you glistring gold, but more to shine.

"Davids Lamentation for Saul and Jonathan."

2. Sam. 1. 19.

TEXT: Ellis, pp. 363-364.

Alas slain is the Head of Israel,
Illustrious *Saul* whose beauty did excell,
Upon thy places mountainous and high,
How did the Mighty fall, and falling dye?
In *Gath* let not this things be spoken on,
Nor published in streets of *Askalon,*
Lest daughters of the Philistines rejoyce,
Lest the uncircumcis'd lift up their voice.
O *Gilbo* Mounts, let never pearled dew,
Nor fruitfull showres your barren tops bestrew,
Nor fields of offrings ever on you grow,
Nor any pleasant thing e're may you show;
For there the Mighty Ones did soon decay,

The shield of *Saul* was vilely cast away,
There had his dignity so sore a foyle,
As if his head ne're felt the sacred oyle.
Sometimes from crimson, blood of gastly slain,
The bow of *Jonathan* ne're turn'd in vain:
Nor from the fat, and spoils of Mighty men
With bloodless sword did *Saul* turn back agen.
Pleasant and lovely, were they both in life,
And in their death was found no parting strife.
Swifter then swiftest Eagles so were they,
Stronger then Lions ramping for their prey.
O Israels Dames, o'reflow your beauteous eyes
For valiant *Saul* who on Mount *Gilbo* lyes,
Who cloathed you in Cloath of richest Dye,
And choice delights, full of variety,
On your array put ornaments of gold,
Which made you yet more beauteous to behold.
O! how in Battle did the mighty fall
In midst of strength not succoured at all.
O lovely *Jonathan!* how wast thou slain?
In places high, full low thou didst remain.
Distrest for thee I am, dear *Jonathan,*
Thy love was wonderfull, surpassing man,
Exceeding all the love that's Feminine,
So pleasant hast thou been, dear brother mine,
How are the mighty fall'n into decay?
And warlike weapons perished away?

"To my Dear and loving Husband." [1]

TEXT: Ellis, p. 394.

If ever two were one, then surely we. '
If ever man were lov'd by wife, then thee;
If ever wife was happy in a man,
Compare with me ye women if you can.
I prize thy love more then whole Mines of gold,
Or all the riches that the East doth hold.
My love is such that Rivers cannot quench,
Nor ought but love from thee, give recompence.

Thy love is such I can no way repay,
The heavens reward thee manifold I pray.
Then while we live, in love lets so persever,
That when we live no more, we may live ever.

"Another."

TEXT: Ellis, pp. 397-398.

As loving Hind that (Hartless) wants her Deer,
Scuds through the woods and Fern with harkning ear,
Perplext, in every bush & nook doth pry,
Her dearest Deer, might answer ear or eye;
So doth my anxious soul, which now doth miss,
A dearer Dear (far dearer Heart) then this.
Still wait with doubts, & hopes, and failing eye,
His voice to hear, or person to discry.
Or as the pensive Dove doth all alone
(On withered bough) most uncouthly bemoan
The absence of her Love, and loving Mate,
Whose loss hath made her so unfortunate:
Ev'n thus doe I, with many a deep sad groan
Bewail my turtle true, who now is gone,
His presence and his safe return, still wooes,
With thousand dolefull sighs & mournfull Cooes.
Or as the loving Mullet, that true Fish,
Her fellow lost, nor joy nor life do wish,
But lanches[1] on that shore, there for to dye,
Where she her captive husband doth espy.
Mine being gone, I lead a joyless life,
I have a loving phere, yet seem no wife:
But worst of all, to him can't steer my course,
I here, he there, alas, both kept by force:
Return my Dear, my joy, my only Love,
Unto thy Hinde, thy Mullet and thy Dove,
Who neither joyes in pasture, house nor streams,
The substance gone, O me, these are but dreams.
Together at one Tree, oh let us brouze,
And like two Turtles roost within one house,
And like the Mullets in one River glide,

Let's still remain but one, till death divide.
{ *Thy loving Love and Dearest Dear,*
{ *At home, abroad, and every where.*

A.B.

"Before the Birth of one of her Children."

TEXT: Ellis, pp. 393-394.

All things within this fading world hath end,
Adversity doth still our joyes attend;
No tyes so strong, no friends so dear and sweet,
But with deaths parting blow is sure to meet.
The sentence past is most irrovocable,
A common thing, yet oh inevitable;
How soon, my Dear, death may my steps attend,
How soon't may be thy Lot to lose thy friend,
We both are ignorant, yet love bids me
These farewell lines to recommend to thee,
That when that knot's unty d that made us one,
I may seem thine, who in effect am none.
And if I see not half my dayes that's due,
What nature would, God grant to yours and you;
The many faults that well you know I have,
Let be interr'd in my oblivions grave;
If any worth or virtue were in me,
Let that live freshly in thy memory
And when thou feel'st no grief, as I no harms,
Yet love thy dead, who long lay in thine arms:
And when thy loss shall be repaid with gains
Look to my little babes my dear remains.
And if thou love thy self, or loved'st me
These O protect from step Dames injury.
And if chance to thine eyes shall bring this verse,
With some sad sighs honour my absent Herse;
And kiss this paper for thy loves dear sake,
Who with salt tears this last Farewel did take.

A.B.

". . . some verses upon the burning of our house, July 10th, 1666."

TEXT: Ellis, pp. 40-42.

In silent night when rest I took,
For sorrow neer I did not look,
I waken'd was with thundring nois
And Piteous shreiks of dreadfull voice.
That fearfull sound of fire and fire,
Let no man know is my Desire.

I, starting up, the light did spye,
And to my God my heart did cry
To strengthen me in my Distresse
And not to leave me succourlesse.
Then coming out beheld a space,
The flame consume my dwelling place.

And, when I could no longer look,
I blest his Name that gave and took,
That layd my goods now in the dust:
Yea so it was, and so 'twas just.
It was his own: it was not mine;
Far be it that I should repine.

He might of All justly bereft,
But yet sufficient for us left.
When by the Ruines oft I past,
My sorrowing eyes aside did cast,
And here and there the places spye
Where oft I sate, and long did lye.

Here stood that Trunk, and there that chest;
There lay that store I counted best:
My pleasant things in ashes lye,
And them behold no more shall I.
Under thy roof no guest shall sitt,
Nor at thy Table eat a bitt.

No pleasant tale shall 'ere be told,
Nor things recounted done of old.
No Candle 'ere shall shine in Thee,

Nor bridegroom's voice ere heard shall bee.
In silence ever shalt thou lye;
Adeiu, Adeiu; All's vanity.

Then streight I gin my heart to chide,
And did thy wealth on earth abide?
Didst fix thy hope on mouldring dust,
The arm of flesh didst make thy trust?
Raise up thy thoughts above the skye
That dunghill mists away may flie.

Thou hast an house on high erect
Fram'd by that mighty Architect,
With glory richly furnished,
Stands permanent tho: this bee fled.
'Its purchaséd, and paid for too
By him who hath enough to doe.

A Prise so vast as is unknown,
Yet, by his Gift, is made thine own.
Ther's wealth enough, I need no more;
Farewell my Pelf, farewell my Store.
The world no longer let me Love,
My hope and Treasure lyes Above.

"The Flesh and the Spirit."

TEXT: Ellis, pp. 381-385.

In secret place where once I stood
Close by the Banks of *Lacrim* flood
I heard two sisters reason on
Things that are past, and things to come;
One flesh was call'd, who had her eye
On worldly wealth and vanity;
The other Spirit, who did rear
Her thoughts unto a higher sphere:
Sister, quoth Flesh, what liv'st thou on
Nothing but Meditation?
Doth Contemplation feed thee so
Regardlessly to let earth goe?
Can Speculation satisfy

Notion without Reality?
Dost dream of things beyond the Moon
And dost thou hope to dwell there soon?
Hast treasures there laid up in store
That all in th' world thou count'st but poor?
Art fancy sick, or turn'd a Sot
To catch at shadowes which are not?
Come, come, Ile shew unto thy sence,
Industry hath its recompence.
What canst desire, but thou maist see
True substance in variety?
Dost honour like? acquire the same,
As some to their immortal fame:
And trophyes to thy name erect
Which wearing time shall ne're deject.
For riches dost thou long full sore?
Behold enough of precious store.
Earth hath more silver, pearls and gold,
Then eyes can see, or hands can hold.
Affect's thou pleasure? take thy fill,
Earth hath enough of what you will.
Then let not goe, what thou maist find,
For things unknown, only in mind.
Spir. Be still thou unregenerate part,
Disturb no more my setled heart,
For I have vow'd, (and so will doe)
Thee as a foe, still to pursue.
And combate with thee will and must,
Untill I see thee laid in th' dust.
Sisters we are, ye twins we be,
Yet deadly feud 'twixt thee and me;
For from one father are we not,
Thou by old Adam wast begot,
But my arise is from above,
Whence my dear father I do love.
Thou speak st me fair, but hat st me sore,
Thy flatt'ring shews Ile trust no more.
How oft thy slave, hast thou me made,
When I believ'd, what thou hast said,
And never had more cause of woe
Then when I did what thou bad'st doe.

Ile stop mine ears at these thy charms,
And count them for my deadly harms.
Thy sinfull pleasures I doe hate,
Thy riches are to me no bait,
Thine honours doe, nor will I love;
For my ambition lyes above.
My greatest honour it shall be
When I am victor over thee,
And triumph shall, with laurel head,
When thou my Captive shalt be led,
How I do live, thou need'st not scoff,
For I have meat thou know'st not off;
The hidden Manna I doe eat,
The word of life it is my meat.
My thoughts do yield me more content
Then can thy hours in pleasure spent.
Nor are they shadows which I catch,
Nor fancies vain at which I snatch,
But reach at things that are so high,
Beyond thy dull Capacity;
Eternal substance I do see,
With which inriched I would be:
Mine Eye doth pierce the heavens, and see
What is Invisible to thee.
My garments are not silk nor gold,
Nor such like trash which Earth doth hold,
But Royal Robes I shall have on,
More glorious then the glistring Sun;
My Crown not Diamonds, Pearls, and gold,
But such as Angels heads infold.
The City where I hope to dwell,
There's none on Earth can parallel;
The stately Walls both high and strong,
Are made of pretious *Jasper* stone;
The Gates of Pearl, both rich and clear,
And Angels are for Porters there;
The Streets thereof transparent gold,
Such as no Eye did e're behold,
A Chrystal River there doth run,
Which doth proceed from the Lambs Throne:
Of Life, there are the waters sure,

Which shall remain for ever pure,
Nor Sun, nor Moon, they have no need,
For glory doth from God proceed:
No Candle there, nor yet Torch light,
For there shall be no darksome night.
From sickness and infirmity,
For evermore they shall be free,
Nor withering age shall e're come there,
But beauty shall be bright and clear;
This City pure is not for thee,
For things unclean there shall not be:
If I of Heaven may have my fill,
Take thou the world, and all that will.

"As weary pilgrim, now at rest."

TEXT: Ellis, pp. 42-44.

As weary pilgrim, now at rest,
    Hugs with delight his silent nest
His wasted limbes, now lye full soft
    That myrie steps, have troden oft
Blesses himself, to think upon
    his dangers past, and travailes done
The burning sun no more shall heat
    Nor stormy raines, on him shall beat.
The bryars and thornes no more shall scratch
    nor hungry wolves at him shall catch
He erring pathes no more shall tread
    nor wild fruits eate, in stead of bread,
for waters cold he doth not long
    for thirst no more shall parch his tongue
No rugged stones his feet shall gaule
    nor stumps nor rocks cause him to fall
All cares and feares, he bids farwell
    and meanes in safity now to dwell.
A pilgrim I, on earth, perplext
    with sinns with cares and sorrows vext
By age and paines brought to decay
    and my Clay house mouldring away
Oh how I long to be at rest

and soare on high among the blest.
This body shall in silence sleep
    Mine eyes no more shall ever weep
No fainting fits shall me assaile
    nor grinding paines my body fraile
With cares and fears ne'r cumbred be
    Nor losses know, nor sorrowes see
What tho my flesh shall there consume
    it is the bed Christ did perfume
And when a few yeares shall be gone
    this mortall shall be cloth'd upon
A Corrupt Carcasse downe it lyes
    a glorious body it shall rise
In weaknes and dishonour sowne
    in power 'tis rais'd by Christ alone
Then soule and body shall unite
    and of their maker have the sight
Such lasting joyes shall there behold
    as eare ne'r heard nor tongue e'er told
Lord make me ready for that day
    then Come deare bridgrome Come away.
Aug: 31, 69.

"The Author to her Book."

TEXT: Ellis, pp. 389-390.

THou ill-form'd offspring of my feeble brain,
Who after birth did'st by my side remain,
Till snatcht from thence by friends, less wise then true
Who thee abroad, expos'd to publick view,[1]
Made thee in raggs, halting to th'press to trudg,
Where errors were not lessened (all may judg)
At thy return my blushing was not small,
My rambling brat (in print) should mother call,
I cast thee by as one unfit for light,
Thy Visage was so irksome in my sight;
Yet being mine own, at length affection would
Thy blemishes amend, if so I could:
I wash'd thy face, but more defects I saw,
And rubbing off a spot, still made a flaw.

I stretcht thy joynts to make thee even feet,
Yet still thou run'st more hobling then is meet;
In better dress to trim thee was my mind,
But nought save home-spun Cloth, i'th' house I find
In this array, 'mongst Vulgars mayst thou roam
In Criticks hands, beware thou dost not come;
And take thy way where yet thou art not known,
If for thy Father askt, say, thou hadst none:
And for thy Mother, she alas is poor,
Which caus'd her thus to send thee out of door.

Nathaniel Ward

(1578-1652)

TEXT: Ellis, p. 85.

Mercury shew'd *Apollo, Bartas* Book,
Minerva this, and wisht him well to look,
And tell uprightly which did which excell,
He view'd and view'd, and vow'd he could not tel.
Thy bid him Hemisphear his mouldy nose,
With's crackt leering glasses, for it would pose
The best brains he had in's old pudding-pan,
Sex weigh'd, which best, the Woman, or the Man?
He peer'd and por'd, & glar'd, & said for wore,[2]
I'me even as wise now, as I was before:
They both 'gan laugh, and said it was no mar'l
The Auth'ress was a right *Du Bartas* Girle.
Good sooth quoth the old *Don,* tell ye me so,
I muse whither at length these Girls will go;
It half revives my chil frost-bitten blood,
To see a Woman once, do ought that's good;
And chode[2] by *Chaucers* Boots, and *Homers* Furrs,
Let Men look to't, least Women wear the Spurrs.

Anonymous

TEXT: Ellis, p. 92.

> *Anna Bradestreate*   Deer neat *An Bartas*.
> So *Bartas* like thy fine spun Poems been,
> That *Bartas* name will prove an Epicene.
> Another.
> *Anna Bradstreate*   Artes bred neat *An*.

Michael Wigglesworth
(1631-1705)

"GOD'S CONTROVERSY WITH NEW-ENGLAND."

Written in the time of the great drought Anno 1662.
By a lover of New England's prosperity.

TEXT: *Proceedings of the Massachusetts Historical Society, 1871-1873* (Boston, 1873), pp. 83-93.

Isaiah, 5.4.—What could have been done more to my vineyard that I have not done in it? wherefore when I looked that it should bring forth grapes, brought it forth wilde grapes?

The Authors Request Unto the Reader.

> Good christian Reader judge me not
>   As too censorious,
> For pointing at those faults of thine
>   Which are notorious.
> For if those faults be none of thine
>   I do not thee accuse:
> But if they be, to hear thy faults
>   Why shouldest thou refuse.
>
> I blame not thee to spare my self:
>   But first at home begin,
> And judge my self, before that I
>   Reproove anothers sin.

Nor is it I that thee reproove
　　Let God himself be heard
Whose awfull providence's voice
　　No man may disregard.

Quod Deus omnipotens regali voce minatur,
Quod tibi proclamant uno simul ore prophetae,
Quodq' ego cum lachrymis testor de numinis irâ,
Tu leve comentu ne ducas, Lector Amice.[1]

New-England Planted, Prospered, Declining, Threatned, Punished.

Beyond the great Atlantick flood
　　There is a region vast,
A country where no English foot
　　In former ages past:
A waste and howling wilderness,
　　Where none inhabited
But hellish fiends, and brutish men
　　That Devils worshiped.

This region was in darkness plac't
　　Far off from heavens light,
Amidst the shaddows of grim death
　　And of eternal night.
For there the Sun of righteousness
　　Had never made to shine
The light of his sweet countenance,
　　And grace which is divine:

Until the time drew nigh wherein
　　The glorious Lord of hostes
Was pleasd to lead his armies forth
　　Into those forrein coastes.
At whose approach the darkness sad
　　Soon vanished away,
And all the shaddows of the night
　　Were turnd to lightsome day.

The dark and dismal western woods
　　(The Devils den whilere)

Beheld such glorious gospel-shine,
    As none beheld more cleare.
Where sathan had his scepter sway'd
    For many generations,
The King of Kings set up his throne
    To rule amongst the nations.

The stubborn he in pieces brake,
    Like vessels made of clay:
And those that sought his peoples hurt
    He turned to decay.
Those curst Amalekites, that first
    Lift up their hand on high
To fight against Gods Israel,
    Were ruin'd fearfully.

Thy terrours on the Heathen folk,
    O Great Jehovah, fell:
The fame of thy great acts, o Lord,
    Did all the nations quell.
Some hid themselves for fear of thee
    In forrests wide & great:
Some to thy people croutching came,
    For favour to entreat.

Some were desirous to be taught
    The knowledge of thy wayes,
And being taught, did soon accord
    Therein to spend their dayes.
Thus were the fierce & barbarous
    Brought to civility,
And those that liv'd like beasts (or worse)
    To live religiously.

O happiest of dayes wherein
    The blind received sight,
And those that had no eyes before
    Were made to see the light!
The wilderness hereat rejoyc't,
    The woods for joy did sing,
The vallys & the little hills
    Thy praises ecchoing.

Here was the hiding place, which thou,
    Jehovah, didst provide
For thy redeemed ones, and where
    Thou didst thy jewels hide
In per'lous times, and saddest dayes
    Of sack-cloth and of blood,
When th'overflowing scourge did pass
    Through Europe, like a flood.

While almost all the world beside
    Lay weltring in their gore:
We, only we, enjoyd such peace
    As none enjoyd before.
No forrein foeman did us fray,
    Nor threat'ned us with warrs:
We had no enemyes at home,
    Nor no domestick jarrs.

The Lord had made (such was his grace)
    For us a Covenant
Both with the men, and with the beasts,
    That in this desert haunt:
So that through places wilde and waste
    A single man, disarm'd,
Might journey many hundred miles,
    And not at all be harm'd.

Amidst the solitary woods
    Poor travellers might sleep
As free from danger as at home,
    Though no man watch did keep.
Thus were we priviledg'd with peace,
    Beyond what others were.
Truth, Mercy, Peace, with Righteousness,
    Took up their dwelling here.

Our Governour was of our selves,
    And all his Bretheren,
For wisdom & true piety,
    Select, & chosen men.
Who, Ruling in ye fear of God,

The righteous cause maintained,
And all injurious violence,
   And wickedness, restrained.

Our temp'rall blessings did abound:
   But spirituall good things
Much more abounded, to the praise
   Of that great King of Kings.
Gods throne was here set up; here was
   His tabernacle pight:[2]
This was the place, and these the folk
   In whom he took delight.

Our morning starrs shone all day long:
   Their beams gave forth such light,
As did the noon-day sun abash,
   And's glory dazle quite.
Our day continued many yeers,
   And had no night at all:
Yea many thought the light would last,
   And be perpetuall.

Such, o New-England, was thy first,
   Such was thy best estate:
But, Loe! a strange and suddain change
   My courage did amate.[3]
The brightest of our morning starrs
   Did wholly disappeare:
And those that tarried behind
   With sack-cloth covered were.

Moreover, I beheld & saw
   Our welkin overkest,
And dismal clouds for sun-shine late
   O'respread from east to west.
The air became tempestuous;
   The wilderness gan quake:
And from above with awfull voice
   Th' Almighty thundring spake.

Are these the men that erst at my command
   Forsook their ancient seats and native soile,

To follow me into a desart land,
  Contemning all the travell and the toile,
Whose love was such to purest ordinances
  As made them set at nought their fair inheritances?

Are these the men that prized libertee
  To walk with God according to their light,
To be as good as he would have them bee,
  To serve and worship him with all their might,
Before the pleasures which a fruitfull field,
  And country flowing-full of all good things, could yield,

Are these the folk whom from the brittish Iles,
  Through the stern billows of the watry main,
I safely led so many thousand miles,
  As if their journey had been through a plain?
Whom having from all enemies protected,
  And through so many deaths and dangers well directed,

I brought and planted on the western shore,
  Where nought but bruits and salvage wights did swarm
(Untaught, untrain'd, untam'd by vertue's lore)
  That sought their blood, yet could not do them harm?
My fury's flaile them thresht, my fatall broom
  Did sweep them hence, to make my people elbow-room.

Are these the men whose gates with peace I crown'd,
  To whom for bulwarks I salvation gave,
Whilst all things else with rattling tumults sound,
  And mortall frayes send thousands to the grave?
Whilest their own brethren bloody hands embrewed
  In brothers blood, and fields with carcases bestrewed?

Is this the people blest with bounteous store,
  By land and sea full richly clad and fed,
Whom plenty's self stands waiting still before,
  And powreth out their cups well tempered?
For whose dear sake an howling wildernes
  I lately turned into a fruitfull paradeis?

Are these the people in whose hemisphere
  Such bright-beam'd, glist'ring, sun-like starrs I placed,

As by their influence did all things cheere,
    As by their light blind ignorance defaced,
As errours into lurking holes did fray,
    As turn'd the late dark night into a lightsome day?

Are these the folk to whom I milked out
    And sweetnes stream'd from consolations brest;
Whose soules I fed and strengthened throughout
    With finest spirituall food most finely drest?
On whom I rained living bread from Heaven,
    Withouten Errour's bane, or Superstition's leaven?

With whom I made a Covenant of peace,
    And unto whom I did most firmly plight
My faithfulness, If whilst I live I cease
    To be their Guide, their God, their full delight;
Since them with cords of love to me I drew,
    Enwrapping in my grace such as should them ensew.

Are these the men, that now mine eyes behold,
    Concerning whom I thought, and whilome spake,
First Heaven shall pass away together scrold,
    Ere they my lawes and righteous wayes forsake,
Or that they slack to runn their heavenly race?
    Are these the same? or are some others come in place?

If these be they, how is it that I find
    In stead of holiness Carnality,
In stead of heavenly frames an Earthly mind,
    For burning zeal luke-warm Indifferency,
For flaming love, key-cold Dead-heartedness,
    For temperance (in meat, and drinke, and cloaths)
                                      excess?

Whence cometh it, that Pride, and Luxurie
    Debate, Deceit, Contention, and Strife,
False-dealing, Covetousness, Hypocrisie
    (With such like Crimes) amongst them are so rife,
That one of them doth over-reach another?
    And that an honest man can hardly trust his Brother?

How is it, that Security, and Sloth,
        Amongst the best are Common to be found?
That grosser sins, in stead of Graces growth,
        Amongst the many more and more abound?
I hate dissembling shews of Holiness.
        Or practise as you talk, or never more profess.

Judge not, vain world, that all are hypocrites
        That do profess more holiness than thou:
All foster not dissembling, guilefull sprites,
        Nor love their lusts, though very many do.
Some sin through want of care and constant watch,
        Some with the sick converse, till they the sickness catch.

Some, that maintain a reall root of grace,
        Are overgrown with many noysome weeds,
Whose heart, that those no longer may take place,
        The benefit of due correction needs.
And such as these however gone astray
        I shall by stripes reduce into a better way.

Moreover some there be that still retain
        Their ancient vigour and sincerity;
Whom both their own, and others sins, constrain
        To sigh, and mourn, and weep, and wail, & cry:
And for their sakes I have forborn to powre
        My wrath upon Revolters to this present houre.

To praying Saints I always have respect,
        And tender love, and pittifull regard:
Nor will I now in any wise neglect
        Their love and faithfull service to reward;
Although I deal with others for their folly,
        And turn their mirth to tears that have been too jolly.

For thinke not, O Backsliders, in your heart,
        That I shall still your evill manners beare:
Your sinns me press as sheaves do load a cart,
        And therefore I will plague you for this geare
Except you seriously, and soon, repent,
        Ile not delay your pain and heavy punishment.

And who be those themselves that yonder shew?
    The seed of such as name my dreadfull Name!
On whom whilere compassions skirt I threw
    Whilest in their blood they were, to hide their shame!
Whom my preventing love did neer me take!
    Whom for mine own I mark't, lest they should me
                                forsake!

I look't that such as these to vertue's Lore
    (Though none but they) would have Enclin'd their ear:
That they at least mine image should have bore,
    And sanctify'd my name with awfull fear.
Let pagan's Bratts pursue their lusts, whose meed
    Is Death: For christians children are an holy seed.

But hear O Heavens! Let Earth amazed stand;
    Ye Mountaines melt, and Hills come flowing down:
Let horrour seize upon both Sea and Land;
    Let Natures self be cast into a stown.[4]
I children nourisht, nurtur'd and upheld:
    But they against a tender father have rebell'd.

What could have been by me performed more?
    Or wherein fell I short of your desire?
Had you but askt, I would have op't my store,
    And given what lawfull wishes could require.
For all this bounteous cost I lookt to see
    Heaven-reaching-hearts, & thoughts, Meekness,
                       /   Humility.
But lo, a sensuall Heart all void of grace,
    An Iron neck, a proud presumptuous Hand;
A self-conceited, stiff, stout, stubborn Race,
    That fears no threats, submitts to no command:
Self-will'd, perverse, such as can beare no yoke;
    A Generation even ripe for vengeance stroke.

Such were that Carnall Brood of Israelites
    That Josua and the Elders did ensue,
Who growing like the cursed Cananites
    Upon themselves my heavy judgements drew.
Such also was that fleshly Generation,
    Whom I o'rewhelm'd by waters deadly inundation.

They darker light, and lesser meanes misused;
    They had not such Examples them to warn:
You clearer Rules, and Precepts, have abused,
    And dreadfull monuments of others harm.
My gospels glorious light you do not prize:
    My Gospels endless, boundless grace you clean despize.

My painfull messengers you disrespect,
    Who toile and sweat and sweale[5] themselves away,
Yet nought at all with you can take effect,
    Who hurrie headlong to your own decay.
In vain the Founder melts, and taketh pains:
    Bellows and Lead's consum'd, but still your dross
                                                    remains.

What should I do with such a stiff-neckt race?
    How shall I ease me of such Foes as they?
What shall befall despizers of my Grace?
    I'le surely beare their candle-stick away,
And Lamps put out. Their glorious noon-day light
    I'le quickly turn into a dark Egyptian night.

Oft have I charg'd you by my ministers
    To gird your selves with sack cloth, and repent.
Oft have I warnd you by my messengers;
    That so you might my wrathfull ire prevent:
But who among you hath this warning taken?
    Who hath his crooked wayes, & wicked works
                                                    forsaken?

Yea many grow to more and more excess;
    More light and loose, more Carnall and prophane.
The sins of Sodom, Pride, and Wantonness,
    Among the multitude spring up amain.
Are these the fruits of Pious Education,
    To run with greater speed and Courage to Damnation

If here and there some two, or three, shall steere
    A wiser course, then their Companions do,
You make a mock of such; and scoff, and jeere
    Becaus they will not be so bad as you.
Such is the Generation that succeeds
    The men, whose eyes have seen my great & awfull
                                                    deeds.

Now therefore hearken and encline your ear,
    In judgement I will henceforth with you plead;
And if by that you will not learn to fear,
    But still go on a sensuall life to lead:
I'le strike at once an All-Consuming stroke;
    Nor cries nor tears shall then my fierce intent revoke.

    Thus ceast his Dreadful-threatning voice
        The High & lofty-One.
    The Heavens stood still Appal'd thereat;
        The Earth beneath did groane:
    Soon after I beheld and saw
        A mortall dart come flying:
    I lookt again, & quickly saw
        Some fainting, others dying.

    The Heavens more began to lowre,
        The welkin Blacker grew:
    And all things seemed to forebode
        Sad changes to ensew.
    From that day forward hath the Lord
        Apparently contended
    With us in Anger, and in Wrath:
        But we have not amended.

    Our healthfull dayes are at an end,
        And sicknesses come on
    From yeer to yeer, becaus our hearts
        Away from God are gone.
    New-England, where for many yeers
        You scarcely heard a cough,
    And where Physicians had no work,
        Now finds them work enough.

    Now colds and coughs, Rhewms, and sore-throats,
        Do more & more abound:
    Now Agues sore & feavers strong
        In every place are found.
    How many houses have we seen
        Last Autumn, and this spring,
    Wherein the healthful were too few
        To help the languishing.

One wave another followeth,
    And one disease begins
Before another cease, becaus
    We turn not from our sins.
We stopp our ear against reproof,
    And hearken not to God:
God stops his ear against our prayer,
    And takes not off his rod.

Our fruitful seasons have been turnd
    Of late to barrenness,
Sometimes through great & parching drought,
    Sometimes through rain's excess.
Yea now the pastures & corn fields
    For want of rain do languish:
The cattell mourn, & hearts of men
    Are fill'd with fear & anguish.

The clouds are often gathered,
    As if we should have rain:
But for our great unworthiness
    Are scattered again.
We pray & fast, & make fair shewes,
    As if we meant to turn:
But whilst we turn not, God goes on
    Our field, & fruits to burn.

And burnt are all things in such sort,
    That nothing now appears,
But what may wound our hearts with grief,
    And draw foorth floods of teares.
All things a famine do presage
    In that extremity,
As if both men, and also beasts,
    Should soon be done to dy.

This O New-England hast thou got
    By riot, & excess:
This hast thou brought upon thy self
    By pride & wantonness.
Thus must thy worldlyness be whipt.

They, that too much do crave,
Provoke the Lord to take away
Such blessings as they have.

We have been also threatened
With worser things then these:
And God can bring them on us still,
To morrow if he please.
For if his mercy be abus'd,
Which holpe us at our need
And mov'd his heart to pitty us,
We shall be plagu'd indeed.

Beware, O sinful Land, beware;
And do not think it strange
That sorer judgements are at hand,
Unless thou quickly change.
Or God, or thou, must quickly change;
Or else thou art undon:
Wrath cannot cease, if sin remain,
Where judgement is begun.

Ah dear New England! dearest land to me;
Which unto God hast hitherto been dear,
And mayst be still more dear than formerlie,
If to his voice thou wilt incline thine ear.

Consider wel & wisely what the rod,
Wherewith thou art from yeer to yeer chastized,
Instructeth thee. Repent, & turn to God,
Who wil not have his nurture be despized.

Thou still hast in thee many praying saints,
Of great account, and precious with the Lord,
Who dayly powre out unto him their plaints,
And strive to please him both in deed & word.

Cheer on, sweet souls, my heart is with you all,
And shall be with you, maugre Sathan's might:
And whereso'ere this body be a Thrall,
Still in New-England shall be my delight.

"A Farewel to the World"

TEXT: *The Day of Doom,* 7th ed. enlarged (Boston, 1751), pp. 97-99.

NOw farewel World, in which is not my Treasure,
I have in thee enjoy'd but little Pleasure.
And now I leave thee for a better Place,
Where lasting Pleasures are before CHRIST's Face.

Farewel, ye Sons of Men, who do not favour
The things of God; who little prize his Favour.
Farewel, I say with your *Fools Paradise,*
Until the King of Terrors you Surprise,
And bring you trembling to CHRIST's Judgment seat,
To give Account of your Transgressions Great.

Farewel, *New-England,* which hast long Enjoy'd
The Day of Grace, but hast most vainly toy'd,
And trifled with the Gospels Glorious Light;
Thou mayst expect a dark *Egyptian* Night.

Farewel, *Young* Brood and Rising Generation,
Wanton and Proud, Ripe for Gods Indignation;
Which neither you, nor others can prevent,
Except in Truth you speedily Repent.

Farewel, sweet Saints of God, Christ's little Number,
Beware lest ye thro' sloth securely Slumber.
Stand to your Spiritual Arms, and keep your Watch,
Let not your Enemy you napping catch.
Take up your Cross, prepare for Tribulation,
Thro' which doth ly the way unto Salvation.
Love JESUS CHRIST, with all Sincerity:
Eschew Will-Worship and Idolatry.
Farewel again, until we all appear
Before our Lord, a *Well-done* there to hear.

Farewel ye faithful Servants of the Lord,
Painful dispensers of His Holy Word;
From whose Communion and Society
I once was kept thro' long Infirmity;

This of my Sorrows was an Aggravation;
But, Christ be thanked, thro' whose Mediation,
I have at length obtained Liberty
To dwell with Soul-delighting Company,
Where many of our Friends are gone before,
And you shall follow with as many more.
Mean while stand fast, the Truth of God maintain,
Suffer for Christ, and great shall be your Gain.

Farewel, my natural Friends and dear Relations,
Who have my Trials seen and great Temptations;
You have no Cause to make for me great Moan;
My Death to you is little Loss or none.
But unto me it is no little Gain;
For Death at once frees me from all my Pain.
Make Christ your greatest Friend, who never dies;
All other Friends are fading Vanities.
Make him your Light, your Life, your End, your All:
Prepare for Death, be ready for his call.

Farewel, vile Body subject to Decay,
Which art with lingering Sickness worn away,
I have by thee much Pain and Smart endur'd,
Great Grief of Mind thou hast to me Procur'd;
Great Grief of Mind, by being impotent,
And to Christ's Work an awkward Instrument.
Thou shalt not henceforth be a clog to me,
Nor shall my Soul a burthen be to thee.

Rest in thy Grave, until the Resurrection,
Then shalt thou be revived in Perfection:
Endow'd with wonderful Agility,
Cloathed with Strength, and Immortality;
With shining brightness, gloriously array'd,
Like to Christ's glorious Body, glorious made.
Thus Christ shall thee again to me restore,
Ever to live with Him, and part no more.
Mean while my Soul shall enter into Peace,
Where Fears and Tears, where Sin & Smart shall cease.

"Meditation"

TEXT: *Meat out of the Eater,* 4th ed. (Boston, 1689), pp. 9-12.

(1)

GOd doth chasten his own
    In Love' their souls to save:
And lets them not run wild with them
    That no Correction have.
    Now as the Rod restrains   *Prov.* 2
    From posting down to Hell;   14.
So by the same God doth Excite
    And teach us to do well.

(2)

Affliction is Christ's School,
    Wherein He teacheth His   *Psa.* 94
To know and do their duty, and   12.
    To mend what is amiss.
    For though Afflictions may
    Unto the Flesh be painful;
David and other Saints of God
    Have found them very gainful.

(3)

Ps. 119.   Before I was chastis'd,
67.   Saith he, I went astray:
               But since I've learnt with better Care
                    To keep Thy Precepts way.
Ver. 71.   'Tis good for mee that I
                    Have been afflicted sore
               That I might learn to know thy Lawes
                    And swerve therefrom no more

(4)

Isa. 48.   These are God's Fining Pot,
10.   Wherein He melts His Gold,
               Consumes the Dross and maketh it
                    More lovely to behold.

Mal. 3.   These are His Fullers Sope[1]
2, 3.   To wash our spots away.
Dan. 11   That being thus refin'd and Wash'd
35.   Him glorifie we may.

(5)

As sharpest Winter Frosts
Do clarifie the Aire
And cleanse our blood, soften the earth
And it for seed prepare,
Making it fruitfuller:
So do Afflictions sore
Correct the Rankness of our hearts,
Cleanse and Subdue them more.

(6)

Much Honey turns to Gall
And Cholerick Excess;
And too-too-much Prosperity   *Deut.* 32
Breeds Pride and Wantonness: 15.
Afflictions purge them out,   *Isa.* 27
Like bitter Aloe.   9.
Which though unpleasant to the Taste,   *Heb.* 12.
Far wholesomer may be.   10. 11.

(7)

Full Diet, dainty Fare,
With Idleness and Ease
Heap up bad Humours and Contract,   *Ezek.* 16
Many a foul Disease,   49, 50.
To Soul and Body too,
Dang'rous and Troublesome,
Which must be purged out in time
With some *Catholicum*.[2]

(8)

Strong wine makes weak heads *giddy,*
Procuring Drunkenness;

Long peace and plenty likewise breed
   Intemperance and Excess.   *Jer.* 7.
We soon are surfeited   7, 8.
   With strong delicious matter:
And therefore God who, *knowes our frame*
   Mingleth our Wine with Water.

(9)

Afflictions are like Ballast
   I'th' Bottom of a Ship;
For tho perhaps without the same
   We might more lightly Skip:
   Yet every little puff
   Would quickly set us over.
And sink us in the Ocean Sea
   No more for to Recover.

(10)

            Our hearts are over-run
Jer. 4.   Much like a Fallow-field,
3, 4.   Which must be broke and plowed up
           Before it Fruit can yeild:
Ps. 129.   Afflictions are God's Plough
2, 3.   Where-with He breaketh us,
Jer. 31.   Tears up our *lusts* those noisome *weeds*
18, 19.   And fitteth us for Use.

(11)

Grace in prosperity
   Lies hid unoccupy'd:
But is by Chastening set to work,
   And by the Cross descri'd.
   The Cross to Vertue trains;
   It Tries, it makes to grow;
It sanctifies, purgeth and heals;
   It humbleth and layes low.

Jonathan Mitchell

(1624-1668)

"On the following Work,
and
It's AUTHOR:"

TEXT: Michael Wigglesworth, *The Day of Doom,* 5th ed. enlarged
(Boston, 1701), pp. B-B1.

A Verse may find him who a Sermon flies,
Saith *Herbert* well. Great Truths to dress in Meeter;
Becomes a Preacher; who mens Souls doth prize,
That Truth in Sugar roll'd may taste the sweeter,
　　No Cost too great, no Care too curious is
　　To set forth Truth, and win mens Souls to bliss.

In Costly Verse, and most laborious Rymes,
Are dish't up here Truths worthy most regard:
No Toyes, nor Fables (Poets wonted Crimes)
Here be; but things of worth with Wit prepar'd.
　　Reader, fall too; and if thy tast be good,
　　Thou'lt praise the Cook, & say, 'Tis choisest Food.

David's affliction bred us many a *Psalm,*
From Caves, from mouth of Graves that Singer sweet
Oft tun'd his Soul felt Notes: For not in's Calm,
But Storms, to write most Psalms God made him meet
　　Affliction turn'd this Pen to Poetry,[1]
　　Whose serious streins do here before thee ly.

This Man with many griefs afflicted sore,
Shut up from speaking much in sickly Cave:
Thence painful leisure hath to write the more,
And sends thee Counsels from the mouth o' th' Grave.
　　One foot i'th' other World long time hath been:
　　Read, and thou'lt say, His heart is all therein.

Oh, happy Cave, that's to mount *Nebo* turn'd!
Oh, happy Pris'ner that's at liberty
To walk through th' other World! the Bonds are burn'd
(But nothing else) in Furnace fiery.
     Such Fires unfetter Saints, and set more free
     Their unscorch'd Souls for Christ's sweet companie.

Cheer on, sweet Soul, although in briny tears
Steept is thy seed, though dying every day;
Thy Sheaves shall joyful be, when Christ appears
To change our death and pain to life for ay.
     The weepers now shall laugh; the jovial laughter,
     Of vain ones here, shall turn to tears hereafter.

Judge right, and his restraint is our Reproof;
The Sins of Hearers, Preachers Lips do close,
And make that Tongue to cleave unto its roof,
Which else would check and cheer full freely those
     That need. But from this Eater comes some Meat,[2]
     And sweetness good from this affliction great.

In these vast Woods a Christian Poet Sings
(Where whilome Heathen wild were only found)
Of things to come, the last and greatest things,
Which in our Ears aloud should ever sound.
     Of Judgment dread, Hell, Heaven, Eternity;
     Reader, think oft, and help thy thoughts hereby.

John Saffin
(1626-1710)

"An Epithalmium or wedding Song"

TEXT: MS, The Rhode Island Historical Society.

Come Brave Gallants come away,
it quickly will be Break of Day;
Sweet virgins and fair Ladys all
hark: for it is the Bridgrooms Call;
hast, if you will be Dignifi'd

t'attend the Bridegroom and the Bride:
with all your Rich Attire, and Dress,
See who can best, their love Express;
for Neptune now hath lay'd aside
His Seagreen Mantle, Thetis pride:
to grace the Bride with good Intents
betake them Silver ornaments;
the pretty Birds, that Sing most rare:
Retaine their Notes, and lend an Eare
to hear the Sweet Hermonious Noise,
of the fair Bride, and Bridegrooms voice;
and Everything doth motion move,
with awefull due Respect, and Love
To Honour this their Nuptiall Tye
that thence may Spring a Progenie
which may in Vertue Ever Shine
like Pha'bus in Meridian line;
meanwhile wee'll Sing on Every side
Joyes to the Bridegroom & the Bride.

"From Virginia, 1654"

TEXT: MS, The Rhode Island Historical Society.

Sweetly (my Dearest) I left thee asleep
Which Silent parting made my heart to weep,
Faine would I wake her, but Love did Reply
O wake her not, So sweetly let her Lye.
But must I goe, ô must I Leave her So,
So ill at Ease: involv'd in Slumbering wo
Must I goe hence: and thus my Love desert
Unknown to Her, ô must I now Depart;
Thus was I hurried with such thoughts as these,
Yet loath to Rob the of thy present Ease,
Or rather Senceless payn: farewell thought I,
My Joy my Deare in whom I live or Dye
Farewell Content, farewell fare Beauty's light
And the most pleasing Object of my Sight;
I must begone, Adeiu my Dear, Adieu
Heavens grant good Tideings I next heare from you
Thus in sad Silence I alone and mute,

My lips bad thee farewell, with a Salute.
And so went from thee: turning back againe
I thought one kiss to little then Stole twaine
And then another: but no more of this,
Count with your Self how many of them you miss.
And now my Love soon let me from the heare
Of thy good health, that may my Spirits Cheare
Acquaint me with such passages as may
Present themselves since I am come away
And above all things let me thee Request
To bee both Chearfull quiet and at Rest
In thine own Spirit, and let nothing move
Thee unto Discontent my Joy my Love.
Hopeing that all things shall at last Conduce
Unto our Comfort and a Blessed use
Considering that those things are hardly gain'd
Are most Delightfull when they are Attain'd.
Gold Crowns are heavy: Idalian Burn's
And Lovers Days are good, and bad by turn's
But yet the Consummation will Repay
The Debt that's due many a happy Day
Which that it may so be, Ile Heaven Implore
To grant the same henceforth forever more
And so farewell, farewell fair Beautys light
Ten thousand times Adieu my Dear Delight.
　　　Your Ever loveing friend whilest Hee
　　　Desolved is: or Cease to bee.
　　　　　　　　　　　　　　J.S.

"A Letter to his Dear Martha 1660"

TEXT: MS, The Rhode Island Historical Society

Joy of my Life

When I think of those Charming Joys which I
use to possess in thy Societie
I Envy not the greatest in their places
Who ne'r perhaps Enjoy such sweet Embraces
But are meer Strangers to it, and ne'r prove
Those true Delights that founded are in Love

the true fruition of all Earthly Bliss
being not ample, without haveing this.
Reciprocall, intire affection Sound
Which to Each other doth so much Abound
But oh! I think the time almost ill Spent
That doth obstruct our Mutuall sweet Content
Deeming my Self, as of my Self Depriv'd
Liveing (me thinks) as one but Semi-liv'd
acting like him that is now here now there
being in an place in Body: heart Else where
Counting the tedious Months, the weeks, the Days
Nilling the Distance, or what else Delays
me from Enjoyment of thy Self who art,
My Love, my Joy, my Dear, my Better part.
But then againe think I, what would some give
to be assured ever while they live
Once to Enjoy at length that Happiness
Which we in other doe allways possess.
for thô thing in [blank] all men Crave
of whatsoever wealth, or Store they have
yet that in [blank] allso is well known
to be as well undoubted their owne.
A King whose Subjects Number doth amount
To an Exceeding Numerous account
Joys he hath people, and can pleased bee
Thô many of them he doe never See.
He that hath Store of money Gold or ware
Lands, Rents (perhaps) dispersed here & there
Joys that he has it, thô (perhaps) indeed
He hath no more in hand then what his Need
Serves to Supply; yet who will say that He
is not more Richer far, than many be
that have more Wealth at present in their hand
yet are no Owners of a house or Land.
So he, or She, that hath of the Most High
the Blessing of a happy Nuptiall Tye
Thô sometime absent from their dear Delight
and for a while, Deprived of their Sight
yet Joyes in this that they have such an One
thô out of Sight, assuredly their Owne;
And that in Gods due time they shall attaine

the Sweet fruition of their Loves againe
Even so it is my Dear Delight with mee
who takes more pleasure oft, to think on thee:
than doth the Greedy Miser, to behold
The full Cram'd Baggs, of his beloved Gold.
Meanwhile my Johnny-Boy is not forgott
Him I Remember thô he heeds it not;
Sweet Babe! how doe I mind thy perking Smiles
and pretty Toys thou usest other whiles.
Thy harmless quarrells, which so long Remaine
untill a Teat, doe make thee friends againe;
I likewise feel those paines that have opprest,
thy tender Body with whole Nights unrest:
and then thy pittious lookes, methinkes I see,
which language of those lookes, Afflicted mee.
Thy Mothers teares dry'd with her Sighs so deep:
(Enough to make a Marble Heart to weep;)
And such like Symtomes as these Ever are
the Marks of Love, and of Paternall Care;
Methinks I hear thy Mother to the prate
like to thy Self, that thou mayest imitate
and then againe to joy that other while,
thy wonton Inocence should laugh, & smile
and notice take of what may seem to high
for thy Juviniller, Capacity.
Thy promiseing perfection every way:
Seems to bespeake thee faine another Day.
And so Adieu my Dove, Heavens grant that wee
may with our Wonted Joy, Each other see.
          Thine or not his own   J.S.

"Cankers touch fairest fruites"

TEXT: MS, The Rhode Island Historical Society.

Cankers touch fairest fruites, by their Infection
A feavers Seize those of the best Complection.
So long the foolish Fly, plays with the flame,
till her light wings are singed with the same;
if Cupid then be blinde, how blinde are we,
that will be caught, by one that cannot See;

are women Woe to men? No, they'r the way
to bring them homeward, when they goe Astray.
Look all about yee: who so young that Loves-not
And who so Old, a Comely Feature moves

"The Painters Premonition."

TEXT: MS, The Rhode Island Historical Society.

There was a Gentlewoman came into a Painters room & turn'd a Picture,
and behold the Genitiles of a man at which Shee blusht) & was laugh't
into Shame.

Take heed, who in this Room appear
You Don't presume to turn a Picture here
Without the Speciall Licence of the Owner
Least you Displease him, and your Selves dishonour.

"on a Rogue that abus'd the people of N.E. of all Ranks
and sexes, in a printed Scurrillous pamphlett"

TEXT: MS, The Rhode Island Historical Society.

This Indigent Romantick Lowsey Lecher,
Belyes both sexes, Magistrate, & preacher;
So gross, malicious Serpentinely-fell:
Proceeding from Abaddon, hatch'd in Hell.

"To the Revd: Mr Wm Hubbard on his Exact History of
New Englands Troubles &c."

TEXT: MS, The Rhode Island Historical Society.

When thy Rare piece unto my view once came,
it made my Muse that Erst did Smoke, to flame:
Raiseing my fancie so sublime, that I
that famous Forked Mountaine did Espy,
Thence in an Extasie, I softly fell
downe, neare unto the Helliconian well:
where Poetry in prose (made) I did see,
By a Mercurian braine which sure was thee;

Such is thy modest Stile, Enrich'd with sense
Invention fine, faced with Eloquence;
Thy Flored Language quaintly doth Express,
the truth of matter, in a Comely Dress;
Couching the sense in such a pleaseing Straine,
as makes the Readers Heart to Leap againe:
And Sweetly drawes him, like those lotteries,
that never miss, but allwayes winnes the prize.
But whither Roves my Muse? what can be done
by him augments the Sea, or lights the Sun.
Goe on Brave Worthy, and let these Essayes
Like fair Aurora usher the Rayes:
of a Refulgent Sun, ariseing Clear
Hence to Illuminate our Hemisphere;
That th' after Ages may Extoll the High-one
For's loveing kindness to our little Sion.
And may our Senatours with due regard
These and thy future Labours all Reward:
Thô not in full yet such Encouragment
as may in them be just, to Thee Content.
For th' present age, and them that shall Ensue
Will be perpetuall Debtors unto you.
Fame shall with Honour Crown thee, & wee'll Raise
Thy lasting Monument in Groves of Bayes.
Heavens bless Thee in thy worke, & may Success
Attend thee here: Hereafter Happiness.

"A lamentation on my Dear Son Simon who dyed of the Smallpox
on the 23 November 1678"

TEXT: MS, The Rhode Island Historical Society.

Simon my son, Son of my Nuptiall knott—
ah! Simon's gone, Simon my son is not—
whose Heaven-born Soul in full ripe fruit appears
wherein he liv'd an age above his years.
whose pregnant witt, quick Genius, parts sublime
facill'd his Books, made him Pernassus clime
and Dare Apelles to were he alive
Who best should Lym, or Rarest piece contrive
He unappall'd with humble Confidence

could to's Superiours speak without Offence
So free and unconcern'd as one had been
conversing with his Equalls Dayly seen
his Towering Fancy, and his quaint invention
Excell'd most of his Standing and pretention
Lovely in's features his Complection fair
of comely Jeasture, flaxen was his haire
But that which Crowneth all the Rest
In his own language better is Exprest.

"One presenting a rare Book to Madam Hull Senr:
his Vallintine"

TEXT: MS, The Rhode Island Historical Society.

Here's Witts Extraction Morall & Divine
Presented to you, by your Vallintine
Here's Florid Language Suiting well your Straine
The Pallas of a Rare Mercurian Braine
Appollo's Darlings & th' Hesperedes
Doe with the Graces joyntly seeke to please
Your Towering fancy & Ingenious Spirit
You by the favour of the Gods Inherit
And I in Honour of my Vallintine
Leave Her Devoted at Minerva's Shrine

"Consideratus Considerandus"

TEXT: MS, The Rhode Island Historical Society.

What pleasure can this gaudy world afford?
what true delight does Teeming Nature hoard?
In Her great Store-house, where She lays her Treasure
Alas! tis all the Shaddow of a Pleasure;
No true content in all Her works are found
No solled joys in all Earths Spacious Round
For Labouring Man, who toyles himself in vaine
Eagerly grasping what creates his paine
How false and feeble, Nay scarce worth a Name
Are Riches, Honour Power, and Babling fame
Yet tis for those Men wade through Seas of Blood,

And bold in Mischief, Storm to be withstood
Which when Obtaind breed but Stupendious feare
Strife, jealousies, and Sleep-Disturbing Care;
No Beam of Comfort, not a Ray of Light
Shines thence to guide us thrô Fates Gloomy Night
But lost in Dismall Darkness there we Stay
Bereft of Reason in an Endless way
Vertu's the Souls true good if any bee
Tis that creats us true filicitie
Thô we despise, Contemn, and cast it by
As worthless, or Our fatalst Enemy
Because our Darling Lusts it dare Controule
And bound the Roveings of the wandering Soul.
Therefore in Garments poor it still appears
And sometimes (Naked) it no garment weares
Shun'd by the Great, and worthless deem'd by most ⎫
Urg'd to be gone, or wish'd forever Lost   ⎬
Yet it is Loath to leave our wretched Coast   ⎭
But in Disguise does here, and there intrude,
Striveing to Conquer base Ingrattitude
And boldly ventures now & then to Shine
So to make known it is of Birth Divine
But clouded oft it like the Lightning plays
Looseing as sone as seen its poynted Rays
Which scarceness makes those that are weak in witt
For vertues Self admire its Counterfiete
With Damned Hipocrites the world Delude
As men on Indians Glass, for Gems obtrude.

Benjamin Tompson
(1642-1714)

"New-Englands Crisis"

TEXT: *Benjamin Tompson 1642-1714,* ed. Howard J. Hall (Boston, 1924), pp. 49-71.

THE PROLOGUE.

The times wherein old *Pompion*[1] was a Saint,

When men far'd hardly yet without complaint
On vilest *Cates;* the dainty *Indian Maize*
Was eat with *Clamp-shells* out of wooden Trayes
Under thatcht *Hutts* without the cry of *Rent,*
And the best *Sawce* to every Dish, *Content.*
When Flesh was food, & hairy skins made coats,
And men as wel as birds had chirping Notes.
When Cimnels[2] were accounted noble bloud
Among the tribes of common herbage food.
Of *Ceres* bounty form'd was many a knack
Enough to fill *poor Robins Almanack.*
These golden times (too fortunate to hold)
Were quickly sin'd away for love of gold.
Twas then among the bushes, not the street
If one in place did an inferiour meet,
Good morrow Brother, is there ought you want?
Take freely of me, what I have you ha'nt.
Plain *Tom* and *Dick* would pass as currant now,
As ever since *Your Servant Sir* and bow.
Deep-skirted doublets, *puritanick* capes
Which now would render men like upright Apes,
Was comlier wear our wiser Fathers thought
Than the cast fashions from all *Europe* brought.
Twas in those dayes an honest *Grace* would hold
Till an hot puddin grew at heart a cold.
And men had better stomachs to religion
Than I to capon, turkey-cock or pigeon.
When honest Sisters met to pray not prate
About their own and not their neighbours state.
During *Plain Dealings* Reign, that worthy Stud
Of th'ancient planters race before the flood
These times were good, Merchants car'd not a rush
For other fare than *Jonakin*[3] *and Mush.*
Although men far'd and lodged very hard
Yet Innocence was better than a Guard.
Twas long before spiders & wormes had drawn
Their dungy webs or hid with cheating Lawne
New-Englands beautyes, which stil seem'd to me
Illustrious in their own simplicity.
Twas ere the neighbouring *Virgin-land* had broke
The Hogsheads of her worse than hellish smoak.

Twas ere the Islands sent their Presents in,
Which but to use was counted next to sin.
Twas ere a *Barge* had made so rich a fraight
As *Chocholatte,* dust-gold and bitts of eight.
Ere wines from *France* and *Moscovadoe* too
Without the which the drink will scarsly doe,
From western Isles, ere fruits and dilicacies,
Did rot maids teeth & spoil their hansome faces.
Or ere these times did chance the noise of war
Was from our towns and hearts removed far.
No Bugbear Comets[4] in the chrystal air
To drive our christian Planters to despair.
No sooner pagan malice peeped forth
But Valour snib'd[5] it; then were men of worth
Who by their prayers slew thousands Angel like,
Their weapons are unseen with which they strike.
Then had the Churches rest, as yet the coales
Were covered up in most contentious souls.
Freeness in Judgment, union in affection,
Dear love, sound truth they were our grand protection
These were the twins which in our Councells sate,
These gave prognosticks of our future fate,
If these be longer liv'd our hopes increase,
These warrs will usher in a longer peace:
But if *New-Englands* love die in its youth
The grave will open next for blessed Truth.
This *Theame* is out of date, the peacefull hours
When Castles needed not but pleasant bowers.
Not ink, but bloud and tears now serve the turn
To draw the figure of *New-Englands* Urne.
New Englands hour of passion is at hand,
No power except Divine can it withstand;
Scarce hath her glass of fifty years run out,
But her old prosperous Steeds turn heads about,
Tracking themselves back to their poor beginnings,
To fear and fare upon their fruits of sinnings:
So that the mirrour of the Christian world
Lyes burnt to heaps in part, her Streamers furl'd
Grief reigns, joyes flee and dismal fears surprize,
Not dastard spirits only but the wise.
Thus have the fairest hopes deceiv'd the eye

Of the big swoln Expectant standing by.
Thus the proud Ship after a little turn
Sinks into *Neptunes* arms to find its Urn.
Thus hath the heir to many thousands born
Been in an instant from the mother torn.
Ev'n thus thine infant cheeks begin to pale,
And thy supporters through great losses fail.
This is the *Prologue* to thy future woe,
The *Epilogue* no mortal yet can know.

New-Englands Crisis.

In seventy five the *Critick* of our years
Commenc'd our war with *Phillip* and his peers.
Whither the sun in *Leo* had inspir'd
A feav'rish heat, and *Pagan* spirits fir'd?
Whither some Romish Agent hatcht the plot?
Or whither they themselves? appeareth not.
Whither our infant thrivings did invite?
Or whither to our lands pretended right?
Is hard to say; but *Indian spirits* need
No grounds but lust to make a Christian bleed.

And here methinks I see this greazy *Lout*
with all his pagan slaves coil'd round about,
Assuming all the majesty his throne
Of rotten stump, or of the rugged stone
Could yield; casting some bacon-rine-like looks,
Enough to fright a Student from his books,
Thus treat his peers, & next to them his Commons,
Kennel'd together all without a summons.
My friends, our Fathers were not half so wise
As we our selves who see with younger eyes.
They sel our land to english man who teach
Our nation all so fast to pray and preach:
Of all our countrey they enjoy the best,
And quickly they intend to have the rest.
This no wunnegin,[6] so big matchit law,
Which our old fathers fathers never saw.
These english make and we must keep them too,
Which is too hard for them or us to doe,

We drink we so big whipt, but english they
Go sneep, no more, or else a little pay.
Me meddle Squaw me hang'd, our fathers kept
What Sqaws they would whither they wakt or slept.
Now if you'le fight Ile get you english coats,
And wine to drink out of their Captains throats.
The richest merchants houses shall be ours,
Wee'l ly no more on matts or dwell in bowers
Wee'l have their silken wives take they our Squaws,
They shall be whipt by virtue of our laws.
If ere we strike tis now before they swell
To greater swarmes then we know how to quell.
This my resolve, let neighbouring *Sachems* know,
And every one that hath club, gun or bow.
This was assented to, and for a close
He strokt his smutty beard and curst his foes.
This counsel lightning like their tribes invade,
And something like a muster's quickly made,
A ragged regiment, a naked swarm,
Whome hopes of booty doth with courage arm,
Set forthwith bloody hearts, the first they meet
Of men or beasts they butcher at their feet.
They round our skirts, they pare, they fleece they kil,
And to our bordering towns do what they will.
Poor Hovills (better far then *Caesars* court
In the experience of the meaner sort)
Receive from them their doom next execution,
By flames reduc'd to horror and confusion:
Here might be seen the smoking funeral piles
Of wildred towns pitcht distant many miles.
Here might be seen the infant from the breast
Snatcht by a pagan hand to lasting rest:
The mother *Rachel*-like shrieks out my child
She wrings her hands and raves as she were wild.
The bruitish wolves suppress her anxious moan
By crueltyes more deadly of her own.
Will she or nill the chastest turtle must
Tast of the pangs of their unbridled lust.
From farmes to farmes, from towns to towns they post,
They strip, they bind, they ravish, flea and roast.
The beasts which wont their masters crib to know,

Over the ashes of their shelters low.
What the inexorable flames doe spare
More cruel *Heathen* lug away for fare.
These tidings ebbing from the outward parts
Makes trades-men cast aside their wonted Arts
And study armes: the craving merchants plot
Not to augment but keep what they have got.
And every soul which hath but common sence
Thinks it the time to make a just defence.
Alarums every where resound in streets,
From *west* sad tidings with the *Eastern* meets.
Our common fathers in their Councels close
A martial treaty with the pagan foes,
All answers center here that fire and sword
Must make their *Sachem* universal Lord.
This armes the english with a resolution
To give the vaporing *Scab* a retribution.
Heav'ns they consult by prayer, the best design
A furious foe to quel or undermine.
RESOLV'D that from the *Massachusets* bands
Be prest on service some *Herculean* hands
And certainly he wel deserv'd a jerke
That slipt the Collar from so good a work.
Some Volunteers, some by compulsion goe
To range the hideous forest for a foe.
The tender Mother now's all bowels grown,
Clings to her son as if they'd melt in one.
Wives claspe about their husbands as the vine
Huggs the fair elm, while tears burst out like wine.
The new-sprung love in many a virgin heart
Swels to a mountain when the lovers part.
Nephews and kindred turn all springs of tears,
Their hearts are so surpriz'd with panick fears.
But dolefull shrieks of captives summon forth
Our walking castles, men of noted worth,
Made all of life, each Captain was a *Mars,*
His name too strong to stand on waterish verse:
Due praise I leave to some poetick hand
Whose pen and witts are better at command.
Methinks I see the *Trojan-horse* burst ope,
And such rush forth as might with giants cope:

These first the natives treachery felt, too fierce
For any but eye-witness to rehearse.
Yet sundry times in places where they came
Upon the Indian skins they carv'd their name.
The trees stood Centinels and bullets flew
From every bush (a shelter for their crew)
Hence came our wounds and deaths from every side
While skulking enemies squat undiscri'd,
That every stump shot like a musketeer,
And bowes with arrows every tree did bear
The swamps were Courts of Guard, thither retir'd
The stragling blew-coats when their guns were fir'd,
In dark Meanders, and these winding groves,
Where Beares & panthers with their Monarch moves
These far more cruel slily hidden lay,
Expecting english men to move that way.
One party lets them up, the other greets
Them with the next thing to their winding-sheets;
Most fall, the rest thus startled back return,
And from their by past foes receive an urn.
Here fel a Captain, to be nam'd with tears,
Who for his Courage left not many peers,
With many more who scarce a number left
To tell how treacherously they were bereft.
This flusht the pagan courage, now they think
The victory theirs, not lacking meat or drink.
The ranging wolves find here and there a prey,
And having fil'd their paunch they run away
By their Hosts light, the thanks which they return
Is to lead Captives and their taverns burn.
Many whose thrift had stor'd for after use
Sustain their wicked plunder and abuse.
Poor peeple spying an unwonted light,
Fearing a Martyrdom, in sudden fright
Leap to the door to fly, but all in vain,
They are surrounded with a pagan train;
Their first salute is death, which if they shun
Some are condemn'd the Gauntelet to run;
Death would a mercy prove to such as those
Who feel the rigour of such hellish foes.
Posts daily on their *Pegasean* Steeds

Bring sad reports of worse than *Nero's* deeds,
Such bruitish Murthers as would paper stain
Not to be heard in a Domitians Reign.
The field which nature hid is common laid,
And Mothers bodies ript for lack of aid.
The secret Cabinets which nature meant
To hide her master piece is open rent,
The half formd Infant there receives a death
Before it sees the light or draws its breath,
Many hot welcomes from the natives arms
Hid in their sculking holes many alarms
Our brethren had, and weary weary trants,[7]
Sometimes in melting heats and pinching wants:
Sometimes the clouds with sympathizing tears
Ready to burst discharg'd about their ears:
Sometimes on craggy hills, anon in bogs
And miery swamps better befitting hogs,
And after tedious Marches little boast
Is to be heard of stewd or bakt or roast,
Their beds are hurdles, open house they keep
Through shady boughs the stars upon them peep,
Their chrystal drink drawn from the mothers breast
Disposes not to mirth but sleep and rest.
Thus many dayes and weeks, some months run out
To find and quell the vagabonding rout,
Who like inchanted Castles fair appear,
But all is vanisht if you come but near,
Just so we might the *Pagan* Archers track
With towns and merchandize upon their back;
And thousands in the *South* who settled down
To all the points and winds are quickly blown.
At many meetings of their fleeting crew,
From whom like haile arrows and bullets flew:
The *English* courage with whole swarms dispute,
Hundreds they hack in pieces in pursuit.
Sed haud impunè, English sides do feel
As well as tawny skins the lead and steel
And some such gallant Sparks by bullets fell,
As might have curst the powder back to Hell:
Had only Swords these skirmishes decided
All *Pagan Sculls* had been long since divided.

The lingring war out-lives the Summer sun,
Who hence departs hoping it might be done,
Ere his return at *Spring* but ah hee'l find
The Sword still drawn, men of unchanged mind.
Cold winter now nibbles at hands and toes
And shrewdly pinches both our friends and foes.
Fierce *Boreas* whips the *Pagan* tribe together
Advising them to fit for foes and weather:
The axe which late had tasted Christian bloud
Now sets its steely teeth to feast on wood.
The forests suffer now, by waight constrein'd
To kiss the earth with souldiers lately brain'd.
The lofty oakes and ash doe wagge the head
To see so many of their neighbours dead;
Their fallen carcasses are caried thence
To stand our enemies in their defence.
Their Myrmidons inclos'd with clefts of trees
Are busie like the ants or nimble bees:
And first they limber poles fix in the ground,
In figure of the heavens convex: all round
They draw their arras-matts and skins of beasts,
And under these the Elves do make their nests.
Rome took more time to grow then twice six hours,
But half that time will serve for indian bowers.
A Citty shall be rear'd in one dayes space
As shall an hundred english men out-face.
Canonicus precincts there swarmes unite,
Rather to keep a winter guard then fight.
A dern and dismal swamp some Scout had found
Whose bosome was a spot of rising ground
Hedg'd up with mighty oakes, maples and ashes,
Nurst up with springs, quick boggs & miery plashes,
A place which nature coyn'd on very nonce
For tygers not for men to be a sconce.
Twas here these Monsters shapt and fac'd like men
Took up there Rendezvouz and brumal den,
Deeming the depth of snow, hail, frost and ice
Would make our Infantry more tame and wise
Then by forsaking beds and loving wives,
Meerly for indian skins to hazzard lives:
These hopes had something calm'd the boiling passion

Of this incorrigible warlike nation.
During this short *Parenthesis* of peace
Our forces found, but left him not at ease.
Here english valour most illustrious shone,
Finding their numbers ten times ten to one.
A shower of leaden hail our captains feel
Which made the bravest blades among us reel.
Like to some ant-hill newly spurn'd abroad,
Where each takes heels and bears away his load:
Instead of plate and jewels, indian trayes
With baskets up they snatch and run their wayes.
Sundry the flames arrest and some the blade,
By bullets heaps on heaps of Indians laid.
The Flames like lightening in their narrow streets
Dart in the face of every one it meets.
Here might be heard an hideous indian cry,
Of wounded ones who in the Wigwams fry.
Had we been *Canibals* here might we feast
On brave *Westphalia* gammons ready drest.
The tauny hue is Ethiopick made
Of such on whome *Vulcan* his clutches laid.
There fate was sudden, our advantage great
To give them once for all a grand defeat;
But tedious travell had so crampt our toes
It was too hard a task to chase the foes.
Distinctness in the numbers of the slain,
Or the account of Pagans which remain
Are both uncertain, losses of our own
Are too too sadly felt, too sadly known.
War digs a common grave for friends and foes,
Captains in with the common souldier throws.
Six of our Leaders in the first assault
Crave readmission to their Mothers Vault
Who had they fell in antient *Homers* dayes
Had been enrol'd with *Hecatombs* of praise.
As clouds disperst, the natives troops divide,
And like the streames along the thickets glide.
Some breathing time we had, & short God knowes
But new alarums from recruited foes
Bounce at our eares, the mounting clouds of smoak
From martyr'd townes the heav'ns for aid invoke:

Churches, barns, houses with most ponderous things
Made volatile fly ore the land with wings.
Hundreds of cattle now they sacrifice
For aiery spirits up to gormandize;
And to the *Molech* of their hellish guts,
Which craves the flesh in gross, their ale in butts.
Lancaster, Medfield, Mendon wildred *Groton,*
With many Villages by me not thought on
Dy in their youth by fire that usefull foe,
Which this grand cheat the world will overflow.
The wandring Priest to every one he meets
Preaches his Churches funeral in the streets.
Sheep from their fold are frighted, Keepers too
Put to their trumps not knowing what to doe.
This monster Warre hath hatcht a beauteous dove
In dogged hearts, of most unfeigned love,
Fraternal love the livery of a Saint
Being come in fashion though by sad constraint,
Which if it thrive and prosper with us long
Will make *New-England* forty thousand strong.
    But off the Table hand, let this suffice
    As the abridgment of our miseryes.
    If Mildew, Famine, Sword, and fired Townes,
    If Slaughter, Captivating, Deaths and wounds,
    If daily whippings once reform our wayes,
    These all will issue in our Fathers Praise;
    If otherwise, the sword must never rest
    Till all New-Englands *Glory it divest.*

A Supplement.

WHat meanes this silence of *Harvardine* quils
While *Mars* triumphant thunders on our hills.
Have pagan priests their Eloquence confin'd
To no mans use but the mysterious mind?
Have Pawaws charm'd that art which was so rife
To crouch to every Don that lost his life?
But now whole towns and Churches fire and dy
Without the pitty of an *Elegy.*
Nay rather should my quils were they all swords
Wear to the hilts in some lamenting words.

I dare not stile them poetry but truth,
The dwingling[9] products of my crazy youth.
If these essayes shall raise some quainter pens
Twil to the Writer make a rich amends.

Marlburyes Fate.

When *Londons* fatal bills[10] were blown abroad
And few but Specters travel'd on the road,
Not towns but men in the black bill enrol'd
Were in *Gazetts* by *Typographers* sold:
But our *Gazetts* without *Errataes* must
Report the plague of towns reduct to dust:
And feavers formerly to tenants sent
Arrest the timbers of the tenement.
Ere the late ruines of old *Groton's* cold,
Of *Marlbury's* peracute disease we're told.
The feet of such who neighbouring dwellings urnd
Unto her ashes, not her doors return'd.
And what remaind of tears as yet unspent
Are to its final gasps a tribute lent.
If painter overtrack my pen let him
An olive colour mix, these elves to trim;
Of such an hue let many thousand thieves
Be drawn like Scare-crows clad with oaken leaves,
Exhausted of their verdant life and blown
From place to place without an home to own.
Draw Devils like themselves, upon their cheeks
The banks for grease and mud, a place for leeks.
Whose locks *Medusaes* snakes, do ropes resemble,
And ghostly looks would make *Achilles* tremble.
Limm them besmear'd with Christian Bloud & oild
With fat out of white humane bodyes boil'd.
Draw them with clubs like maules & full of stains,
Like *Vulcans* anvilling *New-Englands* brains.
Let round be gloomy forrests with crag'd rocks
Where like to castles they may hide their flocks,
Till oppertunity their cautious friend
Shall jogge them fiery worship to attend.
Shew them like serpents in an avious path
Seeking to sow the fire-brands of their wrath.

Most like Aeneas in his cloak of mist,
Who undiscover'd move where ere they list
Cupid they tell us hath too sorts of darts.
One sharp and one obtuse, one causing wounds,
One piercing deep the other dull rebounds,
But we feel none but such as drill our hearts.
From Indian sheaves which to their shoulders cling,
Upon the word they quickly feel the string.
Let earth be made a screen to hide our woe
From Heavens Monarch and his Ladyes too;
And least our Jealousie think they partake,
For the red stage with clouds a curtain make.
Let dogs be gag'd and every quickning sound
Be charm'd to silence, here and there all round
The town to suffer, from a thousand holes
Let crawle these fiends with brands and fired poles,
Paint here the house & there the barn on fire,
With holocausts ascending in a spire.
Here granaries, yonder the Churches smoak
Which vengeance on the actors doth invoke.
Let *Morpheus* with his leaden keyes have bound
In feather-beds some, some upon the ground,
That none may burst his drowsie shackles till
The bruitish pagans have obtain'd their will,
And *Vulcan* files them off then *Zeuxis* paint
The phrenzy glances of the sinking saint.
Draw there the Pastor for his bible crying,
The souldier for his sword, The Glutton frying
With streams of glory-fat,[11] the thin-jaw'd Miser
Oh had I given this I had been wiser.
Let here the Mother seem a statue turn'd
At the sad object of her bowels burn'd.
Let the unstable weakling in belief
Be mounting *Ashurs* horses for relief.
Let the half Convert seem suspended twixt
The dens of darkness, and the Planets fixt,
Ready to quit his hold, and yet hold fast
By the great *Atlas* of the Heavens vast.
Paint Papists muttering ore their apish beads
Whome the blind follow while the blind man leads.
Let *Ataxy* be mounted on a throne

Imposing her Commands on every one,
A many-headed monster without eyes
To see the wayes which wont to make men wise.
Give her a thousands tongues with wings and hands
To be ubiquitary in Commands,
But let the concave of her skull appear
Clean washt and empty quite of all but fear,
One she bids flee, another stay, a third
She bids betake him to his rusty sword,
This to his treasure, th'other to his knees,
Some counsels she to fry and some to freeze,
These to the garison, those to the road,
Some to run empty, some to take their load:
Thus while confusion most mens hearts divide
Fire doth their small exchecquer soon decide.
Thus all things seeeming ope or secret foes,
An Infant may grow old before a close,
But yet my hopes abide in perfect strength.

The Town called *Providence*

Its Fate.

Why muse wee thus to see the wheeles run cross
Since *Providence* it self sustaines a loss:
And yet should *Providence* forget to watch
I fear the enemy would all dispatch;
Celestial lights would soon forget their line,
The wandering planets would forget to shine,
The stars run all out of their common spheres,
And quickly fall together by the eares:
Kingdoms would jostles out their Kings and set
The poor Mechanick up whome next they met,
Or rather would whole kingdoms with the world
Into a *Chaos* their first egge be hurl'd.
Ther's none this Providence of the Most High
Who can survive and write its Elegie:
But of a solitary town I write,
A place of darkness yet receiving light
From pagan hands, a miscellanious nest
Of errors Hectors, where they sought a rest
Out of the reach of Lawes but not of God,

Since they have felt the smart of common rod.
Twas much I thought they did escape so long,
Who Gospel truth so manifestly wronge:
For one *Lots* sake perhaps, or else I think
Justice did at greatest offenders wink
But now the shott is paid, I hope the dross
Will be cashiered in this common loss.
Houses with substance feel uplifting wings,
The earth remains, the last of humane things:
But know the dismal day draws neer wherein
The fire shall earth it self dissolve and sin.

Seaconk Plain Engagement.

On our *Pharsalian Plaines,* comprizing space
For *Caesars* host brave *Pompey* to outface,
An handfull of our men are walled round
With Indian swarmes; anon their pieces sound
A *Madrigal* like heav'ns artilery
Lightning and thunderbolts their bullets fly.
Her's hosts to handfulls, of a few they leave
Fewer to tell how many they bereave.
Fool-hardy fortitude it had been sure
Fierce storms of shot and arrows to endure
Without all hopes of some requital to
So numerous and pestilent a foe.
Some musing a retreat and thence to run,
Have in an instant all their business done,
They sink and all their sorrows ponderous weight
Down at their feet they cast and tumble straight.
Such who outliv'd the fate of others fly
Into the Irish bogs of misery.
Such who might dye like men like beasts do range
Uncertain whither for a better change,
These Natives hunt and chase with currish mind,
And plague with crueltyes such as they find.
    When shall this shower of Bloud be over? When?
    Quickly we pray oh Lord! say thou Amen.

Seaconk or *Rehoboths* Fate.

I once conjectur'd that those tygers hard
To reverend *Newmans*[12] bones would have regard,

But were all *SAINTS* they met twere all one case,
They have no rev'rence to an Angels face:
But where they fix their griping lions paws
They rend without remorse or heed to laws.
Rehoboth here in common english, Rest
They ransack, *Newmans* Relicts to molest.
Here all the town is made a publick stage
Whereon these *Nimrods* act their monstrous rage.
All crueltyes which paper stain'd before
Are acted to the life here ore and ore.

Chelmsfords Fate.

Ere famous *Winthrops* bones are laid to rest
The pagans *Chelmsford* with sad flames arrest,
Making an artificial day of night
By that plantations formidable light.
Here's midnight shrieks and Soul-amazing moanes,
Enough to melt the very marble stones:
Fire-brands and bullets, darts and deaths and wounds
Confusive outcryes every where resounds:
The natives shooting with the mixed cryes,
With all the crueltyes the foes devise
Might fill a volume, but I leave a space
For mercyes still successive in there place
Not doubting but the foes have done their worst,
And shall by heaven suddenly be curst.

> *Let this dear Lord the sad Conclusion be*
> *Of poor* New-Englands *dismal tragedy.*
> *Let not the glory of thy former work*
> *Blasphemed be by pagan Jew or Turk:*
> *But in its funeral ashes write thy Name*
> *So fair all Nations may expound the same:*
> *Out of her ashes let a Phoenix rise*
> *That may outshine the first and be more wise.*

B. Tompson.

ON *A FORTIFICATION*

At Boston *begun by Women.*
Dux Foemina Facti.

A Grand attempt some Amazonian Dames
Contrive whereby to glorify their names,
A Ruff for *Boston* Neck of mud and turfe,
Reaching from side to side from surfe to surfe,
Their nimble hands spin up like Christmas pyes,
Their pastry by degrees on high doth rise.
The wheel at home counts it an holiday,
Since while the Mistris worketh it may play.
A tribe of female hands, but manly hearts
Forsake at home their pasty-crust and tarts
To knead the dirt, the samplers down they hurle,
Their undulating silks they closely furle.
The pick-axe one as a Commandress holds,
While t'other at her awkness gently scolds.
One puffs and sweats, the other mutters why
Cant you promove your work so fast as I?
Some dig, some delve, and others hands do feel
The little waggons weight with single wheel.
And least some fainting fits the weak surprize,
They want no sack nor cakes, they are more wise.
These brave essayes draw forth Male stronger hands
More like to Dawbers than to Martial bands:
These do the work, and sturdy bulwarks raise,
But the beginners well deserve the praise.

FINIS.

ALMANAC VERSE

Samuel Danforth
(1626-1674)

TEXT: *An* Almanack for the Year of Our Lord 1647 . . .
By Samuel Danforth of Harvard Colledge Philomathemat
(Cambridge, 1647).

[March]

A Coal-white Bird appeares this spring[1]
That neither cares to sigh or sing.

This when the merry Birds espy,
They take her for some enemy.
Why so, when as she humbly stands
Only to shake you by your hands?

[April]

That which hath neither tongue nor wings[2]
This month how merrily it sings:
To see such, out for dead who lay
To cast their winding sheets away?
Freinds! would you live? some pils then take
When head and stomack both doe ake.

[May]

White Coates! whom choose you! whom you list:[3]
Some Ana-tolleratorist:
Wolves, lambs, hens, foxes to agree
By setting all opinion-free:
If Blew-coates doe not this prevent,
Hobgoblins will be insolent.

[June]

Who dig'd this spring of Gardens here,[4]
Whose mudded streames at last run cleare?
But why should we such water drink?
Give loosers what they list to think,
Yet know, one God, one Faith profest
To be New-Englands interest.

[July]

The wooden Birds[5] are now in sight,
Whose voices roare, whose wings are white,
Whose mawes are fill'd with hose and shooes,
With wine, cloth, sugar, salt and newes,
When they have eas'd their stomacks here
They cry, farewell untill next yeare.

[August]

Many this month I doe fore-see
Together by the eares will bee:
Indian and English in the field
To one another wil not yeild.
Some weeks continue wil this fray,
Till they be carted all away.

[September]

Four heads should meet and counsell have,[6]
The chickens from the kite to save,
The idle drones away to drive,
The little Bees to keep i'th hive.
How hony m[a]y be brought to these
By making fish to dance on trees.

[October]

If discontented Bellyes shall
Wish that the highest now might fall:
Their wish fulfilled they shall see,
Whenas within the woods they bee.
Poor Tinker think'st our shrubs will sing:
The Bramble here shall be our King.[7]

[November]

None of the wisest now will crave
To know what winter we shall have.
It shail be milde, let such be told.
If that it be not over cold.
Nor over cold shall they it see,
If very temperate it bee

[December]

It maybe now some enemy—[8]
Not seen, but felt, will make you fly.
Where is it best then to abide:

I think close by the fier side.
If you must fight it out i'th field,
Your hearts let woollen breast-plates shield.

[January]

Great bridges shall be made alone
Without ax, timber, earth or stone,[9]
Of chrystall metall, like to glasse;
Such wondrous works soon come to passe,
If you may then have such a way,
The Ferry-man you need not pay.

[February]

Our Lillyes which refus'd to spin
All winter past, shall now begin
To feel the lash of such a Dame,
Whom some call Idlenes by name.
Excepting such who all this time
Had reason good against my rime.

Samuel Bradstreet
(1633?-1682)

TEXT: *An Almanack for The Year of Our Lord, 1657*
   (Cambridge, 1657).

Aspice venturo latentur ut omnia Seclo.[1]
IT was, when scarce had rang the morning bells
That call the dead to rise from silent tombes,
Whilst yet they were lockt up in darker Cells,
Ne had the light posses'd their shady roomes,
    That slumbring Tellus in a dream did see
    Apollo come to cure her Lethargee.

Strait shee awoke, and lifting up her eyes
To top of tall Mount-AEthers burning brow;
From flaming Globes, the Titans Herauld spies
Herward approach; Then 'fore her shrine to bow;

Who bids her in great Phaebus name to cheer,
For he was coming, and would soon be heer.

Now rapt with joy, she takes her mantle soft,
On colder Couch ne longer will shee lie;
But decks her self by christall glass aloft
That hangs above her spangled Canopie,
  With pearly drops that fall from Limpid stilles
  She dights her too, and then with pleasance smiles.

Whilst fleet-fire-foming-steeds from farre appear
In speedy race the lofty hills to stride:
They Scout the smoaking Plaines, and then draw near
With burning Carre, that none but he can guide
  Who baulks their course with curb & gars[2] them bound
  Whilst he steps down to Sublunary-round:

To greet his Tellus then he hies apace,
Whom sprusely deckt he findes i'th verdant gown
He whilom sent. Each other doth embrace
In loving armes, and then they sitten down
  Whilst high-born states, and low Tellurean bands
  Rejoyce to see sage Hymen joyn their hands.

Eftsoones Apollo gives a Girlond rare
With flowers deckt (for Tellus front alone)
To her: and sayes in mind of me this weare
And Babyes deft will thence arise anon.
  She dons it strait: And buds that erst were green
  Now sucklings at her milkey papps they been.

Daniel Russell

(1642-1679)

TEXT: *An Almanack of Coelestiall Motions For the Year of the Christian Aera, 1671* (Cambridge, 1671).

[March]
  The Starry Monarch now to's full careere,
  Comes marching up to our North Hemisphere,

And by his burning Beams, our Frigid Zone
Doth Metamorphize to a temperate one;
Re-animating with Celestial Fire,
Those liveless Natures *Hyem's*[1] caus'd t'expire:
And causing *Tellus* t'doff her Winter Vest,
For joy of th'Spring; her new-come, welcome guest.

[April]

The Airy Choristers, they now begin
To warble forth their Native Musick in
The new-leaf'd Boughs; and in each pleasant Field,
By Natures Art their curious Nests do build.
Now big with hopes, the toyling Country Swain
Buries in th'Earth his multiplying Grain,
On which the Heavens do fertile Showers distill,
Which th'Earth with fruits, the Swain with joy doth fill.

[May]

Dame *Tellus* cloathed in a grass-green Coat,
By *Flora's* curious Needle-work well wrought,
'Gins to appear; for now the Meads abound
With fragrant Roses, and with Lillies Crown'd.
The Proverb's verifi'd, that *April* Showers
On *Maia's* Fields do rain down glittering Flowers;
And now the croaking Crew, late *All a-Mort,*
By their Night-chantings, their new life report.

[June]

The smiling Fields, attired in their Suits
Of Taste-delighting, and Eye pleasing Fruits;
Their Strawb'ry Mantles now begin to wear,
And many Orchards Cherry-cheekt appear.
Now *Sol* in's Crabbed Throne doth take his place,
Where he performs his Longest daily Race:
Soon after which, the dayes length 'gins to fade,
And *Phoebus, Cancer*-like turns Retrograde.[2]

[July]

Now *Ceres* Offspring's numerous every where,
And mighty Armies of Tall Blades appear
In many Fields, all Rank'd and Fil'd they stand

Ready for Battel: With whom hand to hand
Fierce Husbandmen with crooked Cutlash meet,
And being Victors lay them at their feet.
This don't suffice; together th'Blades are bound,
Transported home, and soundly thresh'd on th'ground.

[August]

Now *Sol* and *Mercury* near th'*Virgin* meet,
Where in Conjunction they each other greet,
The best of Aspects; which doth signify,
Advancement to the Sons of *Mercury*.
And now the verdant Meads begin to feel
The sharp encounter of the Mowers Steel:
The Noble Vines with Grapes, the Grapes begin
To swell with *Bacchus,* which is Barell'd in.

[September]

The *Indian* Stalks, now richly fraught with store
Of golden-colour'd Ears, seem to implore
By humble bowing of their lofty Head,
From this their load to be delivered.
Pomona's Daughters now at age, and dight
With pleasing Beauty, Lovers do invite
In multitudes: it's well if they escape
From each of these, without a cruel Rape.

[October]

Now the *Aeolian* Lords and Commons meet
In Parliament, where it is Voted fit,
Yea and Resolv'd upon, what-ere it cost,
They'll King it over all, and rule the Rost.
Which to effect, it is Agreed by all,
That blustring *Boreas* shall be Generall
Of their great Forces; and then to't they go,
And *Tellus* Kingdom first they'll overthrow.

[November]

Where thundring *Boreas,* with his Troops, doth shake
The trembling Woods, and makes the Trees to quake:
The Leaves for very fear the Trees have left,
Which of their *July* garb, now're quite bereft:

The Fruits, those pleasant Fruits, the painted Flowers,
The Flow'ry Meads, gay Fields, and shady Bowers,
Are now destroy'd; and th'Earths depriv'd of all
Her Summer glory by this Wasting FALL.

[December]

Exit Autumnus: Winter now draws neare,
Armed with Frost i'th'Van, with Snow i'th'Rere;
Whose freezing Forces cause men to retire,
For help to th'Fortress of a well-made Fire.
Phoebus himself, as if with pannick feare
Hereat affrighted, now in's full Careere
Doth poste away, and speeds him from our sight
In greatest haste, bidding the World good-night.

[January]

The Northern Captains Siege still fiercely lasts,
And still the Roaring Canons of his Blasts
And fired off; which brings both Land and Sea
His Chained Captives quickly for to be:
And lest they should rebell, if load they lack,
Mountains of Snow are heap'd on *Tellus* back;
The lofty swelling Waves, stout *Neptunes* pride
Are made a packhorse on which men may ride.

[February]

And now the Worlds bright Torch, whose radiant Light
Dispels the gloomy Mists of black-fac'd Night:
The Twelve *Herculean* Labours of his Sphere,
Compleated hath, and Periodiz'd the Year,
But not his Motion: Natures Law commands
That fiery *Phoebus* Charriot never stands,
Without a Miracle; but that it be,
Still termed *Certus: semper Mobile.*

The Puritan Elegy

"I. Sam. 25. 1. And SAMUEL dyed, and all the Israelites were gathered together, and Lamented him."

—Inscription to Cotton Mather's Elegy on Urian Oakes.

The New York Historical Society owns a commonplace book kept by Samuel Sewall in which the great diarist patiently transcribed a few dozen elegies. Whatever in Sewall's temperament accounts for so exclusive a taste, whether morbidity or a sense of the past moved him to copy with the decorative clarity of an engagement notice these testimonials to the New England dead, that mood often guided the literary tastes of New England Puritans. No other form of poetry seemed so natural to them as the elegy. Far from disliking verse they awarded it an important public function. Death tests life. At death a man's lifelong daily struggle for salvation faces God's precalculated judgment. Then the soul knows whether it has won its way to glory or slid to eternal vomit of hell. Because death tested the conduct of a man's whole life, and because the passing of great men showed God's disposition toward the community, the elegy could stake as its province theological doctrine, social theory, and personal grief, while elaborating the ideals of conduct Puritans valued and solidifying the community's scorn for heretics—could in short reach all domains the most public and most private of Puritan life.

New England elegies were modelled on similar poems written by English Puritans. Much of what is to be said about the theory and practice of the New England elegy applies as well to Puritan elegies in England, with several highly important exceptions. John W. Draper, the authority on the English elegy, has shown how in the 1640's English Puritans took over the genre from Cavalier poets, among whom it had lost favor. Then by accentuating the melancholic aspects of the elegy, they sped that generalizing process by which the form, its tone and

121

funerary imagery freed from actual occasions of death, encouraged
Sentimentalism and the melancholy of nascent Romanticism.[1] In New
England, however, the elegy did not follow this course: it resisted the
influence of Neoclassicism and the tendency to Sentimentalism.

The conservatism of the New England elegy was probably due in part
to the cultural lag, partly to the different fate of Puritanism in New
England, and, especially, to the unique purpose New England poets
found for the elegy. In old England, merchant class Puritans used the
theme of the democracy of death to show that their social betters were
their human equals; in New England, class distinctions were less pronounced, and the butts of Puritan loathing were usually other middle-
class dissenter groups. In New England, the elegy spoke less for the
merchant class than for the clergy, to whom the advantage of the form
lay in its didactic possibilities, and who rarely exploited macabre detail
for itself. Equally effective in forestalling the advance of Sentimentalism
was the fact that long after the political effectiveness of Puritanism in old
England was spent, American Puritans persisted in their hope for a
Puritan state. Accordingly the elegy remained an expression of Puritan
aims. But the single most important difference between the Puritan
elegies of old and New England was that in America the elegy became a
vehicle for recording regional history and a means for displaying local
pride.

New England Puritans wrote elegies throughout the seventeenth century. Despite stinging attacks against the form from Benjamin Franklin
and the *New-England Courant,* attacks that by bringing to open expression much latent repugnance for Puritan writing abruptly mark a gradual
shift in colonial taste, the elegy remained popular in New England during the entire colonial period. One stark contrast between Northern and
Southern colonial verse is that the South produced no such elegiac tradition.[2] While it did not decide this contrast, death was observed differently
in the two regions. Puritans regarded death ceremoniously but without
much sentiment. Memorial verses were often part of the ceremony. After
English custom, friends fastened funeral tributes to the pall covering the
casket. At the funeral of Thomas Shepard in 1685, Samuel Sewall re-
called that "there were some Verses; but none pinned on the Herse." [3]
Cotton Mather distributed elegies to the hundred mourners at his wife's
funeral.[4] But funerals in Virginia were less reserved and literary. Mourners oiled parched throats with homebrew, having usually travelled far
over crude roads to attend; and in the mishaps ensuing from the cus-
tomary discharge of guns, the bereaved occasionally ended up dead
themselves.[5]

Puritan Elegiac Theory

Two types of New England elegy ought to be distinguished. Verse written as private, lyric condolence remained mostly in manuscript journals and diaries: such personal elegies as Samuel Torrey's on the insane William Tompson (father of the poet) or John Saffin's on his son Simon. In these moving poems inelegant verse seems the just expression of awkward grief: they are true primitives. Another type of elegy, fastened to the pall, perhaps read at the graveside and later published, served as a public commemoration, to idealize the dead minister or leader as a model of conduct for the community.[6] These are documents for us of the ideals of leadership and conduct many New England Puritans held, portraits of the Saved Soul. The form of many public elegies was patterned after the funeral sermon. Elegists borrowed the formal sermon devices of exhortation and application, calling on their audience, as the minister called on his congregation, to imitate the deceased.[7]

As for everything else, Puritans sought a theoretical basis for the elegy. It had to be justified. Large portions of many elegies are spent defending the poem's right to be. Thirteen stanzas of Urian Oakes' celebrated elegy on Shepard argue the propriety of the remaining forty stanzas. Like all elegists, Puritans worried whether the contrivances of rhyme and meter did not belie a mere toying with cooled-over grief. "He that his crosses wailes / Indeed," Urian Oakes broods, "would vent his griefs without restraints." But the next moment his doubts are halted:

> Stop, stop my Pen! lest *Israel's* singer sweet
> Should be condemn'd, who, in that Song of th' Bow,
> To vent his passionate complaints thought meet,
> And to bewail his great Friends overthrow.

The Bible, source of all law, has elegies. Were elegies vain, or dishonest, David would never have lamented Jonathan in verse. This was the Puritans' key justification for the elegy. Wishing to grieve spontaneously, and distressed by the possibility that grief versified is grief no more, Puritan poets comforted themselves with Biblical precedent. Claiming such precedent was of course not their innovation. Dryden, for one, cited the examples of David and Jesus in *Of Dramatick Poesie* to prove poetry and religion compatible. But Puritans, in old England and New, made the invocation of Biblical precedent a fairly rigid obligation of the elegist. The convention can be documented throughout the history of Puritanism. Percival Lowle, writing in 1649 on the death of John Winthrop, quieted any doubts about rhymed mourning by linking his audience with the messianic Hebrews:

> The Jews did for their *Moses* weep
> Who was their Gubernator
> Let us for Winthrope do the like,
> Who was our Conservator.[8]

Cotton Mather, in his elegy on Urian Oakes (1682), bolstered his belief that "Worthies *to* Praise is a Praise-worthy thing" with the fact that "Christ *did it*." [9] John Danforth later imagined all the Old Testament poets mining the elegiac vein before him, and called "sweet Tongue'd *David,* sad Song'd *Jeremiah,*" as well as Jonathan, Josiah, and Moses to help him *"find* one *Grave,* and 'Grave one Epitaph." [10] The convention was very useful. Aside from granting the elegy a legitimate birth, it served to suggest epic stature for the dead leader. It placed him in the line of Old Testament protagonists and, in America more than in England, flattered its audience's sense of historic mission.

The Biblical example most frequently cited by New England elegists was David's Lament for Jonathan. After proclaiming "Christ *did it,*" Mather adds that "David bid me go." Urian Oakes and many other elegists transformed David into a Puritan muse, an acceptable ideal of inspiration:

> Oh for the Raptures, Transports, Inspirations
> Of *Israel's Singer,* when his *Jon'athans* Fall
> So tun'd his mourning Harp! what Lamentations
> Then would I make for *Shepards* Funerall

Many motifs and even phrases of David's Lament appear in the Puritan elegies. In it, as in all the Biblical episodes, Puritans discovered parallels to their own situation. Jonathan, like Cotton or Winthrop, was a leader; so by anastomasia Winthrop and Cotton became Jonathans. Like David, elegists felt wary of rejoicing the Philistines by announcing the leader's death. Many elegists warn against spreading the news outside the Puritan community; to the profane world, the leader's death is a victory. In his elegiac ode on Sir William Phips, Daniel Henchman realized some of the possible local applications of the convention by equating Philistines with French and Indians, who will have cause to celebrate the knight-governor's death:

Rejoyce, Messieurs; Netops, Rejoyce; 'Tis True;
Ye Philistines, None will Rejoyce, but you;

....

O Dont his Death to the Blind Heathen shew,
Least they thereby, Their Courage do renew;
Nor let in Ask'lons Streets, the Deadly Voice
of it be heard, Least at it they Rejoyce.

After three quarters of a century of elegiac writing in New England,
Puritans no doubt felt the convention of citing Biblical precedent a bur-
den. In some introductory remarks to his elegy on Nathanael Collins,
Cotton Mather disclaimed any need for justifying his poem, since "to
Lament the *Dead* in *Verse* [has] been even from the dayes of *David*
until Now, in some sort almost *as Common as Death itself* . . ." [11] (thus
excusing himself for the obligatory excuse). The patterning of the New
England elegy on the model of David's lament did linger into the eighteenth century, where the most elaborate example is the minister John
Adams' elegy on Josiah Winslow (1725). But by then the Biblical idiom
no longer served to remind the elegist's audience of its historic mission,
nor was the conduct it valued any longer practicable in ever more worldly
New England.

The Elegy and the Plain Style

The elegy raised all the problems of the plain style in a highly charged
context. Exotics like allusion and metaphor seemed inappropriate to
sincere grief, to the humanity of the subject's death and, above all, to
the didactic function of the elegy. Oakes presents himself as unwilling
to write but overmastered by grief, which "forc'd a verse . . . whether
th'Learned Sisters would or no." He means equally, of course, that he
wrote under the force of passion and that passion forced him to write
without poetic machinery. As Puritans dismissed "arts" of preservation,
they dismissed elegiac rhetoric. Oakes adds that no "Spices, Odours,
curious Arts" are needed, "No skill of *Egypt,* to embalm the Name / Of
such a Worthy." Artificiality is unjust to the dead himself: "Least I
offend his Ghost, plainly I write," [12] one elegist explains; "Plain honest
Rhimes," says another, "best becomes a *Prophets Urn.*" [13] Most important extravagant artifice can only hamper the instructional benefits the
elegy offers. For the New England elegy was primarily (and unlike its
English model, remained) a didactic instrument: to teach is to teach
everyone, to reach the meanest intelligence. Jewelled rhetoric puts the

subject at a remove from the reader, and by lending him an aura of
uncommon learning discourages imitation. In his poem on Joseph Green,
Nicholas Noyes sums up the whole didactic argument against artifice:

> God Hates a Lye, my muse well knows,
> Whether it be in Verse or Prose.
> His praise was in the Church before,
> He needed not a Gilding o'er.
> By over-praising of the Dead,
> Nor they or we are Bettered.
> Poetic Raptures Scandalize,
> And pass with most for learned Lies:
> Whilst others are discouraged,
> And think Saints can't be Imited:
> Such high Flights seem Designed to raise
> The *Poet's,* not the Person's praise.
> Whereas Plain Truth gives no offence,
> And doth effect the Conscience;
> To Imitation doth excite,
> Unflorished Copies Teach to Write.[14]

By the force of his unadorned example, the dead will move our grief
and excite us to imitation.

But, as one expects, many of their elegies are everything the Puritans
insisted elegies should not be. John Fiske, perhaps the most gifted New
England elegist, takes death as an occasion for knitting intricate metaphysical conceits. He explains his "crabbed anggry tough unpleasing"
tone by the theory of the 'knot.' It is a recurrent term in Puritan verse,
used brilliantly in Edward Taylor's "Upon Wedlock and the Death of
Children." The course of human events, as man looks upon it to determine its causes, is labyrinthine and perplexing, a knot. The buzzing
confusion of history, however, is only God's revealed will. What is given
to man as a dense tangle is in God's mind, His Hidden Will, a beautiful
plan that man cannot understand. Fiske explains how the gnarled
syntax and teasing imagery of his elegies, while certainly not designed
for the intelligence of the least gifted hearer, mirror the inner snarled
perplexity of all things:

> The knott sometimes seems a deformity
> It's a mistake, tho such be light set by
> The knott it is the Joynt, the strength of parts
> The bodies-beauty. . . .

In the same way the teachings of the lamented John Cotton are for Fiske a 'honied knot,' sweet but difficult, obscure but soothing, delighting the reader by making him experience at the same time man's bewilderingly painful life and God's loving design (the knot is further perplexed by the fact that "Honie Knott" is an anagramatization of 'John Cotton').

This duplicity gives a similarly "crabbed anggry" but sweet tone to nearly everything the Puritans wrote. God, contradictory and apparently willful, certainly arbitrary, is still paternal. Writers like Fiske and the authors of the *Bay Psalm Book* seem to strive in their verse for a deliberate awkwardness, a fervently glad distress appropriate to the Puritan view expressed by Richard Steere that "there's a kind of happiness in Crosses." [15] Not alone the tone and syntax, but the preachments as well of many elegies assert this duplicity. The idealized great man combines gentleness with ferocity, severity toward the profane with kindliness, is good to his own but a scourge to the Philistines, is himself a honied knot. Mather imagines the schoolmaster Cheever advising tutors to "Be *Strict;* But yet be *Gentle* too"; Benjamin Woodbridge recalls how John Cotton "Spake many Tongues in one: one Voice and Sense / Wrought Joy and Sorrow, Fear and Confidence." In lauding such disparate qualities and explaining so contrary a God, Puritan elegists very often found the plain style inferior to knotty conceits and a difficult tone. Other elegists than Fiske write with pleasure in confusion. John Danforth juggles the heterogeneous virtues of the dead John Eliot in the anagram "HONY . . . TOILE" (a version of the honied knot), and the anagram itself is much exploited in its opportunities for wordplay.[16] So, again, while a plain style was often prescribed as an instrument of instruction, elegists found in the meaning of death, and in their borrowed models, permission to be "crabbed anggry tough unpleasing" and difficult.

The Communal Basis of the Elegy

The emphasis on instruction, however qualified, suggests that to the Puritan the elegy was not a personal cry but a communal exercise. John Fiske's poem on Samuel Sharpe opens with the New England elegy's quint-essential phrase:

Us) saies. . . .

"Us) saies": the elegist mourns not a personal but a tribal loss. The imagery of his poem is often determined by a search for figures that visualize the subject's relation to the community. Certain figures are common: the deceased is a pillar upholding the church, a light or star leading the community. The communal diction of New England elegies

is one more expression of Puritan domesticity, of the familial organiza-
tion of church and state, that one-for-all *elan* of a closeknit minority
destined to seize power.[17] And it no doubt gained assurance from the
prescription in David's lament to keep mourning inside the family. So
in "E.B.'s" elegy on Samuel Stone, Cambridge is a weeping mother; the
death of Cotton means for Fiske that "A Father in our Israel's cea'st
to be": for Oakes, "Sister *Charlstown* sits and Moans" the death of
Shepard while Cambridge "Sympathizes with her Sister dear." John
Fiske professes to speak with the combined grief of the mourning community:

> O us! our Losse! our Losse! how sad it is
> this breach in fam'ly greate, in church, in Towne
> who each bereft as of a Father Now
> are forc't to wayle our heavenly-Fathers frowne.
>   oh! who shall us! us! comfort, hope, helpe, give?

Not only is death felt to be a communal loss, but also a communal
punishment. It is a stroke against the living for their sins. Oakes cries
that "Our sins have slain our *Shepard!*" God chastizes the public's
"Prophet-killing" vices by taking away great men: "our sin the cause."

Around 1660, as ministers began heating up their sermons into boiling jeremiads, Puritan elegists found in their sense of communal loss
and communal responsibility ammunition for an onslaught against New
England backsliding. The death of prominent men came to betoken
God's displeasure with his Chosen People, to loom as portents and fore-
casts of coming evil times. For Oakes, the death of Shepard is a cata-
clysmic event, a violence done against nature. Indeed he keys Shepard's
death to the same pitch of emotion as The Day of Doom, making it a
horrendous preview of that catastrophe:

> As when some formidable Comets blaze,
> As when Portentous Prodigies appear,
> Poor Mortals with amazement stand and gaze,
> With hearts affrighted, and with trembling fear:
>   So are we all amazed at this blow,
>   Sadly portending some approaching woe.

After 1660, poets more and more identified the death of leaders with
the fall of Wilderness Zion. In his elegy on Phips, Daniel Henchman
warned that "thy Fate shows in his Funeral" and that his epitaph will be

New England's own. What killed the leader is the community's own sinning and his death is a sign of future, greater loss.

Yet in this, as in much else, Puritans wanted to discourage but not to crush. However bleakly the elegist pictures New England, hope is held out. Although with the death of Shepard Zion's brightest star has set, Oakes sees reason to believe that the Wilderness Errand will be performed:

> Harvard! where's such a fast Friend left to thee
> Unless thy great Friend, LEVERET, it be.

Benjamin Woodbridge, the first graduate of Harvard, takes faith that while Cotton, greatest of New England ministers, is gone, "yet *Joshua* is not dead." Norton, "worthy hee / Successor to our MOSES is to bee." Besides, the community can repent its sin, and presumably repulse God's wrath by practicing what the leader represented.

The Significance of the New England Elegy

By 1720 the vogue of the New England communal elegy was effectually ended. By that time it could no longer focus in the fact of death so many issues crucial to the Puritans' life in the new world. Death was the same, but the new world had changed them, and they had changed it. As in England, in Massachusetts elegies remained popular in subliterary circles throughout the neoclassical era. But by 1720, lamentations over communal woe and exhortations to communal virtue had become a survival, unrelated to the colony's increasingly more complex social and political life. The way a lady poet in 1742 imagined the death of James Davenport allows an easy insight into how far New Englanders, like English elegists fifty years earlier,[18] had come from the "crabbed anggry tough unpleasing" tone of John Fiske:

> The sacred Man is to his Shade convey'd
> On Cammomile his aking Temples laid;
> Here Roses, Honey-Suckles, Jessamine
> In beauteous Arches o'er the Champion twine.[19]

In step with this artificiality in the elegy is its development into a vehicle of burlesque and parody.[20] Joseph Green's elegy on "Mr. Old Tenor" laments not a vanished eminence, but the recall of paper notes. It spoofs the Puritan theme of communal dependence by grieving how New England's prosperity will slide now that the cash is gone.

The concerted ridicule of the New England elegy by Benjamin Franklin and the writers of the *New-England Courant* around 1720 is a momentous event in the placid history of colonial verse. At issue was not merely a form, of course, but the provincial mind the form pleased and the cultural lag its continued practice represented. Franklin's quarrel is with the antiquated spirit of the elegy; it has not caught up with the eighteenth-century manner. In his seventh "Dogood" paper, printed in the *Courant* in 1722, he connects his attack on "Elegiographers" with contempt for rooted institutions like Harvard and ministerial pedantry. Franklin's essay stimulated much risible discussion in the *Courant* of "Kitelick poets" and Kitelick verse, so named from a popular and banal elegy on a Mehitebell Kitel. Some comments show simple boredom with the form and its pinching ideals of conduct. One correspondent noted that New Englanders have been constrained not to do good in order to avoid having elegies written about themselves.[21] Another associated the elegy quite simply with rustic vulgarity, complaining that there is "scarce a Plow-Jogger or Country Cobler that has read our Psalms, and can make two Lines jingle, who has not once in his Life, at least, exercised his Talent this way."[22]

Yet, while Franklin debunked the elegy, he printed many himself later in the *Pennsylvania Gazette*. In truth, Puritan writers had invested in the elegy much of what they felt about their lives in the new world. By the same idealizing process that described socially desirable conduct, the elegies exalted dead ministers and leaders into heroes. In this lay a fertile source of allusion and the nub of a literary tradition. New England writers themselves thought that in one way their pursuit of the genre was unique. As in no other form, in the elegy were the proofs of a continuous and rich local culture. If the English Puritan elegy was, as Draper contends, a goad to Sentimentalism and Romantic Melancholy, the American Puritan elegy was a goad to patriotism. The same writer to the *Courant* who ridiculed the elegies of cobblers and ploughmen acknowledged his awareness of a regional tradition. He had traced "this Spirit of Elegy among us for an hundred Years back," and found that "it came in with the first Planters. *New-England's Memorial* furnishes us with several Elegies made long since by our Fore-Fathers, which our modern *Elegaic* writers imitate." [23] Puritans too had been alive to such a continuity, and of such later imitations, and looked upon them as enrichments of their lives in the new world and a challenge to Europe. Cotton Mather prefaced his own elegy on Jonathan Mitchell by asking why "need I travel, as far as *Europe* for an *Elegy* upon this Worthy Man?" He wanted it known that *"America* can *Embalm* Great Persons, as well as *Produce* them, and *New England* can bestow, an *Elegy,* as well as an *Education,* upon its *Hero's."* [24] To experience the vitality of this tradition one has only to come upon the many echoes of Urian Oakes' elegy in later Puritan poems. The elegy in New England became a place, the place, for flaunting local enthusiasm. Mather writes with an appreciative feeling for the new world writers who have come before him and the traditional value of following in their line:

> *Cotton* Embalms great *Hooker; Norton* Him: And *Norton's* Herse do's *Poet-Wilson* trim With Verses. *Mitchel* writes a Poem on The Death of *Wilson*: and when *Mitchel's* gone, *Shepard* with fun'ral Lamentations gives Honour to Him: and at his Death receives The like from the (*like-Maro*) Lofty Strain Of admirable *Oakes.*[25]

If morbidity moved Samuel Sewall to copy elegies by the dozen into his daybook, he was also clearly guided by a sense of the past.

NOTES

[1] John W. Draper, *The Funeral Elegy and the Rise of English Romanticism* (New York, 1929), *passim.*

[2] Draper attributes this to the absence of Puritanism in the South and the lack of "urban life with its literary inclinations and the absence also of a Grub street with interested motives in the production of such pieces" (p. 156). Actually, Puritan activity in the early South was considerable. See Babette Levy, *Early Puritanism in the southern and island colonies, Proceedings of the American Antiquarian Society* (Worcester, 1960). A simpler explanation is that there was no Southern printing in the seventeenth century. It might be added that the later Southern elegists work less in the metaphysical tradition than in the pastoral tradition of Spenser and Milton.

[3] In Ola Elizabeth Winslow, *American Broadside Verse* (New Haven, 1930), p. xix.

[4] *Diary of Cotton Mather,* ed. Worthington Chauncey Ford (repr. New York, n.d.), I, 449-450.

[5] Philip Alexander Bruce, *The Social Life of Virginia in the Seventeenth Century* (Lynchburg, Va., 1927), p. 223 f.

[6] Broadsides on military heroes by English Puritans reflect a similar idealizing process in the home country. See Draper, p. 88.

[7] Robert Henson, "Form and Content of the Puritan Funeral Elegy," *American Literature,* XXXII (March 1960), 11-27 *passim.*

[8] Winslow, p. 3.

[9] Cotton Mather, "A Poem Dedicated to the Memory of . . . Urian Oakes" (Boston, 1682), p. 1.

[10] John Danforth, *Kneeling to God* (Boston, 1697), p. 66.

[11] Cotton Mather, "An Elegy on . . . Mr. Nathanael Collins," repr. in *Early American Poetry* (Boston, 1896), III, 2.

[12] Benjamin Tompson, "The Character of Mr. Samuel Tompson," *Benjamin Thompson 1642-1714*, ed. Howard Judson Hall (Boston, 1924), p. 137.

[13] Nicholas Noyes, "An Elegy on the Death of . . . John Higginson" (Boston, 1709), n.p.

[14] Nicholas Noyes, "An Elegy upon . . . Joseph Green," *Essex Institute Historical Collections*, VIII (1866), 173.

[15] Similarly, the crabbed verses of the *Bay Psalm Book* are often cited as evidence of the Puritans' lack of poetic talent. They should be cited, on the contrary, as illustrations of their poetic theory, of the "tough unpleasing" tone which they felt expressed their experience. John Cotton, who composed many of the awkward verses, could write as smoothly as any other Puritan. See his prefatory poem to Samuel Stone's "A Congregational Church Is a Catholike Visible Church" (London, 1652).

[16] *Kneeling to God*, p. 72 The strategy of the elegiac anagram is simple. The virtues of the deceased are discovered in his name or its anagram, showing that they were essential to him. The reiterated name or anagram has a structural function as well. It establishes in the poem an incantatory rhythm of grief, a ritual breastbeating, as in "E.B.'s" elegy on Samuel Stone:

> On him, the *Stone* was held a *Light compleat*:
> A *Stone* more than the *Eben-ezer* fam'd;
> *Stone* splendent Diamond, right *Orient* nam'd;
> A *Cordiall Stone* . . . etc.

[17] And the New England elegist was addressing a much more compact group than was the English Puritan. He knew his audience by face and name, as an English Puritan did not. He spoke to a community, the English Puritan to a party.

[18] Draper finds that "as early as the reign of Charles II, the funeral elegy began to mark the new tendency toward the Sentimental" (p. 320).

[19] "To the Reverend Mr. James Davenport . . . *By a Female Friend*" (Boston, 1742), p. 2.

[20] The elegy became an instrument of burlesque in England too, although again much earlier. During the reign of Charles II, the Royalists often parodied the elegy to ridicule their opponents.

[21] *The New-England Courant*, 5 Aug. 1723, n.p.

[22] *Ibid.*, 5 Nov. 1722, n.p.

[23] *Ibid.*

[24] Cotton Mather, *Ecclesiastes* (Boston, 1697), p. 109.

[25] Cotton Mather, "A Poem . . . to . . . Oakes," p. A2.

Anonymous

(1645)

"Thomas Dudley" [1]

TEXT: Harold S. Jantz, *The First Century of New England Verse* (Worcester, 1944), p. 34.

Thomas Dudley
ah! old, must dye
A deaths head on your hand you neede not weare
a dying hand you on your shoulders beare
you need not one to minde you, you must dye
you in your name may spell mortalitye
younge men may dye, but old men these dye must
t'will not be long before you turne to dust.
before you turne to dust! ah! must; old! dye!
what shall younge doe, when old in dust doe lye?
when old in dust lye, what N. England doe?
when old in dust doe lye, it's best dye too.

Benjamin Woodbridge
(1622-1684)

"Upon the TOMB of the most Reverend Mr. *John Cotton,* late Teacher
of the Church of *Boston* in *New-England.*"

TEXT: Nathaniel Morton, *New Englands Memoriall* (Cambridge,
1669), pp. 137-139.

HEre lies magnanimous Humility,
Majesty, Meekness; Christian Apathy
On soft Affections: Liberty in thrall;
A Noble Spirit, Servant unto all.
Learnings great Master-piece; who yet would sit
As a Disciple at his Schollars feet.
A simple Serpent, or Serpentine Dove,
Made up of Wisdome, Innocence, and Love.
Neatness Embroider'd with *it self* alone;
And Civils Canonized in a Gown:
Embracing old and young, and low and high;
Ethicks imbodyed in Divinity:
Ambitious to be lowest, and to raise
His Brethrens Honour on his own Decayes.
Thus doth the *Sun* retire into his bed,

That being gone, the *Stars* may shew their head.
Could wound at Argument without Division;
Cut to the quick, and yet make no Incision;
Ready to Sacrifice Domestick Notions
To Churches Peace, and Ministers Devotions.
Himself indeed (and singular in that)
Whom all admired, he admired not.
Liv'd like an Angel of a Mortal Birth,
Convers'd in Heaven while he was on Earth:
Though not (as *Moses*) radiant with Light,
Whose Glory dazell'd the beholders sight;
Yet so divinely beautifi'd, youl'd count
He had been born and bred upon the Mount.
A living breathing Bible: Tables where
Both Covenants at large engraven were;
Gospel and *Law* in's Heart had each its Colume
His Head an Index to the Sacred Volume.
His very Name a *Title Page;* and next,
His Life a *Commentary* on the Text.
O what a Monument of glorious worth,
When in a *New Edition* he comes forth
Without *Errata's,* may we think hee'll be,
In *Leaves* and *Covers* of Eternitie!
A man of Might at heavenly Eloquence,
To fix the Ear, and charm the Conscience,
As if *Apollos* were reviv'd in him,
Or he had learned of a *Seraphim.*
Spake many Tongues in one: one Voice and Sense
Wrought Joy and Sorrow, Fear and Confidence.
Rocks rent before him, Blinde receiv'd their sight;
Souls levell'd to the dunghil, stood upright.
Infernal Furies burst with rage to see
Their Pris'ners captiv'd into Libertie.
A *Star* that in our Eastern *England rose,*
Thence hurry'd by the Blast of stupid foes,
Whose foggy Darkness, and benummed Senses,
Brook'd not his daz'ling fervent Influences.
Thus did he move on Earth from East to West;
There he went down, and up to Heaven for Rest.
Nor from himself, whilst living doth he vary,
His Death hath made him an *Ubiquitary*:

Where is his Sepulchre is hard to tell,
Who in a thousand Sepulchres doth dwell;
(Their *Hearts,* I mean, whom he hath left behind,)
In them his Sacred Relique's now Enshrin'd.
But let his Mourning Flock be comforted,
Though *Moses* be, yet *Joshua* is not dead:
I mean Renowned NORTON;[1] worthy hee
Successor to our MOSES is to bee,
O happy *Israel* in AMERICA,
In such a MOSES such a JOSHUA.

John Fiske
(1608-1677)

"Upon the much-to be lamented desease
of the Reverend Mr. John Cotton
late Teacher to the church at Boston N.E.
who departed this Life 23 of 10. 52."

TEXT: Harold S. Jantz, *The First Century of New England Verse*
(Worcester, 1944), pp. 118-121.

John ⎰ Cotton
     ⎱ Kotton after the old English writi'g

Anagr:
O, Honie knott

With Joy erst while, (when knotty doubts arose)
To thee we calld, o Sir, the knott disclose:
But now o and alasse to thee to call
In vayne tis thou no Answer give or shall.
Could loud Shrickes, could crys recall thee back
From deaths estate we wold our eye ne're slack
O, this our greife it is, lament shall we
A Father in our Israel's cea'st to be
even hee that in the Church a pillar was

A gurdeon knot of sweetest graces as
He who set fast to Truths so clossly knitt
as loosen him could ne're the keenest witt
Hee who his Flesh together bound ful-fast
no knott more sure whilest his life did last
Hee who the knotts of Truth, of Mysteries
sacred, most cleerely did ope' fore our eyes
even hee who such a one, is ceas'd to bee
'twixt whose life, death, the most sweete harmony
Knotts we doe meet with many a cue daily
which crabbed anggry tough unpleasing bee
But we as in a honi-comb a knott
of Hony sweete, here had such sweetenes Gott
the knotts and knobbs that on the Trees doe grow
the bitterest excressences we know.

                his soule Embalmd with grace
                        was fit to soare on high
                and to receive its place
                        above the starry skie.
                now grant O G[od that we]
                        may follow afte[r him]
                surviving worlds ocean unto thee
                        our passage safe may swim.

A vine tree seene, a plant of Gods owne hand
In it this knott of sweetest parts did stand.
The knott in place sublime: most eminent
As, his, no Branch could challeng like extent
The knott sometimes seems a deformity
It's a mistake, tho such be light set by
The knott it is the Joynt, the strength of parts
the bodies-beauty, so this knott out-starts
What others in that place, they ought to bee
even such a knott exemplar'ly was hee
Knotts now adayes affrayd of are most men
of Hony if expose'd feare none would then
I guesse why knotty Learning downe does goe
'twould not, if as in him 'twere sweetned soe
Meeknes Humility forebearance too
this lovely knott to love the most did woe

In knotts what greate adoe to gayne the hearte
yee had it heere, he did it free impart
When knotty theames and paynes some meet with then
as knotty and uncouth their tongue and pen
so 'twas not heere, he caus'd us understand
and tast the sweetnes of the knott in hand.
When knotty querks and quiddities broacht were
by witt of man he sweetely Breathed there.
His charity his wisdom meeknes eke
left none that loved light, in knotts to seeke
Hee tho invincible thrô softnes did
the knottiest peeces calme and cleave amid
Such was hee of such use in these last dayes
Whose want bewayle, o, and alas alwaies
This knott so we have seen lien broknly
By knotts so breathlesse, so crookt, crackt, or fly
This knott thereof so surfetted we see
By hony surfetted we know som bee
The cause nor in the knott nor hony say
Thrô Temper bad, unskilfulnes this may
O knott of Hony most delightfull when
Thou livd'st, thi death a sad presage hath ben
Have Ben? yea is, and is, and is alas
For woe to us, so greate a Breach when was
Woe to that knotty pride hee ne're subdude
Woe they who doe his Truthes dispenct exclude
and woe to them that factions there contrive
woe them whose wayes unrighteous survive
Woe they that by him warning did not take
Woe to us all if mercy us forsake
A Mercy once New England thou hast had
(you Boston cheifly) in thi Cotton clad
Some 'gan to count't too meane a dresse and sought
Silk Velvetts Taffeties best could be bought
these last will soyle, if first doe soyle also
how can we think but Naked we shall goe
must silken witts, must velvet tongues be had
and shall playne preaching be accounted bad
I feare a famine, pinching times t'ensue
Time Such may have, slighted mercy to Rue
My wakened muse to rest, my moystned pen

mye eye, my hearte which powred out this have ben
cease try no more, for Hee hath gayn'd his prize
His heavenly mansion 'bove the starry skie
Returne thee home and wayle the evills there
Repent breake off thi sins Jehovah feare
    O Jehovah feare: this will thi wisdom bee
    And thou his waies of mercy yet maust see
    Returne thou mee;   And turned bie
    Lord unto thee: even so shall I.

"Upon the decease of the Reverend
Mr Tho: Hooker &c"

TEXT: Jantz, p. 123.

Thomas Hooker
Anagr.
A Rest; oh com'! oh

A Rest's at hand after thy weary dayes
After thy Tossings heere in wildernes:

A rest is it? oh com'! oh, no delayes
let bee! of this life end the wretchednes.

"Upon the departure
of
the worthy aged useful servant of god Mr Sa: sharp
late ruling-Elder to the Church at Salem.
deceased the 72. y. of his age.
when he had borne office 26. yeeres in the church
upon the 3d. of 3d. mo. 1655."

TEXT: Jantz, pp. 125-126.

Samuel Sharpe
Anagr.
Us! Ample-share.

Us) saies, whose is the losse: The Gayner Hee
Whom changd for ample-share of Blisse you see
Alias

Whil'st we Thee mind, Deere Sharpe, whose presence sweete
Erstwhile did us refresh, whose watchfull eye
holpe to prevent exorbitances greate
and to relax them [that] in snare did Lye

O us! our Losse! our Losse! how sad it is
this breach in fam'ly greate, in church, in Towne
who each bereft as of a Father Now
are forc't to wayle our heavenly-Fathers frowne

oh! who shall us! us! comfort, hope, helpe, give?
who shew shall what hath us of him depriv'd?
where may supply? how may the worke be done?
our safety peace, tell us, which way contriv'd

Looke here seeke there, sorrow doth us beset
us, God corrects in this a stroke so greate
our sin the cause, no cause we should forget
Mercy alone tis that we need entreate

The Losse is ours who survive, and who
unto this Brother did erst'while relate
The losse not his, of all whose toylesome care
and weary-warefare and his pilgrime state

Of all whose Teares, conflicts, and watchfull paynes
Suffering for christ, hard measure heere below
wants, weaknesses, Temptations, and what else
done, borne by him, or what he did bestow

What counsells, prayers, comforts, or reproofes
what censures, Tryalls, faithfulnes in these,
what diligence, what travel, meeknes, Zeale
He now of all, reapes the reward in blesse.

An Ample share he had indeed i'th' first
whilest heere he liv'd, and served all his dayes;
And in a good old age (with patience firme
his station kept) departs, no longer staies

An Ample-share in the Reward he has
which layd up is in Heaven, therefore none should

his Losse Lament; A Gayner Hee, and then
not greive, but Joy on his behalfe Love would

Love leave thy fruits, Love speake and act thy kind
to those of His which may him soonest want
Eye those Relicts which hee hath left behind
find they an Ample share in it, not scant:

The larger share they find in that they Love
the larger testimony thou shalt give
of thy Repentance for the Sin that strove
Thee, Thee of such a blessing to deprive

So much the more as thou a comfort art
the widdow orphane by such fruits unto:
so much the more Ample a share thou shalt
of blessing reape, even thou when hence thou goe.

"Upon the decease of Mris Anne Griffin
(the wife of Mr. Richard Griffin late Ruling Elder
to the Church in Concord) departing this life
upon 23 of 10. 55 being about 96 yeers of Age"

TEXT: Jantz, pp. 130-131.

Anne Griffin
Anagr
In Fanne: Rig.

Canst thinke the Cargoe wherewith ship is fraught
pure wheate should bee, and shee unrig'd? And why
should't once be thought, the Soule which Grace hath caught,
and stor'd its ship therewith, unrig'd should Lye.

Whil'st wheate in Fanne, the ship in Rigging is
the Tackling fitt and fastned to there use
When Season is, that it set forth, amisse
that nought there bee, to gayne the haven it chuse

Like to the wheate, Thy wheate appeare that't may
as twere in Fanne; thou now at last hast ben

Even such a Fanne, none like to it they say
Thou knew'st before; in yeeres nigh ten times ten

O're all Thy changes Chelmesford Granary
must be where Fanne caus'd Thee Repose to have
Yet still the Fanne, thy portion there doth Lye
Thy seas nor calme, tho Thou heere Rest didst crave

Yea that thy ship, (wherein thy soule Imbarkt)
had heere as in a hoped safe Port, cast
Her Anchor, found fresh feares in eares were har[kt]
Heere no abode, up, Rig, to flight make hast.

Time calls, be Gone, hoyse yards, out, get the home
longer abroad tis not for Thee to bee
Deathes Summons tells thee when wilbe Thy Dome
and Thou an End of weary dayes shalt see.

See! now Thou seest, Thou feels't, Thou find'st thy Re[st]
the sweetest Rest, the surest Anchorage
in such a haven, in Earth as not exprest
where Rockes endanger not nor Billowes Rage

We who surevive, hence double duty ken
Her change, her Gayne to Count: her blest to Judg[e]
We must the Fanning heere expect till done
Hye Time, when once in Fanne, thinke hence to Trudg[e]

When once Afflictions doe thee seaze, thinke then
Death will ere long approach, to thy long home
Thee hence to fetch: to Rest prepar'd who ben
who Tyrant-like to unprepared come.

                                                    JF.

But more, in Fanne of tryalls seest a saint
Yea one whose aged yeers the Deeps might know
think't time for us to Rig, for us acquaint
will God with Tryalls such, And lay us Low

Yea lay us Low, and humble us Hee will
or first or Last ere that he us will rayse

and follow us with waves and billowes still
Ere that for aye him we in Glory prayse.

JF.

What thou heere soughtst pray'd for, hop'd for, desir'd
which heere is not our portion to Enjoy
that there Thou hast more fully then requir'd
or understood could bee whilst sin annoy

"E. B."

(probably EDWARD BULKELEY)

(1614-1696)

"A *Threnodia* upon our Churches second dark Eclipse, happening *July* 20. 1663. by Deaths Interposition between us and that Great Light and Divine Plant, Mr. *Samuel Stone,* late of *Hartford* in *New-England."*

TEXT: Nathaniel Morton, *New Englands Memoriall* (Cambridge, 1669), pp. 168-169.

LAst Spring this Summer may be *Autumn* styl'd,
Sad withering *Fall* our Beauties which despoyl'd:
Two choicest *Plants,* our *Norton*[1] and our *Stone,*
Your *Justs* threw down; remov'd, away are gone.
One Year brought *Stone* and *Norton* to their Mother
In one Year *April July* them did smother.
Dame *Cambridge* Mother to this darling Son;
Emmanuel, Northampt' that heard this one,
Essex, our *Bay, Hartford,* in Sable clad,
Come bear your parts in this *Threnodia* sad.
In losing *One,* Church *many lost*: O then
Many for *One* come be sad singing men.
May *Nature, Grace* and *Art* be found in *one*
So high, as to be found in *few* or *none?*
In him these *Three* with full-fraught hand contested
With which by each he should be most invested.
The *Largess* of the *Three* it was so great
On him, the *Stone* was held a *Light compleat*:

A *Stone* more then the *Eben-ezer*[2] fam'd;
Stone splendent Diamond, right *Orient* nam'd;
A *Cordiall Stone,* that often cheared hearts
With pleasant Wit, with Gospel rich imparts;
Whet-Stone, that Edgefi' a th'obtusest Minde:
Load-Stone, that drew the Iron Heart unkinde;
A *Ponderous Stone,* that would the Bottom sound
Of Scripture-depths, and bring out *Arcan's*[3] found;
A *Stone* for Kingly *David's* use so fit,
As would not fail *Goliah's* Front to hit;
A *Stone* an *Antidote,* that brake the course
Of Gangrene Errour by Convincing force;
A *Stone Acute,* fit to divide and square;
A *Squared Stone,* became Christs Building rare;
A *Peter's Living lively Stone,* (so Reared)
As *'live,* was *Hartfords* life; *dead,* death is feared.
In *Hartford* old, *Stone* first drew Infant-breath;
In *New* effus'd his last: O there beneath
His Corps are laid, near to his darling Brother,   Mr. *Hooker.*
Of whom dead oft he sigh'd, *Not such another.*
Heaven is the more desireable (said he)
For Hooker, Shepard, *and* Haynes *Company.*

Samuell Torrey

(1632-1707)

"Upon the Death of Mr William Tompson . . .
Etati sue 68. 1666."

TEXT: Kenneth B. Murdock, *Handkerchiefs from Paul* (Cambridge,
1927), pp. 18-19.

Epitaph

Here lies his corps, who, while he drew his breath,
He lived the lively portrature of Death,
A walking tomb, a liveing sepulcher,
In which blak meloncholy[1] did interr
A blessed soule, which god & nature have

By Death deliverd from yt liveing grave.
By this thine epitaph, now thou art gon:
Thy death it was thy resurection.

Here lyes his Corps, whose spirit was divine,
Too rich a relict for an earthly shrine,
A secret temple closd, where in his god
By solitudes of fellowship abode.
His gifts, his grace, his life, his light, retird,
He livd by life immediatly inspird.
Black darkness oft the Child of light befalls,
Yet he had sumtimes lucid entervales.
Then let this epitaph to him be given:
Darkness dispelled by the light of heaven.

He did outlive his life; twas time to dye,
He shall out live his death eternally.
Wele not lament his timely Death, for why
Twas death to live, his life to dye;
But yet we cannot Chuse but sigh to se
A saint to make a Dark Catastrophe.
Then sleep, swete saint, & rest thy weary dust;
Sing requems to thy selfe among the just.
We hope ere longe with ye to bear our part[s];
This epitaph to wright upon our hearts:
Sleep in this tomb till Christ ungrave thy dust,
Untill the resurection of the just.

Benjamin Tompson

(1642-1714)

"Gulielmi Tompsoni Braintreensis"

Ecclesiae Pastoris in Angliâ utraque
Celeberimi vice. Epitaphium

TEXT: *Benjamin Tompson 1642-1714,* ed. Howard J. Hall (Boston, 1924), pp. 107-108.

Judicious Zeale: New-Englands Boanerges[1]
Lies Tombles: not to spare the Churches Charges
But that the world may know he lacks no Tomb
Who in Ten thousand hearts commanded room
While thus the thundring Textman hidden lies
Some Virgins slumber: Others wantonize.

"*Upon the setting of that Occidental Star*
John Winthrop *Esq; Governour of* Connecticott
Colony, Member of the Royal Society;
who deceased in his Countreys Service
6 April 1676."

TEXT: Hall, pp. 84-86.

NIne Muses, get you all but one to sleep,
But spare *Melpomene,* with me to weep.
From you whose bleared Eyes have Lectures read,
Of many of our *English* Heroe's dead.
I beg a glance from Spectacles of Woe,
(Quotidian Gazets) Brave *Winthrop* to.
Whose death Terrestrial Comets did portend,
To every one who was his Countreys friend.
The Blaze of Towns was up like Torches light,
To guide him to his Grave, who was so fit
To rule, or to obey, to live or die:
(A special Favorite of the Most High)
Monarch of Natures Secrets, who did hold,
Its grand Elixir named the *Star* of GOLD.
Or else the World mistakes, and by his deeds,
Of Daily Charities Expence he needs.
But had he it, he wiser was than so,
That every Ape of Artists should it know.
He had the System of the Universe,
Too Glorious for any to Rehearse.
As *Moses* took the Law in Clouds and Fire;
Which Vulgars barr'd at distance much admire.
Thus was he taught the precious Art of healing,
(Judge we but by success) at Gods revealing.
He mounted up the Stairs of Sciences,
Unto the place of Visions which did please.

Where on the Pinacle of worldly skill,
On Kingdoms of all Arts, he gaz'd his fill.
Into his Thoughts Alembick we may think,
He crouded Stars to make a Diet Drink.[1]
(I mean) Terrestrial Stars which in the Earth,
Receive their vitals and a Mineral Birth:
That *Proteus, Mercury,* he could compel,
Most soberly well fixt at home to dwell.
Of Salt (which Cooks do use for Eggs and Fishes)
He made a Balsom better than all Riches;
And Sulphur too provided for mens woe,
He made an Antidote Diseases to.
This Terrene three, were made by Fire his friends,
To bring about his *ARCHIATRICK*[2] ends.
He saw the World, which first had only shade,
And after rich Embroideries on it laid,
Of Glorious Light; how the Homogeneal spark,
Did first Rebell against the Central dark.
He saw the Jemms how first they budded, and
The Birth of Minerals, which put to stand
Natures grand Courtiers. He knew the Womb
From whom the Various Tribes of Herbs did come.
He had been round the Philosophick sea,
And knew the Tincture if there any be:
But all his Art must lie, there's no Disease
Predominant, where he doth take his Ease:
Outliving *Theophrast,* he shew'd thereby
Himself Hermetick, more surpassing high
TRISMEGESTOS I'll stile him; first in Grace,
Thrice great in *ART,* the next deserving place;
Thrice High in humble Carriage, and who,
Would not to Highest Meekness ready bow?
England and *Holland* did great *Winthrop* woe;
Both had experienc'd Wonders he could doe.
But poor *New-England* stole his humble Heart,
From whose deep Wounds he never would depart:
His Councel Balsome like, he poured in,
And plaistred up its Breaches made by sin.
Natives themselves, in parlies would confess,
Brave *Winthrops* Charity and Holiness.
The Time he rul'd, War never toucht his bound,

When Fire, and Sword, and Death, raged all round.
Above whose reach he reigns in Glories Rays,
Singing with all the Saints his Makers praise.

EPITAPHIUM

GReater Renown than Boston *could contain,*
Doth underneath this Marble-stone remain:
Which could it feel but half so well as we,
'Twould melt to Tears and let its Prisoner free.

Urian Oakes

(1631-1681)

"An Elegie upon the Death of the Reverend
Mr. Thomas Shepard,"

TEXT: *AN ELEGIE upon The Death of the Reverend Mr. THOMAS
SHEPARD, Late Teacher of the Church at Charlstown in New-
England* (Cambridge, 1677).

To the Reader.

(1)

Reader! I am no Poet: but I grieve!
Behold here, what that passion can do!
That forc'd a verse, without *Apollo's* leave,
And whether th'Learned Sisters would or no.
    My Griefs can hardly speak: my sobbing Muse
    In broken terms our sad bereavement rues.

(2)

I wonder what the learned World still ailes,
To tune and pace their sorrows and complaints
In Rhythm and Verse! He that his crosses wailes
Indeed, would vent his griefs without restraints.
    To tye our grief to numbers, measures, feet,
    Is not to let it loose, but fetter it.

(3)

Is this it? that a Poets softer heart
Of great impressions susceptible is?
He wisely doth perform his mourning part
In Verse, lest grief should time and measure miss.
　　　But griefs unmeasurable would not be
　　　Curb'd, and rein'd-in by measur'd Poetry.

(4)

Stop, stop my Pen! lest *Israel's* singer sweet
Should be condemn'd, who, in that Song of th'Bow,
To vent his passionate complaints thought meet,
And to bewail his great Friends overthrow.
　　　King *David* in an Elegiack Knell,
　　　Rung out his dolours, when dear *Jona'than* fell.

(5)

No matter what's the trifling Poets Use,
Th'Imperious Law of custome we deride:
We have Diviner Warrant to produce,
Th: Soveraign, Sacred Poet is our guide.
　　　He wept his Friend in verse: then let us try,
　　　Now *Shepard's* faln, to write his Elegy.

---

(1)

OH! that I were a Poet now in grain!
How would I invocate the Muses all
To deign their presence, lend their flowing Vein,
And help to grace dear *Shepard's* Funeral!
　　　How would I paint our griefs, and succours borrow
　　　From Art and Fancy, to limn out our sorrow!

(2)

Now could I wish (if wishing would obtain)
The sprightli'est Efforts of Poetick Rage,

To vent my Griefs, make others feel my pain,
For this loss of the Glory of our Age.
    Here is a subject for the loftiest Verse
    That ever waited on the bravest Hearse.

(3)

And could my Pen ingeniously distill
The purest Spirits of a sparkling wit
In rare conceits, the quintessence of skill
In *Elegiack Strains;* none like to it:
    I should think all too little to condole
    The fatal loss (to us) of such a Soul.

(4)

Could I take highest Flights of Fancy, soar
Aloft; If Wits Monopoly were mine:
All would be much too low, too light, too poor,
To pay due tribute to this great Divine.
    Ah! Wit avails not, when th' Heart's like to break,
    Great griefs are Tongue-ti'ed, when the lesser speak.

(5)

Away loose rein'd Careers of Poetry,
The celebrated Sisters may be gone;
We need no *Mourning Womens* Elegy,
No forc'd, affected, artificial Tone.
    Great and good *Shepard's* Dead! Ah! this alone
    Will set our eyes abroach, dissolve a stone.

(6)

Poetick Raptures are of no esteem,
Daring *Hyperboles* have here no place,
Luxuriant Wits on such a copious Theme,
Would shame themselves, and blush to shew their face
    Here's worth enough to overmatch the skill
    Of the most stately Poet *Laureat's Quill.*

(7)

Exube'rant Fancies useless here I deem,
Transcendent vertue scorns feign'd Elogies:
He that gives *Shepard* half his due, may seem,
If Strangers hear it, to Hyperbolize.
      Let him that can, tell what his vertues were,
      And say, this Star mov'd in no common Sphere.

(8)

Here need no Spices, Odours, curious Arts,
No skill of *Egypt,* to embalm the Name
Of such a Worthy: let men speak their hearts,
They'l say, He merits an Immortal Fame.
      When *Shepard* is forgot, all must conclude,
      This is prodigious ingratitude.

(9)

But live he shall in many a gratefull Breast,
Where he hath rear'd himself a Monument,
A Monument more stately than the best,
On which Immensest Treasures have been spent.
      Could you but into th'Hearts of thousands peep,
      There would you read his Name engraven deep.

(10)

Oh! that my head were Waters, and mine Eyes
A flowing Spring of Tears, still issuing forth
In streams of bitterness, to solemnize
The *Obits* of this Man of matchless worth!
      Next to the Tears our sins do need and crave,
      I would bestow my Tears on *Shepards* Grave.

(11)

Not that he needs our Tears: for he hath dropt
His measure full; not one Tear more shall fall
Into God's Bottle from his eyes; *Death* stopt

That water-course, his sorrows ending all.
    He Fears, he Cares, he Sighs, he Weeps no more:
    Hee's past all storms, Arriv'd at th'wished Shoar.

(12)

Dear *Shepard* could we reach so high a strain
Of pure Seraphick love, as to devest
Our selves, and love, of self-respects, thy gain
Would joy us, though it cross our interest.
    Then would we silence all complaints with this,
    Our Dearest Friend is doubtless gone to Bliss.

(13)

Ah! but the Lesson's hard, thus to deny
Our own dear selves, to part with such a Loan
Of Heaven (in time of such necessity)
And love thy comforts better than our own.
    Then let us moan our loss, adjourn our glee,
    Till we come thither to rejoice with thee.

(14)

As when some formidable Comets blaze,
As when Portentous Prodigies appear,
Poor Mortals with amazement stand and gaze,
With hearts affrighted, and with trembling fear:
    So are we all amazed at this blow,
    Sadly portending some approaching woe.

(15)

We shall not summon bold Astrologers,
To tell us what the Stars say in the case,
(Those Cousin-Germans to black Conjurers)
We have a sacred Oracle that says,
    When th'Righteous perish, men of mercy go,
    It is a sure presage of coming wo.

(16)

He was (ah woful word! to say he was)
Our wrestling *Israel,* second unto none,
The man that stood i'th'gap, to keep the pass,
To stop the Troops of Judgments rushing on.
   This Man the honour had to hold the hand
   Of an incensed God against our Land.

(17)

When such a Pillar's faln (Oh such an one!)
When such a glorious, shining Light's put out,
When Chariot and Horsemen thus are gone;
Well may we fear some Downfal, Darkness, Rout.
   When such a Bank's broke down, there's sad occasion
   To wail, and dread some grievous Inundation.

(18)

What! must we with our God, and Glory part?
Lord! Is thy Treaty with *New-England* come
Thus to an end? And is War in thy Heart?
That this Ambassadour is called home.
   So Earthly Gods (Kings) when they War intend,
   Call home their Ministers, and Treaties end.

(19)

Oh for the Raptures, Transports, Inspirations
Of *Israel's Singers,* when his *Jon'athan's* Fall
So tun'd his mourning Harp! what Lamentations
Then would I make for *Shepards* Funerall
    How truly can I say, as well as He?
    My *Dearest Brother I'am distress'd for thee.*

(20)

How Lovely, Worthy, Peerless, in my view?
How Precious, Pleasant hast thou been to me?
How Learned, Prudent, Pious, Grave, and True?

And what a Faithful Friend? who like to thee?
    Mine Eye's desire is vanish'd: who can tell
    Where lives my dearest *Shepard's* Parallel?

(21)

'Tis strange to think: but we may well believe,
That not a few of different Perswasions
From this great Worthy, do now truly grieve
I'th' Mourning croud, and joyn their Lamentations.
    Such Powers Magnetick had He to draw to Him
    The very Hearts, and Souls, of all that knew Him!

(22)

Art, Nature, Grace, in Him were all combin'd
To shew the World a matchless *Paragon*:
In whom of Radiant Virtues no less shin'd,
Than a whole Constellation: but hee's gone!
    Hee's gone alas! Down in the Dust must ly
    As much of this rare Person as could dy.

(23)

If to have solid Judgement, Pregnant Parts,
A piercing Wit, and comprehensive Brain;
If to have gone the *Round* of all the Arts,
Immunity from Deaths Arrest would gain,
    Shepard would have been Death-proof, and secure
    From that All-conquering Hand, I'm very sure.

(24)

If Holy Life, and Deeds of Charity,
If Grace illustrious, and Virtue tri'ed,
If modest Carriage, rare Humility,
Could have brib'd Death, good *Shepard* had not di'ed.
    Oh! but inexorable Death attacks
    The best Men, and promiscu'ous havock makes.

(25)

Come tell me, Criticks, have you ever known
Such Zeal, so temper'd well with moderation?
Such Prudence, and such Inno'cence met in one?
Such Parts, so little Pride and Ostentation?
　　　Let *Momus* carp, and *Envy* do her worst,
　　　And swell with *Spleen* and *Rancour* till she burst.

(26)

To be descended well, doth *that* commend?
Can Sons their Fathers Glory call their own?
Our *Shepard* justly might to this pretend,
(His Blessed Father was of high Renown,
　　　Both *Englands* speak him great, admire his Name)
　　　But his own pers'onal worth's a better claim.

(27)

Great was the Father, once a glorious Light
Among us, Famous to an high Degree:
Great was this Son: indeed (to do him right)
As Great and Good (to say no more) as He.
　　　A double portion of his Fathers Spirit
　　　Did this (his Eldest) Son, through Grace, inherit.

(28)

His Look commanded Reverence and Awe,
Though Mild and Amiable, not Austere:
Well Humour'd was He (as I ever saw)
And rul'd by Love and Wisdome, more than Fear.
　　　The Muses, and the Graces too, conspir'd
　　　To set forth this Rare Piece, to be admir'd.

(29)

He govern'd well the Tongue (that busie thing,
Unruly, Lawless and Pragmatical)
Gravely Reserv'd, in Speech not lavishing,

Neither too sparing, nor too liberal.
    His Words were few, well season'd, wisely weigh'd,
    And in his Tongue the Law of kindness sway'd.

(30)

Learned he was beyond the common Size,
Befriended much by Nature in his Wit,
And Temper, (Sweet, Sedate, Ingenious, Wise)
And (which crown'd all) he was Heav'ens Favourite:
    Or whom the God of all Grace did command,
    And show'r down Blessings with a lib'eral hand.

(31)

Wise He, not wily, was; Grave, not Morose;
Not stiffe, but steady; Seri'ous, but not Sowre;
Concern'd for all, as if he had no Foes;
(Strange if he had!) and would not wast an Hour.
    Thoughtful and Active for the common good:
    And yet his own place wisely understood.

(32)

Nothing could make him stray from Duty; Death
Was not so frightful to him, as Omission
Of Ministerial work; he fear'd no breath
Infecti'ous, i'th' discharge of his Commission.
    Rather than run from's work, he chose to dy,
    Boldly to run on Death, than duty fly.

(33)

(Cruel Disease! that didst (like *High-way-men*)
Assault the honest Trav'eller in his way,
And rob dear *Shepard* of his life (Ah!) then,
When he was on the Road, where Duty lay.
    Forbear, bold Pen! 'twas God that took him thus,
    To give him great Reward, and punish us.)

(34)

Zealous in God's cause, but meek in his own;
Modest of Nature, bold as any Lion,
Where Consc'ience was concern'd: and there were none
More constant Mourners for afflicted Sion:
    So gene'ral was his care for th'Churches all,
    His Spirit seemed Apostolical.

(35)

Large was his Heart, to spend without regret,
Rejoycing to do good: not like those *Moles*
That root i'th' Earth, or roam abroad, to get
All for themselves (those sorry, narrow Souls!)
    But He, like th' Sun (i'th' Center, as some say)
    Diffus'd his Rayes of Goodness every way.

(36)

He breath'd Love, and pursu'd Peace in his day,
As if his Soul were made of Harmony:
Scarce ever more of Goodness crouded lay
In such a piece of frail Mortality.
    Sure Father *Wilsons*[1] genuine Son was he,
    New-England's Paul had such a *Timothy*.

(37)

No Slave to th'Worlds grand *Idols;* but he flew
At *Fairer Quarries,* without stooping down
To Sublunary prey: his great Soul knew
Ambition none, but of the Heave'nly Crown.
    Now he hath won it, and shall wear't with Honour,
    Adoring Grace, and God in Christ, the Donour.

(38)

A Friend to Truth, a constant Foe to Errour,
Pow'erful i' th' *Pulpit,* and sweet in converse,
To weak ones gentle, to th'Profane a Terrour.

Who can his vertues, and good works rehearse?
   The Scripture-Bishops-Character read o're,
   Say this was *Shepards*: what need I say more?

(39)

I say no more: let them that can declare
His rich and rare endowments, paint this Sun,
With all its dazling Rayes: But I despair,
Hopeless by any hand to see it done.
   They that can *Shepards* goodness well display,
   Must be as good as he: But who are they?

(40)

See where our Sister *Charlstown* sits and Moans!
Poor Widowed *Charlstown!* all in Dust, in Tears!
Mark how she wrings her hands! hear how she groans!
See how she weeps! what sorrow like to hers!
   Charlstown, that might for joy compare of late
   With all about her, now looks desolate.

(41)

As you have seen some Pale, Wan, Ghastly look,
When grisly Death, that will not be said nay,
Hath seiz'd all for it self, Possession took,
And turn'd the Soul out of its house of Clay:
   So Visag'd is poor *Charlstown* at this day;
   Shepard, her very Soul, is torn away.

(42)

Cambridge groans under this so heavy cross,
And Sympathizes with her Sister dear;
Renews her Griefs afresh for her old loss
Of her own *Shepard,* and drops many a Tear.
   Cambridge and *Charlstown* now joint Mourners are,
   And this tremendous loss between them share.

(43)

Must Learnings Friend (Ah! worth us all) go thus?
That Great Support to *Harvards* Nursery!
Our *Fellow* (that no Fellow had with us)
Is gone to Heave'ns great University.
        Our's now indeed's a lifeless *Corporation,*
        The Soul is fled, that gave it *Animation!*

(44)

Poor *Harvard's* Sons are in their Mourning Dress:
Their sure Friend's gone! their Hearts have *put on Mourning;*
Within their Walls are Sighs, Tears, Pensiveness;
Their new Foundations dread an overturning.
        Harvard! where's such a fast Friend left to thee
        Unless thy great Friend, LEVERET,[2] it be.

(45)

We must not with our greatest Soveraign strive,
Who dare find fault with him that is most High?
That hath an absolute Prerogative,
And doth his pleasure: none may ask him, why?
        We're Clay-lumps, Dust-heaps, nothings in his sight:
        The Judge of all the Earth doth always right.

(46)

Ah! could not Prayers and Tears prevail with God:
Was there no warding off that dreadful Blow!
And was there no averting of that Rod!
Must *Shepard* dy! and that good Angel go!
        Alas! Our heinous sins (more than our hairs)
        It seems, were louder, and out crie'd our Prayers.

(47)

See what our sins have done! What Ruines wrought:
And how they have pluck'd out our very eyes!
Our sins have slain our *Shepard!* we have bought,

And dearly paid for, our Enormities.
    Ah Cursed sins! that strike at God, and kill
    His *Servants,* and the Blood of *Prophets* spill.

(48)

As you would loath the Sword that's warm and red,
As you would hate the hands that are embru'd
I' th' Hearts-blood of your dearest Friends: so dread,
And hate your sins; Oh! let them be pursu'd:
    Revenges take on bloody sins: for there's
    No Refuge-City for these Murtherers.

(49)

In vain we build the Prophets Sepulchers,
In vain bedew their Tombs with Tears, when Dead;
In vain bewail the Deaths of Ministers,
Whilest Prophet-killing sins are harboured.
    Those that these Murth'erous Traitors favour, hide;
    Are with the blood of Prophets deeply di'ed.

(50)

New-England! know thy Heart-plague: feel this blow;
A blow that sorely wounds both Head and Heart,
A blow that reaches All, both high and low,
A blow that may be felt in every part.
    Mourn that this *Great Man's* faln in *Israel:*
    Lest it be said, *with him New-England fell!*

(51)

Farewel, Dear *Shepard!* Thou art gone before,
Made free of *Heaven,* where thou shalt sing loud *Hymns*
Of *High triumphant Praises* evermore,
In the sweet Quire of *Saints* and *Seraphims.*
    Lord! look on us here, clogg'd with sin and clay,
    And we, through Grace, shall be as happy as they.

(52)

My Dearest, Inmost, Bosome-Friend is Gone!
Gone is my sweet Companion, Soul's delight!
Now in an Huddling Croud I'm all alone,
And almost could bid all the World *Goodnight*:
    Blest be my Rock! God lives: Oh let him be,
    As He is All, so All in All to me.

                                    The Bereaved, Sorrowful
                                    Urian Oakes.

Daniel Henchman

(1677-1708)

"LAMENTAT[I]ONS Upon The Death of Sir
WILLIAM PHIPS, Knight Governour. Who
Expired in London February 18 1694, 5."

TEXT: Harold S. Jantz, *The First Century of New England Verse*
(Worcester, 1944), pp. 171-174.

And is He Mortal too, whose Life maintain'd
The Breath and Joy of ours? He who had gain'd
His Monarchs Favour, and his country's Love
By Glorious Actions, Registred above?
HE who himself did so Immortalize
By his All made one Glorious Sacrifice
To his lov'd Peoples Weal? . . .

Rejoyce, Messieurs; Netops,[1] Rejoyce; 'Tis True;
Ye Philistines, None will Rejoyce, but you;
Loving of all HE dy'd; who love him not
Now have the Grace of Publicans forgot.
Our Almanack's foretold a great Eclipse.
This they foresaw not of our Greater PHIPS.
Phips, our great Friend, our Wonder, and our Glory,
The Terrour of our Foes, the Worlds rare story.
England will boast him too, whose Noble Mind,

Impell'd by Angells, did those Treasures find,
Long in the bottom of the Ocean laid,
Which her three Hundred Thousand Richer made
By Silver yet nev' Canker'd, nor defil'd
By honour, nor betray'd when Fortune Smil'd.[2]

Since this bright Phoebus visited our Shoar
We saw no Foggs, but what were rais'd before:
Those vanish'd too; Harrass'd by bloody Wars
Our Land saw peace by his most Generous Cares.
The Wolvish Pagans at his dreaded Name
Tam'd, Shrunk before him, and his Doggs became.

Fell Moxus, and Feirce Docawando, fall,
Charm'd at the feet of our brave General.
O Dont his Death to the Blind Heathen shew,
Least they thereby, Their Courage do renew;
Nor let in Ask'lons Streets, the Deadly Voice
of it be heard, Least at it they Rejoyce.
Fly-blow the Dead, Pale Envy, let him not
(What Hero ever did?) escape a Blot.
All his distort with an Inchanted Eye;
And Height will make what's right still stand Awry.
HE was, O that he was? His faults we'l tell,
Such faults as these; we knew and lik'd 'em well
Just to an Injury; Denying none
Their Dues; but self denying oft his Own.
Good, to a Miracle; Resolv'd to do
Good unto all, whether they would or no.
To make us good, great, Wise, and all things else,
He wanted but the Gift of Miracles.
On him vain Mob, they Mischeifs cease to throw;
Bad but in this alone, the tims were so.
Stout to a prodigy; living in pain
To send back Quebeck Bullets once again
Thunder his Musick; Sweeter than the Spheres
Chim'd Roaring Cannons in his Martial Ears.
Frigats of Armed men could not withstand
'Twas try'd, the force of his one Swordless Hand:
Hand which in one all of Briareus had,
And Hercules' Twelve Toyls but Pleasure made.

Too Humble; In brave Stature not so tall,
As low in Carriage, stopping unto all:
Raisd in Estate, in Figure, in Renown,
Not pride; Higher and yet not prouder grown.
Of Pardons full; ner' to Revenge at all,
Was that which He would satisfaction call.
True to his Mate; from whom though often flown,
A stranger yet to every love but one.
Write him not Childless, whose whole people were,
Sons, Orphans, now of his Paternal Care.
Now least Ungratfull Brands, we still incurr,
Your Salary, we'l pay in tears, Great Sir!
To England often blown, and by his Prince
Often sent laden with Preferments thence:
Preferr'd each Time He went: when all was done
That Earth could doe, Heaven fetch'd him to a Crown.
'Tis he: with him interr'd how great Designs!
Stand fearless now Ye eastern Firrs and Pines,
with naval Stores not to enrich the Nation,
Stand for the Universal Conflagration.
Mines, opening unto none but Him, now lay
Close under lock, and Key, 'till the last Day.
In this, like to the grand Aurifick Stone,
By any but Great Souls not to be known.
And thou, Rich Table,[3] with Bodilla lost,
In the Rich Galeon, on the Spanish Coast,
In weight three Thousand and Three Hundred Pound,
But of pure Massie Gold, lye Thou not found;
Safe since He's laid under the Earth asleep,
Who learn't where thou dost under water keep.
But Thou Chief looser Poor New England, speek
Thy Dues to such as did thy Welfare seek.
The Governour, that Vow'd to Rise and Fall
With Thee, thy Fate shows in his Funeral.
Write now his Epitaph; 'twill be thy own:
Let it be this; A PUBlick Spirits gone.
or, but name PHIPS; more need's not be exprest,
Both ENGLANDS, and next Ages tell the Rest.

                                        Sic Lamentatus est
                                        D. Hincsman.

John James
(1633-1729)

"Of John Bunyans Life &c"

TEXT: Jantz, p. 150.

Wel mended Tinker! sans dispute
Brasse into Gold Grace can transmute.
Its hammer rings upon thy breast
so sanctifyed wert and blest
In thee an happy change was made
And thou becamest an other blad
Unswaupt,[1] instampt & meliorate
By such means was thy wretched state
So sovereigne a Mastery
Has Grace to cure debauchery.

Nov-8-1702

Cotton Mather
(1663-1728)

"Epitaph"

TEXT: *Magnalia Christi Americana*, Bk. 7 (London, 1702), p. 78.

DUMMER[1] the *Shepherd* Sacrific'd
By *Wolves,* because the *Sheep* he priz'd.
The *Orphans* Father, Churches *Light,*
The *Love* of *Heav'n,* of *Hell* the *Spight.*
The Countries *Gapman,* and the *Face*
That *Shone,* but knew it not, with *Grace.*
Hunted by *Devils,* but Reliev'd
The Martyr'd *Pelican,* who Bled

Rather than leave his Charge Unfed.
A proper *Bird of Paradise,*
Shot, and Flown thither in a Trice.

Lord, hear the Cry of *Righteous* DUMMER'S Wounds.
Ascending still against the *Salvage Hounds,*
That Worry thy dear *Flocks,* and let the *Cry*
Add Force to *Theirs* that at thine *Altar* lye.

"*The Excellent* WIGGLESWORTH,
Remembred by some Good Tokens."

TEXT: *A Faithful Man, Described and Rewarded* (Boston, 1705),
p. 48.

His Pen did once MEAT FROM THE EATER fetch;
And now he's gone beyond the *Eaters* reach.
His *Body,* once so *Thin,* was next to *None;*
From Thence, he's to *Unbodied Spirits flown.*
Once his rare skill did all *Diseases* heal;
And he does nothing now *uneasy* feel.
He to his *Paradise* is Joyful come;
And waits with Joy to see his DAY OF DOOM.

"GRATITUDINIS ERGO.
An ESSAY on the Memory of my Venerable MASTER;
EZEKIEL CHEEVER."[1]

TEXT: *Corderius Americanus* (Boston, 1708), pp. 26-33.

Augusto perstringere Carmine Laudes.
Quas nulla Eloquij vis Celebrare queat.[2]

YOU that are *Men,* & Thoughts of *Manhood* know,
Be Just now to the *Man* that made you so.
Martyr'd by *Scholars* the stabb'd *Castian*[3] dies,
And falls to cursed Lads a Sacrifice.
Not so my CHEEVER; Not by *Scholars* slain,
But Prais'd, and Lov'd, and wish'd to *Life* again.

A mighty *Tribe* of Well-instructed Youth
Tell what they owe to him, and Tell with Truth.
All the *Eight parts of Speech* he taught to them
They now Employ to *Trumpet* his Esteem.
They fill still *Fames Trumpet,* and they spread a Fame
To last till the *Last Trumpet* drown the same.
Magister pleas'd them well, because 'twas *he;*
They saw that *Bonus* did with it agree.
While they said, *Amo,* they the Hint improve
Him for to make the Object of their *Love.*
No *Concord* so Inviolate they knew
As to pay Honours to their Master due.
With *Interjections* they break off at last,
But, *Ah,* is all they use, *Wo,* and *Alas!*
We Learnt *Prosodia,* but with that Design
Our Masters Name should in our *Verses* shine.
Our Weeping *Ovid* but instructed us
To write upon *his* Death, *De Tristibus.*
Tully we read, but still with this Intent,
That in *his* praise we might be Eloquent.
Our Stately *Virgil* made us but Contrive
As our *Anchises* to keep *him* Alive.
When *Phoenix* to *Achilles* was assign'd
A *Master,* then we thought not *Homer* blind.
A *Phoenix,* which Oh! might his *Ashes* shew!
So rare a Thing we thought *our Master* too.
And if we made a *Theme,* 'twas with Regret
We might not on *his* Worth show all our Wit.
    Go on, ye Grateful Scholars, to proclame
To late Posterity your *Masters* Name.
Let it as many Languages declare
As on *Loretto*-Table[4] do appear.
    Too much to be by any *one* exprest:
I'll tell my share, and *you* shall tell the rest.
Ink is too vile a Liquor; *Liquid Gold*
Should fill the Pen, by which such things are told.
The Book should *Amyanthus*-Paper be
All writ with *Gold,* from all corruption free.
    A Learned Master of the *Languages*
Which to Rich *Stores* of Learning are the *Keyes*
He taught us first *Good Sense* to understand

And put the *Golden Keyes* into our Hand,
We but for him had been for Learning *Dumb,*
And had a sort of *Turkish Mutes* become.
Were *Grammar* quite Extinct, yet at his Brain
The *Candle* might have well been lit again.
If *Rhet'rick* had been stript of all her *Pride*
She from his *Wardrobe* might have been Supply'd.
Do but Name CHEEVER, and the *Echo* straight
Upon that Name, *Good Latin,* will Repeat.
A *Christian Terence,* Master of the *File*
That arms the Curious to Reform their *Style.*
Now *Rome* and *Athens* from their Ashes rise;
See their *Platonick Year* with vast surprize:
And in our *School* a *Miracle* is wrought;
For the *Dead Languages* to *Life* are brought.

His *Work* he Lov'd: Oh! had we done the same:
Our *Play-dayes* still to him ungrateful came.
And yet so well our *Work* adjusted Lay,
We came to *Work,* as if we came to *Play.*

   Our *Lads* had been, but for his wondrous Cares,
   Boyes of my Lady *Mores* unquiet Pray'rs.
   Sure were it not for such informing *Schools,*
   Our *Lat'ran* too would soon be fill'd with *Owles.*
   Tis CORLET's[5] pains, & CHEEVER's, we must own,
   That thou, *New-England,* are not *Scythia* grown.
   The *Isles* of *Silly* had o're-run this Day
   The *Continent* of our *America.*
Grammar he taught, which 'twas his work to do:
But he would *Hagar*[6] have her place to know.
   The *Bible* is the Sacred *Grammar,* where
   The *Rules of speaking well,* contained are.
He taught us *Lilly,*[7] and he *Gospel* taught;
And us poor Children to our *Saviour* brought.
Master of Sentences, he gave us more
Then we in our *Sententiae* had before.
We Learn't Good Things in *Tullies Offices;*
But we from *him* Learn't Better things than these.
With *Cato's* he to us the *Higher* gave
Lessons of JESUS, that our Souls do save.
We Constru'd *Ovid's Metamorphosis,*
But on our selves charg'd, not a *Change* to miss.

Young *Austin* wept, when he saw *Dido* dead,
Tho' not a Tear for a *Lost Soul* he had:
Our Master would not let us be so vain,
But us from *Virgil* did to *David* train,
Textors Epistles would not *Cloathe* our Souls;
Pauls too we heard; *we went to School at Pauls.*
   Syrs, Do you not Remember well the Times,
When us he warn'd against our *Youthful Crimes*:
What *Honey dropt* from our old *Nestors* mouth
When with his Counsels he Reform'd our Youth:
How much he did to make us *Wise* and *Good;*
And with what *Prayers,* his work he did conclude.
Concern'd, that when from him we *Learning* had,
It might not *Armed Wickedness* be made!
The *Sun* shall first the *Zodiac* forsake,
And *Stones* unto the *Stars* their Flight shall make:
First shall the *Summer* bring large drifts of *Snow,*
And beauteous Cherries in *December* grow;
E're of those Charges we Forgetful are
Which we, *O man of God,* from thee did hear.
   Such *Tutors* to the *Little Ones* would be
   Such that *in Flesh* we should *their Angels* see;
   Ezekiel should not be the Name of such;
   We'd *Agathangelus*[8] not think too much,
Who Serv'd the *School,* the *Church* did not forget;
But Thought, and Pray'd, and often wept for it.
Mighty in Prayer: How did he wield thee, Pray'r!
Thou Reverst Thunder: CHRIST's-Sides-piercing Spear?[9]
Soaring we saw the *Bird of Paradise;*
So Wing'd by Thee, for Flights beyond the Skies.
How oft we saw him tread the *Milky Way,*
Which to the Glorious *Throne of Mercy* lay!
   Come from the *Mount,* he shone with ancient Grace,
Awful the *Splendor* of his Aged Face.
Cloath'd in the *Good Old Way,* his Garb did wage
A War with the Vain Fashions of the Age.
Fearful of nothing more than hateful *Sin;*
'Twas that from which he laboured all to win,
Zealous; and in *Truths Cause* ne'r known to trim;
No *Neuter Gender* there allow'd by him.
Stars but a *Thousand* did the Ancients know;

On later Globes they *Nineteen hundred* grow:
Now such a CHEEVER added to the Sphere;
Makes an Addition to the *Lustre* there.
   Mean time *America* a *Wonder* saw;
A Youth in Age, forbid by *Natures* Law.
   You that in t'other Hemisphere do dwell,
Do of *Old Age* your dismal Stories tell.
You tell of *Snowy Heads* and *Rheumy Eyes*
And things that Make a man himself despise.
You say, a *frozen Liquor* chills the Veins,
And scarce the *Shadow* of a *Man* remains.
Winter of Life, that *Sapless Age* you call,
And of all Maladies the *Hospital*:
The *Second Nonage* of the Soul; the *Brain*
Cover'd with Cloud; the *Body* all in pain.
To weak *Old Age,* you say, there must belong
A Trembling Palsey both of *Limb* and *Tongue;*
Dayes all Decrepit; and a Bending *Back,*
Propt by a *Staff,* in *Hands* that ever shake.
   Nay, Syrs, our CHEEVER shall confute you all,
On whom there did none of these Mischefs fall.
He *Liv'd,* and to vast Age no Illness knew;
Till *Times Scythe* waiting for him Rusty grew.
He *Liv'd* and *Wrought;* His Labours were Immense:
But ne'r *Declin'd* to *Praeter-perfect Tense.*
A *Blooming Youth* in him at *Ninety Four*
We saw; But, Oh! when such a sight before!
At Wondrous *Age* he did his *Youth* resume,
As when the *Eagle* mew's his Aged plume.
With Faculties of *Reason* still so bright,
And at Good Services so Exquisite;
Sure our sound *Chiliast,* we wondring thought,
To the *First Resurrection* is not brought!
No, He for That was waiting at the Gate
In the *Pure Things* that fit a *Candidate.*
He in Good Actions did his Life Employ,
And to make others Good, he made his Joy.
Thus well-appris'd now of the *Life to Come,*
To *Live here* was to him a *Martyrdom.*
Our brave *Macrobius* Long'd to see the Day
Which others dread, of being *Call'd away.*

So, Ripe with Age, he does invite the Hook,
Which watchful does for its large Harvest look:
Death gently cut the *Stalk,* and kindly laid
Him, where our God his *Granary* has made.
   Who at *New-Haven* first began to Teach,
Dying *Unshipwreck'd,* does *White-Haven* reach.
At that *Fair Haven* they all Storms forget;
He there his DAVENPORT[10] with Love does meet.
   The *Luminous Robe,* the *Loss* whereof with *Shame*
Our Parents wept, when *Naked* they became;
Those Lovely *Spirits* wear it, and therein
Serve God with *Priestly Glory,* free from Sin.
   But in his *Paradisian Rest* above,
To *Us* does the Blest Shade retain his Love.
With *Rip'ned Thoughts* Above concern'd for Us,
We can't but hear him dart his Wishes, thus.
   'TUTORS, Be *Strict;* But yet be *Gentle* too:
'Don't by fierce *Cruelties* fair *Hopes* undo.
'Dream not, that they who are to Learning slow,
'Will mend by Arguments in *Ferio.*
'Who keeps the *Golden Fleece,* Oh, let him not
'A *Dragon* be, tho' he *Three Tongues* have got.
'Why can you not to Learning find the way,
'But thro' the Province of *Severia?*
''Twas *Moderatus,* who taught *Origen;*
'A *Youth* which prov'd one of the Best of men.
'The Lads with *Honour* first, and *Reason* Rule;
'*Blowes* are but for the *Refractory Fool.*
'But, Oh! First Teach them their Great God to fear
'That you like me, with Joy may meet them here
               H'has said!————
Adieu, a little while, Dear Saint, Adieu;
Your *Scholar* won't be Long, Sir, after you.
In the mean time, with Gratitude I must
Engrave an EPITAPH upon your Dust.
'Tis true, *Excessive Merits* rarely Safe,
Such an *Excess* forfeits an *Epitaph.*
But if Base men the Rules of Justice break,
The *Stones* (at least upon the *Tombs*) will speak.[11]

Joseph Green
(1706-1780)

"A Mournful Lamentation for the sàd and deplorable Death of Mr. Old Tenor,[1] A Native of *New-England,* who, after a long Confinement, by a deep and mortal Wound which he received above Twelve Months before, expired on the 31st Day of *March, 1750.*"

TEXT: *A Mournful Lamentation,* Broadside (Boston, 1750).

> *He lived beloved, and died lamented.*
> To the mournful Tune of, *Chevy-Chace.*

A Doleful tale prepare to hear,
    As ever yet was told:
The like, perhaps, ne'er reach'd the ear
    Of either young or old.
'Tis of the sad and woful death
    Of one of mighty fame,
Who lately hath resign'd his breath;
    OLD TENOR was his Name.

In vain ten thousands intercede,
    To keep him from the grave;
In vain his many good works plead;
    Alas! they cannot save.
The powers decree, and die he must,
    It is the common lot,
But his good deeds, when he's in dust,
    Shall never be forgot.

He made our wives and daughters fine,
    And pleased every body;
He gave the rich their costly wine,
    The poor their flip and toddy.
The labourer he set to work;
    In ease maintain'd the great:
He found us mutton, beef and pork,
    And every thing we eat.

To fruitful fields, by swift degrees,
　　He turn'd our desart land:
Where once nought stood but rocks and trees,
　　Now spacious cities stand.
He built us houses strong and high,
　　Of wood, and brick and stone;
The furniture he did supply;
　　But now, alas! he's gone.

The merchants too, those topping folks,
　　To him owe all their riches;
Their ruffles, lace and scarlet cloaks,
　　And eke their velvet breeches.
He launch'd their ships into the main,
　　To visit distant shores;
And brought them back, full fraught with gain,
　　Which much increas'd their stores.

Led on by him, our Soldiers bold,
　　Against the foe advance;
And took, in spite of wet and cold,
　　Strong CAPE BRETON from *France*.
Who from that *Fort* the *French* did drive,
　　Shall he so soon be slain?
While they alas! remain alive,
　　Who gave it back again.

From house to house, and place to place,
　　In *paper doublet* clad,
He pass'd, and where he shew'd his face,
　　He made the heart full glad.
But cruel death, that spareth none,
　　Hath rob'd us of him too;
Who thro' the land so long hath *gone,*
　　No longer now must *go.*

In *Senate* he, like *Caesar,* fell,
　　Pierc'd thro' with many a wound,
He sunk, ah doleful tale to tell!
　　The *members* sitting round.
And ever since that fatal day,

Oh! had it never been,
Closely confin'd at home he lay,
And scarce was ever seen.

Until the last of *March,* when he
Submitted unto fate;
In anno Regis twenty three,
AEtatis forty eight*
Forever gloomy be that day,
When he gave up the ghost:
For by his death, oh! who can say
What hath *New-England* lost?

Then good OLD TENOR, fare thee well,
Since thou art dead and gone;
We mourn thy fate, e'en while we tell
The good things thou hast done.
Since the bright beams of yonder sun,
Did on *New-England* shine,
In all the land, there ne'er was known
A death so mourn'd as thine.

Of every rank are many seen,
Thy downfal to deplore;
For 'tis well known that thou hast been
A friend to rich and poor.
We'll o'er thee raise a SILVER tomb,
Long may that tomb remain,
To bless our eyes for years to come,
But wishes ah! are vain.

And so God bless our noble state,
And save us all from harm,
And grant us food enough to eat,
And cloaths to keep us warm.
Send us a lasting peace, and keep
The times from growing worse,
And let us all in safety sleep,
With SILVER in our purse.

* Mr. OLD TENOR was born in the year 1702. [Green's note.]

Edward Taylor

"Let a man examine himself, and so let him eat of that bread and drink of that cup. I. Cor. 1.1."

(A favorite Puritan text)

Except that he was the most productive and talented poet of the colonial period, Edward Taylor led a life not at all different from that of many American Puritans. He was born in England in 1642, the first year of civil war. He may have gone to Cambridge. His rigorous Puritan upbringing led him to disavow the Act of Uniformity in 1662 and cost him a teaching post. Six years later he shipped to America, gaining his first sight of Boston, then a city of five to six thousand inhabitants, on the fourth of July. Ominous as the day may seem it counted for nothing. He was to be far less taken with the New World, in his poetry at least, than any other American Puritan poet: it provided his *Meditations* one reference to a rattlesnake and one to a canoe.

Taylor spent the first two nights at Increase Mather's house. Shortly after, he was admitted with advanced standing to Harvard College, where despite duties as college butler he took a degree in slightly over three years, instead of four, for two of them bedding with Samuel Sewall, his lifelong friend. In 1670 he reluctantly accepted a pastorate at Westfield, a ramshackle frontier village on the Connecticut river. There he remained the rest of his life, preaching, working as a physician, and writing verse. At Westfield he courted Elizabeth Fitch and married her in 1674. She bore him eight children; five died. In 1692, three years after her death, he remarried; his second wife bore six children. Although he complained to Sewall of living "far off from the Muses' copses . . . where little save clonian rusticity is à la mode," [1] it was at Westfield that he wrote all of his major works. In 1682 he began the *Preparatory Meditations,* whose composition occupied him, at monthly intervals, for forty-four years. He wrote much else in verse and prose: in eight long sermons on the Lord's Supper (1694) he attacked the liberal views of Solomon Stoddard; a decade later he completed a group of masterfully argued

173

but very taxing discourses on the nature of Christ and the need for imitating him. He wrote his last Meditation in 1725 and after that remained mostly bedridden until his death in 1729. Only three of his poems saw print in his lifetime. He did not and apparently forbade his heirs to publish the rest. A selection of his verse first appeared in 1937; no complete edition existed until 1960. That was a real misfortune for American Puritans. A John Cotton or Anne Bradstreet—any of the first generation of American Puritans—would have found Taylor's work instructive and exciting.

For Taylor was an altogether orthodox, an old-fashioned Puritan.[2] The concerns he shares with earlier American Puritans inspire his protests against deadness of heart, his eight communal elegies, his invocations of David, his virtuoso acrostics and shape verse. (The initial letters of his "acrostic Chronogram" compose a lengthy roman numeral whose digits add up to the year of Charles Chauncy's death.) But on one count Taylor differed from his contemporaries and from earlier Puritans drastically. None of them used verse for working out the esoteric complexities of Puritan theology. He is the sole doctrinal poet of American Puritanism. In his verse the incomprehensible Puritan God is approached through subtle and ambiguous argument. Other Puritan versifiers profess their piety, man's depravity, their hopes for salvation. But no other nails the sentiment of his verse to such strictly reasoned theses. Taylor's dramatic narrative, *God's Determinations* (omitted here, unfortunately, because of its length), grapples with finickey points of the doctrine of Grace and often bends them into poetry.

But in his *Meditations* Taylor does not usually manage doctrine so well. Unsatisfied with one treatment of a delicate point, he treats it again. He never feels wholly licensed to escape doctrinal terms. He repeats himself too much and trusts his novel impulses too little. He impresses us by moments. His images are often superficially related to the argument they decorate, although he often plots some forced link from image to image and stanza to stanza. His diction is a spectacularly discordant array of scholastic terminology, dialect, coinages and colloquialisms. His rough meter and elliptical syntax foster that same knottiness we find in other Puritan poets. Each poem is by fits prudent and wild, and there are many total failures. Scholars have tried to explain the character of Taylor's verse by tracing the quite obvious influences upon it. He has been dubbed a hellenistic poet, a metaphysical or baroque poet, a poet in the tradition of medieval morality plays. He had an appetite for third-rate poets like Robert Wild, and for the emblem writers; he knew the works of Anne Bradstreet, at his death the only English poems in his library. His verse does, at one time or another, recall all the metaphysicals, occasionally Traherne by its brand of mysticism, continually George Herbert, from whose "The Church-Porch" Taylor probably borrowed the six-line stanza of his *Meditations* and the familiar tone of his address to God. Echoes of Herbert fill Taylor's work, as they fill the verse of most other American Puritan writers.

None of these influences, however, define Taylor's verse. To repeat, he is, more strictly perhaps than even Milton, a Puritan poet. He is *the* Puritan poet. His subject is Puritan theology. Because he is a doctrinal poet whose work seldom yields large humanistic propositions, it seems helpful to preface a selection of his verse by reviewing its major doctrinal issue. Nearly all of Taylor's *Meditations* are concerned with the mystery of the Lord's Supper. For Taylor the Supper was the closest experience to that of everlasting life, a penultimate communion.[3] Most Puritans felt troubled by the Supper. While they administered it, they recognized it as a badge of the priesthood. The Pilgrim fathers did not observe the sacrament for nine years. They, already, seem to have thought it a perfunctory ritual, inessential to the Christian life and the being of a church.[4] By Taylor's time the administration of the Supper had become a battleground of intrachurch dispute. The question was, Should the Supper be open to all believers, or only to the Elect? Taylor thought the Supper closed to all but the Elect. Explicating his doctrine of the Supper in "A Particular Church is God's House" (1679) and Meditations 102-111 (1711-12), he challenged the view that because its efficacy was only that of a sermon or a prayer, the table should be opened to anyone who behaved well. Against this, he argued that the Supper is not a spur to faith or cause of faith, but a seal of faith already won, and should receive only the truly faithful.[5] This was no quibble. The dispute was over the preservation of Wilderness Zion itself. For to deny ministers control over their congregations, to open the church to the merely decent, was to deny authority to the group that kept Puritanism to its mark and preserved its ideals in the teeth of ever more secular America. Taylor even claimed that the Puritans left England explicitly for the sake of practicing their own version of the sacrament:

> To avoid such mixt administrations of the Lord's Supper; and to enjoy an holy administrating of it to the visibly worthy was that that brought this people from all things near and dear to them in their native country to encounter with the sorrows and difficulties of the wilderness. . . .[6]

To open the Supper to any but the "visibly worthy" was to defeat the whole purpose of the emigration! Then Taylor's ritual verses on the Supper were an intense, forty-year-long, unpublished protest against what New England was becoming, and did become: under his successor the Westfield congregation opened the communion table to anyone respectable.

The vivid emotional force of the Supper as an experience similar to Glory, and the fact that continued experience of it confirmed the determination of Israel in America to stay pure, explain why Taylor made the Supper the subject of 217 Meditations. And it explains why so much of Taylor's verse sounds the same. Each Meditation is a ritualized struggle to grasp the mystery of communion. Each gropes to understand how finite, depraved man may be joined with infinite Holy God, and through understanding evoke a state of mind proper to administering the sacrament. Two systems of imagery develop the apparent hopelessness of union with God: images for things heavenly (jewels, pearls), and images for things earthly (filth, snakes). The extremes of Taylor's diction reflect his need to encompass and celebrate hopelessly opposed values:

> Should Gold Wed Dung, should Stars woo Lobster Claws,
> It would no wonder, like this Wonder, cause.
>
> (Meditation 33, 2d Series)

Because the opposition is complete, Taylor is faced with the chance that communion is impossible, and with the complete inadequacy of man's language to understand its nature. It is literally impossible to write poems about Him since "Things styld Transcendent, do transcend the Stile / Of Reason. . . ." Taylor is not one of those poets who regard the act of writing as a discovery of meaning. What we know of God we know beforehand in doctrinal terms. The poem adds nothing. Taylor sometimes makes the poet a confounded, lisping child (a favorite persona of Anne Bradstreet's too), whose voice and reason are knotted by the effort to explain:

> In finest Twine of Praise I'm muzzled.
>   My tazzled Thoughts twirld into Snick-Snarls run.
>   Thy Grace, my Lord, is such a glorious thing,
>   It doth Confound me when I would it sing.

The purpose of the Meditation is to overcome this confusion in the hope of re-opening the "Golden Channells" of communion.

Meditation can do this by driving home doctrinal truths to the heart. For the Puritans, Meditation was a verbal art not unlike poetry, a "Preaching to ones self," as Richard Baxter called it.[7] It can "stir up," Taylor wrote, "all sacramental graces,"[8] such as humility, repentance, and faith. He was not the only Puritan who theorized on Meditation. Nicholas Noyes compared Meditation to the philosopher's stone. As that transmutes everything into gold, Meditation scans the sensible world for common objects and converts them to emblems of God. "The touch, the taste, Eye, Ear and Smell," Noyes puns, "Matter provide for *musing well.*" Meditation takes its language from common experience:

> The *Brass,* the *Iron Doggs* and *Tongs,*
> And *Bellows* that have *leather Lungs*
> *Fire, Wood, Brands, Ashes, Coals,* and *Smoke,*
> Do all to *Godliness* provoke!
> The *flame,* the *sparks, light, heat,* and *motion,*
> Are *Metamorphosed* to *Devotion.*[9]

Meditation was the plain style theory inwardly applied. It prescribed familiarity not as a way of reaching the least gifted hearer, but as a means of moving oneself. Since, as Taylor says, Christ "makes use of natural things to illustrate supernaturals by," [10] homely terms make difficult points of doctrine the knowledge of the heart.

The Puritan view of Meditation predicts the kind of familiar language Taylor used in plumbing the profound mysteries of communion. He is a coal that needs fanning, a sluggish windmill awaiting wind, or a bell, chime, spinning wheel, locked box, anything God can rouse, ply, or stir. Or he imagines the communion as a marriage, a marriage whose sexual implications he boldly extends, depicting himself as a wife. That may not have been for Donne, but was for a Puritan, daring; and even Donne might have paused before "The Soule's the Womb. Christ is the Spermodote . . ." (Meditation 80, 2d Series). The imagery of food and feasting that saturates Taylor's verse (a Puritan reduction of the more sensual diction of Catholic mystical poets) insists on the actual taste of communion, and makes his view of the Supper strikingly gay: Christ is "Glory's Chiefest Grape"; the sacramental wine is "beer! no nectar like it";[11] the wafer is "Zions Pasty Plate-Delights." The sacrament is not a moment of repose, as in George Herbert, but a rollicking holiday feast:

Here is a feast indeed! in ev'ry Dish
   A Whole Redeemer, Cookt up bravely, Good,
Is served up in holy Sauce that is,
   A mess of Delicates made of his blood,
   Adornd with graces Sippits; rich Sweet-Meats.

(Meditation 108, 2d Series)

But the image of communion Taylor dotes on is of channels flushed open. With remarkable audacity, the channels range from Christ's veins to sewer pipes. His best figures defy explication but suggest, sometimes in a single phrase, how the opening of channels is attended by a complex psychic state in which the believer feels purged, nourished, illuminated, and aroused. In "The Reflexion," Taylor presents himself as a darkened garden with underground pipes, the scene of the Fall. The opening of the pipes will sweep away his filth (purgation), irrigate the tree—the tree of Life, God—whose fruits he will be fatted on (nourishment). When the pipes (his soul) open, tears will come to his eyes (the rousing of the unregenerate heart); and God, now the sun, will shine over the Garden (illumination). Purgation, nourishment, an ecstatic state, understanding, all the components of communion are suggested in the conceit of the stopped pipe.

    Sewers and spinning wheels—Taylor makes the precious moments of the spirit's life rise from daily existence. He brings into play both domains of Puritan interest, theology and the home. In the moment of communion each ecstatically reveals the other's worth. Then the esoteric is divined in room and board, the workaday soul savors the ineffable God: "beer! no nectar like it." In his poems on the Supper the Puritan idiom of family affection and the mazy logic of Puritan theology join in celebration. By domesticating God, by uniting in a single voice John Cotton and Anne Bradstreet, Taylor's verse becomes the most comprehensive expression of the New England way.

NOTES

[1] In Norman S. Grabo, *Edward Taylor* (New York, 1961), pp. 25-26. The details of my sketch of Taylor's life are taken from Grabo's biography.

[2] Some critics have claimed that Taylor's orthodoxy prevented his development as a poet. See, for instance, Roy Harvey Pearce, "Edward Taylor: The Poet as Puritan," *New England Quarterly*, XXIII (March 1950), 31-46. Pearce describes Taylor as the spokesman of a static culture, echoing accepted beliefs and finding in his own experience, over and over, only what those beliefs told him ought to be there. But Puritan beliefs were not static. They were open to wide disagree-

ment within the Puritan community, and changed constantly as a result of changes in Puritan society. If Puritan doctrine narrowed Taylor's understanding of his actual experience, the controversies that beset Puritan doctrine gave his poems their unique urgency. The voice of his poems does not belong to some complacent moralist, but to a passionate mind sometimes frantically engaged in the dialectics of faith and wresting private certainties from fear, doubt and confusion.

3 Grabo, p. 36.

4 Geoffrey F. Nuttall, *The Holy Spirit in Puritan Faith and Experience* (Oxford, 1946), pp. 93-95. In New England, Puritans followed the custom originated by Zwingli of standing or receiving sacraments in their pews. The sacramental table or shelf was in the deacon's pew near the pulpit, raised a foot or so off the meeting-house floor. The implements were usually pewter, although John Cotton's first church used wooden chalices. Thin cakes of unleavened bread were prepared for the service. The Milton Church in 1734 ordered its deacons to buy canary wine, and other churches presumably did the same. See Alice Morse Earle, *The Sabbath in Puritan New England* (New York, 1892), pp. 113-114.

5 Norman S. Grabo, "Edward Taylor on the Lord's Supper," *Boston Public Library Quarterly,* XII (January 1960), 29.

6 Grabo, *Edward Taylor,* p. 34.

7 *Ibid.,* p. 63.

8 *Ibid.,* p. 35.

9 Nicholas Noyes, untitled prefatory poem to Cotton Mather, *Christianus per Ignem* (Boston, 1702), pp. 2-3.

10 Grabo, *Edward Taylor,* p. 100.

11 The beer may be a recollection of Taylor's days as college butler at Harvard. Richard Baxter, however, also refers to the sacramental wine as beer.

Preparatory Meditations before my Approach to the Lords Supper. Chiefly upon the Doctrin preached upon the Day of administration

"Prologue"

Lord, Can a Crumb of Dust the Earth outweigh,
  Outmatch all mountains, nay the Chrystall Sky?
Imbosom in't designs that shall Display
  And trace into the Boundless Deity?
  Yea hand a Pen whose moysture doth guild ore
  Eternall Glory with a glorious glore.

If it its Pen had of an Angels Quill,
  And Sharpend on a Pretious Stone ground tite,
And dipt in Liquid Gold, and mov'de by Skill

In Christall leaves should golden Letters write
It would but blot and blur yea jag, and jar
Unless thou mak'st the Pen, and Scribener.

I am this Crumb of Dust which is design'd
To make my Pen unto thy Praise alone,
And my dull Phancy I would gladly grinde
Unto an Edge on Zions Pretious Stone.
And Write in Liquid Gold upon thy Name
My Letters till thy glory forth doth flame.

Let not th'attempts breake down my Dust I pray
Nor laugh thou them to scorn but pardon give.
Inspire this Crumb of Dust till it display
Thy Glory through't: and then thy dust shall live.
Its failings then thou'lt overlook I trust,
They being Slips slipt from thy Crumb of Dust.

Thy Crumb of Dust breaths two words from its breast,
That thou wilt guide its pen to write aright
To Prove thou art, and that thou art the best
And shew thy Properties to shine most bright.
And then thy Works will shine as flowers on Stems
Or as in Jewellary Shops, do jems.

From the *First Series*

1. Meditation

What Love is this of thine, that Cannot bee
    In thine Infinity, O Lord, Confinde,
Unless it in thy very Person see,
    Infinity, and Finity Conjoyn'd?
    What hath thy Godhead, as not satisfide
    Marri'de our Manhood, making it its Bride?

N.B. All poems by Taylor are from *The Poems of Edward Taylor,* ed. Donald E. Stanford (New Haven, 1960), reprinted with the generous permission of Professor Stanford and the Yale University Press. See the Preface for copyright attributions of individual poems.

Oh, Matchless Love! filling Heaven to the brim!
    O're running it: all running o're beside
This World! Nay Overflowing Hell; wherein
    For thine Elect, there rose a mighty Tide!
    That there our Veans might through thy Person bleed,
    To quench those flames, that else would on us feed.

Oh! that thy Love might overflow my Heart!
    To fire the same with Love: for Love I would.
But oh! my streight'ned Breast! my Lifeless Sparke!
    My Fireless Flame! What Chilly Love, and Cold?
    In measure small! In Manner Chilly! See.
    Lord blow the Coal: Thy Love Enflame in mee.
                         (1682)

"The Reflexion."

Lord, art thou at the Table Head above
    Meat, Med'cine, sweetness, sparkling Beautys to
Enamour Souls with Flaming Flakes of Love,
    And not my Trencher, nor my Cup o'reflow?
    Be n't I a bidden Guest? Oh! sweat mine Eye.
    Oreflow with Teares: Oh! draw thy fountains dry.

Shall I not smell thy sweet, oh! Sharons Rose?
    Shall not mine Eye salute thy Beauty? Why?
Shall thy sweet leaves their Beautious sweets upclose?
    As halfe ashamde my sight should on them ly?
    Woe's me! for this my sighs shall be in grain
    Offer'd on Sorrows Altar for the same.

Had not my Soule's thy Conduit, Pipes stopt bin
    With mud, what Ravishment would'st thou Convay?
Let Graces Golden Spade dig till the Spring
    Of tears arise, and cleare this filth away.
    Lord, let thy spirit raise my sighings till
    These Pipes my soule do with thy sweetness fill.

Earth once was Paradise of Heaven below
    Till inkefac'd sin had it with poyson stockt
And Chast this Paradise away into

Heav'ns upmost Loft, and it in Glory Lockt.
But thou, sweet Lord, hast with thy golden Key
Unlockt the Doore, and made, a golden day.

Once at thy Feast, I saw thee Pearle-like stand[1]
    'Tween Heaven, and Earth where Heavens Bright
                                  glory all
In streams fell on thee, as a floodgate and,
    Like Sun Beams through thee on the World to Fall.
    Oh! sugar sweet then! my Deare sweet Lord, I see
    Saints Heavens-lost Happiness restor'd by thee.

Shall Heaven, and Earth's bright Glory all up lie
    Like Sun Beams bundled in the sun, in thee?
Dost thou sit Rose at Table Head, where I
    Do sit, and Carv'st no morsell sweet for mee?
    So much before, so little now! Sprindge, Lord,
    Thy Rosie Leaves, and me their Glee afford.

Shall not thy Rose my Garden fresh perfume?
    Shall not thy Beauty my dull Heart assaile?
Shall not thy golden gleams run through this gloom?
    Shall my black Velvet Mask thy fair Face Vaile?
    Pass o're my Faults: shine forth, bright sun: arise
    Enthrone thy Rosy-selfe within mine Eyes.
                            (Undated)

6. Meditation.

Am I thy Gold? Or Purse, Lord, for thy Wealth;
    Whether in mine, or mint refinde for thee?
Ime counted so, but count me o're thyselfe,
    Lest gold washt face, and brass in Heart I bee.
    I Feare my Touchstone touches when I try
    Mee, and my Counted Gold too overly.

Am I new minted by thy Stamp indeed?
    Mine Eyes are dim; I cannot clearly see.
Be thou my Spectacles that I may read
    Thine Image, and Inscription stampt on mee.
    If thy bright Image do upon me stand
    I am a Golden Angell in thy hand.

Lord, make my Soule thy Plate: thine Image bright
    Within the Circle of the same enfoile.
And on its brims in golden Letters write
    Thy Superscription in an Holy style.
    Then I shall be thy Money, thou my Hord:
    Let me thy Angell[1] bee, bee thou my Lord.
                          (Undated)

10. Meditation. Joh. 6.55. My Blood is Drinke indeed.

Stupendious Love! All Saints Astonishment!
    Bright Angells are black Motes in this Suns Light.
Heav'ns Canopy the Paintice[1] to Gods tent
    Can't Cover't neither with its breadth, nor height.
    Its Glory doth all Glory else out run,
    Beams of bright Glory to't are motes i'th' sun.

My Soule had Caught an Ague, and like Hell
    Her thirst did burn: she to each spring did fly,
But this bright blazing Love did spring a Well
    Of Aqua-Vitae in the Deity,
    Which on the top of Heav'ns high Hill out burst
    And down came running thence t'allay my thirst.

But how it came, amazeth all Communion.
    Gods onely Son doth hug Humanity,
Into his very person. By which Union
    His Humane Veans its golden gutters ly.
    And rather than my Soule should dy by thirst,
    These Golden Pipes, to give me drink, did burst.

This Liquour brew'd, thy sparkling Art Divine
    Lord, in thy Chrystall Vessells did up tun,
(Thine Ordinances,) which all Earth o're shine
    Set in thy rich Wine Cellars out to run.
    Lord, make thy Butlar draw, and fill with speed
    My Beaker full: for this is drink indeed.

Whole Buts of this blesst Nectar shining stand
    Lockt up with Saph'rine Taps, whose splendid Flame
Too bright do shine for brightest Angells hands

To touch, my Lord. Do thou untap the same.
Oh! make thy Chrystall Buts of Red Wine bleed
Into my Chrystall Glass this Drink-Indeed.

How shall I praise thee then? My blottings Jar
And wrack my Rhymes to pieces in thy praise.
Thou breath'st thy Vean still in my Pottinger[2]
To lay my thirst, and fainting spirits raise.
Thou makest Glory's Chiefest Grape to bleed
Into my cup: And this is Drink-Indeed.

Nay, though I make no pay for this Red Wine,
And scarce do say I thank-ye-for't; strange thing!
Yet were thy silver skies my Beer bowle fine
I finde my Lord, would fill it to the brim.
Then make my life, Lord, to thy praise proceed
For thy rich blood, which is my Drink-Indeed.

(1684)

29. Meditation. Joh. 20.17. My Father,
and your Father, to my God, and your God.

My shattred Phancy stole away from mee,
(Wits run a Wooling[1] over Edens Parke)
And in Gods Garden saw a golden Tree,
Whose Heart was All Divine, and gold its barke.
Whose glorious limbs and fruitfull branches strong
With Saints, and Angells bright are richly hung.

Thou! thou! my Deare-Deare Lord, art this rich Tree
The Tree of Life Within Gods Paradise.
I am a Withred Twig, dri'de fit to bee
A Chat Cast in thy fire, Writh off by Vice.
Yet if thy Milke white-Gracious Hand will take mee
And grafft mee in this golden stock, thou'lt make mee.

Thou'lt make me then its Fruite, and Branch to spring.
And though a nipping Eastwinde blow, and all
Hells Nymps with spite their Dog's sticks thereat ding
To Dash the Grafft off, and it's fruits to fall,
Yet I shall stand thy Grafft, and Fruits that are
Fruits of the Tree of Life thy Grafft shall beare.

I being grafft in thee there up do stand
    In us Relations all that mutuall are.
I am thy Patient, Pupill, Servant, and
    Thy Sister, Mother, Doove, Spouse, Son, and Heire.
    Thou art my Priest, Physician, Prophet, King,
    Lord, Brother, Bridegroom, Father, Ev'ry thing.

I being grafft in thee am graffted here
    Into thy Family, and kindred Claim
To all in Heaven, God, Saints, and Angells there.
    I thy Relations my Relations name.
    Thy Father's mine, thy God my God, and I
    With Saints, and Angells draw Affinity.

My Lord, what is it that thou dost bestow?
    The Praise on this account fills up, and throngs
Eternity brimfull, doth overflow
    The Heavens vast with rich Angelick Songs.
    How should I blush? how Tremble at this thing,
    Not having yet my Gam-Ut,[2] learnd to sing.

But, Lord, as burnish't Sun Beams forth out fly
    Let Angell-Shine forth in my Life out flame,
That I may grace thy gracefull Family
    And not to thy Relations be a Shame.
    Make mee thy Grafft, be thou my Golden Stock.
    Thy Glory then I'le make my fruits and Crop.
                     (1688)

32. Meditation. 1 Cor. 3.22. Whether
Paul or Apollos, or Cephas.

Thy Grace, Dear Lord's my golden Wrack, I finde
    Screwing my Phancy into ragged Rhimes,
Tuning thy Praises in my feeble minde
    Untill I come to strike them on my Chimes.
    Were I an Angell bright, and borrow could
    King Davids Harp, I would them play on gold.

But plung'd I am, my minde is puzzled,
    When I would spin my Phancy thus unspun,
In finest Twine of Praise I'm muzzled.

My tazzled[1] Thoughts twirld into Snick-Snarls[2] run.
Thy Grace, my Lord, is such a glorious thing,
It doth Confound me when I would it sing.

Eternall Love an Object mean did smite
      Which by the Prince of Darkness was beguilde,
That from this Love it ran and sweld with spite
      And in the way with filth was all defilde
      Yet must be reconcild, cleansd, and begrac'te
      Or from the fruits of Gods first Love displac'te.

Then Grace, my Lord, wrought in thy Heart a vent,
      Thy Soft Soft hand to this hard worke did goe,
And to the Milke White Throne of Justice went
      And entred bond that Grace might overflow.
      Hence did thy Person to my Nature ty
      And bleed through humane Veans to satisfy.

Oh! Grace, Grace, Grace! this Wealthy Grace doth lay
      Her Golden Channells from thy Fathers throne,
Into our Earthen Pitchers to Convay
      Heavens Aqua Vitae to us for our own.
      O! let thy Golden Gutters run into
      My Cup this Liquour till it overflow.

Thine Ordinances, Graces Wine-fats where
      Thy Spirits Walkes, and Graces runs doe ly
And Angells waiting stand with holy Cheere
      From Graces Conduite Head, with all Supply.
      These Vessells full of Grace are, and the Bowls
      In which their Taps do run, are pretious Souls.

Thou to the Cups dost say (that Catch this Wine,)
      This Liquour, Golden Pipes, and Wine-fats plain,
Whether Paul, Apollos, Cephas, all are thine.
      Oh Golden Word! Lord speake it ore again.
      Lord speake it home to me, say these are mine.
      My Bells shall then thy Praises bravely chime.
                                                      (1689)

40. Meditation. 1. Joh. 2.2. He is a Propitiation for our Sin.
Still I complain; I am complaining still.
    Oh! woe is me! Was ever Heart like mine?
A Sty of Filth, a Trough of Washing-Swill
    A Dunghill Pitt, a Puddle of mere Slime.
    A Nest of Vipers, Hive of Hornets; Stings.
    A Bag of Poyson, Civit-Box of Sins.

Was ever Heart like mine? So bad? black? Vile?
    Is any Divell blacker? Or can Hell
Produce its match? It is the very Soile
    Where Satan reads his Charms, and sets his Spell.
    His Bowling Ally, where he sheeres his fleece
    At Nine Pins, Nine Holes, Morrice, Fox and Geese.

His Palace Garden where his courtiers walke.
    His Jewells Cabbinet. Here his Caball
Do sham it, and truss up their Privie talk
    In Fardells of Consults and bundles all.
    His shambles, and his Butchers stale's herein.
    It is the Fuddling Schoole of every sin.

Was ever Heart like mine? Pride, Passion, fell.
    Ath'ism, Blasphemy, pot, pipe it, dance
Play Barlybreaks, and at last Couple in Hell.
    At Cudgells, Kit-Cat, Cards and Dice here prance.
    At Noddy, Ruff-and-trumpet, Jing, Post-and-Pare,
    Put, One-and-thirty, and such other ware.

Grace shuffled is away: Patience oft sticks
    Too soon, or draws itselfe out, and's out Put.
Faith's over trumpt, and oft doth lose her tricks.
    Repentance's Chalkt up Noddy, and out shut.
    They Post, and Pare off Grace thus, and its shine.
    Alas! alas! was ever Heart like mine?

Sometimes methinks the serpents head I mall:
    Now all is still: my spirits do recreute.
But ere my Harpe can tune sweet praise, they fall
    On me afresh, and tare me at my Root.
    They bite like Badgers now nay worse, although
    I tooke them toothless sculls, rot long agoe.

My Reason now's more than my sense, I feele
   I have more Sight than Sense. Which seems to bee
A Rod of Sun beams t'whip mee for my steele.
     My Spirits spiritless, and dull in mee
     For my dead prayerless Prayers: the Spirits winde
     Scarce blows my mill about. I little grinde.

Was ever Heart like mine? My Lord, declare.
   I know not what to do: What shall I doe?
I wonder, split I don't upon Despare.
     Its grace's wonder that I wrack not so.
     I faintly shun't: although I see this Case
     Would say, my sin is greater than thy grace.

Hope's Day-peep dawns hence through this chinck. Christs
                                name
   Propitiation is for sins. Lord, take
It so for mine. Thus quench thy burning flame
     In that clear stream that from his side forth brake.
     I can no Comfort take while thus I see
     Hells cursed Imps thus jetting strut in mee.

Lord take thy sword: these Anakims[1] destroy:
   Then soake my soule in Zions Bucking[2] tub
With Holy Soap, and Nitre, and rich Lye.
     From all Defilement me cleanse, wash and rub.
     Then wrince, and wring mee out till th'water fall
     As pure as in the Well: not foule at all.

And let thy Sun, shine on my Head out cleare.
   And bathe my Heart within its radient beams:
Thy Christ make my Propitiation Deare.
     Thy Praise shall from my Heart breake forth in streams.
     This reeching Vertue of Christs blood will quench
     Thy Wrath, slay Sin and in thy Love mee bench.
                          (1690/1)

From the *Second Series*

3. Meditation. Rom. 5.14. Who is the
Figure of Him that was to come.

Like to the Marigold, I blushing close

My golden blossoms when thy sun goes down:
Moist'ning my leaves with Dewy Sighs, half frose
 By the nocturnall Cold, that hoares my Crown.
 Mine Apples ashes are in apple shells
 And dirty too: strange and bewitching spells!

When Lord, mine Eye doth spie thy Grace to beame
 Thy Mediatoriall glory in the shine
Out Spouted so from Adams typick streame
 And Emblemiz'd in Noahs pollisht shrine
 Thine theirs outshines so far it makes their glory
 In brightest Colours, seem a smoaky story.

But when mine Eye full of these beams, doth cast
 Its rayes upon my dusty essence thin
Impregnate with a Sparke Divine, defacde,
 All Candid o're with Leprosie of Sin,
 Such Influences on my Spirits light,
 Which them as bitter gall, or Cold ice smite.

My brissled sins hence do so horrid peare,
 None but thyselfe, (and thou deckt up must bee
In thy Transcendent glory sparkling cleare)
 A Mediator unto God for mee.
 So high they rise, Faith scarce can toss a Sight
 Over their head upon thyselfe to light.

Is't possible such glory, Lord, ere should
 Center its Love on me Sins Dunghill else?
My Case up take? make it its own? Who would
 Wash with his blood my blots out? Crown his shelfe
 Or Dress his golden Cupboard with such ware?
 This makes my pale facde Hope almost despare.

Yet let my Titimouses Quill suck in
 Thy Graces milk Pails some small drop: or Cart
A Bit, or Splinter of some Ray, the wing
 Of Grace's sun sprindgd out, into my heart:
 To build there Wonders Chappell where thy Praise
 Shall be the Psalms sung forth in gracious layes.
        (1693)

Meditation 44. Joh. 1.14. The word was made Flesh.

The Orator from Rhetorick gardens picks
    His Spangled Flowers of sweet-breathd Eloquence
Wherewith his Oratory brisk he tricks
    Whose Spicy Charms Eare jewells do commence.
    Shall bits of Brains be candid thus for eares?
    My Theme claims Sugar Candid far more cleare.

Things styld Transcendent, do transcende the Stile
    Of Reason, reason's stares neere reach so high.
But Jacob's golden Ladder rounds do foile
    All reasons Strides, wrought of **THEANTHROPIE**.[1]
    Two Natures distance-standing, infinite,
    Are Onifide, in person, and Unite.

In Essence two, in Properties each are
    Unlike, as unlike can be. One All-Might
A Mite the other; One Immortall fair.
    One mortall, this all Glory, that all night.
    One Infinite, One finite. So for ever:
    Yet ONED are in Person, part'd never.

The Godhead personated in Gods Son
    Assum'd the Manhood to its Person known,
When that the Manhoods essence first begun
    That it did never Humane person own.
    Each natures Essence e're abides the same.
    In person joynd, one person each do claim.

Oh! Dignifide Humanity indeed:
    Divinely person'd: almost Deifide.
Nameing one Godhead person, in our Creed,
    The Word-made-Flesh. Here's Grace's 'maizing stride.
    The vilst design, that villany e're hatcht
    Hath tap't such Grace in God, that can't be matcht.

Our Nature spoild: under all Curses groans
    Is purg'd, tooke, grac'd with grace, united to
A Godhead person, Godhead-person owns
    Its onely person. Angells, Lord its so.

This Union ever lasts, if not relate
Which Cov'nant claims Christs Manhood, separate.

You Holy Angells, Morning-Stars, bright Sparks,
    Give place: and lower your top gallants. Shew
Your top-saile Conjues[2] to our slender barkes:
    The highest honour to our nature's due.
    Its neerer Godhead by the Godhead made
    Than yours in you that never from God stray'd.

Here is good anchor hold: and argument
    To anchor here, Lord, make my Anchor stronge
And Cable, both of holy geer, out sent
    And in this anch'ring dropt and let at length.
    My bark shall safely ride then though there fall
    On't th'strongest tempests hell can raise of all.

Unite my Soule, Lord, to thyselfe, and stamp
    Thy holy print on my unholy heart.
I'st nimble be when thou destroyst my cramp
    And take thy paths when thou dost take my part.
    If thou wilt blow this Oaten Straw of mine,
    The sweetest piped praises shall be thine.
                                        (1701)

56. Meditation. Joh. 15.24. Had I not done amongst them the
works, that none other man hath done, etc.

Should I with silver tooles delve through the Hill
    Of Cordilera for rich thoughts, that I
My Lord, might weave with an angelick skill
    A Damask Web of Velvet Verse thereby
    To deck thy Works up, all my Web would run
    To rags, and jags: so snicksnarld to the thrum.

Thine are so rich: Within, Without. Refin'd.
    No workes like thine. No Fruits so sweete that grow
On th'trees of righteousness, of Angell kinde
    And Saints, whose limbs reev'd with them bow down low.
    Should I search ore the Nutmeg Gardens shine
    Its fruits in flourish are but skegs to thine.

The Clove, when in its White-green'd blossoms shoots,
    Some Call the pleasentst sent the World doth show.
None Eye e're saw, nor nose e're smelt such Fruits
    My Lord, as thine, Thou Tree of Life in'ts blow.
    Thou Rose of Sharon, Vallies Lilly true
    Thy Fruits most sweet and Glorious ever grew.

Thou art a Tree of Perfect nature trim
    Whose golden lining is of perfect Grace
Perfum'de with Deity unto the brim,
    Whose fruits, of the perfection, grow, of Grace.
    Thy Buds, thy Blossoms, and thy fruits adorne
    Thyselfe, and Works, more shining than the morn.

Art, natures Ape, hath many brave things done
    As th'Pyramids, the Lake of Meris vast
The Pensile Orchards built in Babylon,[1]
    Psammitich's Labyrinth. (arts Cramping task)
    Archimedes his Engins made for war.
    Romes Golden House. Titus his Theater.

The Clock at Strasburgh, Dresdens Table-Sight
    Regiamonts Fly of Steele about that flew.
Turrian's Wooden Sparrows in a flight.
    And th'Artificiall man Aquinas slew.[2]
    Mark Scaliota's Lock, and Key and Chain
    Drawn by a Flea, in our Queen Betties reign.

Might but my pen in natures Inventory
    Its progress make, 't might make such things to jump
All which are but Inventions Vents or glory
    Wits Wantonings, and Fancies frollicks plump.
    Within whose maws lies buried Times, and Treasures
    Embalmed up in thick dawbd sinfull pleasures.

Nature doth better work than Art: yet thine
    Out vie both works of nature and of Art.
Natures Perfection and the perfect shine
    Of Grace attend thy deed in ev'ry part.
    A Thought, a Word, and Worke of thine, will kill
    Sin, Satan, and the Curse: and Law fulfill.

Thou art the Tree of Life in Paradise,
    Whose lively branches are with Clusters hung
Of Lovely fruits, and Flowers more sweet than spice
    Bende down to us: and doe out shine the sun,
    Delightfull unto God, doe man rejoyce
    The pleasentst fruits in all Gods Paradise.

Lord feed mine eyes then with thy Doings rare,
    And fat my heart with these ripe fruites thou bearst.
Adorn my Life well with thy works, make faire
    My Person with apparrell thou prepar'st.
    My Boughs shall loaded bee with fruits that spring
    Up from thy Works, while to thy praise I sing.
                         (1703)

66. Meditation. Joh. 15.13. Greater Love hath no man than this
That a man lay down his Life for his Friends.

O! what a thing is Love? who can define
    Or liniament it out? Its strange to tell.
A Sparke of Spirit empearld pill like and fine
    In't shugard pargings,[1] crusted, and doth dwell
    Within the heart, where thron'd, without Controle
    It ruleth all the Inmates of the Soule.

It makes a poother[2] in its Secret Sell
    Mongst the affections: oh! it swells, its paind,
Like kirnells soked untill it breaks its Shell
    Unless its object be obtained and gain'd.
    Like Caskd wines jumbled breake the Caske, this Sparke
    Oft swells when crusht: untill it breakes the Heart.

O! Strange Strange Love! 'Stroy Life and't selfe thereby.
    Hence lose its Object, lay down all't can moove.
For nothing rather choose indeed to dy,
    And nothing be, than be without its love.
    Not t'be, than be without its fanci'de bliss!
    Is this Love's nature? What a thing is this?

Love thus ascending to its highest twig,
    May sit and Cherp such ditties. Sing and dy.

This highest Note is but a Black-Cap's jig
    Compar'd to thine my Lord, all Heavenly.
    A greater love than such man ne'er mentain'd.
    A greater Love than such thou yet hast gain'd.

Thy Love laid down thy Life hath for thy Sheep:
    Thy friends by grace: thy foes by Nature's Crimes.
And yet thy Life more precious is and sweet
    More worth than all the World ten thousand times.
    And yet thy Love did give bright Wisdoms Shine
    In laying down thy precious life for thine.

This Love was ne'er adulterate: e're pure.
    Noe Whiffe of Fancy: But rich Wisdomes Beams,
No Huff of Hot affection men endure.
    But sweetend Chimings of Celestiall gleams
    Play'd and Display'd upon the golden Wyer
    That doth thy Human Cymball brave, attire.

Thy Love that laid thy life all down for thine
    Did not thereby destroy itselfe at all.
It was preserved in thy Selfe Divine
    When it did make thy Humane Selfe down fall.
    And when thy body as the Sun up rose
    It did itselfe like flaming beames disclose.

Lord, let thy Love shine on my Soule! Mee bath
    In this Celestiall Gleame of this pure Love.
O! gain my heart and thou my Love shalt have
    Clime up thy golden Stares to thee above.
    And in thy upper Chamber sit and sing
    The glory of thy Love when Entred in.
                             (1705)

82. Meditation. Joh. 6.53. Unless yee eate the Flesh of the Son
of Man, and drinke his blood, ye have no life.

My tatter'd Fancy; and my Ragged Rymes
    Teeme leaden Metaphors: which yet might serve
To hum a little touching terrene Shines.

But Spirtuall Life doth better fare deserve.
This thought on, sets my heart upon the Rack.
I fain would have this Life but han't its knack.

Reason stands for it, moving to persue't.
But Flesh and Blood, are Elementall things.
That sink me down, dulling my Spirits fruit.
Life Animall a Spirituall Sparke ne'er springs.
But if thy Altars Coale Enfire my heart,
With this Blesst Life my Soule will be thy Sparke.

I'm Common matter: Lord thine Altar make mee.
Then sanctify thine Altar with thy blood:
I'l offer on't my heart to thee. (Oh! take mee)
And let thy fire Calcine mine Altars Wood,
Then let thy Spirits breath, as Bellows, blow
That this new kindled Life may flame and glow.

Some Life with Spoon, or Trencher do mentain
Or suck its food through a Small Quill, or Straw:
But make me, Lord, this Life thou givst, sustain
With thy Sweet Flesh, and Blood, by Gospell Law.
Feed it on Zions Pasty Plate-Delights:
I'de suck it from her Candlesticks Sweet Pipes.

Need makes the Old wife trot: Necessity
Saith, I must eate this Flesh, and drinke this blood.
If not, no Life's in mee that's worth a Fly,
This mortall Life, while here eats mortall Foode.
That sends out influences to mentaine,
A little while, and then holds back the same.

But Soule Sweet Bread, is in Gods Back house, made
On Heavens high Dresser Boarde and throughly bakd:
On Zions Gridiron, sapt in'ts dripping trade,
That all do live that on it do partake,
Its Flesh, and Blood even of the Deity;
None that do eat, and Drinke, it, ever dy.

Have I a vitall Sparke even of this Fire?
How Dull am I? Lord let thy Spirit blow

Upon my Coale, untill its heart is higher,
    And I be quickned by the same, and Glow.
    Here's Manna Angells food to fatten them.
    That I must eate or be a witherd stem.

Lord, make my Faith thy golden Quill where through
    I vitall Spirits from thy blood may suck.
Make Faith my Grinders, thy Choice Flesh to chew,
    My Witherd Stock shall with frim Fruits be stuck.
    My Soule shall then in Lively Notes forth ring
    Upon her Virginalls, praise for this thing.
                     (1708)

161A. Meditation. Cant. 2.3. As the apple tree among the trees
of the wood, so is my beloved among the sons.

My double Dear Lord, and doubl't ore and ore
    Ten thousand times it would indeed still rise
A bubbe[1] too small to knock at thy blesst doore
    Of Loveliness, ten thousand times to thy sise.
    It would be a gift ten thousand times too low
    Though 't is the best I have on thee to bestow.

My Love alas is but a shrimpy thing
    A sorry Crickling[2] a blasted bud
A little drachm, too light a gift to bring.
    Its but a grain weight and scarce ever good,
    And shall I then presume thee to obtain
    If I should rob thee of so small a grain.

Thou art as Apple tree 'mong sons of man
    As was the Apple tree amonge the trees
That many are, (the Worlds geese are white swans
    In its account.) but thou excellest all these
    Ten thousand times bearing on every limb
    All golden apples; ripest grace that springs.

Not like the tree that once in Eden grew
    Amongst whose fruits the serpent old soon lops
And in his very teeth the poison threw
    Into our Mother Eves her sorry Chops.

Nor like the Serpents Egge the Squerill held[2]
Secur'd itselfe from th'venom that on it fell.

Lord shake their bower and let these apples fall
    Into my Wicker basket and it fill.
Then I shall have rich spirituall food for all
    Occasions as they essences do still
        And I shall feed on their rich grace my fare
        As they drop from thy Apple tree most rare.

And as thou serv'st up in thy Charger bright
    A messe of these rich apples, sweet imbrace
I tasting them do in their reech delight
    And over them will surely sing thee grace.

Thou tree of Life that ever more dost stand
    Within the Paradise of God and hast
The Promise to him gi'n whose happy hand
    Doth overcome, shall of it eate and tast.
        Lord feed mee with this promisd food of Life
        And I will sing thy praise in songs most rife.

                            (1722)

                Miscellaneous Undated Poems

                "[When] Let[1] by rain."

Ye Flippering Soule,
    Why dost between the Nippers dwell?
Not stay, nor goe. Not yea, nor yet Controle.
    Doth this doe well?
        Rise journy'ng when the skies fall weeping Showers.
        Not o're nor under th'Clouds and Cloudy Powers.

Not yea, nor noe:
    On tiptoes thus? Why sit on thorns?
Resolve the matter: Stay thyselfe or goe.
    Be n't both wayes born.
        Wager thyselfe against thy surplice, see,
        And win thy Coate: or let thy Coate Win thee.

Is this th'Effect,
    To leaven thus my Spirits all?
To make my heart a Crabtree Cask direct?
    A Verjuicte[2] Hall?
            As Bottle Ale, whose Spirits prisond nurst
            When jog'd, the bung with Violence doth burst?

Shall I be made
    A sparkling Wildfire Shop
Where my dull Spirits at the Fireball trade
    Do frisk and hop?
            And while the Hammer doth the Anvill pay,
            The fireball matter sparkles ery way.

One sorry fret,
    An anvill Sparke, rose higher
And in thy Temple falling almost set
    The house on fire.
            Such fireballs droping in the Temple Flame
            Burns up the building: Lord forbid the same.

"Huswifery."

Make me, O Lord, thy Spining Wheele compleate.
    Thy Holy Worde my Distaff make for mee.
Make mine Affections thy Swift Flyers[1] neate
    And make my Soule thy holy Spoole to bee.
    My Conversation make to be thy Reele
    And reele the yarn thereon spun of thy Wheele.

Make me thy Loome then, knit therein this Twine:
    And make thy Holy Spirit, Lord, winde quills:
Then weave the Web thyselfe. The yarn is fine.
    Thine Ordinances make my Fulling Mills.[2]
    Then dy the same in Heavenly Colours Choice,
    All pinkt with Varnisht Flowers of Paradise.

Then cloath therewith mine Understanding, Will,
    Affections, Judgment, Conscience, Memory
My Words, and Actions, that their shine may fill

My wayes with glory and thee glorify.
Then mine apparell shall display before yee
That I am Cloathd in Holy robes for glory.

"Upon Wedlock, and Death of Children."

A Curious Knot God made in Paradise,
    And drew it out inamled neatly Fresh.
It was the True-Love Knot, more sweet than spice
    And set with all the flowres of Graces dress.
    Its Weddens Knot, that ne're can be unti'de.
    No Alexanders Sword can it divide.

The slips here planted, gay and glorious grow:
    Unless an Hellish breath do sindge their Plumes.
Here Primrose, Cowslips, Roses, Lilies blow
    With Violets and Pinkes that voide perfumes.
    Whose beautious leaves ore laid with Hony Dew.
    And Chanting birds Cherp out sweet Musick true.

When in this Knot I planted was, my Stock
    Soon knotted, and a manly flower out brake.
And after it my branch again did knot
    Brought out another Flowre its sweet breathd mate.
    One knot gave one tother the tothers place.
    Whence Checkling smiles fought in each others face.

But oh! a glorious hand from glory came
    Guarded with Angells, soon did Crop this flowre
Which almost tore the root up of the same
    At that unlookt for, Dolesome, darksome houre.
    In Pray're to Christ perfum'de it did ascend,
    And Angells bright did it to heaven tend.

But pausing on't, this sweet perfum'd my thought,
    Christ would in Glory have a Flowre, Choice, Prime,
And having Choice, chose this my branch forth brought.
    Lord take't. I thanke thee, thou takst ought of mine,
    It is my pledg in glory, part of mee
    Is now in it, Lord, glorifi'de with thee.

But praying ore my branch, my branch did sprout
    And bore another manly flower, and gay
And after that another, sweet brake out,
      The which the former hand soon got away.
      But oh! the tortures, Vomit, screechings, groans,
      And six weeks Fever would pierce hearts like stones.

Griefe o're doth flow: and nature fault would finde
    Were not thy Will, my Spell Charm, Joy, and Gem:
That as I said, I say, take, Lord, they're thine.
    I piecemeale pass to Glory bright in them.
    I joy, may I sweet Flowers for Glory breed,
    Whether thou getst them green, or lets them seed.

    "Upon the Sweeping Flood Aug: 13.14. 1683."

Oh! that Id had a tear to've quencht that flame
    Which did dissolve the Heavens above
    Into those liquid drops that Came
      To drown our Carnall love.
Our cheeks were dry and eyes refusde to weep.
Tears bursting out ran down the skies darke Cheek.

Were th'Heavens sick? must wee their Doctors bee
    And physick them with pills, our sin?
    To make them purg and Vomit, see,
      And Excrements out fling?
We've griev'd them by such Physick that they shed
Their Excrements upon our lofty heads.

Later New England Verse

March 25, 1701, at Plimouth, this Libel was handed about. One had lent the Order of the Gospel revived, and it was sent home with this written on it, viz.

"A Simple Poem on the Authors and Designs
of this Booke."

Begging Manifesto proves but a great Pesto
    Blackman is Synodalian.
Pray stay there and stop, lest next hap & hop
Ben't Peters chair Italian.

The old strait Gate is now out of Date,
The street it must be broad;
And the Bridge must be wood, tho not half so good
As firm Stone in the Road.

Relations are Rattle with Brattle & Brattle
Lord Brother mayn't command:
But Mather and Mather had rather & rather
The good old way should stand.

Saints Cotton & Hooker, o look down, & look here
Where's Platform, Way, & the Keys?
O Torey what story of Brattle Church Twattle
To have things as they please

Our Merchants cum Mico do stand Sacro Vico;
Our Churches turn genteel:
Parsons grow trim and trigg with wealth wine & wigg
And their crowns are coverd with meal.

—Memorandum from the Letter-Book of Samuel Sewall.

The verse of New England between 1680 and 1720 chronicles the
waning of Puritan life. Its interests turn ever more worldly, until after
1720 it has ceased dealing with Puritan themes. Think what prophecy
of communal woe Michael Wigglesworth would glean from the drying
up of the river Merrimack; but Samuel Sewall takes the occasion for
fabricating a whimsical "Ambushment" on Mount Powow where, the
Merrimack flowing by, "Hydropick Hampshire Drunk it Up!" "Grace"
in Richard Henchman's ode to Lady Phipps signifies not that inward
motion of the heart assuring election but, the author says, his patron's
loan.[1] And in the verse of the Reverend John Adams, God appears not
as the stormy commander of Wilderness Zion, but as the Muse.

New England poets of the turn of the century did not experience the
Puritan twilight with uniform shock.[2] Some bowed resignedly to the new,
spirit, some welcomed it, many were bitter. One Puritan who moved
unperturbed with the times was the wealthy Long Island merchant
Richard Steere. His blank verse, uncommon for the time, itself suggests
a change in taste. Clinging to Puritan sentiment while abandoning Puritan belief, his theorizing about the plain style is not driven by a larger
yearning for apostolic simplicity. Indeed it no longer has a religious
content. Roger Williams would have applauded Steere's stricture that
verse be "wrapt in *raggs*," not "Cloath'd with *Academick* Skill, / Or
lofty Raptures of a *Poet's* Quill." [3] But the same minister, who saw the
wilderness as an emblem of harsh moral struggle, would have reviled the
self-indulgence Steere's plain words commend:

> The chirping notes of winged *Choresters*,
> And Purling Murmurs of the Gliding *brooks*,
> Modulate Accents of a *well Tun'd voice*,
> Joyn'd with the Sweet *Allurements* of the *Lute*,
> The Gallant noise of Manly Musick, *Bells*
> Belonas voice of *Trumpets, Fifes and Drums*,
> Pleasing discourses, *Histories* and *Novals*,
> Am'rous Converse, when Innocent and clean,
> All give a Charming Sweetness to the Muse.

Steere's verse is a halfway house where the plain style co-habits with
the worldly appetite. Although Steere grants that "there's a kind of
happiness in Crosses," faith and reason both assure him that the "worlds
vast Palace we may freely dwell in." In making this concession, the
leisurely blank verse of his "Earth Felicities, Heavens Allowances"
registers no struggle of conscience. Its level, prosey ambling is the voice

of the "fearless free Contented man," temperate in all things. Steere's fastidious sensualist has come a long journey from the Puritan ideal of life lived in the world but not of it.

Other writers were more unnerved than Steere by the transition. The rocking jeremiad verse of the 1660's already records some of the inner convulsions of Puritanism. Yet the jeremiads, for all their grim assertion of Puritan backsliding, do not drop but rally the cause. In much of the verse between 1690 and 1720 that concerns the dissatisfaction with and within Puritanism, however, the cause itself is forgotten. Absorbed with settling the blame for the present troubles, it limits itself to lashing personal abuse and blind spite. For Sewall, John Saffin was no Cotton to be idealized as a mirror of conduct, but an epitome of "lying Impudence," a "Superanuated Squier, wigg'd and powder'd with pretence." (Sewall, once special commissioner at the Salem trials, connived with the secular geist by investing in a wig and carriage himself.) The biggest prey for the New Backbiting was no less than Cotton Mather. Mather got the snappish ridicule of Benjamin Franklin and his brother, who denounced the great epigone in the *New-England Courant,* earning from him the title, Hell-Fire Club. Not only the Franklins were fed up with Mather. Another writer thumped:

> . . . *Satis fecisti*
> My belly's full of your Magnalia Christi.

According to the new iconoclasm, the author of over four hundred works was no demigod but a glib crook who should take up an honest trade, like rowing: "As for thy Trade of preaching we all see, / It starves mens Souls, and also purses free." [4]

Coincident with this tone of shrill recrimination arose an often ribald ballad and broadside literature. The comic and scatological verse that filled New England newspapers after 1720 was the product of the new tone and the airing of feelings it signified. But the clearest poetic expression of the changed Puritan sensibility—and of the disillusionment behind it—is the eruption at this time of parody and lampoon. Cotton Mather himself ridiculed John Hubbard's "Monumental Gratitude" (1727), a poem describing the near-drowning of seven Yale students in Long Island Sound. On the title page of his copy of the poem Mather wrote:

> Poor Lads! the Storm has whirld your Brains around;
> And all the *Sense* is ship-wrack'd in the *SOUND.*

On the back cover he scrawled his own version of Hubbard's bombastic storm and terrified students—transformed into a clattering pigeon-pie banquet:

> Fall on, Huzza! Break down the Bulwarks Strong
> Let Gravy gush and pidgeons Sprawl along.
> Salt, pepper, Butter, Marrow, Flesh and Bones,
> Mix in the Mouth while Spoons encounter Spoons[5]

This new spirit of irreverence assured an appreciative and continued audience for the parodies of Mather Byles and Joseph Green, and for such versed college wit as "Father Abbey's Will." [6] And it meant that few writers could any longer take seriously the traditionally hallowed Puritan occasions.

Local alarm aroused by interchurch disputes and hostility from non-Puritans does not, of course, account for the kind of verse New Englanders had begun writing. Equally potent was the awakening to new English and continental literary fashions. Together they formed a single disruptive force; for the striking examples of Pope and other eighteenth-century poets helped create disdain for such local products as the communal elegy, whose force for other reasons was already exhausted. One of the first New Englanders to embrace the new manner was the Reverend Mather Byles.[7] He made a career and reputation out of imitating "mighty Pope." Reportedly he carried with him Pope's polite reply to his adoring fanletter until it disintegrated. His zest for pranks, puns, and club-life relate him less to his uncle Cotton Mather than to the loathed Hell-Fire faction. When asked where to have a tooth drawn, Byles sent a distressed friend to the home of John Singleton Copley. In the same high spirits he led Boston's literary life, first as head of the Spy Club at Harvard in the 1720's (where he published the first college periodical, The Telltale),[8] later as a member of the informal literary group including Thomas Prince and Matthew Adams, centered around the New-England Weekly Journal. Byles' verse is far from crude; yet he and his friends regarded poetry as recreation. The topic of his M.A. essay was "polite literature is an ornament to a theologian," and he later professed to write "as the Amusements of looser Hours," as a way of "unbending . . . from severer Studies."[9] Unlike the literary clergy of Puritan New England, Byles felt pressed to explain that poetry came second, always, to preaching: "while I employ the Numbers of the Poet," he remonstrated, "I never forget the character of the Divine." [10]

In this new climate, the hope of a formally Puritan state, the Christian

Israel, expired, although Puritanism in the popular sense lingered. Puritans looked on America as the promised land, England as Egypt; most of their descendents in the early eighteenth century saw themselves as provincial subjects of the king. This raised a delicate problem. Strict loyalty to the home country demanded that America was a kind of mistake. Was not local pride a subtle criticism of England? Why had anyone fled England? The authors of *Pietas et Gratulatio,* a volume of panegyric verse dedicated to the king, tried to reconcile English preeminence with emigration:

> It was the fate of our Ancestors to be driven from their native Country by an Administration very different from that of your MAJESTY. They then complained of their hard treatment, but they saw not the Designs of Providence. Had GREAT-BRITAIN been always governed by Princes like those of your MAJESTY'S illustrious House, its Dominion would have been confined to its own Islands; no one would have been persuaded to have exchanged the happy Country for any other whatsoever.[11]

The original settlers had good reason for emigration. Further emigration, the poets' argument implies, is disloyal. That poses the dilemma many colonists of the mid-eighteenth century found themselves in. It was becoming clear that one could not wholly be an Englishman and celebrate America, that in fact their destinies differed and their interests clashed. The verse of New England after 1740 that deals with America is often addressed to this dilemma. It is not surprising that some poets deny America a special destiny, that some are confused in their loyalties, that some are inflammatory and separatist. What is noteworthy is how the language and imagery of their verse affirm its politics. Most Loyalists used the language of contemporary English verse; separatists very often returned to the idiom of Puritan New England. The first century of New England verse was as much a political as a literary fact. To rework its idiom was to acknowledge a regional continuity, and that was both a claim for membership in a unique poetic tradition and an argument for separation.

One of the many poets who denied the country a special destiny and accordingly stripped the original migration of messianic purpose was Roger Wolcott, a governor of Connecticut from 1751-54. He chooses for his subject not 'Israel in America' but "the *English* in *America.*" The Winthrop of his *chanson de geste* "Winthrop's Agency" is utterly unlike the alchemist of Benjamin Tompson's elegy, the learned voyager "round the Philosophick sea" whose death "Terrestrial Comets did portend." Wolcott's hero is a model of prudent and loyal behavior, prostrating himself before the king, *"Caesar."* Where Puritans and Revolutionists imagined England as stern Egypt, America as the Zion nominated for God's special errand, Wolcott's settlers tell the Indians that they have come "from *England* happiest seat in *Christendom."* Where Michael Wigglesworth saw primeval New England as a howling wilderness, in fact the devil's home, Winthrop sees it "Cloath'd all in *Green,"* lush with "Natures *best Fruits* and Richest *Ornaments."* Wolcott does once compare America to the land shown Moses, and once mentions religious motives for emigration. But these are nods to a convention whose once vivid appeal is sapped by the poem's pretty imagery and borrowed diction. For the no longer compelling Puritan view, Wolcott substitutes stock eighteenth-century imagery of no relevance. He compares the settlers' first glimpse of the land with that of a beau seeing "His Smiling Fortune in his Ladys Eye." Elaborating the amatory figure, emigrants sail "Upon the Virgin Stream" which had not yet "been Violated with a Ship," reducing the settlement from a crusade to a flirtation.

By denying the migration ideals it meant to realize, Wolcott was also denying America demands about its future many colonists were in fact making. As the friction between American and British interests increased, as the mere choice of local themes came to present tests of loyalty, some colonial poets who wrote about America turned to pastoral, where the political issues did not have to be faced, or were at least tempered. Thus the Rhode Island physician Benjamin Church[12] professes to be writing "on native Verdure"; yet his imitation of Pomfret's "The Choice" (1751) lacks local reference. Its commendation of the social virtues— the "calm good Temper" and "mutual Ease" society affords—its longing to dally with a library of choice authors at a country seat, compose a picture of ideal English living with no likeness to the colonial scene. And one could not be an Englishman in theory while paying special taxes to a real throne. A contributor to *Pietas et Gratulatio,* Church rescinded his praise at the time of the Stamp Act, regretted dressing "a gay idol in the garb of God," and decided to "weep my folly past." In his poem on the tax (1765), he no longer resides at a country seat but in a "humble cot." No longer espousing "calm good Temper" he feels "wild as the soil," "rudely rough." Speaking as a "wild exotic neighbour to the bear," he offers a new version of the migration: the forefathers fled for that same liberty now denied by the tax. The reversal of loyalties between Church's two poems suggests how volatile the colonists' dilemma was, despite the serene diction the authors of *Pietas et Gratulatio* posed it in. Volatile indeed: having sworn loyalty to the Crown, then renounced it, Church still later was exposed as a fifth columnist, deviously promoting British interests while fanning revolutionary ardor.

Church's verse appeared when many New England poets were again taking their language from the idiom of the Puritan mission. This verse of the early 1750's forms the only clear instance in colonial literature of the evolution of a style. (In addition it supplies a further regional distinction; it has no exact Southern counterpart.)[13] From one standpoint the rediscovery of the Puritan tone was the effect on poetry of the messianic atmosphere of the Great Awakening. Throughout the colonies, the Awakening prompted verse on pious subjects, and scores of poems on George Whitefield. But only in New England did these poems have the Puritan ring. In "New England's Misery, the procuring Cause and Remedy Proposed" (Boston, 1758), the tone and matter are precisely that of the jeremiads a century earlier:

> Behold, and see how deeply we
> do feel divine Displeasure;
> > Our land before has never bore
> > of Wrath so great a Measure.

With the logic of a Michael Wigglesworth, the same writer recommends that to halt the French and Indian wars his readers should "refrain from Speech profane" and "shun all filthy Talking." In the same period many earlier Puritan works achieved a new vogue. A Connecticut lady poet, Martha Brewster, composed in 1757 a volume of poems consciously in imitation of Anne Bradstreet, a third edition of whose works appeared in Boston a year later. Michael Wigglesworth was widely quoted and often reprinted. An eighth edition of *The Day of Doom* appeared in Boston in 1751, the first since 1715; another was published in Norwich in 1774. In 1770 a sixth edition of *Meat out of the Eater* was issued at New London, the first since 1717. Lesser Puritan works also had their day, such as Isaac Wiswall's 1680 verse on a comet, in the foreboding manner of *The Day of Doom,* reprinted at Boston in 1759.

These dates, clustering around the Great Awakening and the looming Revolution, are telling. For in retrospect, the revival of the Puritan idiom was a regional testing of the Revolutionary tone. Later, that habit of narrating colonial doings in Old Testament parallels lent moral force to often utilitarian arguments on the necessity of revolution. And its reminder of traditional, uniquely local ways of thought subtly justified separation. Thus a Revolutionary minister preached on "The Separation of the Jewish Tribes, after the death of Solomon, accounted for, and applied to the present day."[14] Samuel Adams shrewdly chose for one of his firebrand pen-names, "Cotton Mather." In 1772, a committee of Bostonians drew on the rallying power of a shared past when they published a poem by James Allen, beginning:

> From realms of bondage and a Tyrant's reign,
> Our Godlike Fathers bore no slavish chain,
> To *Pharoah's* face th'inspired *Patriarch's* stood,
> To seal their virtue, with a Martyr's blood:
> But lives so precious, such a sacred seed,
> The source of empires, Heav'n's high will decreed;
> He snatch'd the SAINTS from *Pharoah's* impious hand,
> And bid his chosen seek this distant land.[15]

As James I was Pharoah in 1640, in hundreds of pamphlets and verses in 1776, George III was Pharoah; the Atlantic was once again the Red Sea; England once again Egypt; George Washington, as John Winthrop before him, was Joshua; America, if not Zion this time, was Canaan. That idiom persisted through the early careers of the Connecticut Wits. Like Charles Morton and James Allen before them, they retold the Biblical stories with contemporary patriotic implications. But theirs was an epic investigation of national origins. Its freedom in handling scripture was un-Puritan, its ambition outran any Puritan undertaking, and its insinuation that the heritage and destiny of America were not British marks the end of colonial verse.

NOTES

[1] Richard Henchman, "Vox Oppressi," MS, Boston Public Library.

[2] Nor, apparently, did it overtake all of New England at the same time. Inland communities seem to have held on to the orthodox spirit longer than coastal communities. See Allan I. Ludwig, *Graven Images* (Middletown, Conn., 1966).

[3] Richard Steere, *A Monumental Memorial of Marine Mercy* (Boston, 1684), p. 1.

[4] According to another versifier, Mather was conniving with Presbyterians to realize his single consuming ambition, "To write C. Mather first and then D.D." Judging from Mather's correspondence with the Scottish clergy, this charge was not inaccurate. Despite for Mather, however, was of course not universal. Perry Miller points out that the paramount image of Mather at his death was that of a "gentleman." The shrillness of Mather's detractors at any rate illustrates the stresses in a society that had become, Miller says, a "time-bomb, packed with

dynamite, the fuse burning close." *The New England Mind: From Colony to Province* (Cambridge, 1953), p. 484.

5 Cotton Mather, "The Pidgeon Py," written on John Hubbard, *A Monumental Gratitude* (New London, 1727), in *Photostat Americana.*

6 "Father Abbey's Will," fourteen stanzas of doggerel purporting to be the last will and testament of the Harvard College bedmaker, won a prompt reply from some Yale wits, who courted in identical doggerel Father Abbey's prospering widow. The exchange is one sign of increasing literary commerce among the colonies. Such commerce was encouraged by a new demand for literary journalism; the whole of *Jonathan Wild* appeared serially in the *New-England Courant.*

7 See Arthur Eaton, *The Famous Mather Byles* (Boston, 1914).

8 Byles' classmate, Jeremiah Gridley, published one of Boston's most literary papers, the *Weekly Rehearsal* (1731-37).

9 Mather Byles, *Poems on Several Occasions* (Boston, 1744), n.p.

10 Mather Byles, "To his Excellency Governour Belcher" (Boston, 1736), p. 4.

11 *Pietas et Gratulatio* (Boston, 1761), pp. iv-v.

12 See "Benjamin Church," *Dictionary of American Biography.*

13 Southerners of the period wrote evangelical verse, to be sure; but no Southern poem of the period has a title like Francis Worcester's "Sabbath-Profanity, The most Crying Sin of *New-England*" (1760) or John Fiske's "A Poem upon the taking of CAPE BRETON, or, a Representation of the Fall of ANTICHRIST" (1761). As Cotton Mather might have explained the birth of Siamese twins, Fiske shows how from sinning ensue death by lightning, snakebite, war, and in fact deformed births.

14 William Gordon, "The Separation of the Jewish Tribes" (Boston, 1777). The idiom remained useful until late in the eighteenth century. "A Discourse Delivered Near York in Virginia" (Philadelphia, 1782) begins:
> To him who led in ancient days
> The Hebrew tribes, your anthems raise;
> The God who spoke from Sinai's hill
> Protects his chosen people still.

15[James Allen], "The Poem which the committee of the Town of *Boston* had voted unanimously to be Published with the late Oration" (Boston, 1772), p. 7.

Richard Steere

(1643-1721)

"On a Sea-Storm nigh the Coast."

TEXT: *The Daniel Catcher. The Life of the Prophet Daniel: In A Poem* (Boston, 1713), p. 89.

> ALL round the Horizon black Clouds appear;
> A Storm is near:
> Darkness Eclipseth the Sereener Sky,

The Winds are high;
Making the Surface of the Ocean Show
Like mountains Lofty, and like Vallies Low.

The weighty Seas are rowled from the Deeps
                In mighty heaps,
And from the Rocks Foundations do arise
                To Kiss the Skies:
Wave after Wave in Hills each other Crowds,
As if the Deeps resolv'd to Storm the Clouds.

How did the Surging Billows Fome and Rore
                Against the Shore
Threatning to bring the Land under their power
                And it Devour:
Those Liquid Mountains on the Clifts were hurld
As to a Chaos they would shake the World.

The Earth did Interpose the Prince of Light
                'Twas Sable night.
All Darkness was but when the Lightnings fly
                And Light the Sky,
Night, Thunder, Lightning, Rain, & *raging* Wind,
To make a Storm had all their forces joyn'd.

From "Earth Felicities,
Heavens Allowances. A
BLANK POEM."

TEXT: *The Daniel Catcher,* pp. 55-60.

UPon the Earth there are so many Treasures
Various Abounding objects of Delight,
That to Enumerate, would be a Task
Too ponderous for my Imperfect Skill,
Or Pen, to Charactise Effect'ally.
     Yet these felicities may be Reduc'd
Under three heads; As, *Riches, Honours, Pleasures*:
Whence as from fountains, All External good
Riseth, and flows to us in many Streams;
And whosoe'er possesseth these, Enjoys

The fulness of all Temporary good.
   The good Effects which doth from *Riches* spring
Are not a few, nor of a mean Account;
As Education, Friends Acquaintance, Lovers,
With Dignity, Authority; Command,
And many other worthy our Esteem.
   From *Honour* comes Renown and Reputation,
Which when from worthy Actions it proceeds,
It's still accompanied with inward Joy;
And brighter shines in men of Noble birth;
When they shall not Degenerate from those,
Their worthy Ancestors, whose virt'ous Acts
Lifted them to those Honours, and that trust,
Which gives these titles to the Name of great;
Nothing can more Imbellish noble Souls,
Than when their merits challenge honours crown.
   Pleasures are many and of Divers Kinds,
Riches and *Honour* only serve to *please;*
And ev'ry good seems to this end ordain'd;
How many sweet felicities are found
Contributing to pleasure ev'ry scence
Visus, Auditus, Gustus, & Olfactus.
   To please the *Eye* how many various Sights?
The fair and glorious Aspect of the *Heav'ns,*
The Darling brightness of the *Sun Moon Stars,*
The naked *Air,* the Curled Silver *Streams,*
The *Birds* Enamel'd with their Divers *Plumes;*
Orchards, whose *Trees,* with *blossoms, leaves & fruit*
Of various Kinds, all pleasing to the Eye,
The ev'n *Meadows,* in their Tap'stry green,
All Diapred with beauty blooming flow'rs;
The spacious *Ocean,* spreads her wat'ry vail
From shore, to shore, out of whose bowels come
Of sundry Creatures, Infinite in number,
As doth the Land afford, of Diff'rent *figures*:
Ships, Cities, Towns, Castles, and *Monuments;*
Gold, Pearls, and Rare Inestimable *Jems,*
Do all Contribute to delight the *Opticks.*
   Likewise to please, & charm the List'ning *Ears,*
Sweet Musicks pleasant and harmonious Sounds;

The chirping notes of winged *Choresters,*
And Purling Murmurs of the Gliding *brooks,*
Modulate Accents of a *well Tun'd voice,*
Joyn'd with the Sweet *Allurements* of the *Lute,*
The Gallant noise of Manly Musick, *Bells*
Belonas voice of *Trumpets, Fifes* and *Drums,*
Pleasing discourses, *Histories* and *Novals,*
Am'rous Converse, when Innocent and clean,
All give a Charming Sweetness to the Muse.
    Also to Gratifie the sence of *Tasting,*
Are various sorts of *Flesh, Fish, Fowl,* and *Fruits;*
Delicious Banquets, with their pleasing *Sauces,*
With Life refreshing neat brisk Sparkling *Wines,*
Of Divers kinds, both Simple and Compound;
And many more unite to please the *Taste*
    So, the *Olfactal* faculty's Supply'd,
With Oderiferous, and Choice *perfumes,*
Of *Myrrh,* of *Cassia,* and of *Bruised Spices;*
Sweet Smelling *Gums,* from the Arabian Coast,
Or our Domestick *Violets, Pinks,* and *Roses;*
With Fragrant *Herbs,* & *Blossoms* of our *Gardens.*
In fine, the pleasure of the Earth are such,
So good, so many, Common, yet so Sweet,
That should I Dwell for ever on Discourse,
It would surpass the skill of Tongue or Pen,
Sufficiently their value to relate.
    Yet let me add to these a pleasure more,
Of Loving *Parents,* Counter Loving *Children;*
Husband and *Wife,* in Mut'al one-ness knit;
Friends during Life sharing each others Joys
Injoying Each the Others happy Love,
With Delectation: When we make our selves
Sensible, of the sweetness all affords;
We may perceive a Possibility
By bounteous Heav'ns Allowance, on the Earth,
To find in Temp'ral good felicity.
    Having thus Transciently, in brief Survey'd,
Wherein all Earthly Happiness consists;
To the intent we may therein be safe,
We with Content must fortify our minds,

That in all Stations, Accidents, Conditions,
We may Enjoy this worlds felicities,
Abstracted from the Ills that do accrue.
   He is the Richest, and most happy man,
Who is most moderate in his Desire:
Can be Content and sweetly satisfy'd
In ev'ry State, Condition, and degree;
For he that Covets not possesseth all,
And may be truely call'd the Richest man;
When he that has abundance, and yet fears
The loss or want of them, is truely poor;
By his Ambitious and Intemp'rate mind,
Grieving for want of what his heart Desires,
Is in more Poverty, than he that wants,
Yet is Content to want. It grieves not him,
Who makes his little with Content Enough:
Whoso lets Loose th'unruly Appetite,
Desiring first a *Lordship* to possess
Then next a *Kingdom;* After that a *World*
Which if he had, he would Account too Little,
Or grieve, and pine, because it was no better,
Troubling his Restless mind still with desire;
Such in no State can meet with Satisfaction:
Mind with how little nature is supply'd,
If we that little always have at hand,
We have as much in our Sufficiency,
As if possess'd with all the world affords.
   The silent Shade, the Quiet Country life,
Free from the Troubles of the *Crowded Town,*
Or the Perplexing Cares of State affairs,
And deep Projections of great *Politicians;*
Under that bush where *Tityrus* did Sing,
Amidst the sweets of satisfy'd Delights,
With no more wealth than Riseth from Content,
This is a happy State: We often hear
The unperplexed plowmans Thoughtless note,
Tuneing his whistle to his working Teame,
In him behold the Emblem of Content,
A state of Happiness which we should seek,
Tho' Troubles cross the Road that leads thereto.
   Crosses and *Troubles* Common are to men,

No one is free: *Crosses* sometimes he needs
To mix with pleasures, Pleasures else were bitter,
And would grow Stale, and Cloy the Appetite,
But relish sweeter when with *Crosses* mixt;
And tho our Troubles should be very Tart,
Yet being past we relish pleasures better.
   Wisdom and fortitude will us assist,
To raise our minds to such a noble Temper.
And fix such Peace, and Courage in our Souls,
That we shall dare to slight the *world* when't *frowns,*
And with Contempt shall look on its Insults;
Scorning those Stroaks that Conquer feeble minds,
And thereby Crown our selves with Happiness.
   True Piety will Equally Contribute,
To make us face adversity with boldness,
Yielding to *God* Depend on him alone,
Who always what is best for us, will give;
Subject our wills to his, Let the world frown,
We shall from all Afflictions be releas'd.
And relish Joy, when Sorrow's gone the better.
   Since there's a kind of happiness in Crosses,
Let no Condition find us discontent:
None can more Earths Felicities Enjoy,
Than doth the fearless free Contented man,
Who whether want, or have, or Loss, or gain,
He's of an even temper in all States,
All are alike to him, he's always happy.
   Would we on Earth be happy, we must then
Use Earthly happiness without abuse;
All our Intemperate desires will prove,
Disturbers of our Peace and happiness,
Griefs, Cares, Distemp'red Passions, Anguish, Fears,
Are very Incident to vicious men;
They'r not Content with vice, tho it seem pleasant;
None like the virt'ous man can live Content,
He's most secure, lives Healthy, Happy, Free,
Pleasantly Chearful always Dwells in peace;
The Treasures, Riches, pleasures of his mind
Are Durable: In all things he delights,
His way to Heaven seems a pleasant path,
And all his Journey as in Summer time.

....

Samuel Sewall

(1652-1730)

"WEDNESDAY, *January* 1. 1701. A little before Break-a-Day,
at *Boston* of the *Massachusets.*"

TEXT: *WEDNESDAY, January 1. 1701,* Broadside (Boston, 1713).

ONCE more! Our GOD, vouchsafe to Shine:
Tame Thou the Rigour of our Clime.
Make haste with thy Impartial Light,
And terminate this long dark Night.

Let the transplanted *ENGLISH* Vine
Spread further still: still Call it Thine.
Prune it with Skill: for yield it can
More Fruit to Thee the Husbandman.

Give the poor *INDIANS* Eyes to see
The Light of Life: and set them free;
That they Religion may profess,
Denying all Ungodliness.

From hard'ned *JEWS* the Vail remove,
Let them their Martyr'd JESUS love;
And Homage unto Him afford,
Because He is their Rightful LORD.

So false Religions shall decay,
And Darkness fly before bright Day:
So Men shall GOD in CHRIST adore;
And worship Idols vain, no more.

So *ASIA,* and *AFRICA,*
EUROPA, with *AMERICA;*
All Four, in Consort join'd, shall Sing
New Songs of Praise to CHRIST our KING.

"Epitaph on Tom Child, the Painter"

TEXT: *Diary of Samuel Sewall, 1674-1729, Collections of the Massachusetts Historical Society,* 5th Ser., II (1879), 170.

> Tom Child had often painted Death,
> But never to the Life, before:
> Doing it now, he's out of Breath;
> He paints it once, and paints no more.

"Upon the drying up that Ancient River, The River MERRYMAK."

TEXT: *Upon the drying up that Ancient River,* Broadside (Boston,
1720).

> LONG did *Euphrates* make us glad,
> Such pleasant, steady Course he had:
> Fight *White,* fight *Chesnut;* all was one,
> In Peace profound our River Run
> From his remote, and lofty Head,
> Until he with the Ocean Wed.
> Thousands of Years ran parallel,
> View'd it throughout, and lik'd it well.
> Herbs, Trees, Fowls, Fishes, Beasts, and Men,
> Refresh'd were by this goodly Stream.
> Dutiful *Salmon,* once a Year,
> Still visited their *Parent* dear:
> And royal *Sturgeon* saw it good
> To Sport in the renowned Flood.
> All sorts of *Geese,* and *Ducks,* and *Teal,*
> In their Allotments fared well.
> Many a *Moose,* and Thirsty *Dear,*
> Drank to full Satisfaction here.
> The *Fox,* the *Wolf,* the angry *Bear,*
> Of Drink were not deny'd their share.
> The Strangers, late Arrived here,
> Were Entertain'd with Welcom chear;
> The *Horse,* and *Ox,* at their own will,
> Might taste, and drink, and drink their fill.
> Thus *Merrymak* kept House secure,
> And hop'd for Ages to endure;
> Living in Love, and Union,
> With every Tributary Son.

At length, an Ambushment was laid
Near *Powwaw Hill,* when none afraid;
And unawares, at one Huge Sup,
Hydropick *Hampshire* Drunk it Up!
Look to thy self! *Wadchuset* Hill;
And Bold *Menadnuck,* Fear some Ill!
Envy'd *Earth* knows no certain Bound;
In HEAV'N alone, CONTENT is found.

"Upon the Springs issuing out from the foot of Plimouth
   Beach, and running out into the Ocean."

TEXT: *Diary,* I, 27.

The humble Springs of stately Plimouth Beach,
To all Inferiors, due Observance teach.
Perpetually Good Humour'd they concur,
Praying the Sea, Accept our Duty, Sir!
He, mild severe, I've now no need: and When . . .
As you are come, Go back, and come agen.

"To John Saffin"

TEXT: *Diary,* II, 79.

Superanuated Squier, wigg'd and powder'd with pretence,
Much beguiles the just Assembly by his lying Impudence.[1]
None being by, his sworn[2] Attorneys push it on with might and main
By which means poor simple Adam sinks to slavery again.

THREE POEMS ON COTTON MATHER

Anonymous

"On C. Mr.'s Diploma."

TEXT: *The Letter-Book of Samuel Sewall, Collections of the Massachusetts Historical Society,* 6th Ser., I (1886), 407.

The mad enthusiast, thirsting after fame,
By endless volum'ns thought to raise a name.
With undigested trash he throngs the Press;

Thus striving to be greater, he's the less,
But he, in spight of infamy, writes on,
And draws new Cullies in to be undone.
Warm'd with paternal vanity, he trys
For new Suscriptions, while the Embryo lyes
Neglected—Parkhurst[1] says, *Satis fecisti,*
My belly's full of your Magnalia Christi.
Your crude Divinity, and History
Will not with a censorious age agree.
Daz'd with the stol'n title of his Sire,
To be a Doctor he is all on fire;
Would after him, the Sacrilege commit
But that the keeper's care doth him affright.
To Britain's Northern Clime in haste he sends,
And begs an Independent boon from Presbyterian friends;
Rather than be without, he'd beg it of the Fiends.
Facetious George brought him this Libertie
To write C. Mather first, and then D.D.

"*T. M.*"

(Probably Thomas Maule of Salem)

"To Cotton Mather, from a Quaker"

TEXT: *An Abstract of a Letter to Cotton Mather* (n. pl., 1701),
pp. 18-19.

Hebrew, Greek or Latin, I have not,
Learning have, which by the Truth I got
As in true verse, here is this time to thee,
The Truth of which thou in my verse may see.
While thou keep on thy lying Trade to gain:
I thee withstand, the Truth for to maintain;
A Servant fit thou art for evil work,
To deal well sharp with thee will not thee hurt?
Thou Lives at ease, while others Plow and Sow,
Their labour give, for what well do not know,
The love of Money leads thee for to preach:
Keep that from thee, thou wil't no longer teach;
And as to all thy Marchandizing ware,

Such men that buy, their Souls have but ill fare.
Which Trade of thine cannot continue long,
As men see thy deceit will from thee throng:
And those that live to God will search thee out;
Yea, those of thy own Trade will help to rout;
For those of thy own Trade much disagree.
Which shews their fall is near, Gods People see,
It is a Money Trade that with some wit,
With which dishonest men themselves do fit:
Thou hath thy masters way to deal with *Maule,*
As in thy Book without thy name at all,
That is, to *Boston* Wood, the Gallows there:
It shews thou art both void of Grace and fear;
A better way he finds to deal with thee;
To do some good, as all men hear may see,
To leave deceit, and in some boat to row,
Until a good be, then unto preaching go:
If boating work, with thee will not agree;
Take other honest Trade, and honest be.
As for thy Trade of preaching we all see,
It starves mens Souls, and also purses free.
But if resolve not with the Truth to dwell:
Thou must take part with them that go to Hell;
Many things I have against thee more,
And value not the study of thy store.
Thou at the first hath wrong with me begun,
Truth will me right so far may see it done.
Which to conclude with Letters of my name;
That thou may certain be from whom it came.

T.M.

Nicholas Noyes

(1647-1717)

"A Prefatory Poem, on that
Excellent Book, Entituled, *Magnalia Christi Americana*"

TEXT: Cotton Mather, *Magnalia Christi Americana* (London, 1702),
pp. B-B2.

Struck with huge Love, of what to be possest,
I much despond, good Reader, in the *quest;*
Yet help me, if at length it may be said,
Who first the *Chambers of the South* display'd?
Inform me, Whence the *Tawny People* came?
Who was their Father, *Japhet, Shem,* or *Cham?*
And how they straddled to th' *Antipodes,*
To look *another World* beyond the Seas?
And when, and why, and where they last broke ground,
What Risks they ran, where they first Anchoring found?
Tell me their Patriarchs, Prophets, Priests and Kings,
Religion, Manners, Monumental things:
What *Charters* had they? What Immunities?
What Altars, Temples, Cities, Colonies,
Did they erect? Who were their publick Spirits?
Where may we find the *Records* of their Merits?
What Instances, what glorious Displayes
Of Heav'ns high Hand, commenced in their dayes?
These things in *Black Oblivion* covered o'er,
(As they'd ne er been) lye, with a thousand more.
A vexing Thought, that makes me scarce forbear
To stamp, and wring my Hands, and pluck my Hair,
To think, what Blessed *Ignorance* hath done,
What fine Threads *Learnings* Enemies have spun,
How well Books, Schools, and Colledge may be spar'd,
So *Men* with *Beasts* may fitly be compar'd!
Yea, how *Tradition* leaves us in the lurch,
And who, nor stay at home, nor go to Church:
The *Light-within-Enthusiasts,*[1] who let fly
Against our *Pen and Ink Divinity;*
Who boldly do pretend but who'll believe it?)
If *Genesis* were lost, they could retrieve it;
Yea, all the *Sacred Writ;* Pray let them try
On the *New World,* their *Gift of Prophecy.*
For all them, the *New Worlds Antiquities,*
Smother'd in everlasting Silence lies;
And its *First Sachims* mention'd are no more,
Than they that *Agamemnon* liv'd before.
The poor *Americans* are under blame,
Like them of old, that from *Tel-melah*[2] came,
Conjectur'd once to be of *Israel's* Seed,

But no *Record* appear'd to prove the Deed:
And like *Habajah's* Sons,[3] that were put by ⎫
The *Priesthood,* Holy things to come not nigh, ⎬
For having lost their *Genealogy.* ⎭
Who can past things to memory command,
Till one with *Aaron's Breast-plate* up shall stand?
Mischiefs Remediless such Sloth ensue;
God and their Parents lose their Honour due,
And Childrens Children suffer on that Score,
Like Bastards cast forlorn at any Door;
And they and others put to seek their Father,
For want of such a *Scribe* as COTTON MATHER;
Whose Piety, whose Pains, and peerless Pen,
Revives *New-England's* nigh-lost Origin.

    Heads of our *Tribes,* whose *Corps* are under ground,
Their Names and Fames in *Chronicles* renown'd,
Begemm'd on *Golden Ouches*[4] he hath set,
Past Envy's Teeth, and Times corroding Fret:
Of *Death* and *Malice,* he' has brush'd off the Dust,
And made a *Resurrection of the Just:*
And clear'd the Lands Religion of the Gloss,
And *Copper-Cuts* of *Alexander Ross.*
He hath related *Academic* things,
And paid their *First-Fruits* to the King of Kings;
And done his *Alma Mater* that just Favour,
To shew *Sal Gentium* hath not lost its Savour.
He writes like an *Historian,* and *Divine,*
Of *Churches, Synods, Faith,* and *Discipline.*
Illustrious Providences are display'd,
Mercies and Judgments are in colours laid;
Salvations wonderful by Sea and Land,
Themselves are *Saved* by his Pious Hand.
The *Churches Wars,* and various *Enemies,* ⎫
Wild *Salvages,* and wilder *Sectaries,* ⎬
Are notify'd for them that after rise. ⎭

    This *well-instructed Scribe* brings *New* and *Old,*
And from his *Mines* digs richer things than Gold;
Yet freely gives, as *Fountains* do their Streams,
Nor more than they, Himself, by giving, drains.
He's all *Design,* and by his *Craftier Wiles*
Locks fast his Reader, and the Time beguiles:

Whilst *Wit* and *Learning* move themselves aright, ⎫
Thro' ev'ry line, and *Colour* in our sight,   ⎬
So interweaving *Profit* with *Delight;*   ⎭
And curiously inlaying both together,
That he must needs find Both, who looks for either.
    His *Preaching, Writing,* and his Pastoral Care,
Are very much, to fall to one Man's share.
This added to the rest, is admirable,
And proves the Author *Indefatigable.*
Play is his Toyl, and *Work* his Recreation,
And his *Inventions* next to Inspiration.
His *Pen* was taken from some *Bird of Light,*
Addicted to a swift and lofty Flight.
Dearly it loves *Art, Air,* and *Eloquence,*
And hates *Confinement,* save to *Truth* and *Sense.*
    Allow what's known; they who write Histories,
Write many things they see with others Eyes;
'Tis fair, where nought is feign'd, nor undigested,
Nor ought, but what is credibly attested.
The Risk is his; and seeing others do,
Why may not I speak mine Opinion too?
    The *Stuff* is true, the *Trimming* neat and spruce,
The Workman's good, the Work of publick use;
Most piously design'd, a publick Store,
And well deserves the publick Thanks, and more.

Roger Wolcott
(1679-1767)

From "A Brief Account of the Agency of the Honourable John
Winthrop, Esq; in the Court of King Charles the Second, *Anno Dom.*
1662. When he Obtained for the Colony of *Connecticut* His Majesty's
Gracious CHARTER."

TEXT: *Poetical Meditations, being the Improvement of Some Vacant
      Hours* (New London, 1725), pp. 19-36.

      THE Night is Past, & Civil Wars o're-blown,
      And the *right Heir* advanced to the Throne,

A general Joy runs thro' Great-*Brittany,*
At the appearance of His Majesty:
Loud Canons from the Ships upon the *Thames,*
And from the Batteries fill'd the Air with Flames:
Whilst from *the Tower* such mighty Thunders went
As shook the Islands, Seas, and Continent.
The Rich, the Poor, the Old, the Young, agree,
To Celebrate a joyful Jubilee:
And to the utmost all themselves Employ,
To make free Demonstrations of their Joy.
Some quaff full Goblets of the Richest Wine;
And others make the blazing Bonfires shine:
Whil'st the Devout their Prayers to Heaven sent,
For Blessings on the King and Government.

These happy Tidings soon found out their way,
Unto the *English* in *America;*
Who join with *Britain* in the Celebration,
Of their just Princes happy Restauration.
The Sages of *Connecticut* do meet,
To pay their Homage at their Princes Feet;
To whom they seek to hasten an Address,
To shew their Duty and their Joys Excess.
Learned *WINTHROP* then by general Consent,
Sat at the Helm to sway the Government;
Who prudently the People doth Advise,
To ask the King for CHARTER Liberties.

All like his Counsel well; and all reply,
Sir, You must undertake our Agency:
For there is none but You we may expect,
Can make the thing you Counsel take Effect:
Your Serving us in this Important Thing,
And Personating Us before the KING,
Will sure Endear a *WINTHROP*'s Memory
To Us, and to our Last Posterity.

His Mind, vast as the Heavenly Spheres above,
Was all bespangled with the Stars of Love;
And Zealous Care for their Posterity,
Of all his Acts the *Primum Mobile;*

Led on by these bright Stars kind Influence,
He hastens to the Palace of his Prince;
   There waiting for an Opportunity,————

   E're long, Great CHARLES was in his Council sat
With some Choice Nobles of his Cabinet:
His Royal Mind Intent on his Affairs,
He thus Unbosoms to his Counsellers;

   What News, My Lords? *How go Affairs Abroad?*
What more Remains to do for Englands Good?
Do distant Parts of our Dominion
Want farther Help or Favour from the Throne?

   At this arose one of the Lords of Trade,
And to His Majesty this Answer made,
An Agent from *Connecticut* doth wait,
With an Address before your Palace Gate.

   Let him come in, says CHARLES, *and let us Hear.*
What has been done, and what's a doing there?

   Winthrop brought in before his Princes Feet,
Prostrates himself with Reverence, the *King* to *Greet;*
And thanks His Majesty for his Access:
Then for his People offers this Address;

   'GREAT SIR, Since Reconciled Heaven Restores
'YOU to the Throne of Your High Ancestors,
'See how each Subject Emulating tries,
'To Express our National Felicities:
'The Joy of Your Accession to the Throne,
'Is like the Lustre of the Morning Sun;
'Which from the East Salutes the Western Shores,
'Still trampling under foot Nights horrid Powers:
'So the loud Accents of this boundless Joy,
'Ecchoing in our Ears from *Britanny,*
'Gave Light & Gladness where-so'ere it came,
'And fill'd our joyful Hearts with equal Flame.
'The sad Remembrance of those days of Wo,
'Which in Your Absence we did undergo,

'Transports our present Joys to that Excess,
'As passeth all Expressions to express.
'May Heaven preserve Your Majesty, and Bless
'Your Reign with Honour, & with Length of Days;
'And in Your Line the Regal Power extend,
'Until the Suns last Revolution end.

   'And since we are at Mighty *Caesar's* Feet,
'O may He Pardon us, while we Entreat,
'Your Royal Favour in the thing we want;
'T'Incorporate us by Your CHARTER-Grant.
'The Land we've Purchas'd, or Subdu'd by Fight,
'And Bought of *Fenwick* what was *Warwick's* Right,
'And all at the Endeavour of our Own,
'Without the least Dis-bursment from the Throne.

   Rise up, Quoth *Charles; My Liberal Hand Supplies,*
All needful Help to every One that Cries;
Nor shall I be Illiberal to You:
But, Prithee, Winthrop, *Please to let me Know,*
By whom it was your Place did first Commence,
Your Patriarchs that Led your Tribes from Hence?

   'If to declare their Worth, is what You ask,
'Then I must beg Your Pardon. That's a task,
'So Worthy due Performance, and so Great,
'As goes beyond my Utterance and Conceipt:
'But Vertue never fails, succeeding Days
'Shall much regard their Merits, and shall Raise
'Men of bright Parts and moving Oratory;
'Who shall Emblazon their immortal Glory.

   'But if You ask to gain Intelligence,
'What were the *Reasons,* why they went from hence,
'What *Straits* they met with in their *Way,* & *There?*
'These Facts I think I'm able to declare.

   'RELIGION was the Cause; *Divinity*
'Having declared the Gospel shine should be,
'Extensive as the Suns Diurnal Shine;
'This mov'd our Founders to this Great design.

'And sure the Holy Spirit from above,
'That first did Quickning on the Waters move,
'Inspir'd their Minds & fill'd them with Intents,
'To bring to pass such Glorious Events.
'And now they wholly to this Work devote,
'Mind not the Country they are going out:
'Their Ancient Homes they leave to come no more.
'Their Weeping Friends & Kindred on the shore
'They bid adieu, and with an aking Heart
'*Shake Hands,* 'tis hard when *dearest Friends* must part.
'But here they part and leave their Parent Isle,
'Their whilome Happy Seat. The Winds a while
'Are Courteous and Conduct them on their way,
'To near the midst of the *Atlantick* Sea,
'When suddenly their Pleasant Gales they Change
'For dismal Storms that on the Ocean Range.
'For Faithless *AEolus* Meditating Harms,
'Breaks up the Peace and Priding much in Arms,
'Unbars the great *Artillery* of Heaven
'And at the fatal Signal by him given,
'The *Cloudy Chariots* Threatning take the Plains;
'Drawn by *wing'd Steeds,* hard pressing on their reins.
'These Vast *Battalions* in dire Aspect rais'd,
'Start from the Barriers-night with *Lightning blaz'd*
'Whil'st *clashing Wheels* resounding Thunder cracks,
'Struck Mortals deaf, & Heaven astonished shakes.

    'Here the *Ship Captain* in the midnight Watch,
'Stamps on *the Deck* & thunders up *the Hatch;*
'And to the *Mariners* aloud he Cries,
'Now all from Safe-recumbency arise:
'*All Hands aloft,* & stand well to your Tack,
'*Engendring Storms* have cloath'd the Sky with black,
'Big Tempests threaten to Undo the World:
'*Down Top-sail,* let the *Main-sail* soon be furl'd,
'Hast to the *Fore-sail,* there take up a Rief:
' 'Tis time, Boys, now if ever to be brief:
'Aloof for Life; lets try to stem the Tide,
'The Ship's much Water, thus we may not Ride:
'Stand roomer then, let's run before the Sea,
'That so the Ship may feel her Stearage-way:

'Steady at Helm! Swiftly along she Scuds,
'Before the Wind, and cuts the foaming Suds.
'Somtimes aloft she lifts her Prow so high,
'As if she'd run her Bowsprit thro' the Skie.
'Then from the summit Ebbs and hurries down,
'As if her way were to the Center shown.

'Mean while our Founders in the Cabbin sat,
'Reflecting on their true and sad Estate.
'Whilst holy *Warham's*[1] Sacred lips did treat,
'About GOD's Promises, and Mercies Great.

'Still more *Gigantick Births* spring from the Clouds,
'Which tore the tatter'd Canvis from the Shrouds,
'And dreadful Balls of *Lightning* fill the Air,
'Shot from the Hand of the *Great Thunderer.*

'And now a mighty Sea the *Ship* or'e rakes,
'Which falling on the Deck the Bulk-head breaks;
'The Sailors cling to Ropes and frighted Cry,
'The Ship is Foundered, We dy! we dy!

'Those in the Cabbin heard the Sailors Screech,
'All rise and Reverend *Warham* do beseech,
'That he would now lift up to Heaven a Cry,
'For Preservation in Extremity.
'He with a Faith sure bottom'd on the Word,
'Of Him that was of *Sea* and *Winds* the LORD,
'His Eyes lifts up to Heaven, his hands Extends,
'And fervent Prayers for deliverence sends.
'The Winds abate, the Threatning Waves appease,
'And a sweet Calm sits Regent on the Seas.
'They bless the Name of their Deliverer,
'Who now they found a God that heareth Prayer.

'Still further *West-ward* on they keep their way,
'Plowing the Pavement of the briny Sea.
'Till the vast Ocean they had overpast,
'And in *Connecticut* their Anchors cast.

'Here came *Soheage* and told the Company,
'The Garden of *America* did Ly,

'Further up Stream near Fifty Miles from hence,
'Part of which Country he himself was Prince.
'Much ask'd o'th Soil, much of the Government,
'What Kings were there? the Land of what Extent?
'All which by his free answers when they knew,
'They or'e his back a Scarlet Mantle threw.

  'And now invited with fresh Southern Gales,
'They weigh their Anchors & they hoise their Sails,
'And Northward for th'Expected Country stood,
'Upon the smiling Pavement of the Flood.
'At length they Entered those awful Streights,
'Where the Stream runs thro' Adamantine Gates.
'Twas strange to see the Banks advanc'd so high,
'As if with *Atlas* they bore up the Sky.
'But when those dismal Streights were passed thro',
'A Glorious Country opens to their view,
'Cloath'd all in *Green* and to the Eye presents,
'Natures *best Fruits* and Richest *Ornaments.*

  'Chear'd with the sight they set all Sails a-trip,
'And rais'd the *English Ensign* on their Ship.
'Brave Youths with eager Strokes bend knotty Oars,
'Glad shouts bring chearful Eccho's from the Shores.

  'As when the Wounded Amorous doth spy,
'His Smiling Fortune in his Ladys Eye,
'O how his Veins and Breast swell with a Flood,
'Of pleasing Raptures that revive his Blood?
'And grown Impatient now of all Delays,
'No longer he Deliberating stays;
'But thro' the Force of her resistless Charms,
'He throws him Soul & Body in her Arms.

  'So we amazed at these seen Delights,
'Which to fruition every sense Invites,
'Our eager Mind already Captive made,
'Grow most Impatient now to be delay'd.
'This most Delightful Country to Possess,
'And forward with Industrious speed we press
'Upon the Virgin Stream who had as yet,
'Never been Violated with a Ship;

'Upon the Banks King *Aramamet* Stood,
'And round about his Wondering Multitude,
'Greatly Amazed at such an uncouth show,
'What is't they Cry'd? Some say, A great *Canoe*.
'Others, a *Bird* that in the Air doth Fly,
'With her Long Bill, and Wings up to the Skie.
'But other some, whom Fear did Terrify
'Cry'd, tis some Ill Presaging *Prodigie*.
'Nothing on Earth more Impetuous we find,
'Than Terror when it Seiseth on the Mind.
'Dreadful Effects of this did soon Appear,
'The Multitude Surpriz'd with chilling Fear;
'With Looks Distracted, & out-staring Eyes,
'Each Scares himself and others Terrifys;
'Only the *King* who had within his Breast,
'A Heart which foolish fear could not Infest;
'Perceiv'd the Matter, and the Ship he hails,
'Now drop your Anchors, and unbend your Sails;
'And if for Peace and Friendship you are come,
'And do Desire this Land shou'd be your Home;
'Let some of your Chief Leaders come to Land,
'And now with Me join their right *Hand* to *Hand*.

'Sails lower amain, nor Oars now touch the Flood,
'Down drop the Anchors deep into the Mud.
'Their Chiefs Repair to Land, & with them bring
'Obliging Presents for the *Indian King*.
'Majestick *Aramamet* with his Lords,
'Steps forth to meet those Guests without his Guards
'Meeting he paus'd, astonish'd at the sight,
'Such Men, such Airs with Countenances bright,
'He ne'er had seen, nor now to see Expecting;
'Amaz'd he stood! a while, but recollecting,
'His Scattered Intellect, he crys, Who's there?
'Whence come you? Seek you with us *Peace* or *War?*

    '*Brittons* you see, say they, and we are come,
'From *England* happiest Seat in *Christendom,*
'Where Mighty CHARLES Obligeth *Sea & Land*
'To yield Obedience to his Scept'red Hand,
'Nor came we here to Live with you in Wars,
'As He knows best that made Sun Moon & Stars,

'But rather here to Live with you in Peace,
'Till Day and Nights Successive Changes cease.
'This we propose, and this if you approve
'And do Respect our Neighbourhood and Love,
'Then Sell us Land, whereon we *Towns* may Plant,
'And join with us in Friendly Covenant.

'What you propose, (quoth he,) is Just & Good,
'And I shall e're Respect your Neighbourhood;
'Land you may have, we Value not the Soil,
'Accounting Tillage too severe a Toil.

'Then he his own Right hand to theirs doth join,
'Of his sure Friendship the undoubted sign,
'Then brings them to his House, & from his Boards
'Feasts them with what his Country best affords,
'Whilst here they stay at *Aramamets* Court,
'Hither the Neighbouring *Indian Kings* resort,
'And join with them in Articles of Peace,
'And of their Lands make firm Conveyances,
'And being now by Deeds and Leagues Secure,
'Their *Towns* they *Build,* their *Purchas'd Land Manure.*

Thus far he said; Then said his Majesty,
Methinks, I have a Curiosity,
To know this Country, that for Ages Past,
Lay hid and you have now found out at last;
This New-found River, *Is it Fresh and Fair?*
What Land adjoins to it? Has't a Pleasant Air?

Learn'd *Winthrop* bow'd with humble Reverence,
T'Express his Loyalty unto his Prince.
And then these His demands to Satisfy,
He with a Chearful air made this reply;

'This Your Desire, *Great* SIR, bears me in mind,
'What in the Ancient Register we find.
'Of the first King in *Jesurun* from whose breast,
'Such vast and ample thoughts themselves exprest,
'That they have by the World been held e're since,
'Of Truth and Wisdom clearest Evidence.

'This mighty Man desired of his GOD
'That he before his Lifes last Period,
'Might be Permitted once to look upon
'The Land, that goodly *Mount* and *Lebanon,*
'Which his desire was thus Accomplished,
'After his Charge was done, then he was led
'Up to the top of *Pisgah* and his Eye,
'From thence was well enabled to Discry
'The Land of Promise in its full extent,
'And all things in it that were Excellent.
'Long did he Feast his hungry Eyes and gaz'd
'Upon those Objects, until all amaz'd
'And Ravisht with the sight thus to him given,
'His vast Capacious Soul flew up to Heaven.
'But thus to view fine Countrys from a far
'Must still remain that Man's Peculiar;
'And tho' I think, our Land is near as Good
'As that which then was unto *Moses* shew'd,
'Yet may it not from me be now expected
'It's worth should be so amply Dissected,
'Yet will I do my best to satisfy
'What is Demanded by Your Majesty.

'This gallent *Stream* keeps running from the Head
'Four Hundred Miles ere it with *Neptune* bed,
'Passing along hundreds of *Rivolets,*
'From either bank its Christial waves besets,
'Freely to pay their Tributes to this Stream,
'As being Chief and Sovereign unto them,
'It bears no torrent nor Impetuous course
'As if 'twere driven to the Sea by force.
'But calmly on a gentle wave doth move;
'As if 'twere drawn to *Thetis* house by love.

'The Waters Fresh and Sweet, & he that swims
'In it, Recruits and Cures his Surfeit Limbs.
'The *Fisherman* the *Fry* with Pleasure gets,
'With Seins, Pots, Angles, and his Tramel-nets,
'In it Swim *Salmon, Sturgion, Carp* and *Eels,*
'Above fly *Cranes, Geese, Duck, Herons* and *Teals;*
'And *Swans* which take such Pleasure as they fly,
'They Sing their Hymns oft long before they Dy.

'The Grassy Banks are like a Verdant Bed,
'With Choicest Flowers all Enameled,
'O're which the winged *Choristers* do fly,
'And Wound th'Air with wonderous Melody.
'Here *Philomel* high Perch't upon a Thorn,
'Sings chearful Hymns to the approaching Morn.
'The Song once set, each Bird Tunes up his Lyre,
'Responding Heavenly Musick through the quire.
'Within these Fields, fair Banks of *Violets* grows;
'And near them stand the Air Perfuming *Rose,*
'And Yellow *Lilies* fair Enameled,
'With Ruddy Spots here Blushing hang the Head.

'These Meadows serve not only for the sight,
'To Charm the Eye with wonder and delight,
'But for their *Excellent Fertility,*
'Transcends each spot that ere beheld Sol's Eye.
'Here Lady *Flora's* richest Treasure grows,
'And here she bounteously her Gifts bestows.
'The *Husband-Man* for all his Diligence,
'Receives an ample Liberal *Recompence,*
'And Feasting on the Kidneys of the Wheat,
'Doth soon his Labour and his Toil forget.

'After the *Meadows* thus have took their Place,
'The Champion Plains draw up to fill the space.
'Fair in their Prospect, Pleasant, Fruitful, Wide,
'Here *Tellus* may be seen in all his Pride.
'Cloud kissing Pines in stately Man groves stand,
'Firm *Oaks* fair *Branches* wide and large extend.
'The *Fir,* the *Box,* the *Balm-Tree* here stand mute,
'So do the *Nut-Trees* Laden down with Fruit.
'In shady Vales the Fruitful *Vine* o're whelms,
'The Weaving Branches of the bending *Elms.*

'Within the Covert of these shady Boughs,
'The Loving *Turtle* and his Lovely Spouse.
'From Bough to Bough in deep Affection move,
'And with Chast Joy reciprocate their Love.
'At the Cool Brooks, the *Beavers* and the *Minks*
'Keep House, and here the *Hart & Panther* Drinks.

'And *Partridges* here keep in Memory,
'How to their Loss they soared once too high.

   'Within these Spacious Forests, Fresh & Green,
'No Monsters of Burn *Africk* may be seen.
'No hissing *Bassalisk* stands to affright.
'Nor *Seps,* nor *Hemorhus*[2] with Mortal bite,
'The Lybian *Lyon* n'er set Footing here,
'Nor *Tygers* of *Numedia* do appear.
'But here the *Moose* his spreading *Antlers* sways,
'And bears down Stubborn standels with their *sprays,*
'These sport themselves within these *Woods* & here
'The Fatted *Roe-buck* and the *Fallow Deer,*
'Yield Venison as good as that which won
'The Partriarchial Benediction.

   'Each Plain is bounded at its utmost Edge
'With a long Chain of Mountains in a ridge,
'Whose Azure tops advance themselves so high
'They seem like Pendants hanging in the Skie.
'Twenty Four Miles, Surveyers do account
'Between the *Eastern* and the *Western* Mount;
'In which vast Interspace, Pleasant and Fair,
'Zephirus* Whispers a Delightful Air.
'These Mountains stand at Equi-distant space,
'From the fair Flood in such Majestick Grace.
'Their looks alone are able to Inspire
'An Active Brain with a Mercurial Fire.
'The Muses hence their ample Dews Distil,
'More than was Feigned from the twy topt Hill.
'And if those Witty Men that have us told
'Strange Tales of Mountains in the Days of Old,
'Had they but seen how these are Elevated,
'We should have found them far more Celebrated,
'In the Fine Works that they have left to us,
'Than high *Olimpus* or long *Cancassus;*
'Or *Latmos* which *Diana* stops upon,
'There to Salute her dear *Endimion.*

   'Hither the *Eagles* fly and lay their Eggs,
'Then bring their *Young* ones forth out of those *Crags*

'And force them to behold *Sols* Majesty,
'In mid-noon Glory with a steady Eye.
'Here the old *Eagle* his long beak belays,
'Upon a rock till he renews his days.
'And hence they from afar behold their Prey
'And with a steady pinion wing their way.
'But why so Excellent a Land should Lie,
'So many Ages in Obscurity,
'Unseen, Unheard of, or Unthought upon?
'I think there's no good reason can be shown.
'Unless 'twere as it seems the mind of Fate,
'Your Royal Name long to perpetuate,
'So ordered it that such a land might own,
'Thanks for it's Libertys, *Great* SIR, to You.

'The *English* Settlements when thus begun,
'Were blest and prospered in their carrying on.
'Churches Embody, Heaven they address,
'For Preservation in the Wilderness.
'The *Heathen* they Invite unto the Lord,
'And teach them the good Knowledge of his word.
'Heav'n heard their *Pray'rs* & their Labour Crown'd,
'With *Health* & *Peace* with all their Nei'bors round.
....

Psalm LXIV. 6.

The Heart is Deep.

TEXT: *Poetical Meditations*, p. 12.

HE that can trace a Ship making her way,
Amidst the threatening Surges on the Sea;
Or track a Towering Eagle in the Air,
Or on a Rock find the Impressions there
Made by a Serpents Footsteps. Who Surveys
The Subtile Intreagues that a Young Man lays,
In his Sly Courtship of an harmless Maid,
Whereby his Wanton Amours are Convey'd
Into her Breast; Tis he alone that can
Find out the Cursed Policies of Man.

Mather Byles

(1707-1788)

"To PICTORIO, *on the Sight of his Pictures.*"

TEXT: *Poems on Several Occasions* (Boston, 1744), pp. 89-93.

AGES our Land a barbarous Desart stood,
And savage Nations howl'd in ev'ry Wood;
No laurel'd Art o'er the rude Region smil'd,
Nor bless'd Religion dawn'd amidst the Wild;
Dulness and Tyranny confederate reign'd,
And Ignorance her gloomy State maintain'd.

An hundred Journies now the Earth has run,
In annual Circles, round the central Sun,
Since the first Ship the unpolish'd Letters bore
Thro' the wide Ocean to the barb'rous Shore.
Then Infant-Science made it's early Proof,
Honest, sincere, tho' unadorn'd, and rough;
Still thro' a Cloud the rugged Stranger shone,
Politeness, and the softer Arts unknown:
No heavenly Pencil the free Stroke could give,
Nor the warm Canvass felt its Colours live.
No moving Rhet'rick rais'd the ravish'd Soul,
Flourish'd in Flames, or heard it's Thunder roll;
Rough horrid Verse, harsh, grated thro' the Ear,
And jarring Discords tore the tortur'd Air;
Solid, and grave, and plain the Country stood,
Inelegant, and rigorously good.

Each Year, succeeding, the rude Rust devours,
And softer Arts lead on the following Hours;
The tuneful Nine begin to touch the Lyre,
And flowing Pencils light the living Fire;
In the fair Page new Beauties learn to shine,
The Thoughts to brighten, and the Style refine,

Till the great Year the finish'd Period brought;
PICTORIO painted, and MAECENAS wrote.

   Thy Fame, PICTORIO, shall the Muse rehearse,
And sing her Sister-Art in softer Verse:
'Tis your's, great Master, in just Lines to trace
The rising Prospect, or the lovely Face.
In the fair Round to swell the glowing Cheek,
Give Thought to Shades, and teach the Paints to speak.
Touch'd by thy Hand, how *Sylvia's* Charms engage!
And *Flavia's* Features smile thro' ev'ry Age.
In *Clio's* Face, th'attentive Gazer spies
Minerva's reasoning Brow, and azure Eyes,
Thy Blush, *Belinda,* future Hearts shall warm,
And *Celia* shine in *Citherea's* Form.
In hoary Majesty, see CATO here;
Fix'd strong in Thought, there NEWTON'S Lines appear;
Here in full Beauty blooms the charming Maid;
Here *Roman* Ruins nod their awful Head;
Here gloting Monks their am'rous Rights debate,
The *Italian* Master sits in easy State,
VANDIKE and RUBENS show their rival Forms,
And CAESAR flashes in the Blaze of Arms.

   But cease, fond Muse, nor the rude Lays prolong,
A thousand Wonders must remain unsung;
Crowds of new Beings lift their wond'ring Heads,
In conscious Forms, and animated Shades.
What Sounds can speak, to ev'ry Figure just,
The breathing Statue, and the living Bust?
Landskips how gay! arise in ev'ry Light,
And fresh Creations rush upon the Sight;
Thro' fairy Scenes the roving Fancy strays,
Lost in the endless, visionary Maze.

   Still, wondrous Artist, let thy Pencil flow,
Still, warm with Life, thy blended Colours glow,
Raise the ripe Blush, bid the quick Eye-balls roll
And call forth every Passion of the Soul.
Let thy soft Shades in mimick Figures play,
Steal on the Heart, and catch the Mind away.

Yet *Painter,* on the kindred Muse attend,
The Poet ever proves the Painter's Friend.
In the same Studies Nature we pursue,
I the Description touch, the Picture you;
The same gay Scenes our beauteous Works adorn,
The purple Ev'ning, or the flamy Morn:
Now, with bold Hand, we strike the strong Design;
Mature in Thought, now soften every Line;
Now, unrestrain'd, in freer Airs surprize,
And sudden, at our Word, new World's arise.
In gen'rous Passion let our Breasts conspire,
As is the Fancy's, be the Friendship's Fire;
Alike our Labour, and alike our Flame:
'Tis thine to raise the Shape; 'tis mine to fix the Name.

"Written in the Blank Leaf of a POEM intitled Aetna.*"*

TEXT: *Poems on Several Occasions,* p. 98.

THat first of Beauties in your Numbers shines,
You suit your Theme with correspondent Lines.
As sounding Aetna thunders from below,
And Smoke, majestick, hovers round its Brow, }
While its tall Head shines with eternal Snow: }
    Each various Scene your answ'ring Lines unfold,
So *rough* you write, so *cloudy,* and so *cold.*

"Commencement."

TEXT: *A Collection of POEMS. By several Hands.* (Boston, 1744),
    pp. 46-54.

I Sing the day, bright with peculiar charms,
Whose rising radiance ev'ry bosom warms;
The day when *Cambridge* empties all the towns,
And youths commencing, take their laural crowns:
When smiling joys, and gay delights appear,
And shine distinguish'd, in the rolling year.

    While the glad theme I labour to rehearse,
In flowing numbers, and melodious verse,

Descend immortal nine, my soul inspire,
Amid my bosom lavish all your fire,
While smiling *Phoebus,* owns the heavenly layes
And shades the poet with surrounding bayes.
But chief, ye blooming nymphs of heavenly frame,
Who make the day with double glory flame,
In whose fair persons, art and nature vie,
On the young muse cast an auspicious eye:
Secure of fame, then shall the goddess sing,
And rise triumphant with a tow'ring wing,
Her tuneful notes wide-spreading all around,
The hills shall echo, and the vales resound.

   Soon as the morn in crimson robes array'd
With chearful beams dispels the flying shade,
While fragrant odours waft the air along,
And birds melodious chant their heavenly song,
And all the waste of heav'n with glory spread,
Wakes up the world, in sleep's embraces dead.
Then those whose dreams were on th'approaching day,
Prepare in splendid garbs to make their way
To that admir'd solemnity, whose date,
Tho' late begun, will last as long as fate.
And now the sprightly Fair approach the glass
To heighten every feature of the face.
They view the roses flush their glowing cheeks,
The snowy lillies twining round their necks.
Their rustling manteaus huddled on in haste,
They clasp with shining girdles round their waist.
Nor less the speed and care of every beau,
To shine in dress, and swell the solemn show.
Thus clad, in careless order mixt by chance,
In haste they both along the streets advance;
'Till near the brink of *Charles's* beauteous stream,
They stop, and think the lingring boat to blame.
Soon as the empty skiff salutes the shore,
In with impetuous haste they clustering pour,
The men the head, the stern the ladies grace,
And neighing horses fill the middle space.
Sunk deep, the boat floats slow the waves along,
And scarce contains the thickly crowded throng;

A gen'ral horror seizes on the fair,
While white-look'd cowards only not despair.
'Till row'd with care, they reach th'opposing side,
Leap on the shore, and leave the threat'ning tide.
While to receive the pay the boat-man stands,
And chinking pennys jingle in his hands.
Eager the sparks assault the waiting cars,
Fops meet with fops, and clash in civil wars.
Off fly the wigs, as mount their kicking heels,
The rudely bouncing head with anguish swells,
A crimson torrent gushes from the nose,
Adown the cheeks, and wanders o'er the cloaths.
Vaunting, the victor's strait the chariots leap,
While the poor batter'd beau's for madness weep.

Now in calashes shine the blooming maids,
Bright'ning the day which blazes o'er their heads;
The seats with nimble steps they swift ascend,
And moving on the crowd, their waste of beauties spend,
So bearing thro' the boundless breadth of heav'n,
The twinkling lamps of light are graceful driv'n;
While on the world they shed their glorious rays,
And set the face of nature in a blaze.

Now smoak the burning wheels along the ground,
While rapid hoofs of flying steeds resound,
The drivers by no vulgar flame inspir'd,
But with the sparks of love and glory fir'd,
With furious swiftness sweep along the way,
And from the foremost chariot snatch the day.
So at olympick games when heros strove,
In rapid cars to gain the goal of love.
If on her fav'rite youth the goddess shone
He left his rival and the winds out-run.

And now thy town, O *Cambridge!* strikes the sight
Of the beholders with confus'd delight;
Thy green campaigns wide open to the view,
And buildings where bright youth their fame pursue,
Blest village! on whose plains united glows,
A vast, confus'd magnificence of shows.

Where num'rous crowds of different colours blend,
Thick as the trees which from the hills ascend:
Or as the grass which shoots in verdant spires,
Or stars which dart thro' natures realms their fires.

How am I fir'd with a profuse delight,
When round the yard I roll my ravish'd sight!
From the high casements how the ladies show!
And scatter glory on the crowds below.
From sash to sash the lovely lightening plays
And blends their beauties in a radiant blaze.
So when the noon of night the earth invades
And o'er the landskip spreads her silent shades.
In heavens high vault the twinkling stars appear,
And with gay glory's guild the gleemy sphere.
From their bright orbs a flame of splendors flows,
And all around th'enlighten'd ether glows.

Soon as huge heaps, have delug'd all the plains
Of tawny damsels, mixt with simple swains,
Gay city beau's, grave matrons and coquats,
Bully's, and cully's,[1] clergymen and wits.
The thing which first the num'rous crowd employs,
Is by a breakfast to begin their joys.
While wine, which blushes in a chrystal glass
Streams down in floods, and paints their glowing face.
And now the time approaches when the bell,
With dull continuance tolls a solemn knell.
Numbers of blooming youth in black array
Adorn the yard, and gladden all the day.
In two strait lines they instantly divide,
While each beholds his partner on th'opposing side,
Then slow, majestick, walks the learned *head*,
The *senate* follow with a solemn tread,
Next *levi's* tribe in reverend order move,
Whilst the uniting youth the show improve.
They glow in long procession till they come,
Near to the portals of the sacred dome;
Then on a sudden open fly the doors,
The leader enters, then the croud thick pours.

The temple in a moment feels its freight,
And cracks beneath its vast unweildly weight,
So when the threatning Ocean roars around
A place encompass'd with a lofty mound,
If some weak part admits the raging waves,
It flows resistless, and the city leaves;
Till underneath the waters ly the tow'rs,
Which menac'd with their height the heav'nly pow'rs.

The work begun with pray'r,with modest pace,
A youth advancing mounts the desk with grace,
To all the audience sweeps a circling bow,
Then from his lips ten thousand graces flow.
The next that comes, a learned thesis reads,
The question states, and then a war succeeds.
Loud major, minor, and the consequence,
Amuse the crowd, wide-gaping at their sence.
Who speaks the loudest is with them the best,
And impudence for learning is confest.

The battle o'er, the sable youth descend,
And to the awful chief, their footsteps bend.
With a small book, the laurel wreath he gives
Join'd with a pow'r to use it all their lives.
Obsequious, they return what they receive,
With decent rev'rence, they his presence leave.
Dismiss'd, they strait repeat their backward way,
And with white napkins grace the sumptuous day.

Now plates unnumber'd on the tables shine,
And dishes fill'd invite the guests to dine.
The grace perform'd, each as it suits him best,
Divides the sav'ry honours of the feast,
The glasses with bright sparkling wines abound,
And flowing bowls repeat the jolly round.
Thanks said, the multitude unite their voice,
In sweetly mingled and melodious noise.
The warbling musick floats along the air,
And softly winds the mazes of the ear;
Ravish'd the crowd promiscuously retires,
And each pursues the pleasure he admires.

Behold my muse far distant on the plains,
Amidst a wrestling ring two jolly swains;
Eager for fame, they tug and haul for blood,
One nam'd *Jack Luby*, t'other *Robin Clod*,
Panting they strain, and labouring hard they sweat,
Mix legs, kick shins, tear cloaths, and ply their feet.
Now nimbly trip, now stiffly stand their ground,
And now they twirle around, around, around;
Till overcome by greater art, or strength,
Jack Luby lays along his lubber length.
A fall! a fall! the loud spectators cry,
A fall! a fall! the echoing hills reply.

O'er yonder field in wild confusion runs,
A clam'rous troop of *Affric's* sable sons,
Behind the victors shout, with barbarous roar,
The vanquish'd fly with hideous yells before,
The gloomy squadron thro' the valley speeds
Whilst clatt'ring cudgels battle o'er their heads.

Again to church the learned tribe repair,
Where syllogisms battle in the air,
And then the elder youth their second laurels wear.
Hail! happy laurets! who our hopes inspire,
And set our ardent wishes all on fire.
By you the pulpit and the bar will shine,
In future annals; while the ravish'd nine
Will in your bosom breathe caelestial flames,
And stamp *Eternity* upon your names.
Accept my infant muse, whose feeble wings
Can scare sustain her flight, while you she sings.
With candour view my rude unfinish'd praise
And see my *Ivy* twist around your *bayes*.
So *Phideas* by immortal *Jove* inspir'd,
His statue carv'd, by all mankind admir'd.
Nor thus content, by his approving nod,
He cut himself upon the shining god,
That shaded by the umbrage of his name,
Eternal honours might attend his fame.

Benjamin Church
(1734-1776)

From "The Choice"

TEXT: *The Choice, A Poem.* (Boston, 1757).

IF youthful Fancy might it's Choice pursue,
And act as natural Reason prompts it to;
If Inclination could dispose our State,
And human Will might govern future Fate;
Remote From Grandeur, I'd be humbly wise,
And all the Glitter of a Court despise:
Unskil'd the Proud, or Vicious to commend,
To cringe to Insolence, or Fools attend;
Within myself contented and secure,
Above what mean Ambition can endure:
Nor yet so anxious to obtain a Name,
To bleed for Honour in the Fields of Fame;
Empty Parade, is all that Heroes know,
Unless fair Vertue hover in the Show.

BUT in these Walls, where Heav'n has fix'd my stay,
One half of Life, I'd wish to breath away:
The Fall and Winter of each future Year,
I'd humbly hope to spend contented here;
'Mid the fierce Ravage of a wintry Storm,
Kind Friends to cheer me, moderate Wine to warm;
Securely happy we'd delude the Day,
And smile the Seasons chearfully away.

No needless Show my modest Dome should claim,
Neat and genteel without, within the same;
Decently furnish'd to content and please,
Sufficient for Necessity, and Ease;
Vain is the Pomp of Prodigal Expence,
Frugality denotes the Man of Sense;

My Doors the needy Stranger should befriend,
And Hospitality my Board attend;
With frugal Plenty be my Table spread,
Those, and those only whom I love be fed:
The Meek and Indigent my Banquet share,
Who love the Master, and approve the Fare;
Thy mellow Vintage, *Lisbon!* should abound,
Pouring a mirthful Inspiration 'round;
While laughing *Bacchus* baths within the Bowl,
Love, Mirth and Friendship swallow up the Soul.

I'D have few Friends, and those by Nature true,
Sacred to Friendship, and to Vertue too;
Tho' but to few an Intimate profest,
I'd be no Foe, nor useless to the Rest:
Each Friend belov'd requires a friendly Care,
His Griefs, Dejections, and his Fate to share;
For this my Choice should be to Bounds confin'd,
Nor with a Burst of Passion flood Mankind.

ABOVE the Rest, one dear selected Friend,
Kind to advise, and cautious to offend;
To Malice, Envy, and to Pride unknown,
Nor apt to censure Foibles, but his own;
Firm in Religion, in his Morals just,
Wise in discerning, and advising best;
Learn'd without Pedantry, in Temper kind,
Soft in his Manners, happy in his Mind;
Is there in whom, these social Virtues blend,
The Muse lisps *Pollio,* and she calls him Friend:
To him, when flush'd with Transport I'd repair,
His faithful Bosom should my Solace share;
To him I'd fly when Sorrows prove too great,
To him discover all the Stings of Fate:
His social Soul, should all my Pangs allay,
Tune every Nerve, and charm my Griefs away.

O, HOW I wish to join the friendly Throng,
Elude the Hours, and harmonize the Song;
Each generous Soul still sedulous to please,
With calm good Temper, and with mutual Ease;

Glad to receive and give, the keen Reply,
Nor Approbation to the Jest deny.

BUT at a decent Hour with social Heart,
In Love, and Humour should my Friends depart:
Then to my Study, eager I'd repair,
And feast my Mind with new Refreshment there;
There plung'd in Tho't my active Mind should tread,
Through all the Labours of the learned Dead;
Homer; great Parent of Heroick Strains,
Virgil, whose Genius was improv'd with Pains;
Horace, in whom the Wit and Courtier join'd,
Ovid, the tender, amorous and refin'd;
Keen *Juvenal,* whose all-correcting Page,
Lash'd daring Vice, and sham'd an impious Age;
Expressive *Lucan* who politely sung
With hum'rous *Martial* tickling as he stung;
Elaborate *Terence,* studious where he smil'd,
Familiar *Plautus,* regularly wild;
With frequent Visit these I would survey,
And read, and meditate the Hours away.

NOR these alone, should on my Shelves recline,
But awful *Pope!* majestically shine,
Unequal'd Bard! Who durst thy Praise engage?
Not yet grown reverend with the Rust of Age;
Sure Heav'n alone thy Art unrival'd taught,
To think so well, so well express the Thought;
What Villain hears thee, but regrets the Smart?
But tears the lurking Demon from his Heart?
Virtue attends thee, with the best Applause
Conscious Desert! great Victor in his Cause,
She faithful to thy Worth, thy Name shall grace,
Beyond all Period, and beyond all Space:
Go, shine a Seraph and thy Notes prolong
For Angels only merit such a Song!

HAIL Briton's Genius, *Milton!* deathless Name!
Blest with a full Satiety of Fame:
Who durst attempt Impertinence of Praise?
Or sap insidious thy eternal Bays?

For greater Song, or more exalted Fame,
Exceeds Humanity to make, or claim.
These to peruse, I'd oft forget to dine,
And suck Refection from each mighty Line.
Next *Addison's* great Labours should be join'd
Prais'd by all Tongues and known to all Mankind:
With *Littleton* the tender, and correct,
And copious *Dryden,* glorious in Defect;
Nor would I leave, the great and pious *Young,*
Divinely fir'd, and sublime in Song.
Next would I add the unaffected *Gay,*
And gentle *Waller,* with his flowing Lay;
Last Nature-Limning *Thompson* should appear,
Who link'd Eternity within his Year.
These for Diversion, with the Comic Throng,
Should raise my Fancy, and improve my Song;
Extend my View, 'till opening Visions roll,
And all Piæria bursts upon my Soul.

   BUT to inform the Mind, and mend the Heart,
Great *Tillotson,* and *Butler,* Light impart;
Sagacious *Newton,* with all Science blest,
And *Lock,* who always tho't and reason'd best.

   BUT LO! for real Worth, and true Desert,
Exhaustless Science, and extensive Art,
Boerhaave superior stands; in whom we find,
The other Saviour of diseas'd Mankind;
Whose skilful Hand could almost Life create,
And make us leap the very Bounds of Fate;
Death, Tyrant Death, beholding his decline,
That *Boerhaave* would his Kingdom undermine,
Arm'd with his surest Shafts attack'd his Foe,
Who long eluded the repeated Throw,
At Length fatigu'd with Life, he bravely fell,
And Health with *Boerhaave* bad the World farewell.

   THUS 'till the Year recedes, I'd be employ'd,
Ease, Health and Friendship happily enjoy'd;
But when the Vernal Sun revolves it's Ray,
Melting hoar Winter with her Rage away,

When vocal Groves a gay perspective yield,
And a new Verdure springs from Field to Field;
With the first Larks I'd to the Plains retire,
For rural Pleasures are my chief Desire.

AH doubly blest! on native Verdure laid,
Whose Fields support him, and whose Arbours Shade;
In his own Hermitage in Peace resides,
Fann'd by his Breeze, and slumbring by his Tides;
Who drinks a Fragrance from paternal Groves,
Nor lives ungrateful for the Life he loves.

....

"The Times"

TEXT: *THE TIMES, A POEM. By an American.* (Boston, 1765).

Omnes profecto liberi libentius
Sumus, quam servimus.
Plaut. in Captivis.[1]

POLLIO be kind! nor chide an early crime,
Spawn of chagrine, and labour'd waste of time;
This heart misguides me with a bent so strong,
It mocks restraint, and boldly errs in song:[2]
Thus crimes indulg'd such vig'rous growth obtain,
Your friendly caution frowns rebuke in vain.
    'Tis not great *Churchill's* ghost that claims your ear,
For even ghosts of wit are strangers here;
That patriot-soul to other climes remov'd,
Well-pleas'd enjoys that liberty he lov'd;
No pang resents for W————[3] to exile driven,
Exults that worth and *Pratt*[4] are dear to heaven:
Young sure it is not, from whose honey'd lays
Streams a rank surfeit of redundant praise;
For guilt like his what genius shall atone?
D————n the foul verse that daubs a *Stuart's* throne.

    Curs'd lack of genius, or thou soon should'st know,
This humble cot conceals a tyrant's foe;
By nature artless, unimprov'd by pains,

No favour courts me, and no fear restrains,
Wild as the soil, and as the heav'ns severe,
All rudely rough, and wretchedly sincere;
Whose frowning stars have thrown me God knows where,
A wild exotic neighbour to the bear;
One glebe supports us, brethren cubs we run,
Shoot into form, as foster'd by the sun;
No tutoring hand the tender sapling train'd,
Thro' walks of science, nor his growth sustain'd;
Such fruit he yields, luxuriant wildings bear,
Course as the earth, and unconfin'd as air:
No Muse I court, an alien to the Nine,
Thou chaste instructress, NATURE! thou art mine;
Come, blessed parent, mistress, muse and guide,
With thee permit me wander side by side;
Smit with thy charms, my earliest joy I trace,
Fondly enamour'd of thy angel face;
Succeeding labours smother not the flame,
Still, still the dear attachment lives the same.

     No idle task the earliest MUSE began,
But mark'd the morals, e'er she prais'd the man:
To struggling worth supply'd no feeble aid,
And wove the honest wreath for virtue's head,
Uncourtly grave, or thro' the lessen'd page
Shed wisdom's lore, and humaniz'd the age;
Pour'd wholesome treasures from her magic tongue,
Instructed, rul'd, corrected, blest, by song:
How chang'd! how lost! in these degenerate days,
She stuns me with the clamour of her praise:
Is there a villain eminent in state,
Without one gleam of merit?—she'll create;
Is there a scoundrel, has that scoundrel gold?
There the full tide of panegyrick's roll'd;
From venal quills shall stream the sugar'd shower,
And bronze the wretched Lordling—if in power:
Stamp me that blockhead, which (kind heav'n be blest)
My maker form'd my temper to detest,
If sacred numbers I again desert,
The native byas of an honest heart;
Basely to truckle to a wretch in rule,

Or spread a feast for Gods, to cram a fool;
Not for a Monarch would I forge a lie,
To nestle in the sun-shine of his eye:
The paths of error if in youth I trod,
Dress'd a gay idol in the garb of God,
The pageant shrinks, I weep my folly past,
Heav'n frown me dead, but there I've sinn'd my last:
G————e,[5] scarce one lustrum numbers out its days,
Since every tongue was busy in thy praise;
(O make it nameless in the tale of time,
Nor consecrate to ages such a crime;
We lov'd him, love him still, by heav'ns do more,
But make us B————h subjects, we'll adore)
Successful WAR had added wide domain,
And crouded oceans scarce his fleets sustain,
United *Gaul* and *Spain* his easy prey,
And but *compact* to give their realms away;
Where-e'er he bids, consenting B————s[6] fly,
For G————e they conquer, or for G————e they die;
Bless the glad hour, the glorious strife approve,
That sounds his glory, and proclaims their love:
Ah sad reverse! with doubling sighs I speak,
A flood of sorrow coursing down my cheek,
The salient heart for G———— forgets to bound,
Dark disaffection sheds her gloom around;
Fair LIBERTY our soul's most darling prize,
A bleeding victim flits before our eyes:
Was it for this our great forefathers rode,
O'er a vast ocean to this bleak abode!
When *liberty* was into contest brought,
And loss of life was but a second thought;
By pious violence rejected thence,
To try the utmost stretch of providence;
The DEEP, unconscious of the furrowing keel,
Essay'd the tempest to rebuke their zeal;
The tawny natives and inclement sky
Put on their terrors, and command to fly;
They mock at danger; what can those appall?
To whom fair LIBERTY is all in all.
See the *new world* their purchase, blest domain,
Where *lordly tyrants* never forg'd the chain;

The prize of valour, and the gift of prayer,
Hear this and redden each degenerate heir!
Is it for you their honour to betray?
And give the harvest of their blood away?
Look back with rev'rence, aw'd to just esteem,
Preserve the blessings handed down from them;
If not, look forwards, look with deep despair,
And dread the curses of your beggar'd heir:
What bosom beats not, when such themes excite?
Be men, be gods, be stubborn in the right.

Where am I hurry'd? POLLIO, I forbear,
Again I'm calm, and claim thy sober ear;
To *independence* bend the filial knee,
And kiss her sister sage *oeconomy*.
Oeconomy you frown! "O hide our shame!
" 'Tis vile profusion's ministerial name,
"To pinch the farmer groaning at the press,
"Commission leeches to adopt the peace;
"That peace obtain'd, S———h[7] armies to augment,
"And sink the nation's credit two per cent;
"With barren S———h bards the lists to load,
"Both place and pension partially bestow'd;
"Nay more, the *cave of famine* to translate
"Within the purlieus of the R——l gate;
"While brats from northern hills, full, bat'ning lie,
"Their meagre southern masters pining by."
Peace, peace, my POLLIO! sluice thy sorrows here;
Thy country's ghost now points thee to its bier;
Of foreign wrongs, and unfelt woes no more,
While dogs cry *havock* on thy natal shore;
Yon funeral torch* that dimly glids my cell,
Comes fraught with mischiefs, terrible to tell;
It dawns in sables—too officious ray!
Yet, yet compassionately roll away;
All, all is o'er, but anguish, slavery, fear,
The chains already clanking in my ear;
O *Death!* tho' awful, but prevent this blow,
No more thou'rt censur'd for the human foe;
Oe'r life's last ebbs, thy dregs of sorrow fling.

*November 1st [Church's note].

Point all my pangs, and stab with every sting:
I'll bless th'alternative, if not a slave,
And scorn the wretch who trembles at the grave.

Art thou persuaded, for a moment cool,
That nature made thee slave, and mark'd thee fool,
That what we won by hardy war, was *given,*
That non-resistance is secure of heaven;
That persecution in our infant state,
Was nursing kind compassion in the GREAT;
That emigration was not to secure
Our liberties, but to enslave the more;
That charters, privileges, patents, powers,
Were our's till now, and now no longer our's;
To claim exemption by the charter-seal,
Will rashly violate the common-weal;
Juries are nusances and *Traffick* worse,
And to be blind, sagacity of course;
The STAMP and LAND-TAX are as blessings meant,
And opposition is our free consent;
That where we are not, we most surely are,
That wrong is right, black white, and foul is fair;
That M-nsf—ld's[8] honest, and that Pitt's a knave,
That Pratt's a villain, and that Wilkes's a slave;
That godlike Temple[9] is not greatly good,
Nor B—e[10] a rigid *Jacobite* by blood;
That sordid Gr—v—le[11] lately is become
The patron of our liberties at home,
(For whom, now hear me gods! be hell inflam'd,
And murderers of their country doubly d—d)
Now stretch thy pliant faith, adopt this creed,
And be a J-r-d Ing-rs-l* indeed;
If not thou'rt wretched, crawling in the dust,
Condemn'd, despis'd, and herded with the just:
Frown honest SATYRE! menace what you will,
Rogues rise luxuriant, and defeat you still;

*[Jared Ingersoll, 1722-1781] An ingenious S—— D-str-b-t-r who modestly asserted in the p-bl-c papers that the S——p A—t was design'd to make A—r-ca happy by her indulgent Mother, and that it would certainly prove so, if his country would suffer him to continue in office.

Fatigu'd with numbers, and oppress'd with gall,
One general curse must overwhelm them all:
But O ye vilest vile, detested FEW!
Eager, intent, and potent to undoe;
Come out ye parricides! here take your stand,
Your solemn condemnation is at hand;
Behold your crimes, and tremblingly await
The grumbling thunder of your country's hate;
Accursed as ye are! how durst ye bring
An injur'd people to distrust their K——?
Accursed as ye are, how could ye dare,
To lisp delusion in your M———h's ear?
How do I laugh, when such vain coxcombs lour,
Some grave pretence of dread, from lawless power;
To hear a scribling fry, beneath my hate,
Adopt the fraud, and sanctify deceit;
With mean importance, point regardless stings,
To aid injustice menace mighty things;
Nay to such heights of insolence they're flown,
The knaves crave shelter underneath a throne;
A throne all-gracious, such is GEORGE'S praise,
Nor shall oppression blast his sacred bays.

  Witness ye Fathers! whose protracted time,
Fruitful of story, chronicles the clime;
These howling *Deserts,* hospitably tame,
Erst snatch'd ye, martyrs, from the hungry flame;
'Twas heav'n's own cause, beneath whose shelt'ring pow'r
Ye grew the wonder of the present hour;
With anxious ear we've drank your piteous tale,
Where woes unnumber'd long and loud prevail;
Here savage demons sporting with your pains,
There boding mischief in a *Stuart* reigns;
Mark the glad aera, when prevailing foes,
The state's fell harpies, doubling woes on woes,
Had wing'd destruction—VENGEANCE slept no more,
But flung the *tyrant* from the British shore:
Learn hence ye minions! rev'rence to the law,
Salvation died not with the great NASSAU.[12]
And shall such sons, from such distinguish'd sires,
Nurtur'd to hardships, heirs of all their fires,

Shall they, O pang of heart! thus tamely bear,
Who stalk erect, and toss their heads in air?
Let beasts of burthen meanly woo the chain,
WE talk of masters with a proud disdain.
"Prythee forbear rash youth! conceal thy fears,
"A modest silence best becomes thy years;
"Submit, be prudent—in some future hour,
"You'll feel the iron-gripe of ruthless power:"
Truce spawn of phlegm! thy frozen heart conceal,
Benumb'd, unerring, and unapt to feel;
No deed of glory can that soul intice,
Involv'd in adamantince walls of ice;
Within that bosom is a nook so warm,
That vice or virtue kindles to a storm?
Could nature ever lure thee into sin?
Or bursts of passion thaw the frost within?
Thou happy Cynick! still thy senses lull,
Profoundly cautious, and supinely dull;
And should some heroe start his rash career,
Excentric to thy lazy, drowsy sphere;
Be wondrous wise, thy frigid temper bless,
That never wrought thee to a bold excess:
Call truth a libel, treason, honest zeal,
So strange is virtue, and so few can feel;
Call *Churchill* blockhead, *Freedom,* madness, rage,
Call injur'd Wilkes, a monster of the age;
To make me blest, unite this lay with those,
And then, then kindly rate yourselves my foes.

Fop, witling, fav'rite, st—pm—n,[13] tyrant, tool,
Or all those mighty names in one, thou fool!
Let mean ambition, sordid lust of pride,
League thee vile Pander! to a tyrant's side;
Sport with thy country's groans, and be the first
To stab the bosom which a traitor nurs'd;
Rifle the womb, and on those bowels prey,
To plague mankind, that spawn'd thee into day:
Be eminent, thy little soul exert,
And call forth all the rancour of thy heart:
But should the eye of merit on the lour,
(Tho' lowly crush'd beneath the wheel of power)

Thou art my pity, monster! I forgive,
And beg one only curse, that thou may'st live.

Where lies our remedy, in humble prayer?
Our lordly butchers have forgot to hear;
'Tis rank rebellion, rashness to complain,
And all submission tighter tugs the chain:
Go ask your heart, your honest heart regard,
And manumission is your sure reward;
Would'st thou be blest, thy sov'reign pride lay by,
To tyrant custom give the hardy lie;
Yon shagg will warm thee, in thy country fleece
Sleeps *independence* lin'd with balmy *peace;*
Would'st thou be blest? be diligent! be wise!
And make a chaste sufficiency suffice:
Ye lovely fair! whom heaven's best charms array,
The proud Sultana's of some future day;
Sweet as ye are, compleat in every grace,
That spreads angelic softness o'er the face;
Go ply the loom—there lies the happy art,
By new avenues to attack the heart;
With labours of your own, but deck those charms,
We'll rush with transport to your blissful arms.

Amid this wreck—from all aspersions clear,
Nay blush not *Peter,* honest truths to hear;
Base adulation never stain'd my lay,
But modest merit must be brought to day;
What though thy great DESERT *mounts* far above
The mean expression of thy country's love;
In praise like thine, the rustic muse will soar,
Then damn'd to endless silence—sing no more.
"With great contempt of power, alone to stand.
"Thy life, and spotless honours in thine hand;
"To wage unequal wars—and dare the worst,
"And if thy country perish, perish first;
"With pious vigilance the state to guard,
"And eminent in virtue, shun reward;
"No force of avarice warps thy steady heart,
"To meanness, falshood, or dishonest art;
"A tyrant's mandate, thy supreme disdain,

"Our last, best bulwark in a Sc——h r—n;
These are the honours we to fame consign,
Nay blush not *Peter*—these are *surely* thine.

To close—dread sov'reign at whose sacred seat,
Justice and *Mercy,* spotless maidens meet;
GEORGE! Parent! King! our Guardian, Glory, Pride,
And thou fair REGENT! blooming by his side!
Thy offspring pleads a parent's fostering care,
Reject not, frown not, but in mercy spare;
Besprent with dust, the lowly suppliant lies,
A helpless, guiltless, injured sacrifice:
If e'er our infant efforts could delight,
Or growing worth found favour in thy sight,
If warm affection due returns may plead,
Or faith unshaken ever intercede;
With modest boldness we thy smiles demand,
Nor wish salvation from another hand;
Deprest, not helpless, while a BRUNSWICK reigns,
Whose righteous sceptre, no injustice stains.

Southern Verse

"A Description of Charles Town in 1769."

Black & white all mix'd together,
Inconstant, strange, unhealthful Weather
Burning heat & chilling cold
Dangerous both to young & old
Boisterous winds & heavy raines
Fevers & rhumatic pains
Agues plenty without doubt
Sores, Boils, the Prickling Heat & Gout
Musquitos on the Skin make-blotches,
Centipedes & large Cock-roaches
Frightful creatures in the waters
Porpoises, Sharks & Aligators
Houses built on barren Land
No Lamps or Lights, but Streets of Sand
Pleasant Walks, if you can find 'em
Scandalous Tongues, if any mind 'em
The Markets dear & little money
Large Potatoes, sweet as honey
Water bad, & past all drinking
Men & Women without thinking
Every thing at a high price
But Rum, [illegible] & Rice
Many a Widow not unwilling
Many a Beau not worth a shilling
Many a Bargain, if you strike it,
This is Charles-town, how do you like it.

> ... by "Capt. Martin, Captain of a Man of Wars."
> MS, South Caroliniana Library.

The verse of the colonial South has never been characterized accurately, and attempts to distinguish it from verse of the colonial North have not been convincing. The history of colonial verse itself is sketchy; fine distinctions seem doomed to impressionism. That has been the case. One critic calls Southern poetry "distinctly and essentially lyrical";[1] actually the bulk of Southern verse, like Northern, is public and declamatory. Another finds Southern verse "more graceful"[2] than Northern; actually the verse of the Virginia blacksmith Charles Hansford, nearly the largest body of work by any known Southern colonial poet, matches anything in the period for crudeness.

The fact is that the literary history of the colonial South is only now beginning to be written, and that an adequate understanding of it awaits much further research.[3] But even on the available evidence, one can make out some important differences between the poetry of the two regions.

To begin with, far less verse was printed in the South than in the North. Aside from "Bacons Epitaph" and George Sandys' translation of Ovid, there is little seventeenth-century Southern poetry: there was no seventeenth-century Southern printing. During the colonial period not more than six volumes of verse were printed in the region, and these at great difficulty. In 1757 the *South-Carolina Gazette* advertised "A Collection of POEMS, on *various* SUBJECTS: By a Resident of SOUTH-CAROLINA." A year later the editors explained the delay of the volume by a lack of subscriptions, now being solicited in England. Another year passed before the volume appeared. Other works were promised but apparently never published. Printing in the colonial South —one might on that basis say poetry as well—depended almost entirely on one man, William Parks. Without Parks' presses we would not have the poems of Ebenezer Cooke or Richard Lewis, nor those in the two chief Southern periodicals. Born in England about 1698, Parks became public printer at Annapolis in 1727, where he stayed ten years and founded the *Maryland Gazette,* the first newspaper south of Pennsylvania.[4] Essentially a mercantile sheet, the weekly *Gazette* offered in addition to commercial news, verse and essays in imitation of the *Tatler* and *Spectator,* a mixed dish of scatology and hifaluting that includes comic verses on cooking turds and a treatise about the Poet and the Painter, to which Parks in fact devoted an entire issue. While in Maryland, he brought out *The Maryland Muse* (1731), containing the third edition of Ebenezer Cooke's *Sot-weed Factor* and Cooke's versed history of Bacon's rebellion, the first such volume in a proposed but unrealized annual series. Three years later Parks built the first paper mill in the South, with the aid and encouragement of Benjamin Franklin, who in his own magazines reprinted verse from Parks' two journals.[5]

In 1736 Parks founded the *Virginia Gazette*. Similar in content and
format to the Maryland paper, the *Virginia Gazette* opened its columns
to poets and spurred local controversy by printing versed dunning letters
and a sassy exchange of long essays debating the merits of "The Virginia
Pindar," Samuel Davies. It has been estimated that of the two hundred
poems published in the first three years of the *Gazette,* one-fourth are
by colonists.[6] The only other important Southern journal of this time
was the *South-Carolina Gazette,* founded in Charleston in 1732 by
Thomas Whitmarsh in partnership with Benjamin Franklin. The Carolina paper used poetry mainly as fill, and at least one poet paid to have
his verse inserted.[7]

Perhaps owing to the scarcity of printing, very little broadside verse
appeared in the colonial South, which developed no elegiac tradition
and never until the Revolution turned out popular narrative ballads,
songs, or political verse. The absence of printing in the seventeenth
century, and its scarcity in the eighteenth century, with the resulting
small body of Southern verse, had an important effect. Southern poets
never formed a habit of allusion to the local past, a memory of earlier
writers, in short no literary tradition such as the long succession of New
England elegies provided. They never felt dissatisfied with the local
literary tone handed down to them, as the critics of "Kitelic" poetry
felt in the North. Other arts in the South shared the plight of verse.
There was far less painting than in the North, no distinct furniture style,
and against the wealth of elegant domestic craftsmanship from New
England, we possess from Virginia only three pieces of native silver-
ware.[8]

Partly because of the unfavorable printing situation, poetry in the
South remained the leisure-hour dabbling of unambitious amateurs,
some of whom gathered into literary clubs. The center of club-life was
Annapolis, where the Tuesday Club met between 1745 and 1755,
leaving a 1900-page manuscript journal of its doings, now in the Maryland Historical Society. The tone of the club typifies the rather frivolous
literary atmosphere of the South. Organized by people close to the
governor, the club pretended to be derived from an ancient Scots literary
group, and was led by the Scotch physician Alexander Hamilton, the
same whose testy description of colonial culture we have already met.
The club had twenty-five members, among them Jonas Green, printer
of the *Maryland Gazette* after Parks. Unlike such Northern groups as
William Smith's, the Annapolis Wits made no show of high seriousness.
They awarded themselves burlesque Latin titles, penned anacreontics,
and regaled each other with convivial mock-pindaric odes. A "gelastic

law" provided that any member who broached an unsociable topic be laughed at until he stopped.[9]

A similar trifling afflicted Southern literary life generally. Socially, publication was thought improper and ostentatious for a gentleman; in the North, industrious verse-writing had always been a distinction, even for the most eminent. In the South it was correct, however, for a high-placed planter to throw off some verses. Writing verse one could feel himself, despite the wilderness, a London beau. "Juba" addresses the ladies of Maryland as if lolling at some elegant watering place, advising them to "scorn the fopling Flutters of the town," of which there were no doubt none. William Byrd's verses to Cornelia and Sabina are the bagatelles of a fashionable wit. Such exercises were always proper for men of rank. Francis Nicholson, Royal Governor of Virginia, wrote some poems to court Lucy Burwell, a seventeenth-century belle.[10] A hundred years later, George Washington began a verse in his youth, but did not finish it. Verse from the South resembles colonial Williamsburg itself, a paraphrase of English manner. Northern poets were no doubt often obtuse to their own experience. But Southerners were still more apt to treat the backwoods as if it were London.[11] Many of those who did not claim the South had everything London had, viewed the torpor of Southern culture with good-humored tolerance. Rowland Rugeley of South Carolina asked in the preface to his burlesque poem *Aeneas and Dido* that a committee be appointed to "prevent the landing of any Poets amongst us, with as much care, as we would any dutiable articles whatever." Should any local poets spring up, "though it may not be in our power totally to suppress them, in great measure it will."[12] But his satire has no bite; no poets stood clapping at the gates of Williamsburg.

Rugeley's jest about Southern animus toward poetry covers a sour fact. There seem to have been from the beginning in the South express attempts to discourage learning and the arts. While in the North, Harvard, Yale, the College of Philadelphia, and King's College became centers for young poets, in the South universities never thrived. Governor Berkeley in 1671 wrote to "thank God, *there are no free schools* nor *printing*" in Virginia and hoped that "we shall not have these hundred years." Learning, he said, "has brought disobedience, and heresy, and sects into the world, and *printing* has divulged them . . . God keep us from both!"[13] Later Virginians held similar hopes. In 1693, the same year that the King granted the William and Mary charter requiring that two Latin verses yearly be composed as tribute by students at the college,[14] Attorney General Seymour told James Blair, its founder, that

Virginia had no use for his school. When Blair reminded him that the people needed a ministry, Seymour told him to forget about souls and make tobacco.[15] This scorn in mind, one distrusts the judgment of Richard Lewis, the Maryland poet who for subscriptions to his verse translation, *Muscipulus,* thanked "a *generous Disposition in the Province,* to encourage *Learning.*"[16] Yet Maryland had no college throughout the colonial period. A more reliable witness on Maryland is probably Jonathan Boucher. In 1769 he found no literary man "nearer than the country I had just left [England]: nor were literary attainments beyond merely reading or writing at all in vogue or repute." Poetry in the region, he observed, "may yet be considered only as an exotic." [17] A similar verdict could not have been passed on New England, where the accumulation of nearly a century and a half of verse attested that poetry was a socially useful and personally dignifying work.

How sorely official condemnation of culture inhibited Southern verse one can only guess. One might, however, qualify Daniel Boorstin's thesis that an important result of the colonial period was its new theory of knowledge, its new faith in the public mind. Judging from its verse, the South did not wage such a reform. It had no background of plain style theory to direct the language of poets to the intelligence of the least gifted hearer. Richard Lewis and the other leading Southern poets wrote mainly for the ears of Royal Governors, and their diction was suitably lofty. To the extent that the South lacked this commitment to a universally public style, it was divorced not only from the North but from a major continuity of American verse theory.

Southern Literary Relations with England and the Colonies

Throughout the colonial period, the South was dependent for its culture upon England, as less passively was the North. The list of Southern literary contacts abroad is impressive:[18] William Byrd met Oldmixon, Rowe and Congreve at the Inner Temple, and knew Wycherly well. Charles Carroll of Carrollton dined with Burke. Oglethorpe was a good friend of Johnson's whole circle, and both Pope and Thomson praise him in poems. One of the greatest modern Welsh poets, Gronow Owen (1723-69), the "Vergil of Wales," spent the last twelve years of his life in Virginia, where he became head of the William and Mary grammar school. John Paradise, a Literary Club member mentioned by Boswell in his *Life* of Johnson, owned several houses in Williamsburg. Macpherson passed through Charleston on his way to the West Indies in

1765, and his visit was recorded as headline news by the *South-Carolina Gazette*. The English, for their part, praised Richard Lewis, who together with Thomas Godfrey was probably the colonial poet best known to English audiences. Lewis' "Description of Spring" was first published in England in 1732, and admired for affording "a picture perfectly new to the English reader"; at least four English magazines reprinted it. Two of Lewis' other poems were reprinted in the *Gentleman's Magazine*. The son of the editor of the *London Magazine,* travelling in America in 1746, quoted Lewis' "Description" and confessed taking it from his pocket now and then. For sentiment and piety he found it "one of the best Pieces extant," its pictures "just and fine," offering relief, he added in a minor key, from "a too great Sameness of Prospect."[19]

These direct ties with English literary life prepared a further difference between Northern and Southern verse. The South absorbed the literature of the Restoration, as the North largely did not. The evidence of colonial reading and of literary influences on Southern verse, indicates less of a cultural lag in the Southern colonies. Southerners were caught up with English fashion, perhaps only because their local loyalties were not pronounced. And because of lingering Puritan restrictions in the North, drama arrived thirty years earlier in the South. The many local prologues written for English plays produced in the Southern colonies form one of the more interesting bodies of colonial verse.

Southern literary commerce with other colonies seems to have been limited to Pennsylvania. While much New England verse appeared in magazines and newspapers of the middle colonies, and vice versa, there was little interchange between Boston and the Southern capitals. The sheer distance between them suggests an explanation, but temperamental differences also divided them and, again, their literary fashions were out of step because of the briefer cultural lag in the South. (It is significant that by 1770 Boston poems appear in Southern periodicals, Southern verse in Boston.) A few Puritans had travelled to Virginia, among them Benjamin Tompson's father, and John Saffin. Jonas Green of the *Maryland Gazette* descended from a family of New England printers, stemming from the Samuel Green who opened a press at Cambridge in 1694. But for the most part the list of Southern intercolonial literary ties centers in Pennsylvania. Hugh Jones, the Virginia Anglican clergyman, travelled to Pennsylvania and knew William Smith and Franklin. Two proteges of Franklin at his Philadelphia printshop, Thomas Whitmarsh and Lewis Timothy, became the two successive editors of the *South-Carolina Gazette*. Peter Timothy, Lewis' son, corresponded with Franklin, from whom he bought paper, books, and other supplies.[20]

Richard Lewis' poems were known widely in Pennsylvania. A writer to the *Pennsylvania Gazette* in 1736 castigated an elegy on Lewis that appeared there. In two issues of the *American Weekly Mercury* in 1740, another Philadelphia poet attempted an imitation of Lewis' "Description." Philadelphians also knew the poems of James Sterling, who after publishing plays and poems in England and Ireland moved to Maryland in 1737 as a missionary of the Church of England. In 1757 many of his poems appeared in the Philadelphia *American Magazine*. He visited Pennsylvania often and often wrote on Pennsylvania themes.[21]

America in Southern Colonial Verse

But no difference between the verse of the colonial North and South is more obvious or more profound than their differing attitudes toward America. Southern verse writers rarely idealized the country or, until the mid-eighteenth century, indulged grand speculations over what it might become. Usually Southern poets either wrote about matters unrelated to the new world, or else they dispraised it. Southern dislike for the country radically distinguishes Southern verse from Northern.

The intensity of this dislike must be measured against the surge of chauvinism in other colonies during the first decades of the eighteenth century. By 1730 America is no longer the Wilderness Zion or Cathay but a cultural showplace for all humanity, the Athens of Mankind. The philosophical basis for this ideal was the theory of Translation, the inevitable westward movement of the arts and sciences. Some English writers, notably Bishop Berkeley, had toyed with the theory that the arts moved from Greece to Rome to Britain. Very few, however, were prepared to concede the next step: by design of history, the arts were moving to America. Crèvecoeur proclaimed that "Americans are the western pilgrims, who are carrying along with them that great mass of arts, sciences, vigour and industry which began long since in the east; they will finish the great circle."[22] This prophecy became a commonplace of colonial verse.

Partly it could be validated by experience. America—and many colonists saw deep significance in the fact—had produced the ingenious Franklin. Partly the idea continued in a new idiom the Puritans' own conception of their mission. A 1648 New England Almanac held that peace "bloom'd in Europe once, but now't is gon' / And's glad to find a desart-mansion." At the opening of his *Magnalia* (1702), Cotton Mather professed to write "the *Wonders* of the CHRISTIAN RELIGION, flying from the Depravations of *Europe,* to the *American*

Strand." Whatever its origins, the possibility that historic forces had
assigned America a special destiny as the repository for world culture,
turned colonial poets into local boosters. James Sterling tried to coax
the migration:

> A western course has pleas'd you all along;
> *Greece, Rome,* and *Briton,* flourish all in song.
> Keep on your way, and spread a glorious fame,
> Around the earth let all admire your name
> Chuse in our plains or forests soft retreats;

Most parts of the country revelled in the prospect. In 1733 the Phila-
delphian Joseph Breintnal wished Thomas Penn, "May your Philadelphia
be the future Athens of America."[23] Another Philadelphian, Titan
Leeds, congratulated his city because "*Europe* shall mourn her ancient
Fame declin'd, / And *Philadelphia* be the *Athens* of Mankind." One
South Carolina writer anticipated that America would compete with
Europe, and while granting the meanness of home culture cautioned
his townsmen against spiting it:

> *Athens* from such Beginnings, mean and low!
> Saw *Thespis'* cart a wond'rous Structure grow;

And he exclaimed:

> See! Genius wakes, dispels the former Gloom,
> And sheds Light's Blaze, deriv'd from *Greece* and *Rome!*

From Boston, *A Collection of Poems* (1744) boasted *"New-England's*
sons, e'erwhile of barb'rous name" were now "A match for *Albion,* or
the *Graecian* fame."

As one gathers from these examples, the theory of Translation had
a startling corollary. If of necessity the arts and sciences marched to
America they of necessity left England. So the many colonial poets who
saw themselves transplanting English culture in America, often wrote
of it as an England defunct, of English virtues once prized but no
longer existent. Widespread affirmation of the theory and its corollary
can be documented copiously; the reader will find many instances in the
anthology. Continued interest in the theory is a further unifying theme
in the erratic history of colonial verse. During the Revolution, patriots
seized on such a vague but established expectation to toast prospering

America and gloat over moribund England. A 1774 Liberty Song, "made by a Bostonian" but published in the *Virginia Gazette,* begins:

> That Seat of Science, Athens, and Earth's proud Mistress,
>   Rome,
> Where now are all their Glories? We scarce can find their
>   Tomb.
> Then guard your Rights, Americans, nor stoop to lawless
>   Sway,
> Oppose, oppose, oppose, oppose for North America.[24]

After the Revolution, the theory of Translation became the basis of such epic quests for national origins as Barlow's *Columbiad,* whose intention was to sing the explorer who first unfurled "An eastern banner o'er the western world,/ And taught mankind where future empires lay."

But Southern poets of the first half of the eighteenth century rarely congratulated themselves on their destiny. A few, it is true, looked forward to the Translation. Most Southerners, however, looked at themselves. And they were not cheered. Ebenezer Cooke and Richard Lewis, the two chief Southern colonial poets, viewed their situation with mingled feelings of apprehension and haughty disgust. Cooke typifies that lack in Southern verse of a messianic literature of hope and promise. A sort of colonial Villon, Cooke (or "Cook") refers to himself variously as "Gent" and "Laureat." Whether these are actual titles granted him by Governor Calvert is impossible to say.[25] We know from his treatment of the country in the first version of *The Sot-weed Factor* that the Laureat and Gent loathed the place. Maryland is a run-down sanctuary for runaway scoundrels. Like the forest in some medieval romance, it is remote from civilization, treacherous, threatening, irrational, a deprivation. What greets the emigrant is not the wealth of Cathay and the climate of Eden but rotting food, fevers, wolves, surly peasants, leaky buildings, escaped convicts, frogs, snakes, greasy Indians, rum-benumbed planters, quack lawyers, cockroaches, all-night brawls, and chinces. The reactions of other Southern verse writers, while more restrained, share Cooke's animadversion for "that Shoar, where no good Sense is found, / But Conversation's lost, and Manners drown'd."

Like Cooke, the Etonian schoolmaster Richard Lewis found nothing in the facts of frontier life to suggest that the arts and sciences were preparing to assemble in the South. Arrived in Maryland around 1725, a friend of Governor Calvert (whom he calls in one poem his patron), Lewis mourned how the colony's poverty starved the muse:

> . . . *Here,* rough Woods embrown the Hills and Plains,
> Mean are the *Buildings,* artless are the *Swains*:
> *"To raise the Genius,"* W E no Time can spare,
> A *bare Subsistence* claims our utmost Care.

In 1732, this plaint was a Southern phenomenon: two years earlier,
the Pennsylvanian Titan Leeds had called on the theory of Translation
to declare that in Philadelphia

> . . . *Apollo* does erect his Throne,
> This his *Parnassus,* this his *Helicon:*

And Lewis' dashed view of Southern culture heightens one's doubts
about the "encouragement of learning" he found in Maryland. How
does it jibe with the *"bare Subsistence"* that "claims our utmost Care"?
The contradiction embodies a larger paradox of Southern colonial history. The first Southern settlers all marvelled at the abundance of the
land; yet near-starvation drove them to cannibalism. Lewis too pictures
the land as at once lush and barren, the unfulfilled promise of a rich
life. In *Carmen Seculare* he bids Lord Baltimore welcome to "this fertile Land" with its vast flocks of fowl and fruit and grain. Here, "ev'ry
Planter opens wide his Door,/ To entertain the Stranger, and the Poor."
But, the economic situation in Maryland, Lewis says, is dire. Because
"Arts have rarely visited our shores," settlers lack techniques for mining
nature. Although from one point of view Maryland enjoys voluptuous
plenty, from another its whole energy is spent scratching out existence:

> The plenteous Crops that over-spread our Plains,
> Reward with Poverty the toiling Swains:
> Their sinking *Staple* chills the Planters Hearts,
> Nor dare they venture on unpractis'd Arts;
> Despondent, they impending Ruin view,
> Yet starving, must their old Employ persue.

Almost unanimously, other poets of the eighteenth-century South
echo Lewis' frustration by denouncing the climate, the laziness of the
natives, and the infernal swamps and woods. Markland imagines
"Mournful VIRGINIA, sighing" because it is "numb'd with Winters
cold and bare," its "toilsome Summers fruitless Harvests share." Jonathan Boucher reviles not alone the climate but also the low-bred Southern bumpkin whose complacent wont is to "eat, and loll, and sleep."
Joseph Dumbleton convicts for the failure of agriculture, rum:

In thy Pursuit our Fields are left forlorn,
Whilst giant Weeds oppress the pigmy Corn:
Thou throw'st a Mist before the Planter's Eyes;
The Plough grows idle, and the Harvest dies.

Nature itself seemed inimical. George Seagood and Charles Woodmason regard the land and forests of the South as infernal. Seagood marvels at the courage of Governor Spotswood, who explored the pestiferous wilderness, "to poisonous Snakes and Monsters only known." Reptiles, insects, droughts, Woodmason says, render the vast stores useless:

The planter joyless views luxuriant vines,
And in the myrtle's fragrant shade repines;
Scorch'd in his boasted aromatick grove,
From heat no shelter, no recess for love.

Despite much that he finds attractive in the new world, Woodmason longs to "tread paternal fields again," England, "my country."

Disaffection for the place characterizes the verse of the colonial South. While in the same decades Northerners looked forward to matchless cultural achievements, Southerners indicted a bad climate, a tough soil, unpleasant natives, and a stunted culture. They granted America at best potential good but more often found it poor, rude, dangerous, unhealthy, and hot. England remained, for most of them, "my country."

NOTES

[1] Armistead Gordon, *Virginia Writers of Fugitive Verse* (New York, 1923), p. 4.

[2] Edd Winfield Parks, *Southern Poets* (New York, 1936), p. lxxxv.

[3] A major step toward that history is the important doctoral dissertation by J. A. Leo LeMay, *A Literary History of Colonial Maryland* (University of Pennsylvania, 1964), which attributes many previously unidentified poems to Southern poets, supplies much new biographical material, and gives deserved attention to the essays of Dr. Alexander Hamilton.

[4] "William Parks," *Dictionary of American Biography*.

[5] Alfred Owen Aldridge, "Benjamin Franklin and the *Maryland Gazette*," *Maryland Historical Magazine*, VIL (September 1949), 177-189.

[6] Robert Manson Myers, "The Old Dominion Looks to London: A Study of English Literary Influences upon *The Virginia Gazette* (1736-1766)," *Virginia Magazine of History and Biography*, LIV (July 1946), 195-217.

[7] Hennig Cohen, *The South-Carolina Gazette 1732-1775* (Columbia, S.C., 1953), pp. 10, 12.

[8] Carl Bridenbaugh, *The Colonial Craftsman* (repr. New York, 1961), p .121.

[9] See Walter B. Norris, *Annapolis* (New York, 1925), pp. 61-66. A more favorable estimate of the club appears in LeMay. In 1770 a Homony Club succeeded the Tuesday Club, bringing together Jonathan Boucher, Charles Wilson Peale and others at the Coffee House. It collapsed two years later in political bitterness.

[10] Reprinted in Fairfax Downey, *Our Lusty Forefathers* (New York, 1947), p. 12ff.

[11] In this posture are the beginnings of a uniquely Southern literary tradition. The narrators of such Southern colonial poems as "The Sot-weed Factor" and Jonathan Boucher's "Pastoral" feel themselves morally superior to the world they describe. The distance is that between the educated gentleman and the illiterate slave or poor white, a distance maintained in the fiction of the nineteenth century Southern humorists and in the sketches of Mark Twain. See Kenneth Lynn, *Mark Twain and Southwestern Humor* (Boston, 1959), *passim*.

[12] Rowland Rugeley, *The Story of Aeneas and Dido Burlesqued* (Charlestown, 1774), p. ix. What little information I have been able to uncover about this interesting writer (a son-in-law of William Dawson, poet and Professor of Moral Philosophy at William and Mary), appears in the *South-Carolina Historical and Genealogical Magazine,* X, 224; XI, 105; XX, 17; XXI, 114; XXXIV, 195.

[13] W. W. Henning, ed., *Statutes at Large . . . of Virginia,* II (Richmond and Philadelphia, 1809), 517.

[14] E. M. Counsell, "Latin Verses by Students of William and Mary College," *William and Mary Quarterly,* 2d Ser., X (July 1930), 269-274.

[15] Thomas Jefferson Wertenbaker, *The Shaping of Colonial Virginia* (repr. New York, 1958), II, 136. The interest in education in the colonial South also awaits further study. The first university in America was set up at Henrico in 1619, but was destroyed during the massacre.

[16] Richard Lewis, *Muscipula,* repr. *Maryland Historical Society Fund Publications,* no. 36 (Baltimore, 1900), p. 66.

[17] *Jonathan Boucher's Reminiscences,* ed. Jonathan Bouchier (Boston, 1925), p. 52.

[18] See William L. Sachse, *The Colonial American in Britain* (Madison, Wis., 1956), p. 162; Richard C. Boys, "General Oglethorpe and the Muses," *Georgia Historical Quarterly,* XXXI (March 1947), 20; Arthur Gray, "Gronow Owen in America," *William and Mary Quarterly,* 2d Ser., XI (July 1931), 235-240; Archibald B. Shepperson, *John Paradise and Lucy Ludwell of London and Williamsburg* (Richmond, Va., 1942); Hennig Cohen, " 'Ossian' Visits Charleston 1765," *South Carolina Historical Magazine,* LV (January 1954), 40-41.

[19] C. Lennart Carlson, "Richard Lewis and the Reception of His Work in England," *American Literature,* IX (March 1938), 311.

[20] See Hugh Jones, *The Present State of Virginia* (Chapel Hill, 1956); Frederick Bowes, *The Culture of Early Charleston* (Chapel Hill, 1942), p. 95; Douglas C. McMurtrie, "The Correspondence of Peter Timothy, Printer of Charleston, with Benjamin Franklin," *South-Carolina Historical and Genealogical Magazine,* XXXV (July 1934), 123-129.

[21] Lawrence C. Wroth, "James Sterling: Poet, Priest, and Prophet of Empire," *Proceedings of the American Antiquarian Society,* XLI (1931), 25-76. Many new

poems by Sterling are identified in LeMay, making him perhaps the most prolific Southern poet.

[22] J. Hector St. John de Crèvecoeur, *Letters from an American Farmer* (repr. Dolphin Books, New York, n.d.), p. 49.

[23] Joseph Breintnal, "Directors of Library Company to Thomas Penn," *The Papers of Benjamin Franklin,* ed. Leonard W. Labaree (New Haven, 1959), I, 321.

[24] Arthur M. Schlesinger, "A Note on Songs as Patriot Propaganda 1765-1776," *William and Mary Quarterly,* 3d Ser., XI (1954), 80-81.

[25] Lawrence C. Wroth, "The Maryland Muse by Ebenezer Cooke," *Proceedings of the American Antiquarian Society,* XLIV (1934), 267-335. In an amusing and telling footnote, Cooke says that he excludes from his gallery of Maryland rogues "any of the *English* gentlemen resident there." By implication his whipping boys are not Englishmen but new beings entirely, Americans. More suggestive still are the revisions Cooke made in the 1731 version of the poem, twenty-eight years later. The earlier ending reads: that land "Where no Man's Faithful, nor a Woman Chast." Cooke changed it to: that "Land where Hospitality/ Is every Planter's darling Quality." One cannot say whether some personal change in Cooke's fortunes, or some improvement in living conditions in the colony prompted this change. One supposes that however much most settlers disliked the country they came to terms with it and learned to live in it.

Anonymous

"Bacons Epitaph, made by his Man."

TEXT: *Collections of the Massachusetts Historical Society,* 2d Ser., I (1814), 58-60.

DEATH why soe crewill! what no other way
To manifest thy splleene, but thus to slay
Our hopes of safety; liberty, our all
Which, through thy tyrany, with him must fall
To its late caoss? Had thy rigid force
Bin delt by retale, and not thus in gross
Grief had bin silent: Now wee must complaine
Since thou, in him, hast more then thousand slane
Whose lives and safetys did so much depend
On him there lif, with him there lives must end.
    If't be a sin to think Death brib'd can bee
Wee must be guilty; say twas bribery
Guided the fatall shaft. Verginias foes

To whom for secret crimes, just vengeance owes
Disarved plagues, dreding their just disart
Corrupted Death by Parasscellcian art
Him to destroy; whose well tride curage such,
There heartless harts, nor arms, nor strength could touch.
   Who now must heale those wounds, or stop that blood
The Heathen made, and drew into a flood?
Who i'st must pleade our Cause? nor Trump nor Drum
Nor Deputations; these alass are dumb.
And Cannot speake. Our Arms (though near so strong)
Will want the aide of his Commanding tongue,
Which conquer'd more then Ceaser: He orethrew
Onely the outward frame; this could subdue
The ruged workes of nature. Soules repleate
With dull Child could, he'd annemate with heate
Drawne forth of reasons Lymbick. In a word
Marss and Minerva, both in him Concurd
For arts, for arms, whose pen and sword alike
As Catos did, may admireation strike
Into his foes; while they confess with all
It was their guilt stil'd him a Criminall.
Onely this differance does from truth proceed
They in the guilt, he in the name must bleed.
While none shall dare his obseques to sing
In desarv'd measures; untill time shall bring
Truth Crown'd with freedom, and from danger free
To sound his praises to posterity.
   Here let him rest; while wee this truth report
Hee's gon from hence unto a higher Court
To pleade his Cause where he by this doth know
Whether to Ceaser hee was friend, or foe.

                    "Upon the Death of G.B."

WHETHER to Ceaser he was Friend or Foe?
Pox take such Ignorance, do you not know?
Can he be Friend to Ceaser, that shall bring
The Arms of Hell, to fight against the King?
(Treason, Rebellion) then what reason have
Wee for to waite upon him to his Grave,
There to express our passions? Wilt not bee

Worse then his crimes, to sing his Ellegie
In well tun'd numbers; where each Ella beares
(To his Flagitious name) a flood of teares?
A name that hath more soules with sorow fed,
Then reched Niobe, single teares ere shed;
A name that fil'd all hearts, all eares, with paine,
Untill blest fate proclam'd, Death had him slane.
Then how can it be counted for a sin
Though Death (nay though myselfe) had bribed bin,
To guide the fatall shaft? we honour all
That lends a hand unto a Trators fall.
What though the well paide Rochit¹ soundly ply
And box the Pulpitt, into flattery;
Urging his Rethorick, and strain'd elloquence,
T'adorne incoffin'd filth, and excrements;
Though the Defunct (like ours) nere tride
A well intended deed untill he dide?
'Twill be nor sin, nor shame, for us, to say
A two fould Passion checker workes this day
Of Joy and Sorow; yet the last doth move
On feete impotent, wanting strength to prove
(Nor can the art of Logick yield releife)
How Joy should be surmounted, by our greafe.
Yet that wee Greave it cannot be denide,
But 'tis because he was, not cause he dide.
So wep the poore distressed, Ilium Dames
Hereing those nam'd, their Citty put in flames,
And countrey ruin'd; If we thus lament
It is against our present Ioyes consent.
For if the rule in Phisick, trew doth prove,
Remove the cause, th'effects will after move,
We have outliv'd our sorows; since we see
The causes shifting of our miserey.
    Nor is't a single cause, that's slipt away,
That made us warble out, a well-a-day.
The Branes to plot, the hands to execute
Projected ills, Death Ioyntly did nonsute
At his black Bar. And what no Baile could save
He hath commited Prissoner to the Grave;
From whence there's no repreive. Death keep him close
We have too many Divells still goe loose.

William Byrd
(1674-1744)

"Long has the Furious Priest"

TEXT: *William Byrd's Dividing Line Histories* (Raleigh, 1929), p. 120.

Long has the Furious Priest assay'd in Vain,
With Sword and Faggot, Infidels to gain,[1]
But now the Milder Soldier wisely tryes
By Gentler Methods to unveil their Eyes.
Wonders apart, he knew 'twere vain t'engage
The fix'd Preventions of Misguided Age.
With fairer Hopes he forms the Indian Youth
To early Manners, Probity and Truth.
The Lyon's whelp thus on the Libian Shore   )
Is tam'd and Gentled by the Artful Moor,   }
Not the Grim Sire, inured to Blood before.)

"A Song"

TEXT: MS, University of North Carolina Library

Sabina with an Angels face,
    By Love ordaind for Joy,
Seems of the Syren's cruel Race,
    To Charm and then destroy.

With all the arts of Look and dress,
    She fans the fatal fire:
Thro Pride, mistaken oft for Grace,
    She bids the Swain expire.

The God of Love inrag'd to see,
    The Nymph defy his flame;
Pronounc'd this merciless Decree,
    Against the haughty Dame

Let Age with double Speed oretake her;
    Let Love the room of Pride supply;

And when the Fellows all forsake her,
Let her gnaw the Sheets & dy.

"Upon a Sigh"[1]

TEXT: MS, University of North Carolina Library

Gentlest Air Thou Breath of Lovers,
　　Vapour from a Secret Fire:
Which by Thee it Self discovers,
　　E'r yet daring to aspire.

Softest noat of Whisperd anguish,
　　Harmony's refinedst part:
Strikeing Whilst Thou Seemst to languish,
　　Full upon the Listeners heart.

Safest Messenger of Passion,
　　Steeling thro a Crowd of Spys:
Which constrain the outward fashion,
　　Close the Lips and guard the Eys.

Shapeless Sigh! we ne'er can Show Thee,
　　Form'd but to assault the Ear:
Yet 'eer to their loss, they know Thee
　　Every Nymph may read Thee there

"Upon a Fart"

TEXT: MS, University of North Carolina Library

Gentlest Blast of ill concoction,
　　Reverse of high-ascending Belch:
Th'only Stink abhorr'd by Scotsman,
　　Belovd and practic'd by the Welch.

Softest noat of Inward Gripeing
　　Sr Reverences finest part,
So fine it needs no pains of Wipeing,
　　Except it prove a Brewers fart.

Swiftest Ease of Cholique pain,
　　Vapour from a Secret Stench,
Is rattled out by th'unbred Swain,
　　But whisperd by the Bashfull wench.

Shapeless Fart! we ne'er can show Thee
　　But in that merry Female Sport
In which by burning blew we know Thee
　　Th'Amuzement of the Maids at Court.

"A Poem upon Some Ladys at Tunbridge 1700"

TEXT: MS, University of North Carolina Library

Lady C.D.　Upon the Walks Cornelia moves,
　　　　　　　With such a soft engageing Grace:
　　　　　　Her Ayr and easy manner proves
　　　　　　　Her high descent from Royal Race.

Lady S.　　Plautinas wit divinely draws,
　　　　　　　Our adoration and Surprize:
　　　　　　Her charms invite, her Conduct aws,
　　　　　　　And wounds like Parthians as she flys.

Mrs W....　Cold Phebe's too neglectfull air,
　　　　　　　The humble Crowd of Lovers mourn:
　　　　　　Obsequiously her Chains they wear,
　　　　　　　And much for Eys & acres burn.

Mrs E..k　　Drusilla warms us with her fire,
　　　　　　　Which her too Icey breast denys:
　　　　　　At every smile, some swains expire,
　　　　　　　At every frown some Hero dys.

Lady Sm.　　Foul Madget bursting at such sights,
　　　　　　　Confesst her malice and dispair:
　　　　　　The Poplars on the walks she bites,
　　　　　　　And with these words she blasts ye Air.

　　　　　　What have not I and Envy done?
　　　　　　　Bright looks thro me their bloom forsake:

Whole Familys my Rancour own,
    And each grey hair that's left's a Snake.

Ease o ye Powers a restless mind,
    Some vengeance on these nymphs decree:
Or make their curst Adorers blind,
    Or make their features loath'd like mee.

The Naiid Phoce then appears,
    Which Goddess guards these healing springs:
Her head above the Surface rears,
    And bubling in these Accents Sings.

Quick to the neighbouring Grove begon,
    A bleak & barren Rock you'll find:
Thence throw your crippl'd carcase down,
    And ease your self & all mankind.

J. Markland

(fl. 1730)

"TYPOGRAPHIA.
An Ode, on Printing."

TEXT: *TYPOGRAPHIA. An Ode, on Printing.* (Williamsburg, 1730).

YE NYMPHS, who o'er *Castalian Springs,*
    With joint Command preside,
    Who trill the Lyre's sonorous Strings,
Record the great and glorious Things,
Of Godlike *Rulers,* matchless *Kings,*
    And poetic Numbers guide;
    Daughters of eternal *Jove,*
    Gently to my Assistance move:
Whether on *Pindus'* lofty Top you play,
    Or, with Heav'n-kindled Fire,
    Mæonian Notes inspire,
And shew another *Ilium's* fatal Day;

Or, if upon the *Elian* Plain
You sing the Victor's glorious Deeds,
Where *Pindar* lash'd his fiery-footed Steeds,
His fiery-footed Steeds impatient of the Rein.

II.

Or, if your more exalted Will
To those sweet Seats of blissful Quiet leads,
Where gentle CAM the flow'ry Meads
With genial Moisture overflows;
Or, where the Silver ISIS, smooth and still,
Does, like a bashful Bride,
Into the Arms of amorous THAME
Without a Murmur glide:
Hence ADDISON, the *British Maro,* rose,
Thence DRYDEN soar'd the highest Pitch of Fame:
Leave, leave awhile those blest Abodes,
To view a new-arising *Land,*
A *Land,* whose fertile Plains,
And peaceful shady Woods,
May well demand
Your sweetest Notes, and loftiest Strains,
Where, with supreme Command, your own AUGUSTUS reigns.

III.

AUGUSTUS reigns;
His far-extended Sway,
Nor Length of boundless Land restrains,
Nor separating Sea.
But oh! much more extended is the Pow'r,
Than o'er the Length of boundless Land,
Or o'er the Sea's remotest Strand,
Where Goodness and paternal Care
The Sovereign's native Vertues are,
And Subjects Hearts with Loialty run o'er:
Where envious Thoughts abortive die,
Nor Malice rowls her low'ring Eye:
Where, with contending Zeal,
The *Prince* and *People* strive,

The *Prince* to make his *People* thrive,
    Their Grievances to heal;
And all their good and adverse Fortune shares;
    They, in Return to *Him,*
    Pay mutual Rev'rence and Esteem,
And all his Pow'r, his Honour, Happiness, is theirs.

IV.

Such BRITAIN *is,* —— "Oh happy envy'd Isle,
"Sea-wall'd Commander of EUROPA's Trade,
    (Mournful VIRGINIA, sighing said)
    "Plac'd in thy Sovereign's Smile,
    "Whose Presence, like th'enliv'ning Sun,
    ("Who, where his genial Rays appear,
    "Productive of a fruitful Year,
"The lab'ring Hind's most greedy Hopes does bless)
"Does a diffusive Course of Goodness run,
"And ripens all thy Hopes into Success.
"Whilst I——and yet thy *eldest* Foreign Care—
    "Am numb'd with Winters cold and bare,
"And toilsome Summers fruitless Harvests share.
"O happy were my Lot,
    "Would that kind *Sun* dispense
"On me a nearer Ray of his mild Influence!
"I see his Light, I guess his Warmth,——I feel it not.

V.

She said, she sigh'd, ——AUGUSTUS heard;
    And straight, with willing Mind,
    For her Relief prepar'd,
    Her Sufferings to remove;
    He knew the MAN design'd
To be VIRGINIA's future Boast and Love;
He knew His native Vertue and His Worth;
    Nor long He staid,
    But all Things ready made,
With eager Haste He sent Him forth.

VI.

He came, He saw, and was belov'd;
    Like Lightning, quick, but strong,
An universal Gladness mov'd
    Throughout th'admiring Throng.
    No sooner was He seen,
    His calm, yet awful Look,
    Majestic, yet serene,
The very Pow'r of Prejudice remov'd,
    And ev'n His *Silence* spoke.
    But when His graceful *Tongue,*
Copious of Reason, did display
To Happiness, our nearest, surest Way,
    Ev'n Party-Rancour dy'd away,
    And private Spleen.
We found whence *Britain* is so blest,
Which had so much our Envy bore,
We found—and griev'd we found it not before——
    We found, that when by Love and Peace,
    A Prince has fix'd his Throne
    In ev'ry Subject's loial Breast,
No wonder Factions end, and Murmurs cease,—
Since now, what GEORGE is there, GOOCH[1] here has amply shewn.

VII.

Great REPRESENTATIVE!
What Thanks shall we return? What Honours shew?
To whom our *Staple* does its Being owe,
    By whom our Hopes revive:
    By whom all *Arts* recov'ring live,
That erst like drooping Plants had dropt their Head,
And once again, with native Vigour thrive;
    From whom VIRGINIA's Laws, that lay
    In blotted *Manuscripts* obscur'd,
    By vulgar Eyes unread,
Which whilome scarce the Light endur'd,
Begin to view again the Day,
    As rising from the Dead.

For this the careful *Artist* wakes,
And o'er his countless Brood he stands,
His numerous Hoards,
Of *speechless* Letters, *unform'd* Words,
Unjointed Questions, and *unmeaning* Breaks,
Which into Order rise, and Form, at his Commands.

VIII.

At his Commands they rise,
And cloath themselves with Sense,
Whether an antient Law that dormant lies,
The *sage judicious* FIVE revise,
(Great is your Care, your Pains be blest,
In all you undertake or do,
Ye *separated* FEW
Collective Genius of the rest!)
Or where the newer Acts commence:
Or where, on *solemn Subjects* to enlarge,
In more harmonious Words they shine;
New Beauties crowding every Line
Come forth their *Patron's* CHARGE.
There, PARKS,[2] thy Pains are lost—We find
The *Eloquence* employs the Mind,
The *Artist* lags behind.
HIS lab'ring Thoughts with Wisdom teem,
And struggle with the mighty Birth;
Thy *Art* does like *Lucina* seem,
And only helps to send the perfect *Embrio* forth.

IX.

Yet fair befal His Fame,
And may his Mem'ry long
In latest Annals live,
Who first contriv'd the *wondrous Frame,*
That to *dead Types* supply'd a *Tongue,*
And *Speech* to *lifeless Characters* could give.
O well was he employ'd the while,
And happy was the vent'rous Toil!

His Breast had compass'd some great Thought,
    Tho' formless yet, and void,
His busy Faculties were all employ'd,
How future Ages might be surest taught,
    By old Examples, long since done,
    What Paths to follow, what to shun,
    How Vertue ev'n in Death befriends,
      And how Ambition ends,
How *Socrates* instructed, *Caesar* fought;
    Long Time, his swelling Breast
    The great *Idea* had opprest,
'Till, fix'd at Length, he in a Rapture bid,
Come up a *glorious, great Design,* —And so it did.

X.

With less Expence of Care and Thought
    Did th'antient *Sage* surmise
The *Frame,* (thus *Epicurus* taught)
    And *Order* of the Earth to rise;
    And first he told the *Dance*
Of *Atoms* through th'expanded *Vast,*
    With *Accidents* endu'd,
Of *Figure, Gravity,* and *Magnitude;*
    By whose *Cohesion* fast,
As each to other did advance,
The *homogeneous Parts* ally'd,
Were in the strictest *Closure* ty'd,
    And *Matter* hence arose:
    Directed thence by sightless *Chance,*
The jumbled Mass *fortuitous* was hurl'd,
Where *Hap* a beauteous Fabric did compose,
    And made an *accidental World.*

XI.

Thus sung *Neocles'* unenlighten'd Son,
    When *Nature,* not improv'd by *Grace,*
But dimly on her *Vot'ries* shone,
    And half conceal'd her Face:

Foolish Wise-men! Nor was their Sense
Acuter to perceive a *Providence.*
　　To *Us,* a surer Doctrine's shewn,
　　　　Which *Truth* it self has spoke;
　　And faithful TYPES, by Time unbroke,
　Through many Ages have continu'd down
　　　The mighty Works to *Them* unknown.
In Clouds of wilful Ignorance *They* err'd,
Peccant in wild Conjectures of their own,
　　　　And each his own preferr'd.
　Hence *some* the World *eternal* Thought,
　To *discord some* its *Origin* assign'd,
　Others a perfect *Harmony* could find,
　　　　Destructive of that Scheme;
　　All with delusive Fancies fraught,
Dreamt idle Whims——*Creation* only was *no Dream.*

XII.

　　Happy the *Art,* by which we learn
　　　The Gloss of Errors to detect,
　　　The Vice of Habits to correct,
　And sacred Truths, from Falshood to discern!
　　By which we take a far-stretch'd View⎫
　And learn our Fathers Vertues to pursue, ⎬
　　　　Their Follies to eschew. ⎭
　And may that *Art* to latest Times proclaim
　　Its PATRON's Honourable Name.
　　As some *Sybillin* Book of old,
　　　Had *Sybils* known the Times to come,
　　　Wrapt in *Futurity's* dark Womb,
　Would thus these happy Days have told:
　　　"Revolving Ages hence,
　　　"In Climates now unknown,
　　"A *Ruler's* gentle Influence
　　"Shall o'er his Land be shewn;
　　"*Saturnian Reigns* shall be renew'd,
　　"Truth, Justice, Vertue, be pursu'd,
　　"Arts flourish, Peace shall crown the Plains,
"Where GOOCH administers, AUGUSTUS reigns.

Ebenezer Cooke

(fl. 1708-1732)

"The Sot-weed Factor"[1]

(London, 1708).

COndemn'd by Fate to way-ward Curse,
Of Friends unkind, and empty Purse;
Plagues worse then fill'd *Pandora's* Box,
I took my leave of *Albion's* Rocks:
With heavy Heart, concern'd that I
Was forc'd my Native Soil to fly,
And the *Old World* must bid good-buy.
But Heav'n ordain'd it should be so,
And to repine is vain we know:
Freighted with Fools, from *Plymouth* sound,
To *Mary-Land* our Ship was bound;
Where we arriv'd in dreadful Pain,
Shock'd by the Terrours of the Main;
For full three Months, our wavering Boat,

Did thro' the surley Ocean float,
And furious Storms and threat'ning Blasts,
Both tore our Sails and sprung our Masts:
Wearied, yet pleas'd, we did escape
Such Ills, we anchor'd at the (*a*) *Cape;*
But weighing soon, we plough'd the *Bay,*
To (*b*) Cove it in (*c*) *Piscato-way,*
Intending there to open Store,
I put myself and Goods a-shore:
Where soon repair'd a numerous Crew,
In Shirts and Drawers of (*d*) *Scotch-cloth* Blue.
With neither Stockings, Hat, nor Shooe.

N.B. The lettered footnotes are Cooke's own; the numbered notes are the editor's.

(*a*) By the *Cape,* is meant the *Capes* of *Virginia,* the first Land on the Coast of *Virginia* and *Mary-Land.*

(*b*) To *Cove* is to lie at Anchor safe in Harbour.

(*c*) The Bay of *Piscato-way,* the usual place where our Ships come to an Anchor in *Mary-Land.*

(*d*) The Planters generally wear Blue *Linnen.*

These *Sot-weed* Planters Crowd the Shoar,
In Hue as tawny as a Moor:
Figures so strange, no God design'd,
To be a part of Humane Kind:
But wanton Nature, void of Rest,
Moulded the brittle Clay in Jest.
At last a Fancy very odd
Took me, this was the Land of *Nod;*
Planted at first, when Vagrant *Cain,*
His Brother had unjustly slain:
Then conscious of the Crime he'd done,
From Vengeance dire, he hither run;
And in a Hut supinely dwelt,
The first in *Furs* and *Sot-weed* dealt.
And ever since his Time, the Place,
Has harbour'd a detested Race;
Who when they cou'd not live at Home,
For Refuge to these Worlds did roam;
In hopes by Flight they might prevent,
The Devil and his fell intent;
Obtain from Tripple Tree[2] repreive,
And Heav'n and Hell alike deceive:
But e're their Manners I display, ⎫
I think it fit I open lay   ⎬
My Entertainment by the way;   ⎭
That Strangers well may be aware on,
What homely Diet they must fare on.
To touch that Shoar, where no good Sense is found,
But Conversation's lost, and Manners drown'd.
I crost unto the other side,   ⎫
A River whose impetuous Tide,   ⎬
The Savage Borders does divide; ⎭
In such a shining odd invention,
I scarce can give its due Dimention.
The *Indians* call this watry Waggon
(*e*) *Canoo,* a Vessel none can brag on;
Cut from a *Popular-Tree,* or *Pine,*
And fashion'd like a Trough for Swine:
In this most noble Fishing-Boat,

(*e*) A *Canoo* is an *Indian* Boat, cut out of the body of a Popler-Tree.

I boldly put myself a-float;
Standing Erect, with Legs stretch'd wide,
We paddled to the other side:
Where being Landed safe by hap,
As *Sol* fell into *Thetis* Lap.
A ravenous Gang bent on the stroul,
Of (*f*) Wolves for Prey, began to howl;
This put me in a pannick Fright,
Least I should be devoured quite:
But as I there a musing stood,
And quite benighted in a Wood,
A Female Voice pierc'd thro' my Ears,
Crying, *You Rogue drive home the Steers.*
I listen'd to th'attractive sound,   ⎫
And straight a Herd of Cattel found   ⎬
Drove by a Youth, and homewards bound: ⎭
Cheer'd with the sight, I straight thought fit,
To ask where I a Bed might get.
The surley Peasant bid me stay,
And ask'd from whom (*g*) I'de run away.
Surpriz'd at such a saucy Word,
I instantly lugg'd out my Sword;
Swearing I was no Fugitive,   ⎫
But from *Great-Britain* did arrive,   ⎬
In hopes I better there might Thrive. ⎭
To which he mildly made reply,
I beg your Pardon, Sir, *that I*
Should talk to you Unmannerly;   ⎫
But if you please to go with me   ⎬
To yonder House, you'll welcome be. ⎭
Encountring soon the smoaky Seat,
The Planter old did thus me greet:
"Whether you come from Goal or Colledge,
"You're welcome to my certain Knowledge;
"And if you please all Night to stay,
"My Son shall put you in the way.

(*f*) Wolves are very numerous in *Mary-Land.*

(*g*) 'Tis supposed by the Planters, that all unknown Persons are run away
from some Master.

Which offer I most kindly took,
And for a Seat did round me look:
When presently amongst the rest,
He plac'd his unknown *English* Guest,
Who found them drinking for a whet,[3]
A Cask of (*h*) Syder on the Fret,[4]
Till Supper came upon the Table,
On which I fed whilst I was able.
So after hearty Entertainment,
Of Drink and Victuals without Payment;
For Planters Tables, you must know,
Are free for all that come and go.
While (*i*) Pon and Milk, with (*k*) Mush well stoar'd,
In wooden Dishes grac'd the Board;
With (*l*) Homine and Syder-pap,
(Which scarce a hungry Dog wou'd lap)
Well stuff'd with Fat, from Bacon fry'd,
Or with *Molossus* dulcify'd.
Then out our Landlord pulls a Pouch,
As greasy as the Leather Couch
On which he sat, and straight begun,
To load with Weed his *Indian* Gun;[5]
In length, scarce longer than ones Finger,
Or that for which the Ladies linger:
His Pipe smoak'd out with aweful Grace,
With aspect grave and solemn pace;
The reverend Sire walks to a Chest,
Of all his Furniture the best,
Closely confin'd within a Room,
Which seldom felt the weight of Broom;
From thence he lugs a Cag of Rum,
And nodding to me, thus begun:
I find, says he, you don't much care,
For this our *Indian* Country Fare;

(*h*) Syder-pap is a sort of Food made of Syder and small Homine, like our Oat-meal.

(*i*) Pon is Bread made of *Indian-Corn*.

(*k*) Mush is a sort of Hasty-pudding made with Water and *Indian* Flower.

(*l*) Homine is a Dish that is made of boiled *Indian* Wheat, eaten with Molossus, or Bacon-Fat.

But let me tell you, Friend of mine, ⎫
You may be glad of it in time,   ⎬
Tho' now your Stomach is so fine;   ⎭
And if within this Land you stay,
You'll find it true what I do say.
This said, the Rundlet up he threw,
And bending backwards strongly drew:
I pluck'd as stoutly for my part,
Altho' it made me sick at Heart,
And got so soon into my Head
I scare cou'd find my way to Bed;
Where I was instantly convey'd
By one who pass'd for Chamber-Maid;
Tho' by her loose and sluttish Dress,
She rather seem'd a *Bedlam-Bess*:
Curious to know from whence she came,
I prest her to declare her Name.
She Blushing, seem'd to hide her Eyes,
And thus in Civil Terms replies;
In better Times, e'er to this Land,
I was unhappily Trapann'd;[6]
Perchance as well I did appear,   ⎫
As any Lord or Lady here,   ⎬
Not then a Slave for twice two (*a*) Year. ⎭
My Cloaths were fashionably new,
Nor were my Shifts of Linnen Blue;
But things are changed now at the Hoe,
I daily work, and Bare-foot go,
In weeding Corn or feeding Swine,
I spend my melancholy Time.
Kidnap'd and Fool'd, I hither fled,
To shun a hated Nuptial (*b*) Bed,
And to my cost already find,
Worse Plagues than those I left behind.
Whate'er the Wanderer did profess,
Good-faith I cou'd not choose but guess
The Cause which brought her to this place,

(*a*) 'Tis the Custom for Servants to be obliged for four Years to very servile Work; after which time they have their Freedom.

(*b*) These are the general Excuses made by *English* Women, which are sold, or sell themselves to *Mary-Land*.

Was supping e'er the Priest said Grace.
Quick as my Thoughts, the Slave was fled,
(Her Candle left to shew my Bed)
Which made of Feathers soft and good,
Close in the (c) Chimney-corner stood;
I threw me down expecting Rest,
To be in golden Slumbers blest:
But soon a noise disturb'd my quiet,
And plagu'd me with nocturnal Riot;
A Puss which in the ashes lay,
With grunting Pig began a Fray;
And prudent Dog, that Feuds might cease,
Most strongly bark'd to keep the Peace.
This Quarrel scarcely was decided,
By stick that ready lay provided;
But *Reynard* arch and cunning Loon,
Broke into my Appartment soon;
In hot pursuit of Ducks and Geese,
With fell intent the same to seize:
Their Cackling Plaints with strange surprize,
Chac'd Sleeps thick Vapours from my Eyes:
Raging I jump'd upon the Floar,
And like a Drunken Saylor Swore;
With Sword I fiercely laid about,
And soon dispers'd the Feather'd Rout:
The Poultry out of Window flew,
And *Reynard* cautiously withdrew:
The Dogs who this Encounter heard,
Fiercly themselves to aid me rear'd,
And to the Place of Combat run,
Exactly as the Field was won.
Fretting and hot as roasting Capon,
And greasy as a Flitch of Bacon;
I to the Orchard did repair,
To Breathe the cool and open Air;
Expecting there the rising Day,
Extended on a Bank I lay:
But Fortune here, that saucy Whore,
Disturb'd me worse and plagu'd me more, }
Than she had done the night before.

(c) Beds stand in the Chimney-corner in this Country.

Hoarse croaking (d) Frogs did 'bout me ring, ⎫
Such Peals the Dead to Life wou'd bring,   ⎬
A Noise might move their Wooden King.   ⎭
I stuff'd my Ears with Cotten white
For fear of being deaf out-right,
And curst the melancholy Night:
But soon my Vows I did recant,
And Hearing as a Blessing grant;
When a confounded Rattle-Snake,
With hissing made my Heart to ake:
Not knowing how to fly the Foe,
Or whether in the Dark to go;
By strange good Luck, I took a Tree,
Prepar'd by Fate to set me free;
Where riding on a Limb a-stride,   ⎫
Night and the Branches did me hide, ⎬
And I the Devil and Snake defy'd. ⎭
Not yet from Plagues exempted quite,
The curst Muskitoes did me bite;
Till rising Morn' and blushing Day,
Drove both my Fears and Ills away;
And from Night's Errors set me free.
Discharg'd from hospitable Tree;
I did to Planters Booth repair, ⎫
And there at Breakfast nobly Fare, ⎬
On rashier broil'd of infant Bear: ⎭
I thought the Cub delicious Meat,
Which ne'er did ought but Chesnuts eat;
Nor was young Orsin's flesh the worse,
Because he suck'd a Pagan Nurse.
Our Breakfast done, my Landlord stout,
Handed a Glass of Rum about;
Pleas'd with the Treatment I did find,
I took my leave of Oast so kind;
Who to oblige me, did provide,
His eldest Son to be my Guide,
And lent me Horses of his own, ⎫
A skittish Colt, and aged Rhoan, ⎬
The four-leg'd prop of his Wife *Joan*. ⎭

(d) Frogs are called *Virginea* Bells, and make, (both in that Country and *Mary-Land*) during the Night, a very hoarse ungrateful Noise.

Steering our Barks in Trot or Pace,
We sail'd directly for a place
In *Mary-Land* of high renown,
Known by the Name of *Battle-Town*.
To view the Crowds did there resort, ⎫
Which Justice made, and Law their sport, ⎬
In that sagacious County Court: ⎭
Scarce had we enter'd on the way,
Which thro' thick Woods and Marshes lay;
But *Indians* strange did soon appear,
In hot persuit of wounded Deer;
No mortal Creature can express,
His wild fantastick Air and Dress;
His painted Skin in colours dy'd, ⎫
His sable Hair in Satchel[7] ty'd, ⎬
Shew'd Savages not free from Pride: ⎭
His tawny Thighs, and Bosom bare,
Disdain'd a useless Coat to wear,
Scorn'd Summer's Heat, and Winters Air;
His manly Shoulders such as please,
Widows and Wives, were bath'd in Grease
Of Cub and Bear, whose supple Oil,
Prepar'd his Limbs 'gainst Heat or Toil.
Thus naked Pict in Battel faught,
Or undisguis'd his Mistress sought;
And knowing well his Ware was good,
Refus'd to screen it with a Hood;
His Visage dun, and chin that ne'er ⎫
Did Raizor feel or Scissers bear, ⎬
Or know the Ornament of Hair, ⎭
Look'd sternly Grim, surpriz'd with Fear,
I spur'd my Horse, as he drew near:
But Rhoan who better knew than I,
The little Cause I had to fly;
Seem'd by his solemn steps and pace,
Resolv'd I shou'd the Specter face,
Nor faster mov'd, tho' spur'd and lick'd,
Than *Balaam's* Ass by Prophet kick'd.
Kekicknitop (*a*) the Heathen cry'd:

(*a*) *Kekicknitop* is an *Indian* Expression, and signifies no more than this, *How
do you do?*

How is it *Tom.* my Friend reply'd,
Judging from thence the Brute was civel,
I boldly fac'd the Courteous Devil;
And lugging out a Dram of Rum,
I gave his Tawny worship some:
Who in his language as I guess,
(My Guide informing me no less,)
Implored the (*b*) Devil, me to bless.
I thank'd him for his good Intent,
And forwards on my Journey went,
Discoursing as along I rode,
Whether this Race was framed by God
Or whether some Malignant pow'r,
Contriv'd them in an evil hour
And from his own Infernal Look;
Their Dusky form and Image took:
From hence we fell to Argument
Whence Peopled was this Continent,
My Friend suppos'd *Tartarians* wild,
Or *Chinese* from their Home exiled;
Wandering thro' Mountains hid with Snow,
And Rills did in the Vallies flow,
Far to the South of *Mexico*:
Broke thro' the Barrs which Nature cast,
And wide unbeaten Regions past,
Till near those Streams the humane deludge roll'd,
Which sparkling shin'd with glittering Sands of Gold;
And fetch (*d*) *Pizarro* from the (*e*) *Iberian* Shoar,

(*b*) These *Indians* worship the Devil, and pray to him as we do to God Almighty. 'Tis suppos'd, That *America* was peopl'd from *Scythia* or *Tartaria*, which Borders on *China*, by reason the *Tartarians* and *Americans* very much agree in their Manners, Arms and Government. Other Persons are of Opinion, that the *Chinese* first peopled the *West Indies;* imagining *China* and the Southern part of *America* to be contiguous. Others believe that the *Phoenicians* who were very skilful Mariners, first planted a Colony in the Isles of *America*, and supply'd the Persons left to inhabit there with Women and all other Necessaries; till either the Death or Shipwreck of the first Discoverers, or some other Misfortune occasioned the loss of the Discovery, which had been purchased by the Peril of the first Adventurers.

(*d*) *Pizzarro* was the Person that conquer'd *Peru;* a Man of a most bloody Disposition, base, treacherous, covetous, and revengeful.

(*e*) *Spanish* Shoar.

To Rob the Natives of their fatal Stoar.
I Smil'd to hear my young Logician,
Thus Reason like a Politician;
Who ne're by Fathers Pains and Earning
Had got at Mother *Cambridge* Learning;
Where Lubber youth just free from birch
Most stoutly drink to prop the Church;
Nor with (*f*) *Grey Groat* had taken Pains
To purge his Head and Cleanse his Reines:
And in obedience to the Colledge,
Had pleas'd himself with carnal Knowledge:
And tho' I lik'd the youngester's Wit,
I judg'd the Truth he had not hit;
And could not choose but smile to think
What they could do for Meat and Drink,
Who o'er so many Desarts ran,
With Brats and Wives in *Caravan;*
Unless perchance they'd got the Trick,
To eat no more than Porker sick;
Or could with well contented Maws,
Quarter like (*g*) Bears upon their Paws.
Thinking his Reasons to confute,
I gravely thus commenc'd Dispute,
And urg'd that tho' a *Chinese* Host,
Might penetrate this *Indian* Coast;
Yet this was certainly most true,
They never cou'd the Isles subdue;
For knowing not to steer a Boat,
They could not on the Ocean float,
Or plant their Sunburnt Colonies,
In Regions parted by the Seas:
I thence inferr'd (*h*) *Phoenicians* old,
Discover'd first with Vessels bold

(*f*) There is a very bad Custom in some Colledges, of giving the Students *A Groat ad purgandas Rhenes,* which is usually employ'd to the use of the *Donor.*

(*g*) Bears are said to live by sucking of their *Paws,* according to the Notion of some Learned Authors.

(*h*) The *Phoenicians* were the best and boldest Saylors of Antiquity, and indeed the only *Persons,* in former Ages, who durst venture themselves on the Main Sea.

These Western Shoars, and planted here,
Returning once or twice a Year,
With *Naval Stoars* and Lasses kind,
To comfort those were left behind;
Till by the Winds and Tempest toar,
From their intended Golden Shoar;
They suffer'd Ship-wreck, or were drown'd,
And lost the World so newly found.
But after long and learn'd Contenion,
We could not finish our dissention;
And when that both had talk'd their fill,
We had the self same Notion still.
Thus Parson grave well read and Sage,
Does in dispute with Priest engage;
The one protests they are not Wise,
Who judge by (*i*) Sense and trust their Eyes;
And vows he'd burn for it at Stake,
That Man may God his Maker make;
The other smiles at his Religion,
And vows he's but a learned Widgeon:
And when they have empty'd all their stoar ⎫
From Books and Fathers, are not more   ⎬
Convinc'd or wiser than before.   ⎭
     Scarce had we finish'd serious Story,
But I espy'd the Town before me,
And roaring Planters on the ground,
Drinking of Healths in Circle round:
Dismounting Steed with friendly Guide,
Our Horses to a Tree we ty'd,
And forwards pass'd amongst the Rout,
To chuse convenient *Quarters* out:
But being none were to be found,
We sat like others on the ground
Carousing Punch in open Air
Till Cryer did the Court declare;
The planting Rabble being met,
Their Drunken Worships likewise set:

(*i*) The *Priests* argue, That our Senses in the point of *Transubstantiation* ought
not to be believed, for tho' the Consecrated Bread has all the accidents of Bread,
yet they affirm, 'tis the Body of Christ, and not Bread but Flesh and Bones.

Cryer proclaims that Noise shou'd cease,
And streight the Lawyers broke the Peace.
Wrangling for Plantiff and Defendant,
I thought they ne'er wou'd make an end on't:
With nonsence, stuff and false quotations,
With brazen Lyes and Allegations;
And in the splitting of the Cause,
They us'd such Motions with their Paws,
As shew'd their Zeal was strongly bent,
In Blows to end the Argument.
A reverend Judge, who to the shame
Of all the Bench, cou'd write his (k) Name;
At Petty-fogger took offence,
And wonder'd at his Impudence.
My Neighbour *Dash* with scorn replies,
And in the Face of Justice flies:
The Bench in fury streight divide,
And Scribbles take, or Judges side;
The Jury, Lawyers, and their Clyents,
Contending, fight like earth-born Gyants:
But Sheriff wily lay perdue,
Hoping Indictments wou'd ensue,
And when————————————
A Hat or Wig fell in the way,
He seiz'd them for the *Queen* as stray:
The Court adjourn'd in usual manner,
In Battle Blood, and fractious Clamour;
I thought it proper to provide,
A Lodging for myself and Guide,
So to our Inn we march'd away,
Which at a little distance lay;
Where all things were in such Confusion,
I thought the World at its conclusion:
A Herd of Planters on the ground,
O'er-whelm'd with Punch, dead drunk we found:
Others were fighting and contending,
Some burnt their Cloaths to save the mending.
A few whose Heads by frequent use,

(k) In the County-Court of *Mary-Land,* very few of the Justices of the *Peace* can write or read.

Could better bare the potent Juice,
Gravely debated State Affairs.
Whilst I most nimbly trip'd up Stairs;
Leaving my Friend discoursing oddly,
And mixing things Prophane and Godly:
Just then beginning to be Drunk,
As from the Company I slunk,
To every Room and Nook I crept,
In hopes I might have somewhere slept;
But all the bedding was possest
By one or other drunken Guest:
But after looking long about,
I found an antient Corn-loft out,
Glad that I might in quiet sleep,
And there my bones unfractur'd keep.
I lay'd me down secure from Fray,
And soundly snoar'd till break of Day;
When waking fresh I sat upright,
And found my Shoes were vanish'd quite,
Hat, Wig, and Stockings, all were fled
From this extended *Indian* Bed:
Vext at the Loss of Goods and Chattel,
I swore I'd give the Rascal battel,
Who had abus'd me in this sort,
And Merchant Stranger made his Sport.
I furiously descended Ladder;
No Hare in *March* was ever madder:
In vain I search'd for my Apparel,
And did with Oast and Servants Quarrel;
For one whose Mind did much aspire
To (*a*) Mischief, threw them in the Fire;
Equipt with neither Hat nor Shooe,
I did my coming hither rue,
And doubtful thought what I should do:
Then looking round, I saw my Friend
Lie naked on a Tables end;
A Sight so dismal to behold,
One wou'd have judg'd him dead and cold;
When wringing of his bloody Nose,

(*a*) 'Tis the Custom of the Planters, to throw their own, or any other Persons Hat, Wig, Shooes or Stockings in the Fire.

By fighting got we may suppose;
I found him not so fast asleep,
Might give his Friends a cause to weep:
Rise (*b*) *Oronooko,* rise, said I,
And from this *Hell* and *Bedlam* fly.
My Guide starts up, and in amaze,
With blood-shot Eyes did round him gaze;
At length with many a sigh and groan,
He went in search of aged Rhoan;
But Rhoan, tho' seldom us'd to faulter,
Had fairly this time slipt his Halter;
And not content all Night to stay
Ty'd up from Fodder, ran away:
After my Guide to ketch him ran,
And so I lost both Horse and Man;
Which Disappointment, tho' so great,
Did only Mirth and Jests create:
Till one more Civil than the rest,
In Conversation for the best,
Observing that for want of Rhoan,
I should be left to walk alone;
Most readily did me intreat,
To take a Bottle at his Seat;
A Favour at that time so great,
I blest my kind propitious Fate;
And finding soon a fresh supply,
Of Cloaths from Stoar-house kept hard by,
I mounted streight on such a Steed,
Did rather curb, than whipping need;
And straining at the usual rate,   }
With spur of Punch which lay in Pate, }
E'er long we lighted at the Gate: }
Where in an antient *Cedar* House,
Dwelt my new Friend, a (*a*) Cockerouse;
Whose Fabrick, tho' 'twas built of Wood,
Had many Springs and Winters stood;

(*a*) Cockerouse, is a Man of Quality.

(*b*) Planters are usually call'd by the Name of *Oronooko,* from their Planting *Oronooko-Tobacco.*

When sturdy Oaks, and lofty Pines
Were level'd with (*b*) Musmelion Vines,
And Plants eradicated were,
By Hurricanes into the air;
There with good Punch and apple Juice,
We spent our Hours without abuse:
Till Midnight in her sable Vest,
Persuaded Gods and Men to rest;
And with a pleasing kind surprize,
Indulg'd soft Slumbers to my Eyes.
Fierce (*c*) *AEthon* courser of the Sun,
Had half his Race exactly run;
And breath'd on me a fiery Ray,   )
Darting hot Beams the following Day, }
When snug in Blanket white I lay:)
But Heat and (*d*) *Chinces* rais'd the Sinner,
Most opportunely to his Dinner;
Wild Fowl and Fish delicious Meats,   )
As good as *Neptune's* Doxy[8] eats, }
Began our Hospitable Treat;   )
Fat Venson follow'd in the Rear,
And Turkies wild Luxurious Chear:
But what the Feast did most commend,
Was hearty welcom from my Friend.
Thus having made a noble Feast;
And eat as well as pamper'd Priest,
Madera strong in flowing Bowls,
Fill'd with extream, delight our Souls;
Till wearied with a purple Flood,
Of generous Wine (the Giant's blood,
As Poets feign) away I made,
For some refreshing verdant Shade;
Where musing on my Rambles strange,
And Fortune which so oft did change;
In midst of various Contemplations

(*b*) Musmilleon Vines are what we call Muskmilleon Plants.

(*c*) *AEthon* is one of the Poetical Horses of the Sun.

(*d*) *Chinces* are a sort of Vermin like our *Bugs* in *England*.

Of Fancies odd, and Meditations,
I slumber'd long———————
Till hazy Night with noxious Dews,
Did Sleep's unwholsom Fetters lose:
With Vapours chil'd, and misty air,
To fire-side I did repair;
Near which a jolly Female Crew,
Were deep engag'd at *Lanctre-Looe;*
In Nightrails white, with dirty Mein,
Such Sights are scare in *England* seen:
I thought them first some Witches bent,
On Black Designs in dire Convent.
Till one who with affected air,
Had nicely learn'd to Curse and Swear:
Cry'd Dealing's lost is but a Flam,[9]
And vow'd by G-d she'd keep her *Pam.*[10]
When dealing through the board had run,
They ask'd me kindly to make one;
Not staying often to be bid,
I sat me down as others did:
We scarce had play'd a Round about,
But that these *Indian* Froes[11] fell out.
D—m you, says one, tho' now so brave,
I knew you late a Four Years Slave;
What if for Planters Wife you go,
Nature design'd you for the Hoe.
Rot you replies the other streight,
The Captain kiss'd you for his Freight;
And if the Truth was known aright,
And how you walk'd the Streets by night,
You'd blush (if one cou'd blush) for shame,
Who from *Bridewell* or *Newgate* came.
From Words they fairly fell to Blows,
And being loath to interpose,
Or meddle in the Wars of Punk,[12]
Away to Bed in hast I slunk.
Waking next day, with aking Head,

(*f*) Wild Turkies are very good Meat, and prodigiously large in *Maryland.*
[No corresponding (*f*) appears in the body of the poem. Cooke or the printer
omitted note (*e*) altogether.]

And Thirst, that made me quit my Bed;
I rigg'd myself, and soon got up,
To cool my Liver with a Cup
Of (a) *Succahana* fresh and clear,
Not half so good as *English* Beer;
Which ready stood in Kitchin Pail,
And was in fact but *Adam's* Ale;
For Planters Cellars you must know,
Seldom with good *October* flow,
But Perry Quince and Apple Juice,
Spout from the Tap like any Sluce;
Untill the Cask's grown low and stale,
They're forc'd again to (b) Goad and Pail:
The soathing drought scarce down my Throat,
Enough to put a Ship a float,
With Cockerouse as I was sitting,
I felt a Feaver Intermitting;
A fiery Pulse beat in my Veins,
From Cold I felt resembling Pains:
This cursed seasoning I remember,
Lasted from *March* to cold *December;*
Nor would it then its *Quarters* shift,
Until by *Cardus*[13] turn'd a drift,
And had my Doctress wanted skill,
Or Kitchin Physick at his will,
My Father's Son had lost his Lands,
And never seen the *Goodwin-Sands*:
But thanks to Fortune and a Nurse
Whose Care depended on my Purse,
I saw myself in good Condition,
Without the help of a Physitian:
At length the shivering ill relieved,
Which long my Head and Heart had grieved;
I then began to think with Care,
How I might sell my *British* Ware,
That with my Freight I might comply,
Did on my Charter-party lie:

(a) *Succahana* is Water.

(b) A *Goad* grows upon an *Indian* Vine, resembling a Bottle, when ripe it is hollow; this the Planters make use of to drink water out of.

To this intent, with Guide before,
I tript it to the Eastern Shoar;
While riding near a Sandy Bay,
I met a *Quaker, Yea* and *Nay;*
A Pious Conscientious Rogue,
As e'er woar Bonnet or a Brogue,
Who neither Swore nor kept his Word,
But cheated in the Fear of God;
And when his Debts he would not pay,
By Light within he ran away.
With this sly Zealot soon I struck
A Bargain for my *English* Truck,
Agreeing for ten thousand weight,
Of *Sot-weed* good and fit for freight,
Broad *Oronooko* bright and sound,
The growth and product of his ground;
In Cask that should contain compleat,
Five hundred of Tobacco neat.
The Contract thus betwixt us made,
Not well acquainted with the Trade,
My Goods I trusted to the Cheat,
Whose crop was then aboard the Fleet;
And going to receive my own,
I found the Bird was newly flown:
Cursing this execrable Slave,
This damn'd pretended Godly Knave;
On due Revenge and Justice bent,
I instantly to Counsel went,
Unto an ambodexter (*c*) *Quack,*
Who learnedly had got the knack
Of giving Glisters, making Pills,
Of filling Bonds, and forging Wills;
And with a stock of Impudence,
Supply'd his want of Wit and Sense;
With Looks demure, amazing People,
No wiser than a Daw in Steeple;
My Anger flushing in my Face,
I stated the preceding Case:
And of my Money was so lavish,

(*c*) This Fellow was an Apothecary, and turn'd an Attorney at Law.

That he'd have poyson'd half the Parish,
And hang'd his Father on a Tree,
For such another tempting Fee;
Smiling, said he, the Cause is clear,
I'll manage him you need not fear;
The Case is judg'd, good Sir, but look ⎫
In *Galen,* No—in my Lord *Cook,*   ⎬
I vow to God I was mistook: ⎭
I'll take out a Provincial Writ,
And Trounce him for his Knavish Wit;
Upon my Life we'll win the Cause,
With all the ease I cure the (*d*) *Yaws*:
Resolv'd to plague the holy Brother,
I set one Rogue to catch another;
To try the Cause then fully bent,
Up to (*e*) *Annapolis* I went,
A City Situate on a Plain,
Where scarce a House will keep out Rain;
The Buildings fram'd with Cyprus rare,
Resembles much our *Southwark* Fair:
But Stranger here will scarcely meet,
With Market-place, Exchange, or Street;
And if the Truth I may report,
'Tis not so large as *Tottenham Court*.
St. *Mary's* once was in repute,   ⎫
Now here the Judges try the Suit,   ⎬
And Lawyers twice a Year dispute: ⎭
As oft the Bench most gravely meet,   ⎫
Some to get Drunk, and some to eat   ⎬
A swinging share of Country Treat.   ⎭
But as for Justice right or wrong,
Not one amongst the numerous throng,
Knows what they mean, or has the Heart,
To give his Verdict on a Stranger's part:
Now Court being call'd by beat of Drum,
The Judges left their Punch and Rum,
When Pettifogger Docter draws,

(*d*) The *Yaws* is the *Pox*.

(*e*) The chief of *Maryland* containing about twenty four *Houses*.

His Paper forth, and opens Cause:
And least I shou'd the better get,
Brib'd *Quack* supprest his Knavish Wit.
So Maid upon the downy Field,
Pretends a Force, and Fights to yeild:
The Byast Court without delay,
Adjudg'd my Debt in Country Pay;
In (*f*) Pipe staves, Corn, or Flesh of Boar,
Rare Cargo for the *English* Shoar:
Raging with Grief, full speed I ran,
To joyn the Fleet at (*g*) *Kicketan;*[14]
Embarqu'd and waiting for a Wind,
I left this dreadful Curse behind.

May Canniballs transported o'er the Sea
Prey on these Slaves, as they have done on me;
May never Merchant's, trading Sails explore
This Cruel, this Inhospitable Shoar;
But left abandon'd by the World to starve,
May they sustain the Fate they well deserve:
May they turn Savage, or as *Indians* Wild,
From Trade, Converse, and Happiness exil'd;
Recreant to Heaven, may they adore the Sun,
And into Pagan Superstitions run
For Vengence ripe————————
May Wrath Divine then lay those Regions wast
Where no Man's (*) Faithful, nor a Woman Chast.

(*f*) There is a Law in this Country, the Plantiff may pay his Debt in Country pay, which consists in the produce of his Plantation.

(*g*) The homeward bound Fleet meets here.

(*) The Author does not intend by this, any of the *English* Gentlemen resident there.

Richard Lewis

(fl. 1725-1746)

"To His Excellency
BENEDICT LEONARD CALVERT, Govern-

our, and Commander in Chief, in and over the
Province of MARYLAND."

TEXT: *Muscipula . . . translated into English by R. Lewis* (Annapolis,
1728), pp. v-ix.

PERMIT GREAT SIR! a Visit from the Muse,
Nor to her *comic Tale* your Smile refuse:
With humble Duty she presumes to lay
Before your curious View,—this FIRST ESSAY
Of *Latin Poetry,* in *English Dress,*
Which MARYLAND hath publish'd from the Press.
Could I preserve that Beauty in *my Lays,*
Which HOLDSWORTH'S[1] bright Original displays;
I need not, then, the *Critick's* Censure fear,
Secure to please the most judicious Ear.
But all TRANSLATORS must with Grief confess,
That while they strive in ENGLISH to express
The pleasing Charms of *Latin* Poesy,
They lose its genuine Life, and Energy:
Some Grace peculiar thro' each Language flows,
Which other Idioms never can disclose.
Besides, in all GOOD POETRY, we find
A *Spirit* of a most exalted kind:
To pour it off, in vain the *Artist* tries,⎫
The *subtile Spirit* in *Transfusion* flies ⎬
And the *insipid Version,* lifeless lies. ⎭
These Hardships, on the *happiest Muse,* attend,
With Candor, then, *my artless Verse* befriend:
Nor *Here,* expect such *"soft enchanting Strains,"*
As once You heard on fair ITALIAN PLAINS;
Where, the kind Climate does the Muse inspire ⎫
With Thoughts sublime, and gay poetic Fire; ⎬
Where VIRGIL, OVID, HORACE, struck the Lyre: ⎭
Who still demand our Wonder, and our Praise;
Nor spite, nor Time, shall ever blast their Bays.

There, PAINTURE breathes, *There,* STATUARY lives,
And MUSIC most delightful Rapture gives:
There, pompous Piles of *Building* pierce the Skies,
And endless Scenes of *Pleasure* court the Eyes.

While *Here,* rough Woods embrown the Hills and Plains,
Mean are the *Buildings,* artless are the *Swains*:
"To raise the Genius," W E no Time can spare,
A *bare Subsistence* claims our utmost Care.
But from the gen'rous Purpose of *Your* Heart,
Which, in *Your Speech* you graciously impart;
To give to VIRTUE its deserv'd Applause,
To punish daring VICE, by wholsom Laws;
To animate the PEOPLE, now dismayed,
And add new Life to our declining TRADE;
We hope to see soft Joys o'erspread the *Land,*
And *happier Times,* deriv'd from *Your Command.*
For should Your EXCELLENCY'S Plan take Place,
Soon will returning *Plenty* shew its Face:
The *Markets* for our STAPLE, would advance,
Nor shall we live, as *now* we do, by CHANCE.
No more, the lab'ring PLANTER shall complain
How *vast* his *Trouble!* but how *small* his *Gain!*
    THE MARINER shall bless you, when releast
From Toil, which sunk him down from *Man* to *Beast.*
The MERCHANT, shall applaud your Care, to free
His freighted Vessel from the *Wintry Sea.*
And *Husbands, Brothers, Sons,* from *Shipwreck* save'd,
In Climes remote, with Joy shall be receiv'd;
And thankful, tell their *Mothers, Sisters, Wives,*
That YOU, next PROVIDENCE, preserv'd their Lives.
    WHEN *Records,* which to *You,* their Being owe,
These *Acts* to *late Posterity* shall show;
Our *Children's Children* shall extol YOUR Name,
And YOUR'S shall equal your great GRANDSIRE'S Fame,
HIM, shall they stile the *Founder* of the *State,*
From YOU its *Preservation* shall they date.
Oh, may kind HEAV'N regard me, while I pray,
That these great Blessings, might attend YOUR Sway!
May *Peace* harmonious, in our *Councils* reign,
And no *Dissensions* make their Meeting vain!
May the PREROGATIVE receive no Wound,
And PRIVILEGE preserve its proper Bound!
May ALL our SENATORS, with honest Zeal,
To PRIVATE GAIN prefer the PUBLIC WEAL!
Then, shall *Their Actions* due Applause obtain,

And ARTS POLITE, shall shine in this DOMAIN;
Then, shall some future *Bard* THEIR Praise rehearse;
And paint YOUR *happy Rule* in *never-dying Verse.*
But while thus fondly I persue my Rhyme,   ⎫
And trespass on Your EXCELLENCY'S Time,   ⎬
Against the PUBLIC I commit a Crime.   ⎭
    YET—hear me!—while I beg you to excuse,
This bold Intrusion of an *unknown Muse;*
And if her Faults too manifest appear,
And her rude Numbers should offend your Ear,
Then, if you please with your forgiving Breath,
Which can reprieve the Wretch condemn'd, from Death,
To speak a Pardon for her Errors past,
This FIRST Poetic Crime, shall prove her LAST.

"CARMEN SECULARE,
For the Year M, DCC, XXXII."

TEXT: *Carmen Seculare, For the Year M, DCC, XXXII* ([Annapolis],
    1732).

        Seculo *festas referente Luces*
        Reddidi Carmen.
                HOR. Ode vi. Lib. iv.[1]

Those who write the Rise and first Progress of an Infant State,
ought to describe It in Language simple and unadorn'd as are its Man-
ners; while the large Accessions of Arts, and Empire, must be painted
in all the Elegance and Sublimity that accompany those happy Periods.
                BACON Advanc. of Learn.

To the Right Honourable C H A R L E S , Absolute Lord and
Proprietary of the Provinces of *Maryland,* and *Avalon,* Lord Baron of
Baltimore, &c.

TO You, My LORD, this Tributary Lay
By Duty prompted, I submissive pay;
And hail You welcom to this fertile Land,
Which yields Obedience to Your just Command.
When You, far distant Regions to explore,
Advent'rous, left your charming native Shore;
To view the Arts, and Customs of Mankind,

And by Experience form your Noble Mind.
We heard your Dangers told, with trembling Ears,
We could not overcome our anxious Fears;
Lest the rough billows which the Deep deform,
Shou'd dash you out from Life, in some sad Storm.
We wish'd that You the Pilot would command,
To steer your Ship to this your subject Land;
To bring her to these Coasts, auspicious Gales
Shou'd crowding wait, to fill her spreading Sails,
And Providence shou'd make your Life its Care, ⎞
If Heav'n, regardful of our Hearts sincere,   ⎬
Indulgent, listen'd to our gen'ral Pray'r.   ⎠
Our Wish is granted!—We behold your Face,
We view your LADY, form'd with beauteous Grace.
In vain the Muse her Colours would employ,
To paint in Verse, the vast diffusive Joy,
Which Your long-wish'd Arrival *now* imparts,
Which *now* dilates your Tenants grateful Hearts.

THE Cannon that with loud-resounding roar,
Cheerful, proclaim'd the News, from Shore to Shore,
Whose Sound, wide-bursting o'er the winding Floods,
Was borne by Echo thro' our lofty Woods.
The gladsom Pyre enkindled, blazing bright,
Th' illumin'd Domes that made a Day of Night,
Were Signals of our Joy, which ill reveal
The inward Pleasure that your People feel.

WHILE thus your faithful Tenants all rejoyce,
And speak You welcom, with united Voice,
Gracious, My LORD, accept my mean ADDRESS,
That wishes You consummate Happiness;
And that each Joy which crowns the Marriage State,
On You, and Your illustrious Bride, may wait:
May ev'ry circling Year Your Bliss improve,
Augment Your Fortune, and exalt Your Love!
May You a graceful, virtuous Offspring see,
And may they as their Parents happy be!
May Your increasing People in this Clime,
Rul'd by Your noble Race, thro' latest Time,
With cordial Love, their wise Behests obey;

And bless their mild Proprietary Sway!

IF in wish'd Progress, thro' these wide Domains,
Our Lord shall pass, to cheer his Tenant Swains;
With Pleasure will he see th' extensive Land,
Adorn'd by Nature with a lib'ral hand.
Of *Cheseapeake,* fair Bay! She justly boasts,
That swells to wash her *East* and *Western* Coasts;
Whose num'rous, gentle, navigable Streams,
In Fame would equal *Po,* or nobler *Thames;*
Smooth-gliding thro' some Poet's deathless Song,
Had they in EUROPE roll'd their Waves along.

VAST Flocks of Fowl each River's surface hide,
Amidst them sails the Swan with graceful Pride;
From these, the Fowler's Gun gains plenteous Prize, ⎫
Those that escape the mimic Thunder rise,   ⎬
And clam'rous, in Confusion, soar the Skies.   ⎭
Each Flood with watry Wealth exhaustless stor'd,
With choicest Cates supplies the Fisher's board.

CERES all bounteous for the Tiller's Toil,
Cloaths with her Corny Stores th'unfallow'd Soil.

POMONA yields delicious Fruitage here,
Unforc'd by Art, nor asks the Gard'ners care;
Our loaded Orchards bend beneath their weight,
And call for Props to bear the dangling freight.

HERE, *Flora,* gaily wild, profusely pours
O'er Woods, and Meadows, Hills and Dales the Flowr's.

INNUM'ROUS Herds amidst our Forests graze,
Fearless the Deer upon their Hunters gaze.
Wolves, Panthers, Bears, and ev'ry Beast of Prey,
Fly the Inhabitants, and shun the Day.
No dreadful Hurricanes disturb our Skies,
No Earthquakes shock the Soul with sad Surprize;
No sulphurous Vulcanos vomit Fire,
To blast the Plains with Devastation dire.
No treach'rous Crocodiles infest our Floods;

And pois'nous Snakes recede to pathless Woods.
The landscap'd Earth shows many a pleasing scene,
And Fogs but rarely hide the blue Serene.
Nor are these Blessings of indulgent Heav'n,
To an ingrateful Race of Mortals given;
Here, ev'ry Planter opens wide his Door,
To entertain the Stranger, and the Poor:
For them, He cheerful makes the downy Bed,
For them, with Food unbought his Board is spread;
No Arts of Luxury disguise his Meals,
Nor poignant Sauce severe Disease conceals;
Such hearty Welcom does the Treat commend,
As shows the *Donor* to Mankind a Friend.
That good *Old-English* Hospitality,
When ev'ry House to ev'ry Guest was free;
Whose Flight from BRITAIN's Isle, her Bards bemone,
Seems here with Pleasure to have fix'd her Throne.

SUCH, gracious Sir, your Province now appears,
How chang'd by Industry, and rolling Years,
From what it was!——————
When, for the Faith your Ancestors had shown,
To serve Two Monarchs on the *English* Throne;
CECILIUS, from the ROYAL MARTYR'S Hand,
Receiv'd the Charter of this spacious Land.[2]
Incult and wild its mazy Forests lay,
Where deadly Serpents rang'd, and Beasts of Prey:
The *Natives* jealous, cruel, crafty, rude,
In daily Wars declar'd their Thirst for Blood.

OH, if the *Muses* would my Breast inflame,
With Spirit equal to the glorious Theme!
My Verse should shew to the succeeding Age,
(Would Time permit my Verse to 'scape its Rage;)
What Toils your Great PROGENITORS sustain'd,
To plant and cultivate the dreary Strand.

WHAT Virtue in CECILIUS' Bosom glow'd?
Who with unsparing Hand his Wealth bestow'd,
Exhausting Treasures from his large Estate,
His Infant-Colony to cultivate;

To humanize a barb'rous, savage race,
And for industrious Men provide a Dwelling-Place.

MATUREST Wisdom did his ACT inspire,
Which Ages must with Gratitude admire;
By which, the Planters of his Land were freed
From Feuds, that made their Parent-Country bleed:
Religious Feuds, which in an evil Hour
Were sent from Hell, poor Mortals to devour!

OH, be that Rage eternally abhorr'd!
Which prompts the Worshippers of one mild LORD,
For whose *Salvation* one REDEEMER dy'd,
By War their *Orthodoxy* to decide:
Falsely religious, human Blood to spill,
And for GOD'S Sake, their Fellow-Creatures kill!
Horrid Pretence!————————

LONG had this impious Zeal with boundless Sway, ⎫
Most dreadful, urg'd o'er half the Earth its Way, ⎬
Tyrannic, on the Souls of Men to prey: ⎭
'Till great CECILIUS, glorious Hero, broke
Her Bonds, and cast away her cursed Yoke.

WHAT Praise, Oh PATRIOT, shall be paid to Thee! ⎫
Within thy Province CONSCIENCE *first was free!* ⎬
And gain'd in MARYLAND *its native Liberty.* ⎭

TO live beneath the Blessings of her Smile,
Numbers of *Albion's* Sons forsook their Isle;
In Ships prepar'd by BALTIMORE'S Command,
They came to cultivate his subject Land:
And All who cou'd not for Themselves provide,
Were by his kind paternal Care supply'd.

THAT Men of diff'rent *Faiths* in Peace might dwell,
And all unite t'improve their public Weal;
Opprobrious Names, by which blind Guides engage
Their blinded Proselytes, in deadliest Rage;
Sunk in *Oblivion,* by the wise *Decree*
Of CALVERT, left his Land from Faction free.[3]

BUT whither flies the Muse?—incurring blame,
While thus she wanders, devious from her Theme,
Above her Flight ascends CECILIUS' Fame!

HIM CHARLES succeeded; the couragious Son
Advanc'd the Work his Parent had begun;
To cheer the Planters by his gracious Smile,
And by his Presence animate their Toil;
Fir'd with the bold Adventure, scorning Ease,
He left the pompous Court, and pass'd the Seas:
His frequent Visits eas'd his Tenants Care,
When they were wounded deep with Grief-severe;
To drive away the Planters from their Lands,
Th' outrageous *Natives* came in hostile Bands;
Revengeful, cruel, restless, they persu'd
Their Enemies, and ruthless, shed their Blood:
Returning from his daily Toil, at Night,
The Husband often saw with wild Affright,
His darling Wife, and Infants, robb'd of breath,
Deform'd, and mangled by dishonest Death.

THE wise PROPRIETOR his Cares addrest,
To stop those Ills; and Heav'n his Labours blest;
Disarming of their Rage the savage race;
Extending o'er the Land the Shield of Peace.
The Planters, of their Foes no more afraid,
In Plenty liv'd, persuing gainful Trade;
And to their Parent-Land large Tribute paid.
But to their LORD, for those incessant Cares,
In which, the Sire, and Son employ'd their Years;
For so much Treasure spent—What Gains accrew?
Small their Amount!—Perhaps, in distant view,
He saw th' advancing Province would afford
An ample Income, to some future LORD:
But e'er his Progeny receiv'd that Gain,
A round of Years had roll'd their Course in vain.

AT length, to YOU, Great Sir, has Fortune paid
The Int'rest of the Debt, so long delay'd;
And ev'ry future Year that runs his Race,
Shall to your Revenue add large Increase:

If You, My LORD, afford your gen'rous Aid,
If You inspirit our decaying Trade.

ALREADY, has your Care for our Repose
Appear'd, in those VICEGERENTS you have chose.

CALVERT, who thro' discordant Parties steer'd
A steady Course, in Government revere'd;
Whose just Decrees his Enemies approv'd,
And who, in Private Life, by All is lov'd.

YOUR noble BROTHER, who unweary'd strove
Our long declining *Staple* to improve,
Whose Speeches to our *Delegates,* reveal
His ardent Wishes for the Public Weal.
The Pris'ner sav'd, whom Law severe decreed
To die; the pining Poor from Famin freed;
To all Mankind his gen'rous Temper prove,
Tho' to conceal his Charities He strove.
His great Accomplishments, most justly claim
My duteous Verse, to celebrate his Name.——

THY Name, Oh BENEDICT, for ever dear!
From Me exacts the grateful, starting Tear.——

BUT cease my *Muse,* nor with thy Sorrows stain
The Work, that *now* requires a cheerful Strain:
Indulge thy Grief in that *Funereal Verse,*
Which shall His Bounty, and thy Loss rehearse.

THE Province owes its Peace to OGLE'S[4] Care:
When Multitudes seduc'd by fierce Despair,
Spread like a Torrent, with tumultuous haste,
To lay the Hopes of future Markets waste;
(Mistaken Men! who while they sought to cure
Our sickly Trade, had made its Ruin sure:)
If OGLE'S Prudence had not stop'd their Force, ⎫
The Mischiefs flowing from this fatal source,   ⎬
Had delug'd all the Country, in their Course.   ⎭

HIS prudent *Rule* long may your Tenants bless,

And all the Fruits of smiling Peace possess!
That Arts may rise, and set the People free
From the surrounding Snares of Poverty:
For tho' by Nature we are blest with Stores;
Yet Arts have rarely visited our Shores.

TOO long, alas! *Tobacco* has engross'd
Our Cares, and now we mourn our Markets lost:
The plenteous Crops that over-spread our Plains,
Reward with Poverty the toiling Swains:
Their sinking *Staple* chills the Planters Hearts,
Nor dare they venture on unpractis'd Arts;
Despondent, they impending Ruin view,
Yet starving, must their old Employ persue.

IN this Distress to YOU they turn their Eyes,
From YOU, My LORD, their Hopes of Comfort rise:
The sweet Humanity that warms your Breast,
Engages you to succour the Distrest;
Your happy Station in the *British* Court,
Enables You your Province to support.

OH, glorious Privilege of being Great!
To raise a Country from its low Estate!
From You, Great Sir, may boundless Blessings flow,
Thousands unborn, to You their Wealth may owe.

IF You, benevolent, afford your Aid,
Your faithful Tenants shall enlarge their Trade:
By You encourag'd, *Artists* shall appear,
And quitting crowded Towns, inhabit here.
Well pleas'd, would they employ their gainful hands,
To purchase and improve your vacant Lands.

WHILE some with sounding Axes thinn'd the Woods,
And built the Ships to traverse briny floods;
Others, industrious, would with hasty Care
The various Cargoes studiously prepare.

WHILE These, for Fish, the watry world explore,
Those, would refine the rich metallic Ore.

THE Husbandman, might from his fertile Field
Raise finer Flax than *Germany* can yield:
And from our Looms, might curious Workmen show,
The Linen, emulous of driving Snow.

TO feed the Worms that form the silky spoil,
Vast Mulb'ry Groves, spontaneous, crown our Soil,
O'er tallest Trees our Vines wild-spreading rise,
And hide their purple Clusters in the Skies:
Did Art reclaim their too-luxuriant Shoots,
And skilful Culture tame their sylvan Fruits;
We might a flood of native Wine produce,
And rival *France* in the nectareous Juice.

THESE Blessings Nature to this Land imparts;
She only asks the Aid of useful Arts;
To make Her with the happiest Regions vye,
That spread beneath the all-surrounding Sky.

AN hundred Suns thro' Summer Signs have roll'd,
An hundred Winters have diffus'd their Cold;
Since MARYLAND has CALVERT's Race obey'd,
And to its noble LORDS her Homage paid:
And now, the Laws of mighty Time decree
This, for the Year of Sacred JUBILEE:
This Year, distinguish'd far above the rest,
That Time hath sent, shall be for ever blest!
From your kind VISIT, shall the People date ⎫
An happier *AEra,* mark'd by smiling Fate,   ⎬
To raise the Province from its languid State. ⎭

YOUR Presence shall disperse the Cloud that spreads,
Threatning to rain down Ruin on our Heads;
And from the breaking Gloom, shall Trade display
Her Beams, and warm us with a golden Ray.

AND here, prophetic of those glorious Times,
The raptur'd *Muse,* in more exalted Rhymes,
With Pleasure might the Book of FATE unfold,
And show the Scenes our Children shall behold!

BUT I, unequal to the arduous Task,
For my protracted Verse forgiveness ask;
May that be granted to my artless Lays!
A nobler *Bard* must sing those golden Days.

Jonathan Boucher

(1738-1804)

"ABSENCE, a Pastoral: drawn from the life, from the manners, customs and phraseology of planters (or, to speak more pastorally, of the rural swains) inhabiting the Banks of the Potomac, in Maryland."

TEXT: *Glossary of Archaic & Provincial Words*, ed. Joseph Stevenson (London, 1833), pp. xlix-1.

'Twas noon, when all alone young *Billsey*[1] sate
Adown to dine, though hardly down to eat:
His *gammon* smok'd in vain,—the *coleworts* too,
Though all with *good clear fat* drench'd through and through:
For, ah! his love had *o'er the river* gone,
And left her swain—to eat and drink alone.

Why stays my *Mollsey* dear? at length he cries,
The big round drops a-streaming from his eyes:
Ah, idle rover, haste, oh hasten, home,
And, ere the cherries all be gone, O, come!
Green pease, my love, are just a-coming in,
And lamb, and quarter'd *shote*,[2] and goslings green;
How fast the season of good eating rolls!—
Our chickens, in a month, will be old fowls:
Love only fix'd, and without changing, stays;
Ah! He remains a chicken all his days.

Four *colour'd hogsheads,* late in week the last,
And ten besides, have, all, *inspection* past:
My *new crap's pitch'd,* from which I hope to *share*
At least *two thousand,* all good *notes,*[3] next year:
Accounts of sales are come, and highly please;
I've got my goods all home,—and cut my cheese.

In vain I thrive,—in vain the world looks gay,
Still, still I *hone*[4] for bliss, while *Mollsey* is away.

Till now ne'er *crazy,* in my bones no pains,
I *never took no truck,* nor doctor's *means*:
Hoddy and *brave,* my careless days I told;
All night I slept,—all day I ate and *loll'd,*
Save when, an ugly fever *brief about,*[5]
I caught it in my toe, just like the gout:
My doctor thought, the neighbours all can tell,
I'd no *election*[6] ever to get well.
Ah, would no greater pains I now endur'd!
My *Mollsey* nurs'd me, and I soon was cur'd.

Strolling, last *fall,*[7] by yon *pacosen*[8] side,
Coil'd in a heap, a rattle-snake I spied:
Was it for me a *rompus*[9] then to make?
I'm *mad*[10] to see some people dread a snake:
Instant I caught a *chunk,*[11] and, at a blow,
To pieces *smash'd*[12] my notice-giving foe.
For this, if merit's aught, to go no higher,
I look to be a col'nel, or a 'squire:
But what are titles to a swain forlorn?
My *Mollsey's* gone, and I all honours scorn.

In *twist-bud, thick-joint, bull-face, leather-coat,*[13]
I'd toil all day; or *fall,* and *mall,* and *tote*:[14]
Brown linen shirts, and cotton jackets wear,
Or only *wring-jaw*[15] drink, and *'simmon beer;*[16]
My *pone,* or *hoe-cake,* without salt, would eat,
And taste but once a week a bit of meat;
Could my *old woman,*[17] whilst I labour'd thus,
At night reward me with a *smouch,* or buss.

For breakfast, *mush*[18] and *th' top o' milk's*[19] a treat,
Or *bonny clabber* with *molasses* sweet:
At dinner, let me that best *buck-skin*[20] dish,
Broth made of bacon, cream, and eke *cat-fish*
With *toss 'em boys,*[21] and *belly bacon* see,
Cushie,[22] and *dough-boys,*[23] and small *homony*:
At night *crab-lanthorn,*[24] and *fried cucumbers;*

Or *milk and peaches mash'd,* and *roasting-ears.*[25]
Sweet are these luscious cates, and sweet the day,
Ere long, when *water-millions* come in play:
But neither *clabber,* with *molasses* sweet,
Nor *mush,* nor *top o' th' milk* for morning treat;
Nor *cat-fish* broth, nor *paune,* with *toss 'em boys,*
Nor *middling,* garnish'd all with dainties nice;
Nor yet *crab-lanthorn,* with *fried cucumbers,*
Nor *milk and peaches mash'd,* nor *roasting-ears;*
Fog-drams[26] i' th' morn, or (better still) *egg-nogg,*[27]
At night *hot suppings,* and at mid-day, *grogg,*
My palate can regale:—my *Mollsey's* gone,
And ev'ry dainty's naught, when ate alone.

   Our *man-boy,*[28] Jack, did, in his *new-ground patch,*[29]
A *runaway* a' *grabbling 'moodies*[30] catch:
The rogues escap'd, but all the *'moodies* I
For *Mollsey,* in my *'tatoe-hole,* put by.
Ah, woe is me! these dainties are no more;
Some *bugs*[31] or grubs did every one devour:—
Just so have I been prey'd upon within;
For Absence is a worm that preys unseen.

   Old Johnny Two-Shoes,—bless his honest soul!
Sent me a *'possum,*[32] dead indeed, but whole;
I never saw a finer with my eyes:—
All full of maggots in the *safe*[33] it lies:
These things won't keep; no more do I, of late,
Know how to keep out maggots from my pate.

   Last *forest-ball,*[34] I felt like one forlorn,
Though *Ebo-Nan* was play'd, and then *Parch'd Corn:*[35]
When Nancy Wriggle slily did advance,
And, bent to shame me, ask'd me out to dance.
Humgh, humgh,[36] said I; and got upon the floor;
But, ah! I found my dancing days were o'er:
Thinking on *Mollsey,* oft I stood *stock still,*
Or danced a minuet, when they play'd a reel.

   'Twas thus, in lowly and unletter'd strain,
Our shepherd long of Absence did complain;

When to his clap-board mansion he withdrew,
To eat, and loll, and sleep,—as he was wont to do.

BOUCHER'S NOTES

1 *Billsey*: this effeminate manner of pronouncing such names was at that time extremely common in the neighbourhood where this was written.

2 *Shote*: a young swine.

3 *Notes*: at that time, no tobacco could be shipped till it had been examined by inspectors, publicly appointed; who, on finding it marketable, received it into their warehouses, and gave a *note* for the re-delivery of it, when demanded.

4 *Hone*: long for.

5 *Brief about*: probably a corruption for *rife about*.

6 *Election*: likelihood, chance, &c.

7 The *fall*: autumn, the *fall* of the leaf.

8 *Pacosen*: an Indian term for a swamp, or marsh.

9 *Rompus*: an uproar.

10 *Mad*: angry, vexed.

11 *Chunk*: a short piece of wood; a thick stick; a bludgeon.

12 *Smash'd*: beat to pieces.

13 *Twist-bud, &c.*: All these are names for different kinds of tobacco.

14 *Fall, mall,* and *tote*: i.e., *fall*, or cut down, a tree; split, or rive it, by means of *mallets* and wedges, into rails, clapboards, staves, shingles, firewood, or any other purpose for which it may be fit and wanted; and then *tote,* or carry it to some pile or heap, from whence it may be carted away.

15 *Wring-Jaw*: hard cider.

16 *'Simmon beer*: beer, made of the *Prunus sylvestris Virginiensis,* or *Persimmon;* a harsh and unpleasant plum, growing in great plenty, but when mellowed by the frosts, and baked into cakes, and then used as malt, yielding a palatable and rich, but heady beer.

17 *Old woman*: a very common term of endearment in the midland colonies.

18 *Mush*: hasty-pudding, made of Indian meal.

19 *Top o' th' milk*: cream.

20 *Buckskins*: Natives of Virginia and Maryland are so called, in contradistinction to *outlandish* persons, or the natives of any other country.

21 *Toss 'em boys*: chickens; so called, it is supposed, because when any unexpected guest is seen coming, a young negro is dispatched to procure more chickens, to be added to the dinner; and these chickens it is common to run down with his dog, whom he sets on, and encourages, by the phrase *Toss 'em, boys.*

22 *Cushie*: a kind of pancake, made of Indian meal.

23 *Dough-boys*: hard, or Norfolk dumplings; not seldom also made of Indian meal.

24 *Crab-lanthorn*: To the best of my recollection, fried apples are so called.

25 *Roasting-ears*: Indian corn, whilst still soft in the ear, is roasted, and eaten as a favourite delicacy; and indeed is delicious food.

[26] *Fog-drams*: *drams* resorted to on the pretence of their protecting from the danger of *fogs*.

[27] *Egg-nogg*: a heavy and unwholesome, but not unpalatable, strong drink, made of rum beaten up with the yolks of raw *eggs*.

[28] *Man-boy*: an hobbete-hoy, an *ephebus, betwixt* boyhood and manhood.

[29] *New-ground patch*: a piece of ground that had never been cultivated before; the *culta novalia* of Virgil.

[30] *'Moodies*: sweet potatoes; first brought from the Bermudas.

[31] *Bugs*: Almost all insects in America are called *bugs;* excepting that particularly offensive insect, so noisome in beds, so called in London.

[32] A *'possum*: an opossum.

[33] A *safe*: a kind of cupboard.

[34] *Forest-ball*: this term is, in Virginia and Maryland, equivalent to *the country* in England, or to *landwart* in Scotland.

[35] *Ebo-Nan,* and *Parch'd Corn*: two favourite tunes, or jigs, among the negros are so called.

[36] *Humgh, humgh*: interjections denoting assent.

SOUTHERN VERSE FROM GAZETTES

Rev. George Seagood

(fl. 1729)

"Expeditio Ultramontana"
From the Latin of Arthur Blackamore[1]

TEXT: *The Maryland Gazette*, No. 93 (June 24, 1729), n.p.

LET other Pens th' ungrateful News declare,
The dire Effects of *Northern* Civil War;
How furious Men by fatal Madness led,
Pull'd down devoted Vengeance on their Head.
Whilst we thy Care, O *Spotswood,* sing thy Toil,
Which bore thee far into a foreign Soil.
Urge thee to quit soft Ease and grateful Home,
O'er Mountains high and rapid Streams to roam;
And thro' thick Woods impervious to the Sun,
To poisonous Snakes and Monsters only known.
    Tell (Goddess Muse) for thy all pow'rful Art
Is only equal to the Godlike Part;

What lonesome Fields, and unfrequented Floods,
Spotswood did pass thro' dark and desert Woods;
Whilst he, intent upon *Virginia's* Good,
O'er Hills and Dales the noble Task persu'd;
Up steepest Mountains in his Course did run,
Whose Tops were 'bove the Clouds, and Rivals to the Moon,
So he might farther stretch his *Royal Master's* Sway.
   Happy *Virginia!* wouldst thou prize thy Friend,
Who labour'd thus thy Borders to extend;
Encourag'd thee to Arts, train'd thee to Arms;
And guarded thee from more than foreign Harms:
Nor were his Thoughts to these alone confin'd,
But higher Cares imploy'd his Christian Mind.
For having read in God's Prophetic Page,
In after-times should come a glorious Age,
In which all Nations should agree as One;
Be all one Flock, of one Religion.
   "O Prospect sweet! he cries, hail happy Days!
"When thus the Sun of Peace shall [cast his rays?];
"When his bless'd Influence shall the Globe controul,
"And his Messias reign from Pole to Pole.
   Unwearied are his Pains, unshaken is his Mind,
To spread this Good to all of *Adam's* Kind:
In this, ambitious of eternal Fame,
T'advance his Sov'reigns and his Saviour's name ,
That GEORGE'S Fame may thro' the World be read,
And CHRIST'S and *Britain's* Cross in faithless Nations spread.
Now then, the Hero for his March prepares,
And t'wards the *Indian* Parts his Course he steers:
And thus begins to move by GOD'S Command;
As once did *Joshua* to the Promis'd Land.
All Things and Places full of GOD appear,
And both his Goodness and his Power declare:
And all his Creatures his Commands fulfil
And act by his Express, or his permissive Will.
   This Expedition was design'd to trace
A Way to some yet undiscover'd Place;
And barb'rous savage Nations to subdue,
Which neither antient *Greece* or *Rome* e'er knew;
Or else *Virginia's* Borders to secure

And fix the Bounds of his deputed Power:
These, Day and Night, the Regent's Studies are,
And his *Virginia* is his constant Care.

And now the Day was come, when his Command
To distant Climes led on a chosen Band;
All Things conspire to favour the Design,
And lucky Omens with their Wishes joyn.

First then, he pass'd the antient Planters Seats,
Whilst each Plantation from his View retreats;
The winding Road thro' thickest Forest leads,
(Whose Trees tow'rds Heaven shoot up their lofty Heads)
And brings him to the Banks declining Side,
Where *Rapidanna* rowls his hasty Tyde;
Whose Current's fiercer than the *Tiber's* was,
When he with headstrong Course his Bounds did pass,
O'erthrew the Rock where *Vesta's* Temple stood,
And mixt the sacred Structure with the Mud.
Kind Nature dreading such Effects as these,
(Whose all-wise Author all Events foresees)
The like in future Ages to prevent,
Cut deep his Banks, and made a steep Ascent,
With rocky Cliffs his Waters did restrain,   )
Lest overcharg'd with sudden Snow or Rain,   }
He might o'erflow, and drown the Neighb'ring Plain.)

Crossing this Stream, he to *Germanna* came,
Which from new *German* Planters takes its Name,
Here taught to dig, by his auspicious Hand
They prov'd the teeming Pregnance of the Land;
For being search'd, the fertile Earth gave Signs
That her Womb swell'd with Gold and Silver Mines:
This Ground, if faithful, may in Time out-do
Potosi, Mexico, and fam'd *Peru.*

When he from hence a hundred Miles had pass'd
T'wards *George's* Hill a wishful Eye he cast:
This Mountain taller than the rest appears,
As to the Sky his stately Front he rears;
Which *Spotswood,* mindful of his Sov'reign's Fame,
Grac'd with the Title of his Royal Name,
As proud *Olympus* 'bove the Hills does rise,
And nearer views the Starry Pole and Skies;
So much thy Mountain upwards does aspire,

And o'er the Highest thrusts his Shoulders higher;
As Thou, Great GEORGE, the Monarchs dost surpass,
In vertuous Deeds familiar to thy Race.
  The steady Spotswood thither bends his Way,
Altho' thro' roughest pathless Woods it lay;
No Sign of Culture wears the desert Ground;
No Print of humane Footsteps to be found:
When streight the Sky is taken from his Sight,
And *Sylvan* Shades obstruct the Mid-day Light:
Yet on he goes, and does a Passage force;
Thro' Dens of Wolves and Bears he clears his Course.
Each Swamp is fill'd with Broods of horrid Snakes,
And savage Beasts lie lurking in the Brakes.
Unmov'd he hears the howling Wolfs shrill Voice,
And slights the roaring Bears more frightful Noise.
Here Snakes, like *Python,* of a monstrous Size,
With brandish'd Tongues dart out a spiteful Hiss;
With twirling Tails these Serpents coil'd, prepare,
(And with their Rattles beat the Alarm) for War;
And bid the wary Traveller retreat,
Or arm'd expect a deadly Foe to meet,
A Weapon on each Willow's to be found,
Which plenteous grow in Vale and swampy Ground:
One stroke of which the Monster's Blood will spill;
Whose mortal Venom with a Touch does kill.
  Yet arn't these Woods without their proper Grace;
The verdant Earth here shews a cheerful Face.
This fruitful Soil with richest Grass is crown'd,
And various Flow'rs adorn the gawdy Ground.
(Neglecting Order) Nature plants this Land,
And strews her Riches with a lavish Hand;
With Fruit her Bounty cloaths each well-deck'd Bush,
The luscious Cherries on the Branches blush.
Here silken Mulb'ries load the bending Boughs,
And there the cluster'd Grape luxuriant grows.
Here Currants, Peaches, Strawb'ries, Nature tends;
And other Dainties to the Hero lends.
  This, to the pleas'd Spectator, seems the Seat
Where rural *Ceres* makes her own Retreat;
Or else the Birth-place of the *Jolly God,*
Or where *Pomona* makes her chief Abode.

These Things, as *Spotswood* and his Train admire,
Towards *Mount-George* their March conveys them nigher:
At length they reach the Bottom, and look up,
And nearer view its long-sought airy top.
Spotswood had long pursu'd it with his Eye;
But as he follow'd, still it seem'd to fly:
His Haste was fruitless, like *Appollo's* Chace,
When *Daphne* shun'd the am'rous Gods embrace.

Now they ascend and up that Mountain go,
Which looks with Scorn upon the World below.
Hard Labour! thus to climb so near the Skies;
But Strength and Honour, Courage fresh supplies:
Hopes of rare Sights, do strong Desires excite;
And so they gain the Mountains utmost Height.
Here are no Woods to intercept the Sight,
And form at Noon an antidated Night:
But freely now they breathe a purer Air,
The cloudless Sky is all serene and fair,
The Sun and Moon by Turns in Pomp appear.

Here Spotswood stood, and looking from this Height,
The beauteous Landskip charm'd his ravish'd Sight,
Much pleas'd to see thro' Woods the Rivers stray,
And long the Vales in wanton Mazes play.

The Hero smil'd, and thus express'd his Thought:
"Had th' antient Poets known this pleasant Spot,
"They here had plac'd their great *Apollo's* Shrine, ⎫
"Or else the Title of the tuneful *Nine*   ⎬
"Had always made it sacred and devine.   ⎭
"But since an higher Honour it does claim,
"Forever let it bear the mighty GEORGE'S Name.
He spoke, then all their joint Assent declare
By joyful Shouts that rend the nitrous Air.

Another Mountain meets their downward Sight;
Tho' lower far than this, yet next in height.
As there thou stoodst in Power, so next in Fame,
Let thine, O *Spotswood!* be its future Name.
Descending, many Fountains they descry,
That largest Rivers plenteously supply:
O'er Roots, o'er Rocks, a rapid Course they gain,
And in the Vales become a liquid Plain:
'Mongst verdant Trees, the Streams look bright and gay,

As in the Skies appears the *Milky Way*.
Here spangled Snakes, and Fish divert their Sight, ⎫
Which, as they swim, reflect a glitt'ring Light,   ⎬
(Like Stars that twinkle in a frosty Night.)   ⎭
Whose various Sorts and Numbers to rehearse,
Would tire the *Muse,* and pass the Bounds of Verse.
  But then, to paint the Joys this Prospect Breeds
From shady Groves, green Banks, and flow'ry Meads,
And all the Beauties that this Par'dice yields,
Be it *His* Task, who knows th' *Elysian* Fields.
After the Hero pass'd the gentle Flood   ⎫
Thro' which directly went their mirey Road   ⎬
Regardful of his Charge, he pausing stood: ⎭
He thought, and soon resolved without Delay,
Homewards to make his retrogressive Way,
Having for GEORGE, his King, Possession took,
And cut *his Name* in *Ultramontane* Rock.
Obeying then the Dictates of his Mind,
He streight returned, and left this Scene behind;
When he, like *Hercules* in former Days,
Had made two Mountains, Pillars of his Praise.

Anonymous

"The Cameleon Lover"

TEXT: *The South-Carolina Gazette,* No. 10 (March 11, 1732), n.p.

If what the *Curious* have observ'd be true,
That the *Cameleon* will assume the *Hue*
Of all the Objects that approach its *Touch;*
No Wonder then, that the *Amours* of *such*
Whose *Taste* betrays them to a close Embrace
With the *dark* Beauties of the *Sable* Race,
(Stain'd with the Tincture of the *Sooty* Sin,)
Imbibe the *Blackness* of their *Charmer's* Skin.

"Sable"

"The Cameleon's Defence"

TEXT: *The South-Carolina Gazette,* No. 11 (March 18, 1732), n.p.

All Men have Follies, which they blindly trace
Thro' the dark Turnings of a dubious Maze:
But happy those, who, by a prudent Care,
Retreat betimes, from the fallacious Snare.
The eldest Sons of Wisdom were not free,
From the same Failure you condemn in Me.
If as the Wisest of the Wise have err'd,
I go astray and am condemn'd unheard,
My Faults you too severely reprehend,
More like a rigid Censor than a Friend.
Love is the Monarch Passion of the Mind,
Knows no Superior, by no Laws confin'd;
But triumphs still, impatient of Controul,
O'er all the proud Endowments of the Soul.

Anonymous

"Prologue spoken to the ORPHAN, *upon it's being
play'd at* Charlestown, *on Tuesday the 24th of Jan. 1734-5."*

TEXT: *The South-Carolina Gazette,* No. 54 (Feb. 8, 1735), n.p.

WHen first Columbus touch'd this distant Shore
And vainly hop'd his Fears and Dangers o'er,
One boundless Wilderness in View appear'd!
No Champain Plains or rising Cities chear'd
His wearied Eye.—
Monsters unknown travers'd the hideous Waste,
And Men more Savage than the Beasts they chac'd.
But mark! how soon these gloomy Prospects clear.
And the new World's late horrors disappear.

The soil obedient to the industrious Swains,)
With happy Harvests crowns their honest Pains, }
And Peace and Plenty triumph o'er the Plains.)
What various Products float on every Tide?
What numerous Navys in our Harbours ride?
Tillage and Trade conjoin their Friendly Aid,
T'enrich the thriving Boy and lovely Maid.
Hispania, it's true, her precious Mines engross'd,
And bore her shining Entrails to its Coast.
Britannia more humane supplys her wants,
The Brittish Sense and Brittish Beauty plants.
The Aged Sire beholds with sweet Surprize
In foreign Climes a numerous Offspring rize.
Sense, Virtue, worth and Honour stand confest,
In each brave Male, his prosp'rous hands have blest,
While the admiring Eye improv'd may trace
The Mother's Charms in each chast Virgins Face.
Hence we presume to usher in those Arts
Which oft have warm'd the best and bravest Hearts.
Faints our endeavours, rude are our Essays;
We strive to please, but can't pretend at praise;
Forgiving Smiles o'erpay the grateful Task;
They're all we hope and all we humbly ask.

"Juba"

"To the LADIES *of* MARYLAND."

TEXT: *The Maryland Gazette,* No. 8 (June 14, 1745), n.p.

WOULD you, my Fair, triumphant lead along
Of sighing, passive Slaves, a shining Throng?
Say, would you learn the happy pleasing Art
To charm, and to secure the captive Heart?
The Muse thro' all her various Maze pursue,
Her Theme is Beauty, and she sings to you.
    SHUN Affection in your Air and Dress;
The clipt, lispt Accent, and the prim set Face:
Easy each Motion, natural and free,
Not pinch'd with cramp, strait-laced Formality:
Bid Grace and Dignity from conscious Worth,

From Virtue, and fair Honour's Spring, beam forth.
Let not your Cheek the painted Falshood know, ⎞
But flame with the pure native Crimson's Glow, ⎬
Whose Tincture does from modest Merit flow: ⎠
A native Grace shall more attractive prove
Than all th'Auxiliaries of Art, to move.
Affect to please the Men of Sense alone,
And scorn the *Foppling Flutters* of the Town:
A Freedom disengaged, and careless Ease,
Shall the unwary Heart, unaiming, seize:
(Love's richest Gift) an easy, graceful Smile,
Pow'rful to charm, proves an alluring Wile;
On which hid Darts shall certain Conquests wait,
While yielding Slaves to you resign their Fate.
Fly Books; they'll turn your Head, and spoil your Charms;
Philosophy your ev'ry Grace disarms;
Yet deign to make the lighter Muse your Care,
'Twill form the Wit, and give the Debonnair:
Mix'd with the social Choir, the Dance now grace;
And artful moving, swim the mystic Maze:
Or with the full join'd Concert tuneful sing,
Or wake, with skilful Touch, the speaking String.
The Parent of the Graces, Smiles and Loves,
Those gay, those Heart-ensnaring Lures approves.
Those fav'rite Arts her Empire's Power sustain,
Those fav'rite Arts her *Cupids* still maintain.
Be neat, not nice; be rather clean than fine;
And let plain Elegance around you shine.
Of Novel Vanities th' Expences shun,
Nor through the Lab'rinths of the Fashion run:
To please the more, be careless still to please;
So shall you charm with more becoming Ease.
With fairer Grace neglected Beauties glow,
And Charms, the less adorn'd, more lovely show.

Joseph Dumbleton

(fl. 1750)

"The PAPER-MILL. Inscrib'd to Mr. Parks."

TEXT: *The American Magazine* (August 1744), p. 523.[1]
In nova, sert Animus, mutates dicere formas, Corpora;
Ovid.[2]

THO' sage Philosophers have said,
Of nothing, can be nothing made:
Yet *much* thy Mill, O *Parks,* brings forth
From what we reckon *nothing worth.*
Hail kind *Machine!*—The Muse shall praise
Thy Labours, that receive her Lays.
Soon as the *Learn'd* denounce the War
From pratling Box, or wrangling Bar,
Straight, Pen and Paper range the Fight;
They meet, they close, in Black & White.
The Substances of what we think,
Tho' born in *Thought,* must live in *Ink.*
Whilst willing *Mem'ry* lends her Aid,
She finds herself by *Time* betray'd.
Nor can thy Name, Dear *Molly,* live
Without those Helps the Mill must give;
The Sheet now hastens to declare,
How lovely Thou, and—my Despair.
   Unwitting Youths, whom Eyes or Breast,
Involve in Sighs, and spoil of Rest;
Unskill'd to say their piteous Case,
But miss the Girl for want of *Brass,*
May paint their Anguish on the Sheet;
For Paper cannot blush, I weet.
And *Phillis,* (for Bissextile Year[3]
Does only once in Four appear,
When Maids, in dread to lie alone
Have Leave to bid the Men *come on,)*
Each Day may write to lure the Youth
She longs to wed, or fool, or—both.
   Ye *Brave,* whose Deeds shall vie with Time,

Whilst Mill can turn, or Poet rhime,
Your Tatters hoard for future Quires;
So Need demands, so *Parks* desires.
(And long that gen'rous Patriot live
Who for soft Rags, hard Cash will give!)
'The Shirt, Cravat, the Cap again
Shall meet your Hands, with *Mails* from *Spain;*
The *Surplice,* which, when whole or new,
With Pride the Sexton's Wife could view,
Tho' worn by Time and gone to rack,
It quits its Rev'rend Master's Back;
The same again the Priest may see
Bound up in Sacred Liturgy.
   Ye Fair, renown'd in *Cupid's* Field,
Who fain would tell what Hearts you've kill'd;
Each Shift decay'd, lay by with Care;
Or Apron rubb'd to bits at—Pray'r,
One Shift ten Sonnets may contain,
To gild your Charms, and make you vain;
One Cap, a *Billet-doux* may shape.
As full of Whim, as when a Cap,
And modest 'Kerchiefs Sacred held
May sing the Breasts they once *conceal'd.*
   Nice *Delia's* Smock, which, neat and whole,
No Man durst finger for his Soul;
Turn'd to *Gazette,* now all the Town,
May take it up, or smooth it down.
Whilst *Delia* may with it dispence,
And no Affront to Innocence.
   The Bards, besure, their Aids will lend;
The Printer is the Poet's Friend;
Both cram the News, and stuff the Mills,
For Bards have Rags, and—little else.

"A RHAPSODY on *RUM*."

TEXT: *The South-Carolina Gazette,* No. 776 (March 20, 1749), n.p.
      ——*Ignigenamque Vocant.* OVID.[1]

GREAT Spirit hail!—Confusion's angry Sire,
And like thy Parent *Bacchus,* born of Fire:

The Goal's Decoy; the greedy Merchant's Lure;
Disease of Money, but Reflection's Cure.
 We owe, great DRAM! the trembling Hand to thee,
The headstrong Purpose; and the feeble Knee;
The Loss of Honour; and the Cause of Wrong;
The Brain enchanted; and the fault'ring Tongue;
Whilst Fancy flies before Thee unconfin'd,
Thou leav'st disabl'd Prudence far behind.
 In thy Pursuit our Fields are left forlorn,
Whilst giant Weeds oppress the pigmy Corn :
Thou throw'st a Mist before the Planter's Eyes;
The Plough grows idle, and the Harvest dies.
 By Thee refresh'd no cruel Norths we fear;
'Tis ever warm and calm when thou art near:
On the bare Earth for Thee expos'd we lie,
And brave the Malice of a weeping Skie.
And seem like those that did of old repent;
We sit in ashes, and our Cloathes are rent.
 From Thee a thousand flatt'ring Whims escape,
Like hasty Births, that ne'er have perfect Shape.
Thine Ideots seem in gay Delusion fair,
But born in Flame, they soon expire in Air.
 O grand Deluder! such thy charming Art,
'Twere good we ne'er should meet, or ne'er should part:
Ever abscond, or ever tend our Call;
Leave us our Sense entire, or none at all.

James Sterling

(1701-1763)

From "A PASTORAL. To his Excellency GEORGE THOMAS,
Esq; formerly Governor of Pennsylvania, and now General of the Lee-
ward Islands."

TEXT: The American Magazine (May 1758), pp. 391-397.

> Hic ver purpureum, various hic flumina circum
> Fundit humus floret: hic candida populus antro
> Imminet, et lentae texunt umbracula vites.

Huc ades——
Tu decus omne tuis: post quam te fata tulerunt,
Ipse Pales agros, atque ipse reliquit Apollo.
Virg.[1]

PIERIAN nymphs that haunt *Sicilian* plains,
And first inspir'd to sing in rural strains;
Vouchsafe to teach my trembling reed to play,
And woods to join in concert with my lay.
Our *Indian* woods, as yet unus'd to sing,
When taught by you, with harmony shall ring.
O waft your way from fam'd Parnassus' height
(The muses love a bold adventrous flight)
And westward steer——*Phoebus* will lead the way,
You'll reach our mountains e'er the close of day;
And there behold, what sure must highly please,
Apollo's steeds plunge in the western seas.
Soon as the ocean hides his sacred head,
You'll see the golden curtains of his bed:
And waiting *Hasper* gather in the day,
Whilst *Cynthia* spreads her silent silver ray.
    A western course has pleas'd you all along;
Greece, Rome, and *Briton,* flourish all in song.
Keep on your way, and spread a glorious fame,
Around the earth let all admire your name.
Chuse in our plains or forests soft retreats;
For here the muses boast no antient seats.
Here fertile fields, and fishy streams abound;
Nothing is wanting but *Poetic* ground.
Bring me that pipe with which *Alexis*[2] charm'd
The *Eastern* world, and every bosom warm'd.
Our *Western* climes shall henceforth own your power;
Thetis shall hear it from her watry bower;
Even *Phoebus* listen as his chariot flies,
And smile propitious from his flaming skies.
    Haste lovely nymphs, and quickly come away;
Our sylvan gods lament your long delay;
The stately oaks that dwell on *Delaware*
Rear their tall heads to view you from afar.
The Naids summon all their scaly crew
And at *Henlopen*[3] anxious wait for you.

Haste lovely nymphs and quickly reach our shore;
Th' impatient river heeds his tides no more,
Forsakes his banks, and where he joins the main,
Heaps waves on waves to usher in your train.
A numerous fleet rich with what *Ceres* yields
(*Ceres* the goddess of our fertile fields)
With ensigns waving in the prosp'rous gale
For want of water scarce can bend a sail;
The goddess vows to stop her liberal hand—
Haste lovely nymphs, and save a sinking land.
Harmonious *Nine,* bring harmony and peace,
Unite our hearts, and bid all discord cease.
 But hark they come!—The *Dryads* crowd the shore,
The waters rise, I hear the billows roar!
Hoarse *Delaware* the joyful tidings brings,
And all his swans, transported, clap their wings.
Our mountains ring with all their savage host—
Thrice-welcome lovely nymphs, to *India's* coast.
Not more parnassian rocks *Phoebus* admire;
Nor *Thracian* mountains *Orpheus'* tuneful lyre;
Not more sad lovers court the darkling note
Of *Philomela's* mournful warbling throat;
Not more the morning lark delights the swains,
Than you sweet maids our *Pennsylvanian* plains!
 Britain's fair offspring, nymphs as angels bright,
In silent rapture, wonder at the sight.
The swarthy race their wampum belts prepare,
And loud YOHAWS[4] shout thro' the trembling air.
What do I see?—From heaven a sudden blaze!
The *Indian* crowds are hush'd in deep amaze!
Stare on each other with attentive eyes,
For wisdom thirst, and their rude state despise!
They call to *Onas:*[5] generous *Onas* hears,
His heart is melted with barbarian tears.
What mean these wonders, say, divinely-sprung!
The virgins smil'd, and thus melodious sung—
 "O mortals blind to gracious heaven's decree,
"Why thus astonish'd at the change you see?
"Look back thro' ages past, you'll find it clear,
"The rude are polish'd soon as we appear.
"Or if barbarian rage must have its time,

"We seek abodes in some more peaceful clime.
"Thus when the north pour'd forth its *Gothic* swarms,
"From lov'd *Ausonia* vanish'd all our charms,
"To visit *Europe's* crimson fields no more,
"Until the general massacre was o'er;
"At length on fair *Britannia* cast a smile,
"And rais'd a *Chaucer* in the fav'rite isle.
"Successive bards, in one continued line,
"Form'd the brave *English* from a *Saxon Mine.*
" 'Tis ours, by gentle means, to tame the heart;
" 'Tis yours, to sing whatever we impart.
"*Onas* shall favour, whose extensive mind,
"Loves not a part, but all the human kind.
   They sung and vanish'd, whilst I gaz'd in vain;
Yet gently whisper'd, still sing on my swain.
Lend then, *Melpomene,* your sacred fire,
And verses fit for THOMAS' ear, inspire.
   O thou distinguish'd by a far-spread fame,
Obtain'd by merit, not thy honour'd name;
Whether you strive, by strong perswasive sense,
To urge a naked province to defence,[6]
Or wisely dreading savage *Indian* foes,
By friendship's chain avert tremendous woes;
Hear and accept my harmless rural lay;
So may you hold a long and happy sway.
'Tis not a *venal minion* fawning sues,
But one who scorns to prostitute his muse.

[The second part of the poem, a lengthy and conventional pastoral elegy, has been omitted here.]

"*The* 22d *Ode of the first Book of* Horace *imitated; and inscribed to the Lady of his late Excellency* SAMUEL OGLE, *Esquire.*"

TEXT: *The American Magazine* (October 1758), pp. 642-643.

1.

THE christian hero, pure from sin,
Serene, and fortify'd within,

Defies the rage of civil jars,
Assembly-feuds, and foreign wars;
    Nor wants the troops, brave *Amherst*[1] led,
He, safe in sanctity of life,
From the *French* sword and *Indian* knife,
Ne'er dreads a circumcision of the head.

2.

    Whether he purposes to go;
Thro' *Apalachian* rocks and snow.
Cannadean-forests, *Funda's* frost,
Or bleak *Ontario's* barbarous coast;
    Or visits *Niagara's Fall*:
With soul, not liable to fear,
He sees tremendous dangers near;
Smiling, he sees; superior to them all.

3.

    'Tis true, *fair Friend;* no evil can
Surprize the heav'n-protected man.
—As thro' thy pleasing lawns I stray'd;
(While *Virtue,* like a blooming maid,
    Employ'd my tho'ts on all her charms)
From neighb'ring groves, with threat'ning eyes,
A *Buffalo* of monstrous size,
Rush'd sudden forth, nor gave my soul alarms!

4.

    Such never drank *Ohio's* floods,
Or bellow'd in *Virginian*-woods;
Such and so fierce did ne'er advance
'Gainst *Spanish Don* with daring lance;
    Such ne'er in *Hole of Hockley*[2] bled.
Yet *me* unarm'd the savage saw,
With fear and reverential awe,
Spurning the ground, he came, he gaz'd, he fled.

5.

Place me on *Hudson's* dreary shore,
Where icy mountains, bursting, roar;
Where Hyperborean tempests blow;
Where tree or shrub can never grow.
    (*Virtue,* bright goddess! I'm prepar'd)
Place me, where howling swamps extend;
A gloomy wild, without an end!
Yet *Virtue* there shall be her vot'ry's guard!

6.

Cast me amidst the hissing brood,
When sultry *Sirius* fires their blood;
Where from th' inhospitable brake
Dire basilisks their rattles shake:
    Yet, *Virtue,* thou shalt cheer the place;
And, strongly imag'd in my mind,
Within my raptur'd heart inshrin'd,
Shalt sweetly talk, and smile with *Ogle's* grace!

Charles Woodmason

(c. 1720-c. 1776)

"C.W. *in* Carolina *to* E.J. *at* Gosport."

TEXT: *The Gentleman's Magazine,* XXIII (July 1753), 337-338.

WHile you, my friend, indulg'd in each desire,
Your blooming bride with rapt'rous love admire;
From grave to gay with various authors change,
Or blithe from concert to assembly range,
Me harder fate to foreign lands conveys;
In foreign lands the muse my call obeys.
The land, tho' foreign, softest seasons bless,
To the pleas'd native bounteous in excess.
Ev'n I, who pine for less indulgent skies,
Am charm'd where'er I turn my wond'ring eyes.

Almost I seem to tread enchanted ground,
And endless beauty fills the circuit round.
  Thy pleasing name I echo thro' the woods,
Then wish thee with me near these chrystal floods,
To view *Santee* tumultuous in its course,
And trace the great *Port Royal* to its source:
To see *Savanna* draw his watry store,
Thro' the long windings of a swampy shore,
And rapid *Ashley* with impetuous tide,
Thro' the long chain of num'rous islands glide.
  With transport fir'd, attentive I survey,
The two *Podees* to *Winyaw's* bason stray,
Parents of floods! who rolling thro' the plain,
The *Cherokees* of half their moisture drain,
And swol'n with rains, or swift dissolving snow,
Distribute wealth and plenty where they flow.
  Their names, enfranchiz'd by the tuneful throng,
Were never yet immortaliz'd in song:
They, lost in silence and oblivion, lye,
Till time ordains to flow in poetry.
Ah! were I blest with tuneful *Gaselee's* skill,
Thy streams, *Black-River,* shou'd my numbers fill,
Where *Cleland, Powel* and *Trapier* reside,[1]
And learning's toil rude savages deride.
Sometimes to *Pon-pon's* banks I calm retire,
Or shallow *Stono's* fertile shores admire.
Stono, a languid stream, derives its course,
From various urns, and from a doubtful source.
When wilt thou, *Wando,* in poetic lays,
Acquire, like *Helicon,* immortal praise?
When shall some deathless muse exalt thy fame,
Fair *Edistow,* and dignify thy stream?
Broad *Waccamow,* which now obscurely strays,
May gain distinction while it yields the bays,
And farther than her *rice* can find its way,
Ashpoo may be convey'd some future day.
  Here could my humble muse, a train run o'er
Of gen'rous names, that honor *Cooper's* shore:
The *Cordes's, Harlstons, Berefords,* and *Beard,*
(By ties of virtuous friendship long endear'd)
With *Broughton, Simmons, Austen,* and *Durand,*[2]

The pride and grace of *Carolina's* land!
Did not the tilting bark unwilling stay,
And southern breezes chide the short delay:
The pleasing talk, at present, I suspend,
And bid a *Langhorn's*[3] pen their worth commend.
    Oh! would a spark of empyreal fire,
With *Parker's*[4] warmth my ravish'd breast inspire,
Unnumber'd beauties in my verse should shine,
And *Carolina* grace each flowing line.
See how her fragrant groves around me smile,
That shun the coast of *Britain's* stormy isle,
Or when transplanted and preserv'd with care,
Curse the cold clime, and starve in northern air.
Here, kindly warmth, their mounting juice ferments,
To taller growth and more exalted scents:
Ev'n loosen'd sands with tender myrtles bloom,
And trodden weeds exhale a rich perfume.
    Bear me, some god, to worthy *Michi's* seat,
Or give me shade in *Taylor's* calm retreat,
Where western gales eternally reside,
And bounteous seasons lavish all their pride;
Blossoms, and fruits, and flow'rs, together rise,
And the whole year in gay confusion lyes.
    What! tho' a second *Carthage* here we raise,
A late attempt, the work of modern days,
Here *Drayton's* seat and *Middleton's*[5] is found,
Delightful villa's! be they long renown'd.
Swift fly the years when sciences retire,
From frigid climes to equinoctial fire:
When *Raphael's* tints, and *Titian's* strokes shall faint,
As fair *America* shall deign to paint.
Here from the mingled strength of shade and light,
A new creation shall arise to sight,
And sculpture here in full perfection shine,
Dug, for her hand, our *Apalachian* mine.
Methinks I see, in solemn order stand,
The first advent'rers to this blooming land:
Ashley and *Archdale, Colleton,* and *Boon,*
Bull, Johnson, Izzard, heroes worthy *Rome,*
See *Indian* chiefs whom cruelties renown,
Submit their country to the *British* crown,

Domes, temples, bridges, rise in distant views,
And sumptuous palaces the sight amuse.
　　How has kind heav'n adorn'd this happy land,
And scatter'd blessings with a lib'ral hand!
But what avail her unexhausted stores,
Her woody mountains, and her sunny shores,
With all the gifts that heav'n and earth impart,
The smiles of nature, and the charms of art?
While noxious reptiles in her vallies reign,
And stinging insects fill the watry plain,
While droughts and hurricanes at once impair,
The smiling prospects of the plenteous year.
The red'ning orange, and the bearded grain
Are scarce enjoy'd, or snatch'd with fear and pain:
The planter joyless views luxuriant vines,
And in the myrtle's fragrant shade repines;
Scorch'd in his boasted aromatick grove,
From heat no shelter, no recess for love.
　　O *Britain!* queen of isles, serenely bright,
Profuse of bliss, and pregnant with delight,
Eternal pleasures in thy borders reign,
And smiling plenty leads thy wanton train.
On foreign mountains may the sun refine
The grapes soft juice, and mellow it to wine,
With citron groves adorn a distant soil,
And the fat olive swell with floods of oil,
Thy sons ne'er envy warmer climes that lye
Stretch'd in bright tracts beneath a cloudless sky,
Nor yet at heav'n with impious frowns repine,
Tho' o'er their heads, the frozen *Pleiades* shine.
　　Struck with thy name, my country, which resounds
From many a voice, to ocean's utmost bounds;
Dear, conscious mem'ry wounds my breast with pain,
I long to tread paternal fields again:
To hear my lisping boy's delight exprest,
And snatch my *Stella* to my panting breast.

"HOR. B. I. Ode iv. *Imitated.*
By a Friend, (whom Providence protect)
now residing in South Carolina.
To JOHN CORDES, *Esq;*"

TEXT: *The Gentleman's Magazine,* XXIII (May 1753), 240-241.

AT length our fine winter for spring has made way,
And full loaded ships without fear put to sea:
Negroes leave their smoak'd huts—cattle quit the rice field,
Myrtles, lawrels, and bays, shady canopies yield.
By moon-light, our ladies, bright, chearful, and gay,
Walk the town round for air, and turn night into day.
Eastern gales cease to blight, or make our *bar* roar,
And *wild-ducks* retire to *Africa's* shore.
    Now in groves and savanna's, 'midst beautiful flow'rs,
And blossoms expanding, enjoy the fleet hours:
Let's each hold a gen'rous *barbicu* feast,
And with toddy and punch drink rich wine of the best;
For death between mortals no diff'rence makes.
A king, or a beggar, he equally takes:
Hope of distant enjoyment, the present allays,
And sickness your vitals may suddenly seize;
Who can tell what delights will attend us below?
Or order'd how soon our last journey to go?
No *Chloe* or *Phillis,* who warm'd your fond breast,
Nor jovial companions whom once you carest,
Will heighten your laughter, distend your fat sides,
Or add to your pleasures where *Pluto* resides.
Then live while you may—make this minute your own,
For the flow'r of life will be quickly o'erblown.

"*To* Benjamin Franklin *Esq; of* Philadelphia, *on his Experiments and Discoveries in Electricity.*"

TEXT: *The Gentleman's Magazine,* XXIV (February 1754), 88.

LET others muse on sublunary things,
The rise of empires and the fall of kings;
Thine is the praise, with bolder flight to soar,
And airy regions, yet untrack'd, explore;
To dictate science with imperial nod,
And save not ruin by an *iron rod.*
    If for thy birth, when latest times draw nigh,

As now for *Homer's,* rival cities vie;
This spot perhaps unmov'd may hear the strife,
Content to claim the vigour of thy life;
To shew thy tomb, like *Virgil's* shewn before,
With laurel, proof to lightning, cover'd o'er.

   Happy that here we boast the guardian friend,
Where most the hostile elements contend:
This hour tremendous thunders strike my ear,
Keen light'nings dart, and threat'ning clouds appear:
Now fly the negroes from the impending storm!
The air how cold! this moment mild and warm.
Now down it pours! the tempest shakes the skies,
On flashes flashes, clouds on clouds arise;
The noxious rattle snake with fear deprest,
Now creeps for safety to his poisonous nest;
Bears, foxes, lynxes, seek the thickest brake,
Wolves, tygers, panthers in their caverns quake:
Now allegators diving quit the strand,
And birds unknown, in flocks repair to land;
Small riv'lets swell to streams, and streams to floods,
Loud whirlwinds rush impetuous thro' the woods,
Huge oaks midst foaming torrents fiercely burn,
And tall pines blasted from their roots are torn:
The bolt descends and harrows up the ground,
And stones and sand are widely scatter'd round;
How near the welkin breaks! now nearer still!
But now askance, it drives o'er yonder hill;
The rain abates, the gloomy clouds retreat,
And all is light, serenity and heat:
The change how sudden! but how frequent too!
The change, at length, without one fear I view:
Sedate, composed, I hear the tempest roll,
Which once with terror shook my boding soul!
No fire I fear my dwelling shou'd invade,
No bolt transfix me, in the dreadful shade;
No falling steeple trembles from on high,
No shivered organs now in fragments fly,
The guardian point erected high in air,
Nature disarms, and teaches storms to spare.
So through the sultry deep unmov'd I sail,
When the wave whitens with a boding gale;
A fire ball strikes the mast a silent blow,

Then thunder speaks—no further shalt thou go;
Quick it descends the wire, around the shrouds,
Which checks the fury of the flaming clouds.
With hallow'd wands strange circles once were made,
To gull an ign'rant crowd, the jugglers trade;
Within the line no blue infernal fire,
Could pierce, but hence, malignant powers, retire;
What these pretended, *Franklin,* thou hast wrought,
And truth is own'd what once was fiction thought;
Within thy magic circle calm I sit,
Nor friends nor business in confusion quit;
What e'er explosions dreadful break around,
Or fiery meteors sweep the crackling ground.
  O friend, at once to science, and to man,
Persue each noble and each gen'rous plan;
With all the bliss beneficence obtains,
Be thine whate'er from gratitude it gains,
Be thine those honours that are virtue's meed,
Whate'er to genius wisdom has decreed!
  Accept this off'ring of an humble mind,
By sickness weaken'd—long to cares confin'd:
Tho' yet untasted the *Pierian* spring,
In lonely woods she thus attempts to sing,
Where seldom muse before e'er tun'd a lay,
Where yet the graces slowly find their way:
Wild as the fragrant shrubs and blooming flow'rs
Which nature scatters round o'er artless bow'rs.
More soft and sweet will be her future strain,
Should this rude note thy approbation gain.

Anonymous

"VERSES *Occasioned by the* SUCCESS *of the*
BRITISH *ARMS in the Year* 1759."

TEXT: *The Maryland Gazette,* No. 765 (January 3, 1760), n.p.

SHALL echoing Joys thro' all the Land rebound,
And roaring Cannon shake the trembling Ground,
Shall th' ambient Air be fill'd with jovial Cries,
And noisy Transports pierce the distant Skies,

Shall ev'ry Place with Gratulation ring,
And shall the Muse alone forbear to sing?
Shall she be silent 'midst the joyous Throng,
"Nor tune her Voice, nor elevate her Song?"
   Louisburg reduc'd and *Quebec* subdu'd,
Our Rights and Liberties at length secur'd:
What Heart that beats not in great BRUNSWICK'S Cause,
What Tongue is silent in wise PITT'S Applause?
Admiring Worlds shall worship GEORGE's Name,
And latest Ages ring with PITTS'S Fame.
   While grateful *Britons,* b'AMHERST'S Arms secur'd,
Shall toast their Gen'ral at each chearful Board,
Yet mindful of *Ticonderoga's* Fate,
Crown-Point's Subjection and *Niagara's* State;
AMHERST, the Soldier's Friend, by Armies lov'd,
Esteem'd by all, and by his King approv'd.
   Mark Westward, where *Britannia's* Standard waves,
And suppliant Nations, STANWIX[1] Mercy saves;
Where *Indian* Chiefs, and trembling Tribes appear,
Confess their Follies past, and cease to fear.
Guardaloupe vex'd awhile with Wars Alarms,
Now submits to GEORGE'S conq'ring Arms,
And blest with Liberty, and inrich'd by Trade,
Beholds unmov'd, the *Gallic* Glories fade.
   But say, lamented WOLFE, for you can tell,
What Glory's theirs, who for their Country fell;
How *British* Souls, with *Roman* Souls unite,
Congenial shining in Effulgence bright.
How CATO with eternal Laurels crown'd,
BRUTUS in endless Liberty enthron'd,
Incircl'd with Heroes, an awful Train,
Who, in Defence of Native Rights, were slain;
Contemptuous smile at *Caesar's* alter'd State,
Wailing in sad Anguish his wretched Fate,
How *Tyrants* their destructive Arts deplore,
And now with mad Ambition soar no more.
   How diff'rent is the Fate of such from thine!
How black their Name, how bright thy Annals shine.
Oh! lend thy Country yet thy martial Fire,
And *British* Hearts in *Britain's* Cause inspire,
At once to bless and to preserve Mankind,

'Twas what HEAVEN and what great GEORGE design'd.
Big with the Prospects which before us rise,
And future Harvests waving in our Eyes,
We view with silent Glee, the chearful Swain
In Safety smiling o'er his teeming Grain;
Nor fears the Harvest lost, or furtive Foe,
Nor shelters more from War's destructive Blow.
His bellowing Kine, conceal'd with prudent Care
While Armies ravag'd and the Foe was near,
At large, they roam again their native Woods,
Feed their own Fields and drink their usual Floods;
Pure and serene they run, as they ran before,
No more polluted now with human Gore.

Hark, fleecy Ewes, their little Lambkins greet,
See, frisking Lambs, their bleeting Mothers meet;
Sated with rich Repast and wholesome Food,
The Cows come lowing for their tender Brood,
Helpless themselves to glean the flow'ry Mead,
The Verdures rich concocted Juices feed
Thro' swelling Teats with Milk nutritious stor'd
From the distended Udders plenteous pour'd.

The *Planter* there amidst his swarthy Slaves,
Proscribes the Ground where yet the Forest waves;
The Slaves obedient to their Lord's Decree,
The keen edg'd Ax apply to ev'ry Tree;
Redoubl'd Blows thro' all the Wood resound,
Redoubl'd Blows the neighb'ring Woods rebound;
The Forest nods and trembles at the Sound,
And cracking, rattling tumbles to the Ground.

The Trees now prostrate, all their Glories fade,
Their branching Honours, once a grateful Shade,
Laid low on Earth, a dreary Thicket gloom
No more to rise, and ne'er again to bloom.

The Parent Birds forsake their downy Nests,
Their Cares all flutt'ring in their little Breasts,
Perch on the neighb'ring Trees, or wing the Skies,
Bemoan their helpless Young, in doleful Cries.

But cease, my Muse, act a more gen'rous Part,
Nor wound, with plaintive Tales, the tender Heart;
Perhaps too soon, thy mournful Lays may flow,
And weep some Friend in elegiack Woe,

Or if thy Wings, with Satyr fledg'd, shall rise
Some Fool or Knave or Hypocrite chastise;
But here, 'tis thine to touch the pleasing String,
And grateful Strains in chearful Notes to Sing.
   The Muse rebuk'd, attends the *Planters* Cares,
Nor minds the Silvans Groans nor heeds their Tears;
By skilful Slaves, th'entangl'd Boughs are cropt,
And from their Trunks, the cleaving Limbs are lopt;
A Waste of Wood, in wild Confusion spread,
Is strewn promiscuous o'er it's native Bed;
But lays not long, burnt with destructive Fire,
The Heaps collected, in a Blaze expire.
   And now the Ground, with Art and Labour clear'd
For Culture by his lab'ring Host prepar'd,
The *Planter* views, his Crops before him rise,
And future Riches sparkle in his Eyes:
Nor envies the *Spaniard* his golden Mine,
Or those who in Power or in Purple shine;
Perhaps more happy, tho' not quite so great,
Free and contented in his own Estate;
Around him, all in chearful Plenty smile,
And various Sports his peaceful Days beguile.
   The Race-Horse here invites him to the Course,
Elate with Hopes, he meditates the Purse;
Now a Hunter, he seeks th'adjacent Woods,
A Fowler now, he haunts the neighb'ring Floods;
There, Fish of various Kinds afford Delight,
Amuse his Hours, and feast his Appetite.
   See, the Sheep, a luscious Victim lies,
Ordain'd for Food, his plenteous Meal supplies;
The fatted Ox now smoak upon his Board,
The Goose, the Turkey, to his Table crowd;
The Pig, the Porket, next present their Meats,
The Chick and Bacon then prefer their Treats.
   The blushing Peach an humble Tribute yields,
And all the Fruits collected from the Fields,
Come smiling to his Board, in one Accord
Join to regale or to refresh their Lord.
   The Orchard too, it's dripping Tax distils,
His crowded Cellars sparkling Cyder fills;
Oft' in *This* his social Friends their Joys steep,

And *oft'* with *This* he lulls his Cares asleep.
    See yon Field with nodding Harvest cloath'd,
This laid in Grass, in *that* Tobacco stor'd;
Source of his Wealth, first Object of his Cares,
The favour'd Plant with tender Art he rears,
And nicely curious, crops each growing Shoot,
Nor suffers baneful Weeds t'approach the Root.
In vain the *Budworm* weaves it's silken Web,
Nor rests th' envenom'd Insect in her Bed;
Crush'd by his Hands, the noxious Vermin dies,
And at his Feet a wretched Victim lies.
The *Hornworm* next, his vengeful Rage assails,
Nor aught it's stiff extended Horn avails;
Pluckt from the juicy Plant, submits to Fate,
Tho' gorg'd with Plenty, dies perhaps too late;
His greedy Jaws soon rib the spreading Leaves,
Elude the Master's Care, and all his Hope deceives.
    Thus, when devouring Wolves have seiz'd the Herd,
Which late the fond Shepherd with Joy survey'd,
Big with the Prospect of th' increasing Young,
And number'd growing Riches yet to come,
One sad Night his pleasing Hope deceives,
His Prospects vanish, and he madly grieves.
    But Foes repell'd, all noxious Insects gone,
And the ripe Plant to full Perfection grown,
Now leaves the Field, and from inclement Skies
To the hospitable Roof's Protection flies;
Whence, cur'd, and neatly packt and priz'd with Care,
Attending Ships receive their freighted Fare,
And wafted by these to *Britannia's* Shore,
Adds to the Masters Wealth, increasing Store.
    See the Maize in extended Rows arise,
Shoot out a Thousand Silks of various Dyes,
It's flower'd Tassils waving in the Wind,
And wanton Blades in am'rous Sports entwin'd,
The Grain in silken Foliages conceal'd,
Wrapt up in State, disdains to be reveal'd:
So Eastern Kings, in lazy Pride enthron'd,
Hid from the Public, beam their Glories round.
    Indians no more their Savage War shall wage,
Nor *Britons* Blood shall glut their cruel Rage;

No more shall mangl'd Carcasses be found,
By Vultures torn, or strew'd upon the Ground;
Mothers no more shall weep their Children gone,
Nor fond Husbands their ravish'd Wives bemoan;
No more shall Christian Scalps their Pride adorn,
Grace their Triumphs, or their Warriors crown.
For STANWIX Prudence sure Protection yields,
And AMHERST'S Care each helpless *Briton* shields.
VIRGINIA'S Zeal approving Worlds shall praise,
And SHARPE'S² Activity our Wonder raise;
Warm'd with Loyalty in the glorious Cause,
Our other Colonies deserve Applause;
In Conduct steady, principled in Right,
They give with Spirit, and with Spirit fight.

   Oh! were my Lines like ADDISON'S inspir'd,
And were my Lays, like his, divinely fir'd,
Or if APOLLO tun'd herself my Notes,
And bid my warbling Numbers run like POPE'S,
Then GEORGE with more and greater Vict'ries crown'd,
Like WILLIAM in immortal Verse shou'd sound;
In equal Numbers emulate his Praise,
And shroud the Glories of great ANNA'S Days;
Then shou'd FERDINAND like MARLBOROUGH shine,
The *Weser* flow as sweetly as the *Rhine*;
*Hock-Kerchien*³ shou'd in golden Numbers roll,
And warm, like *Blenheim,* ev'ry Reader's Soul;
From Pole to Pole my rambling Muse shou'd rove,
And when o'er th' astonish'd World she drove,
In ev'ry Climate as she past along,
Great GEORGE'S Triumphs shou'd adorn her Song.
If chill'd with Cold, and in the *North* she mov'd,
O'er icy Seas and frozen Lakes she rov'd,
Attesting Nations shou'd with her rejoice,
Join in the Concert, and approve her Voice.
If in the *South* to warmer Climes she goes,
BOSCAWEN⁴ rides triumphant o'er his Foes.
POCOCK⁵ in the *East* curbs their lawless Pride,
And *Western* Nations court his conq'ring Side.

   But such Wonders, alas! confound my Lays,
Strike dumb my Muse, or transcend her Praise;
Confin'd to Woods, and us'd to rural Scenes,
She dares not rise in such exalted Strains.

Prologue to The Orphan

"by a Gentleman in this province."

TEXT: *The Maryland Gazette,* No. 774 (March 6, 1760), n.p.

LO, to new Worlds th' advent'rous Muse conveys
The moral Wisdom of dramatic Lays!
She bears thro' Ocean Phoebus' high Command,
And tunes his Lyre in Fair *Maria's* Land:
O'er takes his Sun, communicates his Fires,
And rising Bards in Western Climes inspires!
  See! Genius wakes, dispels the former Gloom,
And sheds Light's Blaze, deriv'd from *Greece* and *Rome!*
With polish'd Arts wild Passions to controul;
To warm the Breast, and humanize the Soul!
By magic Sounds to vary Hopes and Fears;
Or make each Eye dissolve in virtuous Tears!
'Til sympathizing Youths in Anguish melt,
And Virgins sigh for Woes, before unfelt!
Here, as we speak, each *heart-struck* Patriot glows
With real Rage to crush *Britannia's* Foes!
To quell bold Tyrants, and support the Laws,
Or, like brave WOLFE, bleed in his Country's Cause!
  Europe no more, sole Arbitress, shall sit,
Or boast the proud Monopoly of Wit;
Her *youngest Daughter* here with filial Claim,
Asserts her Portion of Maternal Fame!
  Let no nice Sparks despise our humble Scenes,
Half-buskin'd Monarchs, and itin'rant Queens!
Triflers! who boast, they once in Tragic Fury
Heard *Garrick* thund'ring on the Stage of *Drury!*
Or view'd, exulting, o'er each gay Machine,
The Feats of *Covent-Garden's* Harlequin!
  Athens from such Beginnings, mean and low!
Saw *Thespis'* cart a wond'rous structure grow;
Saw Theatres aspire, and with surprize,
Ghosts, Gods, and Daemons, or descend or rise!
  To Taste, from Censure, draw no rash Pretence;

But think Good-Nature the sure Test of Sense!
As *England's* Sons, attend to Reason's strains;
And prove *her* Blood flows richly in *your* Veins;
But what *we* Act, the Heroes of *our* Parts,
And feel, that *Britons* here have *Roman* Hearts!

"Philo Patriae"

"On LIBERTY-TREE."

TEXT: *The South-Carolina Gazette,* No. 1775 (September 21,
     1769), n.p.

> *Honos erit huic quoque* Arbori
> *Quereus* Libertati *Sacra.*[1]

AS Druid Bards, in Times of old,
E'er Temples were enshrin'd with Gold,
Beneath the Umbrage of a Wood,
Perform'd their Homage to their God;
So let the Muse expatiate free,
Under thy Shade, delightful Tree!
Its humble Tribute while it pays
. To LIBERTY in votive Lays.

Some on the *Laurel* fix their Love,
Some of the *Myrtle* do approve,
While others on the *Olive's* Bough,
With lavish Song, their Praise bestow:
But me, nor *Laurel* does delight,
Nor *Cytherea's Grove* invite,
Nor shall *Minerva's Tree* proclaim,
As the LIVE-OAK, so high a Fame.

No Region boasts so firm a Wood,
So fit to cut the crystal Flood,
And Trade's wide Blessings to convey,
From Land to Land, from Sea to Sea.
No Soil e'er grew a Tree so fair,
Whose Beauty can with thine compare.
Unmatch'd thy awful Trunk appears,

The Product of an Hundred Years.
Thy graceful Head's bent gently down,
Which ever-verdant Branches crown.
Thro' thy twinn'd Foliage Zephyrs play,
And feather'd Warblers tune their Lay.

Here LIBERTY, divinely bright,
Beneath thy Shade, enthron'd in Light,
Her beaming Glory does impart
Around, and gladdens ev'ry Heart.

Hail! O Heav'n-born Goddess hail!
Each Bosom warm, each Breast assail,
With Flame, like that which *Greece* inspir'd,
When with thy living Lyre fir'd:
Or, such, as late by thee imprest
Glow'd in a PYM'S and HAMBDEN'S[2] Breast;
Those fav'rite Sons, whose gen'rous Soul,
No Threat cou'd awe, no Bribe controul,
Who nobly brave, did dare arraign
A worthless *Stuart's* tyrant Reign.
Propitious still, thy Vot'ries aid,
Beneath this TREE, Celestial Maid!

Hither to thee, thy SONS repair,
On thee, repose each anxious Care;
Bravely resolv'd to live or die,
As thou shalt guide their Destiny.

No secret Schemes, no sly Intrigues,
No Measures dark, no private Leagues,
(Such as in Courts are daily found)
Do e'er approach thy sacred Ground:
But hither in the Face of Day
Thy genuine SONS they Duty pay.

Hither resort the Friends of Man,
His common Rights and Claims to scan;
United, firmly to maintain
Those RIGHTS, which God and Nature mean.
RIGHTS! which, when truly understood,

Are Cause of universal Good.
RIGHTS! which declare, "That all are free,
"In Person and in Property.
"That Pow'r supreme, when giv'n in Trust,
"Belongs but to the Wise and Just.
"That Kings are Kings for this sole Cause,
"To be the Guardians of the Laws.
"That Subjects only should obey,
"Only submit to sov'reign Sway,
"When Sov'reigns make those Laws their Choice,
"To which the People give their Voice.
"That in free States, 'tis ever meant,
"No Laws should bind, without *Consent*:
"And that, when other Laws take Place,
"Not to *resist,* wou'd be Disgrace;
"Not to *resist,* wou'd, treach'rous be,
"Treacherous to Society."

These, these are RIGHTS, most just and true,
Which FREEDOM'S SONS proclaim their Due.
SONS! not unworthy of their Sires,
Whom ev'ry Spark of Glory fires;
Whom Violence shall ne'er controul,
Nor check the Vigour of their Soul:
Determin'd, to their latest Hour,
T' oppose and check despotic Power.
Sworn Foes to Tyrants lawless Sway,
They'll to Posterity convey
That gen'rous *Plan,* so dearly bought
For which their fam'd Forefathers fought:
That *Plan!* which form'd in NASSAU'S[3] Days,
Will ever gain a Briton's Praise.

Be these your Arts, be these your Laws,
Ye SONS, engag'd in FREEDOM'S Cause;
With zealous Heart, undaunted Breast,
It's sacred Guardians stand confest.

Wide, and more wide, may thy Domain,
O LIBERTY! its Power maintain,
Parent of Life! true Bond of Law!

From whence alone our Bliss we draw.
Thou! who didst onc. in antient *Rome,*
E'er fell Corruption caus'd its Doom,
Reign in a *Cato's* godlike Soul,
And *Brutus* in each Thought controul;
Here, here prolong thy wish'd for Stay,
To bless and cheer each passing Day.
Tho' with no pompous Piles erect,
Nor sculptur'd Stones, thy Shrine is deckt;
Yet here, beneath thy fav'rite Oak,
Thy Aid will all thy SONS invoke.
Oh! if thou deign to bless this Land,
And guide it by thy gentle Hand,
Then shall AMERICA become
Rival, to once high-favour'd *Rome.*

Verse of the Middle Colonies

Goddess of Numbers, who art wont to Rove
O'er the gay Landskip, or the smiling Grove,
Who taughtst me first to sing in humble strains,
Of murm'ring Fountains, and of Flowery Plains,
Assist me now, while I in Verse Repeat
The curious Beauties of thy Fav'rite Seat.

Teach me, O Goddess, in harmonious Lays,
To sing thy much-lov'd *Pennsilvania's* Praise;
Thy *Philadelphia's* Beauties to indite,
In Verse as Tuneful as her Sons can write;
Such as from *B————l's* Pen are wont to flow,
Or more judicious *T————r's* us'd to show.

Stretch'd on the Bank of *Delaware's* Rapid Stream
Stands *Philadelphia,* not unknown to Fame;
Here the Tall Vessels safe at Anchor ride,
And *Europe's* Wealth flows in with every Tide.
Through each wide Ope the distant Prospect's clear;
The Well-built Streets are regular and fair.

The Plan by thee contriv'd, O *Penn,* the Scheme,
A Work immortal, as the Founder's Name.
'Tis here *Apollo* does erect his Throne,
This his *Parnassus,* this his *Helicon:*
Here solid Sense does every Bosom warm,
Here Noise and Nonsense have forgot to charm.

Thy Seers how cautious! and how gravely Wise!
Thy hopeful Youth in Emulation rise;
Who (if the Wishing Muse inspir'd does sing)

351

Shall Liberal Arts to such Perfection bring,
Europe shall mourn her ancient Fame declin'd,
And *Philadelphia* be the *Athens* of Mankind.

Thy lovely Daughters unaffected shine,
In each Perfection, every Grace Divine:
Beauty triumphant sits in every Eye,
And Wit shines forth, but check't with Modesty;
Decently Grave, which shews a sober Sense,
And Chearful too, a sign of Innocence.

But what, O *Pennsilvania,* does declare
Thy Bliss, speaks thee profusely Happy: Here
Sweet Liberty her gentle Influence sheds,
And Peace her Downy Wings about us spreads,
While War and Desolation widely reigns,
And Captive Nations groan beneath their Chains.

While half the World implicitly obey,
Some Lawless Tyrants most imperious Sway,
No threatning Trumpet warns us from afar
Of hastning Miseries or approaching War;
Fearless the Hind pursues his wonted Toil,
And eats the product of his grateful Soil.

No Unjust Sentence we have cause to fear,
No Arbitrary Monarch rules us here;
Our Lives, our Properties, and all that's Ours,
Our happy Constitution here secures.
What Praise and Thanks, O *Penn,* are due to thee!
For this first perfect Scheme of Liberty.

How shall the Muse thy just Applauses sing?
Or in what strains due Acclamations bring?
Who can the Charter read, but with surprize
Must strait Proclaim thee Generous, Just and Wise?
Through every Page, thro' every careful Line,
How does the Friend, the Nursing-Father shine!

What Toils, what Perils didst thou undergo,
Thro' scorching Heats, thro' endless Tracts of Snow?

How scorning Ease, didst tempt the raging Floods?
How hew thy Passage thro' untrodden Woods?
Thine was the Danger, Thine was all the Toil,
While we, ungrateful We divide the Spoil.

Could my Verse a Monument but raise,
Some part, some little sketch of thy due Praise,
When Time, the Tomb or Statue shall destroy,
Or *Philadelphia's* Self in Dust shall lye,
Ages to come shall read thy Favourite Name,
Fresh and immortal in the Book of Fame.

From Titan Leeds, "The American Almanack for . . . 1730"
(Philadelphia, 1729).

The Seventeenth Century

New Yorkers wrote almost no verse throughout the eighteenth century, although on Manhattan Island a century earlier the transplanted poetry of Holland had briefly flourished.[1] While derivative in form and ornate with medieval rhetorical figures, the verse of the Dutch settlers chose its themes from actual conditions in the colony. In the minister Henricus Selijns' "Bridal Torch," Cupid shoots his conventional bow; but the moment of enamorment transpires in no pleasaunce or allegorical garden, rather in bristling Fort New Amsterdam. The lovers' success hangs not on *Daunger* or *Triuwe* but on the Indians, the menace of whose raids delays their match. The Dutch verse is a disarming hybrid of medieval *topoi* and Flatbush Indians. Despite the nostalgia implicit in its rhetoric (and moreso in the windmills and artificial canals that festooned Manhattan Island), it looks on the new world with little sentimentality. Its refrain is "embrace the here and now, for they are good": take with forbearance what the "sweet and alien land" gives. Except in promotional works, it emphasizes not the ideal bounty of America but its hardships, and the command to work: Cupid "puts no sods upon the dyke." Written mainly by Calvinist ministers, it often resembles Puritan verse in thought and technique. In both, for instance, Indian assaults and the failure of crops are blamed on the sinning community. Both relish verbal play. The punning verse on Newenhuysen's ministry (included here), could have been written by a seventeenth-century New Englander. In fact there was some literary exchange between Puritans and Dutch Calvinists: John Eliot and Jacob Steendam traded complimentary verses, and Selijns wrote an introductory Latin poem to Mather's *Magnalia*.[2]

After the close of Dutch rule in 1654, very little verse was written in New York. John Adams, in ill-temper but not unfairly, remarked that at the beginning of the Revolution New York had not a single cultured man.[3] There is no way of estimating how much poetry from the New York colony was lost. A few scurrilous political verses attacking the reign of Governor Cosby are preserved in manuscripts owned by the New York Public Library. But the roster of New York poets is not imposing. The Puritan merchant Richard Steere settled on Long Island, as did Jupiter Hammon, a Negro slave who dedicated verse to the Boston poetess Phillis Wheatley. William Livingston wrote "Philosophic Solitude," a thirteenth edition of which appeared in New York in 1790. It was one of the most popular poems of the colonial period, and one of the least original.[4]

Unlike the Dutch, the early Quakers and the German sects of Pennsylvania cast a cold eye on poetry.[5] "How many plays did Jesus Christ and his apostles recreate themselves at?" William Penn asked, "What poets, romances, comedies, and the like did the apostles and saints make or use to pass away their time withal?"[6] James Logan, Penn's secretary, challenged the Quaker view by writing a verse translation of Cicero's *Cato Major* (1744), which Benjamin Franklin published as a "happy omen that Philadelphia shall become the seat of the American Muses."[7] But the Friends frequently brought Logan before the Philadelphia Monthly Meeting for breaches of discipline. The Pietist and Baptist sects, slightly less wary of belles lettres, produced a voluminous hymn literature, and a German Baptist physician named Christopher Sower inaugurated a German periodical which regularly published local German verse.[8] But even the German sects showed little enthusiasm for the vocation of poetry. The prodigiously learned Francis Daniel Pastorious left for the instruction of his children a bulky manuscript volume of multi-lingual verse and morality entitled *The Bee-Hive*, where he warned them:

> From Pöetry Poverty in all ages arose,
> Therefore my Children Content you with Prose.

If they must write, he said, let "Meeter-making" be recreation only. Besides, he never knew a poet "who was not a Lover of strong Liquor."[9]

Eighteenth-century Pennsylvania: the Junto

But the Pietists were a minority element, and after 1735 the Quakers' social prestige fell off. It passed to a boldly secular element, personified and led by Benjamin Franklin. Between 1720 and 1770, Franklin, Logan, the botanist John Bartram, and the mathematician David Rittenhouse marshalled a scientific avant-garde whose extraordinary achievements in science outshone verse writing in the colony but also stimulated it and shaped it. Joseph Breintnal, one of many Philadelphians who wrote verse on scientific themes, recorded in mechanical couplets, but with exacting fidelity, the "Dwarfish Hairs" and "quinq-angular" leaves of American flora.[10] Science was only one pursuit that made Philadelphia from 1730 to the end of the eighteenth century the liveliest cultural center in America. Commensurate with its growth into one of the largest cities in the British empire, Philadelphia evolved a complex and stylish social life. The ladies who circulated in such country estates as James Logan's Stenton, won renown throughout the colonies, and even abroad, for their literary taste. The flamboyant Elizabeth Graeme—whose own estate boasted a three-hundred-acre deerchase—created a sensation in London in 1764, befriended Sterne, and was granted a special audience with the King. At home she presided over a literary salon for local poets.[11] When William Black of Virginia met some of Philadelphia's "Female Fishers for the Reputation of Wit" he observed that they spiced their conversation with the words "Genius —and no Genius—Invention, Poetry, Fine things, bad Language, no Style, Charming Writing, Imaginary and Diction."[12] The ladies wrote, too. Elizabeth Graeme co-authored poems in a riming game, *les bouts rimez,* with Nathaniel Evans, and at her death left a manuscript translation of Fénelon's *Télémaque* plus a whole volume of verse. The local passion for poetry, complained "Misericordis" in the *Pennsylvania Chronicle,* made many women "more eager to mix the ingredients of a little piece of this manufacture, than to mix the ingredients for a pudding."

Indeed, as Benjamin Franklin learned, nearly everyone in eighteenth-century Philadelphia wrote verse. On the day he arrived in town, Franklin applied for work at the shop of the mystic and printer Samuel Keimer. We saw how Franklin spoofed the provincialism of New England elegies, and fled them. Having fled them, he found Keimer writing one—an authentically "kitelic" elegy for his deceased helper Aquila Rose.[13] A few days later Franklin won the job and printed the poem. In Philadelphia there was no avoiding poets. In verses customarily delivered on New Year's day, newsboys asked subscribers for tips;[14] by verses in a local paper Keimer advertised his arrival in America; for verse posthumously published in 1740, acclaim fell to even his late printer's devil Aquila Rose. With poetry fashionable, and a taste for it socially rewarded, Philadelphia became the nearest approximation in colonial America to a literary center. Between 1740 and 1778 it supported forty-two printers who turned out at least eleven thousand issues. Perhaps because print was no luxury, the verse of Pennsylvania, at least before William Smith's day, is topical and local, written to satirize Quakers or reprove officialdom, a form of public discussion. It lacks the high-mindedness, but also the ostentation, of much eighteenth-century verse elsewhere in the colonies. Nathaniel Evans' epithet, "Swains of the Schuylkil," and the title of "E.M's" "Wits and Poets of Pennsylvania" acknowledge a sense of local literary tradition duplicated in colonial verse only in some Puritan elegies.

The city's poets gathered into clubs and informal groups that by providing common interests and a common tone were something like local schools of verse. The most literary groups were the Junto, organized in the 1730's, and William Smith's less formal but more finished "Swains of the Schuylkil" in the 1750's. The Junto was the invention of Benjamin Franklin. Although Franklin discouraged poetry in the colonies as a profession, the club pleased him enough to merit an account in his *Autobiography*. No wonder: the Junto's "Pennsylvania Wits" were local workers and tradesmen convened for mutual improvement, a projection of Franklin's own experience. Primarily the autodidacts met to discuss weighty philosophical problems. Nicholas Scull says that the tone was elevated:

> . . . Strength of thought in lofty Language shone
> Such as Dean Swift or Addison might own.

Members also met to hear and recite verse. Franklin asked (how seriously one is left guessing), that Breintnal's poem on the Junto "be read once a Month, and hum'd in Consort, by as many as can hum it."[15] Criticism was welcome and plain-spoken. One member was put down when "Faultring Accents shewd his Muse was gone." Occasionally the club feted poets from other colonies. Scull tells how "Denham," a Boston poet, recited verse about New England's tribulations and its defiance of the King.

Seditious guests were probably not the Junto's standard fare; and despite the members' ration of culture and light, it would be generous to call their verse crude. But "Denham's" presence indicates the Wits' sympathies in colonial affairs. And however misbegotten, their poems

have an interest outside literature. It is only to accent that fondness for
the local scene which distinguishes the Pennsylvania Wits from other
groups in eighteenth-century America, that one notes how Leeds sings
his "much-lov'd *Pennsilvania's* Praise," how Breintnal details a single
city street in 1730, how Taylor sees the arts hastening to Philadelphia:

> Let *Europe* then confess declining Days,
> Content with Fame, and so resign the Bays.
> From Eastern Regions, see, the Muse invades
> Our fragrant Groves, and Occidental Shades.

Local accomplishments in science earned such hopes a basis in fact
which no other colony could claim. The hope for peace found a similar
warrant in William Penn's special, pacific relations with nearby Indian
tribes. Many Pennsylvanians viewed the colony as a sanctuary indeed.
Here, Leeds says, "Fearless the Hind pursues his wonted Toil" while in
Europe "War and Desolation widely reigns."[16]

The Swains of the Schuylkil

Of all William Smith's group, only Francis Hopkinson joined this
chorus of provincial self-glorification.[17] Otherwise the twenty years
separating the Wits and Swains created opposition, despite a common
scene and a continuity of membership. Thomas Godfrey's father, an
amateur scientist, belonged to Franklin's club; Smith and Franklin
knew each other well, but disliked each other. Even discounting the
inevitable battle between generations, the two groups had differing back-
grounds, poetic aims, and ideas about America. The Wits were mainly
unlearned and vaguely deist; the Swains were college educated and
Anglican. Both Jacob Duché, professor of oratory at the College of
Philadelphia, and Nathaniel Evans travelled to England for ordination
as Anglican ministers. Thomas Godfrey shared his friends' views but
lacked their advantages.[18] The introduction to his *Juvenile Poems* compares the son with the self-taught father, ranking both "among the
natural curiosities of Pennsylvania"[19] since neither had much learning.
Around the younger Godfrey grew a Franklinian myth of the rude genius
that came to epitomize the lives of many eminent but unbred eighteenth-
century Philadelphians, and many unpredictably gifted Americans since.

But what finally accounted for the difference between the two groups
were the personality and ideals of William Smith.[20] He was an Episcopal
clergyman, student at Oxford and Lincoln's Inn, fellow of the Royal

Society, and a sworn anglophile. Arriving in Philadelphia in 1753, a generation beyond the Junto's heyday, he helped found the college that became the University of Pennsylvania, and started the *American Magazine,* perhaps the most distinguished literary magazine of colonial America. It is a tribute to Smith's power as a literary catalyst that when the *American Magazine* expired in 1758, Philadelphia had no periodical for another decade. Quite apart from its political support of the Crown against France, the magazine publicized the talents of Smith's pupils at the college, printing works by Francis Hopkinson, John Beveridge, Thomas Shippen, and Thomas Godfrey. (Smith himself contributed a series of essays entitled "The Hermit.") His favors in the cause of artistic promise were not confined to the magazine. He acclaimed Benjamin West, almost certainly had Godfrey's "Victory" published in the *Library* in 1762, and certainly had Evans' poems published in the *Liverpool Advertiser* a year later. Unlike the Wits, he spurned a provincial literature and, seeking commerce with other writers, made three trips to England and often visited his intimate New York friend, Samuel Johnson.

But the focus of Smith's devotion was education, and his encouragements to young poets followed from his educational theories. Invoking the Translation, he wrote that on the training of youth depends

> . . . whether our *New-World*
> (When by the sad Vicissitude of Things
> The *Old* has sunk back to its pristin Sloth
> And *Barbarism*) shall be the last Retreat
> of *Arts,* imperial *Liberty* and *Truth;*

Smith urged his pupils to write verse less for their own pleasure than because an appreciation of literature fosters social harmony. In his utopian "Proposal for the College of Mirania," he postulated that literature not only "renders Life comfortable to ourselves, but also contributes highly to the cement of society, and the tranquility of the state." A Miranian fond of poetry, painting and music can never be "a boisterous subject, an undutiful son, a rough husband, an unnatural parent, a cruel master, a treacherous friend, or an unruly and turbulent man."[21] Students at the theoretical school were to write and study poetry for two months. So brief an apprenticeship is made possible by their prior grounding in philosophy and rhetoric. Of these two months, "about a fortnight is enough for . . . the drama and pastoral, and . . . about a month for the epic poem."[22] Because Smith felt oratory a neglected art, he endorsed it especially, with the result that many poems by his pupils are theatrical oratorical exercises, usually in Dialogue-and-Ode form.

In spirit and nearly in detail, Smith's program became a working curriculum at the college of Philadelphia. No other school in the colonies officially sponsored pure literature. Some of one's doubts about the practicality of Smith's plan were anticipated by Benjamin Franklin. He called the classical taste of Smith and his students inappropriate to colonial conditions and against the purposes of the founders. In 1759 he jotted on the cover of a benevolent pamphlet by Smith:

> For all mankind, unknown, his bosom heaves,
> He only injures those with whom he lives.[23]

Franklin's sense of a too theoretical strain in Smith proved oracular. A booster of native talent, Smith was later jailed for royalist sympathies, the same which dampen his account of American prospects. In a poem addressed to the Pennsylvania Legislature, he invites the translation of arts to California, but tactfully disclaims that liberty, commerce, and poetry will leave England. The poets he guided found the local scene uninteresting or unmanageable, by turns too banal and too explosive. Godfrey cursed the havoc of the French and Indian wars for making poetry impossible. The Muse, he wrote to Evans, "Views with contempt the rude unpolish'd shade." More bitterly Evans replied that in commercial Philadelphia the poet's fate is "To loiter in poetic bliss, / And go without a dinner."

Ingenuous Smith was; yet for all its uncritical optimism his program worked. We do not know whether it metamorphosed ordinary humanity, as he hoped, into gentle husbands, dutiful sons, and true friends. It did educate poets. Tirelessly his pupils praised their teacher and college as the inspirations of their verse. In "Il Pensoroso" Hopkinson summoned up Smith to "hear the muse thou taught'st to sing" and saw new poets arise:

> Blest Institution hail! Methinks I see
> The shining Throng ascribe their Birth to THEE.

Whatever its obligations, the verse of Smith's disciples ranks among the very best colonial writing. More praiseworthy than even its craftsmanlike approach, or its nice determinations of language and meter, is its freedom. Godfrey disowned the eighteenth-century manner and experimented with light cavalier lyrics. Evans' career took the course of the romantic movement: his verse travels the shift in feeling from Pope to Collins and Gray. Their novel aims won the Schuylkil poets unprecedented notice, at home and abroad. Subscribers to Godfrey's poems included William Bartram Jr., Jacob Duché, Franklin, Hopkinson, Governor John Penn, Benjamin Rush and Smith. English critics lauded Godfrey's imagination, but faulted his meager learning, "as appears," one wrote, "from his improper accentuation of classical names."[24]

This gain in imaginative freedom was at the expense of the local scene. One could not yet be both novel and native, it was a contradiction in terms. Barbaric yawps awaited a much heightened sense of the national spirit. The only member of Smith's group attuned to its standard of seemly experiment, but also sympathetic with the Wits' chauvinism, was Francis Hopkinson. In John Adams' familiar caricature, he was a "pretty, little, curious, ingenious" man, his head "not bigger than a large apple."[25] A lesser Franklin, Hopkinson became lawyer, federal judge, musician, friend of Washington, Franklin, Jefferson, West, brother-in-law of Duché, member of the first Continental Congress, possible designer of the American flag, inventor of a harpsichord quill, poet. Hopkinson's extensive occasional verse records the growth and character of colonial aversion toward Britain, from mere dismay to the blank hostility of "The Battle of the Kegs," which assured the soldiers who sung it at the front that the enemy were provincial dupes of wily Americans. The transformation of Hopkinson's persona from a lyric swain of the Schuylkil to a rousing patriotic lampooneer implies an enlarged audience, indeed a new public. No longer addressed to local shepherdesses, it speaks to a nation suddenly created by mutual grievance.

Two differing audiences for poetry and two differing conceptions of America lay between the arrival in Keimer's provincial printshop of the boy with the bread in his pocket, and the parade in 1788 celebrating Philadelphia's ratification of the Constitution. Hopkinson directed the extravaganza of floats, bands, allegorical figures, tradesmen, and celebrities. He carried a green bag with parchment scrolls and a gold anchor in his hat as judge of the admiralty. Excelling even these stagey symbols of republican ideals, four horses drew a printer's float mounted by a press that struck an ode Hopkinson had written for the occasion, ten packets of which were later inscribed to the ten states of the union, and bound to the legs of pigeons who sowed across the country the new concept of the national destiny: "Behold!" the ode begins, "Behold! an Empire rise!"

NOTES

[1] On the culture of the Dutch settlers see Ellis Raesly, *Portrait of New Netherland* (New York, 1945).

[2] Mather also consulted Selijns during the Salem witchcraft trials, but their correspondence has been lost.

[3] In Louis B. Wright, *The Cultural Life of the American Colonies* (New York, 1957), p. 22.

[4] In *Poor Richard* for November 1748, Franklin remarks, cryptically, that readers with no taste for blank verse can find jinglers in New York: *"Muse, Shoes; Days, Stays; Serene, between; Air, Fair; Life, Wife; Strife,* etc. etc. Rhimes, you see, are plenty enow; he that does not like blank verse, may add them at his leisure, as the poets do at *Manhatan."* It is unlikely that Franklin had specific poets in mind. The point of the passage seems to be its contempt for the intellectual life of New York.

[5] For their prose, Quaker writers favored a plain style appealing directly to the "inner eye." Still, few Quakers had literary interests apart from reading. See Frederick B. Tolles, "A Literary Quaker: John Smith of Burlington and Philadelphia," *Pennsylvania Magazine of History and Biography,* LXV (July 1941), 300-333.

[6] In Frederick B. Tolles, *Quakers and the Atlantic Culture* (New York, 1960), p. 80.

[7] Benjamin Franklin, preface to Logan's *Cato Major* (Philadelphia, 1744), p. 2. On Logan see Frederick B. Tolles, *James Logan and the Culture of Provincial America* (Boston, 1957).

[8] John Flory, *Literary Activity of the Brethren in the Eighteenth Century* (Elgin, Ill., 1908), p. 28 and *passim.* Sower was the first German printer in America, although both Andrew Bradford and Benjamin Franklin printed German verse and prose earlier.

[9] Marion Learned, *Pastorious Bee Hive, Americana Germanica* (1899), II, 75.

[10] The impact of local scientific interests on poetry appears similarly in George Webb's "Batchelors-Hall." The poem describes a suburban club where young Philadelphians met to discuss philosophy, and to cultivate new world plants for the medicinal benefit of mankind. As late as 1775, Thomas Paine in the *Pennsylvania Magazine* called attention to this "country whose reigning character is the love of science."

[11] The manuscript poems of Elizabeth Graeme are transcribed in the unpublished Master's essay (Columbia, 1927) by Chester Hallenbeck, *Elizabeth Graeme Fergusson.*

[12] In Carl and Jessica Bridenbaugh, *Rebels and Gentlemen: Philadelphia in the Age of Franklin* (New York, 1942), p. 98.

[13] Like James Logan, Keimer was a Quaker literary man whom the Quakers disowned. See Stephen Bloore, "Samuel Keimer," *Pennsylvania Magazine of History and Biography,* LIV (May 1930), 255-287.

[14] Newsboys in New York and Boston did the same. A selection of these New-Year's Day verses appears in Ola Winslow, *American Broadside Verse* (New Haven, 1930), pp. 201-217.

[15] Benjamin Franklin, *The Papers of Benjamin Franklin,* ed. Leonard W. Labaree, I (New Haven, 1959), 259.

[16] Such a conception of the existing scene was remote from the neighboring wilderness, where in 1755 savages slaughtered the army of General Braddock. The Indians appear frequently in Pennsylvania verse, particularly in connection with the Quakers. Nicholas Scull, for example, gave his lengthy anti-Quaker satire the Indian title "Keewanio Chee Keeteru." The Indians and the hope for peace were related political facts, of course, and in Pennsylvania this hope was colored by Quaker notions of the Peacable Kingdom that bring it close to the Puritan Covenant of Peace.

[17] Bridenbaugh describes Philadelphia's literary culture as a dialectic between the Anglican gentry's attempt to reproduce the classical conventions of Europe, and the "practical, useful, unconsciously democratic writings" reproducing the city's daily life. But his formula "Genteel Verse and Rebel Prose" is inaccurate. The voluminous prose of Smith and his group is politically reactionary. And the most notable fact about the verse of the Wits is its fondness for the local scene.

[18] On Evans and Godfrey see Edgar Legare Pennington, *Nathaniel Evans: a Poet of Colonial America* (Ocala, Fla., 1935) and Albert F. Gegenheimer, *Thomas Godfrey: Protege of William Smith* (Philadelphia, 1943).

[19] In Thomas Godfrey, *Juvenile Poems* (Philadelphia, 1765), p. x. The writer continues that "by the peculiar felicity of their natural endowments, each of them were enabled, tho' in different ways, to raise themselves to honour in the learned world."

[20] On Smith see Albert F. Gegenheimer, *William Smith: Educator and Churchman (1727-1803)* (Philadelphia, 1943).

[21] William Smith, "The College of Mirania," *The Works of William Smith, D.D.,* I (Philadelphia, 1803), 192-193.

[22] *Ibid.,* pp. 187-188.

[23] In Horace Wemyss Smith, *Life and Correspondence of the Reverend William Smith, D.D.* (Philadelphia, 1879), p. 341.

[24] Godfrey, p. xiii.

[25] In George Everett Hastings, *The Life and Works of Francis Hopkinson* (Chicago, 1926), p. 266. My sketch of Hopkinson's career is taken from Hastings, *passim.*

Henricus Selijns

(1636-1701)

"Bridal Torch

For Rev. AEgidius Luyck, Rector of the Latin School at New Amsterdam, and Judith Van Isendoorn, Lighted shortly after the Esopus Murder Committed at Wiltwyck, in New Netherland, by the Indians, in the Year 1663."

TEXT: Henry Cruse Murphy, *Anthology of New Netherland* (New York, 1865), pp. 136-147.

How soon the flame of war the flame of love destroys!
For Mars comes wickedly, the innocent to injure;
    Nor does it Cupid please, who peace and love enjoys,
And starts, at sight of arms, to hide himself from danger.
    He sees the treachery, unlooked for, but designed,
And says: "Can this be right, so stealthily to come in?
    They show a friendly smile, but cloak a hostile mind;
'Tis well to fear for Absalom's and Joab's cunning."
    His words are yet still warm, and does he not behold,
Alas! house after house, with Indian monsters posted?
    Child upon child burnt up? and man on man lain cold?
Barn upon barn consumed? and pregnant women roasted?
    They flee, each where he can. "From Wiltwyck is my home,
I go," so speaks the wight, "in woods and hills t'abide in."
    He bow and arrow seeks; but they had both become
The Indian's ready spoil, who here and there were hiding.
    When he is robb'd of these, his weapons are all gone.
And had he not betimes unto his wings betaken,
    They sure had killed or wounded him, or captive borne
For Indian chiefs to serve, or Indian forts to work in.
    But quickly sat he on the mountains of Katskil,
And thus his woe bewailed: "Domestic joys ne'er bless you,
    Till Hymen tends my loves, and wedlock serves my will.
And cursed be you whose thoughts, whence wantonness doth issue;
    Uncleanness, drunkenness and base and sordid pride,—
The land's three crying sins,—this ruin have effected,
    And driven happiness and peace your land aside.
For gross debauchery, such punishment's inflicted;
    Whose warnings often giv'n did little heed command.
"Remember," he continued, "the earth how it was shaken,
    How fires fell from the sky, and small-pox scourged the land;
And then seek for those lives, whose lives have now been taken.
    Insensibly all trade and pleasure go to naught,
And daily wickedness produces daily evil.
    What wind was that?" he asked; "it is with sorrow fraught,
And with repentant sighs; so 't all at last be paid will."
    With these and like complaints the rogue his time did spend,
And then flew back again, to town and hamlet hieing.
    But where he flew nor bow nor arrow had to bend;
And his vocation so with difficulty plying.
    It happened him by chance he soon his arrow found;

Dropped in the way it lies, just where the Indians lost it.
    He hesitates not long, but has it sharply ground.
And this, it seems, his passion and displeasure soothed;
    Although the former is the latter quite unlike,
Who is by love enthralled? Who is he whom love stifles?
    Whate'er love be, it puts no sods upon the dyke,
Its strength is feeble, and its arrows are mere trifles.
    If this the reason be, that fewer married are
And more do journeys make, is worthy of reflection,
    Unless it be, on their account, who boldly dare,
And wrongly too, the right of property to weaken;
    Who force on force employ and thirst for Christian blood,—
(When patience would have served), nor have Christ's flock
                                                        in keeping.
    Although the harmless rogue nor service does, nor good,
'Tis best he leave the savage children sleeping,
    Whoever bides his time, he spends no time, what else he spends.
Why is it then too late, to wait the fitting hour?
    Since that is wisely fixed to suit the country's ends,
The law of higher law, the strength of higher power.
    But Cupid's true design does not this point concern.
At last, our sufferings and punishment diminish;
    The captives, now and then, as from the grave return;
The savage monster's slain; his wife and children vanish;
    His maize is all destroyed; his fort burnt to the ground;
His guns for booty ta'en; his seewan[1] fills our coffers.
    They fly into the woods, wand'ring the land around;
The fugitives not found, no chance for glory offers.
    Oft through interpreters, for terms the Indians sue;
The port of peace to gain they earnestly endeavor.
    When Cupid hears of this, he comes with great ado
And asks, "Who has my bow?" and wails, "Where is my quiver?"
    "What villainy is this, ye scoundrels," cries the wight,
"Have I committed aught, that you should thus reward me?
    Unless it be, my shafts do amorous pains excite?
I shoot you only in the measure you regard me."
    They gave his weapons back, but made him no reply,
Seeking to hush his wrath by thus his arms restoring.
    He quickly seizes them, and draws his bow on high,
As if he wished to pierce some special mark above him.
    The fort, New Amsterdam, is now by all possessed;

While Judith stands beneath, Luyck looks from the embrasure,
    And ere they see or think, he shoots Luyck in the breast.
Nor does one shaft suffice his cov'nant-making pleasure.
    "Where did he shoot? where was 't he shot?" inquire the folks.
Luyck speaks not, for he feels something his heart is boring .
    As all look up at Luyck, so Judith upward looks.
He shoots a second time and pierces Isendooren.
    This great commotion makes and causes, far and wide,
Reëchoings of joy. While speaks he not, the cry
    Resounds throughout the land: "Joy to the groom and bride,
Joy to the married pair, and joy eternally."
    "Blessings a thousand fold, attend them both," they shout,
"In body and in soul, here and hereafter flowing.
    Joy fill the house within: no sorrow lurk without:
Who gives us happiness, the same on them bestowing."[2]
    Now we, who from this rogue, do neither child of Mars,
Nor Venus understand, nor yet the ways of mortals,
    Save what to wedlock leads and from uncleanness bars,
Wish them the best increase, and joy within their portals.
    May this new married pair, peace and salvation know:
The budding hopes of Luyck and worth of Isendooren,
    Develop more and more, and thus with time so grow,
They at the dying hour, the port of heaven may moor in.

"The Brain's Whetstone of Genius"

TEXT: Murphy, p. 145.

> 'Spite all the mist and rain, and winds that blow a gale,
> Or though the head be not inclined to sewing, knitting,
> Ponder this, the brain will do what it finds best.
> Here is its whetstone, sharpening farces, jests, and puns,
> I know not what besides, in time and beat of kisses,
> All that men dream, that dwell in this new wilderness.
>
> Should someone seek the stuff, wherewith to squander praise,
> To edge the tongue, to view a sweet and alien land,
> Recline thee here; this is a school to train the mind,
> Uproot whate'er is bad, keep what is good. Then know,
> Ywis, that good is always good and bears salvation:
> So come, embrace the here and now, for they are good.

"On the Ministry of Domine Newenhuysen."

TEXT: Murphy, p. 147.

How is New Netherland renewed by Newenhuysen?
　　He kills the old man off and then the new directs;
　　He holds old doctrines fast and not the new rejects,
E'er by his new pledged zeal old error ostracising.
　　Now is New Netherland by Newenhuysen's mission,
　　And Newenhuysen by New Netherland's contrition,
Led to the New Jerusalem for new delights.
What church more safety finds than in renewed rites?

"On the Verses by John Wilson, Senior Pastor of New Boston, in which
he praised the Governor of New Belgium."

TEXT: Murphy, pp. 168-169. Translated from the Latin by
　　　John Mulder.

Reverend old man, saintly prophet, voice of authority, master of the
word, and honor of the flock,

Accept the answer this city sends to you, so that your song may not
be without its echo.

Not satisfied to have praised once, Boston sends fresh applause, and
again you address the country in your verses.

Certainly you follow in the footsteps of Isaiah, and you apply skilfully
your knowledge of all the sacred poets.

The man we praise as father, you glorify more lavishly, in a song
by a better hand and from a more faithful heart.

Our governor seeks peace, but you have wandered far in quest of
peace; the sweet joy of peace is for you the source of happiness.

He seeks to effect a bond between the brethren, but you answer that
we belong to one covenant in Christ.

He is beset by the care to govern New Belgium with the help of God,
and you are moved by the cause of God and the spiritual welfare of man.

For him who rules Curaçao and governs far and wide, nothing is more
important than righteousness and piety.

He hates the pestilent breed of men who are shaken by the spirit,
but for you the whole foul throng is a sewer of evil.

They are ashamed of the gospel and the divine law seems paltry to
them; they scorn watchfulness, covenants, and the holy Trinity.

While they teach, evil is abroad. But the Church is still manifest; not for himself but for Christ must everyone live.

We admire you even more for your zeal in theological writing; all your knowledge there lies open for everyone.

Particularly, your instruction in the doctrine and practice of faith uses a new idiom.

It is yet easy to open for the Indians the door to heaven and to increase the chorus of the faithful with the voice of the new race.

However, I must confess that we are not yet blessed in that respect; at least there is no one that now represents the untutored race.

Do not blame me for this, Wilson, nor any of those who have given much, sometimes their life, for the faith.

Of this, however, you may be proud: New England has won, and teaches assiduously those who are conquered.

If therefore Stuyvesant reins in the black fury of his arms, the gateway to hope may widen.

From here I ask for a triumph in the just war for the faith, and pledge that I live for thee and for Christ. Fare well.

Written ad New Amsterdam.

My Epitaph.

If a future age shall ask: where, Selyns, is your grave?
I shall be silent, as becomes a man,
And my silence shall be my grave.

George Webb

(1708?- ?)

"Batchelors-Hall"

TEXT: *Batchelors-Hall* (Philadelphia, 1731).

O SPRING, thou fairest season of the year,
How lovely soft, how sweet dost thou appear!
What pleasing landskips meet the gazing eye!
How beauteous nature does with nature vie:
Gay scenes around the fancy does invite,
And universal beauty prompts to write:

But chiefly that proud dome on *Delaware's* stream,
Of this my humble song the nobler theme,
Claims all the tribute of these rural lays,
And tunes ev'n my harsh voice to sing its praise.

Say, goddess, tell me, for to thee is known,
What is, what was, and what shall e'er be done;
Why stands this dome erected on the plain;
For pleasure was it built, or else for gain:
For midnight revels was it ever thought,
Shall impious doctrines ever here be taught:
Or else for nobler purposes design'd,
To cheer the soul and cultivate the mind;
With mutual love each glowing breast inspire,
Or cherish friendship's now degenerate fire:
Say, goddess, say, do thou the truth reveal,
Say what was the design, if good or ill.

Tir'd with the bus'ness of the noisy town,
The weary Batchelors their cares disown;
For this lov'd seat they all at once prepare,
And long to breath the sweets of country air;
On nobler thoughts their active minds employ,
And a select variety enjoy.
'Tis not a revel, or lascivious night,
That to this Hall the Batchelors invite;
Much less shall impious doctrines here be taught
Blush ye accusers at the very thought:
For other, O far other ends design'd,
To mend the heart, and cultivate the mind.
Mysterious nature here unveil'd shall be,
And knotty points of deep philosophy;
Whatever wonders undiscover'd are,
Deep hid in earth, or floating high in air,
Tho' in the darkest womb of night involv'd,
Shall by the curious searcher here be solv'd.
Close to the Dome a Garden shall be join'd,
A fit employment for a studious mind:
In our vast woods whatever simples grow,
Whose virtues none, or none but *Indians* know,
Within the confines of this Garden brought,

To rise with added lustre shall be taught;
Then cull'd with judgment each shall yield its juice,
Saliferous balsam to the sick man's use:
A longer date of life mankind shall boast,
And death shall mourn her ancient empire lost.

But yet sometimes the all-inspiring bowl
To laughter shall provoke, and cheer the soul;
The jocund tale to humour shall invite,
And dedicate to wit a jovial night:
Not the false wit the cheated World admires,
The mirth of sailors, or of country 'squires;
Nor the gay punster's, whose quick sense affords
Nought but a miserable play on words;
Nor the grave *Quidnunc's,* whose enquiring head
With musty scraps of journals must be fed:
But condescending, genuine, apt and fit;
Good nature is the parent of true wit;
Tho' gay, not loose; tho' learned, yet still clear;
Tho' bold, yet modest; human, tho' severe;
Tho' nobly thirsting after honest fame,
In spight of wit's temptation keeping friendship's name.

O friendship, heavenly flame! by far above
The ties of nature, or of dearer love:
How beauteous are thy paths! how well design'd
To sooth the wretched mortal's restless mind!
By thee inspir'd, we wear a soul sedate,
And cheerful tread the thorny paths of fate.

Then Musick too shall cheer this fair abode,
Musick, the sweetest of the gifts of God;
Musick, the language of propitious love;
Musick, that things inanimate can move.
Ye winds be hush'd, let no presumptuous breeze
Now dare to whistle thro' the rustling trees;
Thou *Delaware* a while forget to roar,
Nor dash thy foamy surge against the shore:
Be thy green nymphs upon thy surface found,
And let thy stagnant waves confess the sound:
Let thy attentive fishes all be nigh;

For fish were always friends to harmony:
Witness the Dolphin which *Arion* bore,
And landed safely on his native shore.

   Let doting cynicks snarl, let noisy zeal
Tax this design with act or thought of ill;
Let narrow souls their rigid morals boast,
'Till in the shadowy name the vertue's lost;
Let envy strive their character to blast,
And fools despise the sweets they cannot taste;
This certain truth let the enquirer know,
It did from good and generous motives flow.

Jacob Taylor

(1685?-1746)

"To George Webb"

TEXT: George Webb, *Batchelors-Hall* (Philadelphia, 1731), p. 6.

IN Ancient *Greece* the Muses flourish'd long,
Inspiring *Homer* with his lofty Song;
From thence to *Rome* they took a generous Flight,
Maro was theirs, and they were his Delight.
Then tow'ring high, to reach immortal Fame,
They saw the Rocks whence *Albion* took its Name:
The Prospect pleas'd; they thither stretch'd a Wing,
And sweetly taught *Britannia's* Sons to sing.
Had not the Tuneful Nine to *England* come,
Th'ingenious Author had been born in *Rome*:
For in the Place the Muses most adorn,
The lovely Bard was fated to be born:
For him this Western World was timely found,
That on a Virgin Shore his Song might sound.
Cælestial Mansions and the Muse presage,
His Genius, rising with encreasing Age,
Will such bright Sparks and lucid Beams disperse,
Such open Scenes of Learning, Wit and Verse,
As will a Thousand generous Youths inspire,

To court the Muse, and feel Poetick Fire.
Let *Europe* then confess declining Days,
Content with Fame, and so resign the Bays.
From Eastern Regions, see, the Muse invades
Our fragrant Groves, and Occidental Shades.

"The *Indian* PROPHECY."

TEXT: *PENSILVANIA, 1743* (Philadelphia, 1742), n.p.

An *Indian,* of this Province, looking at the great Comet *Anno* 1681, and being asked what he thought was the Meaning of that prodigious Appearance; his Answer was, *"It signifies, that we* Indians *shall melt away, and this Country be inhabited by another Sort of People."* This Prediction the *Indian* delivered very grave and positive, to a *Dutchman* of good Reputation, living then and many Years since near *Chester,* on *Delaware;* who related the same punctually to an *Englishman,* now living, whose Veracity, I think, is never questioned.

This *Indian* Prophecy deserves to stand,
Engrav'd in polish'd Brass and *Parian* Stone:
Vast Number then of *Indians* fill'd the Groves,
Their Fields of Maiz in ev'ry fruitful Spot,
Their Towns by Rivers, Cabbins by the Brooks,
A very little Handful now remains.
    This Part of this new World then newly found,
A Wilderness that never felt the Plough,
Was that same Year by Royal Grant assign'd
To diff'rent People, under diff'rent Laws,
With Cultivation strange to *Indian* Eyes.
Then gallant Ships of pond'rous Load set sail,
And willing People left their native Land,
Despising Dangers, pleas'd on rolling Waves,
And landing here like Swarms of frugal Bees,
Increas'd as fast as *Indians* melted down.

Nicholas Scull

(1687-1761)

"The Junto"

TEXT: MS Notebook, The Historical Society of Pennsylvania.

When the Gay Spring had Cloathd her Self in Green
And Blooming Peachtrees in their Prid were Seen
When weried plowmen to their rest repair
And whippoorwill begins his Evening care
Twas then being wearied with a Country ride
I laid me down and cast my cares aside
But Bussie fancy with a Numerous train
of Pleasing Ideas Soon possest my brain
The Junto room did first to View appear
And wheilst I Slept I Saw the Junto there
Three Queerys in Philosophy were first
Gravely considerd & at length Discust
A Declaimation Next was read in Course
wherein keen wit did Virtues laws Enforce
where Strength of thought in lofty Language Shone
Such as Dean Swift or Addison might own
Busseness once ore a Different Scene appears
the Glass goes round heavenly Musik Chears
The Generous Juice the witty Bards Inspire
With Bright Ideas & Poetick fire

Tunefull Timotheus[1] did the Song Commence
Mixing Sweet numbers & Superior Sence
He Sung the Justness of Britanias laws
If not Perverted to Support a Cause
How Gold alone 'tis moves a lawers tongue
And Poor or Rich with him is right or wrong
He also Sung but with a Diff'rent air
That 'mongst the Crowd Some Instances there are
of those who will the poor mans Cause Maintain
Without Mercenary hopes of gain
But here his Numbers flowd Confusdly on
And Faultring Accents shewd his muse was gone

Turnd Waller Next a Pennsylvania Bard
Whos muse Sometimes on Delware banks is heard
Renownd of Old for Soft harmonious lays
Pastorals Sometimes writes and Sometimes plays
he wheilst Sweet Verse flowd freely from his tongue
the pleasing Labour of the Gard'ner Sung
How tender twigs by art are taught to bear
On the Same Stock the apple and the Pear
How passing poers [pores] of Diffrent Shape [,] the Juice
Takes Diffrent forms & Diffrent fruit produce
Then mounting higher his adventrous Muse
To Sing the wonders of the dart did Choose
That tis not Strength alone that Sends but art
So Swift in air the well directed dart
Its thickness length & weight in Verse he gave
And to a grain what force it must receive
To make it fly thro yeilding air before
It wounds the plain two hundred or more

Denham whos Birth is by fair Boston Claimd
And Justly is for a great Genius famd
Proceeded Next. he Sung New Englands fate
Her Case now Des'prate and her foes how great
How B-----r^2 Crost the Seas to plead their Cause
Secure their freedom and Support their laws
How like a Rock unmovd the hero Stod
Exposd to Danger for his Countreys good
And as the only means for her reliefe
Wisely Procurd himself to be her Cheife
Cloath'd now with Power the Case is alterd Quite
He Veiws New England in a Diffrent light
And tells her now two thousand pound is just
The King Commands it & obey She must
But She maintains what her forefathers held
Nor to her Monarch will her freedom yeild
[The MS here breaks down into many trial stanzas and revisions.]

Joseph Breintnal

(1690?-1746)

"A plain Description of one single Street in this City"

TEXT: *The American Weekly Mercury* (June 12-19, 1729), n.p.

At *Delaware's* broad Stream, the View begin,
Where jutting Wharfs, Food-freighted Boats take in.
Then, with th'advancing Sun, direct your Eye;
Wide opes the Street, with firm Brick Buildings high:
Step, gently rising, o'er the Pebbly Way,
And see the Shops their tempting Wares display;
(Chief on the Right, screen'd from rude Winds and blest,
In Frost with Sunshine) Here, if Ails molest,
Plain surfac'd Flags, and smooth laid Bricks invite
Your tender Feet to Travel with Delight.
And Yew-Bow, Distance, from the Key built Strand,
Our Court-house fronts Caesarea's Pine tree Land .
Thro' the arched Dome, and on each Side, the Street
Divided runs, remote again to meet:
Here Eastward stand the Traps to Obloquy,
And Petty Crimes, Stocks, Post and Pillory:
And (twice a Week) beyond, light Stalls are set
Loaded with Fruits and Fowls and *Jersey's* Meat.
Westward, conjoin, the Shambles grace the Court;
Brick Piles their long extended Roof support.
Oft, West from these, the Country Wains are seen
To crowd each Hand, and leave a Breadth between:
Yet wider still (such is the City's Care)
To Right and Left, strong Bars a Passage spare,
South of the Mart a Meeting-house is rear'd,
Where by the Friends (so call'd) is Christ rever'd;
With Stone and Brick, the lasting Walls are made
High-rais'd the Roof, and Wide the Rafters spread.
Within a Voice of this, the Presbyters
Of like Materials, have erected theirs,
Thence, half a Furlong West, declining pace,
And see the Rock-built Prison's dreadful Face.

'Twixt, and beyond all those, near twice as far
As from a Sling a Stone might pass in Air,
The forging Shops of sooty Smiths are set,
And Wheelwrights Frames—with vacant Lots to let:
A Neighbourhood of Smoke, and piercing Dins,
From Trades, from Prison-Grates and Publick Inns.
But ev'n among this Noise, and Dirt, are place'd
Some Buildings Fair, with peaceful Tenants grac'd,
Distant, more West, with unbuilt Grounds between,
The Furnace-House and Woods close up the Scene.
On th'other Side (left in my verse disjoin'd,
But all one Picture in the Poet's Mind)
A comely Row of Tenements unite,
And set their various Goods and Works to Light;
Salesmen and Trades of decent Sorts are mixt,
(A lively place) some Tavern Signs betwixt:
Along their Doors, the clean hard Paving trends, ⎞
'Till at a plashy crossing Street it ends, ⎬
And thence, a short Arm's Throw, renew'd tends. ⎠
Mechanicks, here, in Iron, Brass, Wood and Horn,
Their narrow Shutters, with their Wares adorn.
'Mongst those, a few tall Structures proudly rise;
Th' adjacent Hutts look lessen'd at their Size.
Beyond, the Street is thinly wall'd, but fair,
With Gardens pale'd, and Orchards here and there
On either Side, those beauteous Prospects lie;
And some inclos'd with Hedges please the Eye.

"July 1740. On the lately discover'd
Wild Raspberries."

TEXT: MS, The Library Company of Philadelphia.

High, on a Mount in Oley, have they grown,
The Food of Birds; to Fruiterers unknown;
And hid from Botanists—Rough Rocks surround,
But black and fertile is th'encumber'd Ground.
   Had Bartram's Eye been there, it had descry'd
This curious Plant, which Nature seem'd to hide;
But, as to Chance great Benefits we owe,
Scull was the first, this Rarity to know:

His Business was Dimensions to Survey,
Not Earth's fair Produce view, and then display;
As he encounter'd Stones, Weeds, Bushes, Trees,
He, wond'ring, found, delicious Raspberries:
Too just his Sense t'avoid a Fruit so good,
Or not communicate it, when he cou'd.
 The Dunbrown Stalk no pointed Prickly wears; ⎫
A long stem'd Leaf, at every Curve, it bears; ⎬
Both Stalk and Stems thick set with Dwarfish Hairs; ⎭
Tipt with a viscous Drop, right out they stand,
And Stick, like Bird Lime, to the Touching Hand.
But touch them gently, or the Stem will break;
Strong tho' they look, they are connected weak!
The Trunk's first Coat soon rends, and ragged grows,
And its Successor fresh and smoother shows.
The Leaves, sharp jagg'd, quinq-angular, pale Green,
And nobly broad, & rough, might far be seen,
Seen, to be known from every Kind beside,
Did not th'obstructing Wildernesses hide.
Five-petal'd Roses deck the Branches Heads,
Long in their Bloom, and slow they quit their beds.
The lovely Berries in rich Purple vye,
And tempt the Fingers as they charm the Eye;
But more excel, in Taste and Size, all those,
That Gard'ners in their choicest Walks dispose.

Aquila Rose

(1695-1723)

"To his Excellency Sir WILLIAM KEITH, *Bart.
on his Journey to* Connestogoe, *and Treaty
with the Indians there."*

TEXT: *Poems on Several Occasions* (Philadelphia, 1740), pp. 25-26.

———*Labor omnia vincit Improbus.*———
AS wise *Lycurgus,* thro' unwearied Toil,
Made *Sparta* fertile from a desart Soil,
By his wise Counsels fix'd th' unsetled State

Of human Race, and taught 'em to be great;
In peaceful Ways led on the wond'ring Throng,
Whilst ag'd Experience rul'd the sprightly young;
So thou, great KEITH,[1] thro' Toils and Travels past,
Shalt make an *Eden* of a spacious Waste:
To *Indians* thou shalt a *Lycurgus* be,
Who Ages hence shall almost worship thee.
Tho' from immortal GEORGE your Potence springs,
Here you're obey'd by arbitrary Kings:
Some sacred Pow'r must sure your Wisdom send,
When Virtue, Peace and Concord is the End.
The *Indian* Children shall be taught thy Name,
And Woods and Rivers echo with thy Fame:
The *Sasquehannah* Banks shall take the Sound,
And bear the Echo to the Nations round;
The *Indian* Nations round thy Name applaud,
And call thee, not unjustly, like a God.

"*To* J—n C————dge, *Esq; on his generous*
Entertainment of Sir William Keith,
and his Company, at Conestogoe."

TEXT: *Poems on Several Occasions,* p. 26.

NO sooner KEITH was from *Virginia* come,
But publick Business forc'd him still from Home:
To Woods remote he took a painful Way,
Nor less Provision made than for the Sea.
Those who for kind Respect or Pleasure went,
Thought each beneath a Tree to pitch his Tent;
Eat his own Bisket, Hams, and private Store,
Drink the cool Spring, and hardly dream'd of more.
But (false to all our wretched Thoughts) we found
A House capacious, and a fertile Ground:
Luxurious Dishes grac'd the loaded Board,
With all the Bounties of rich Nature stor'd.
The flowing Cups with sprightly Liquor smil'd,
And pleasant Talk the running Hours beguil'd.
C————dge to thee we owe this gen'rous Treat,
And, forc'd to Praise, thy spreading Name repeat.
The *'Delphian* Town shall know how well we fare,

Since we are sure to feed less sumptuous there.
    May those, who ill requite the Kindness done,
Be doom'd to nought but Hominy and Pone,
And in an *Indian* Cabbin live alone.

"E. M."

"The Wits and Poets of Pennsylvania, a Poem."

TEXT: *The American Weekly Mercury,* (April 29–May 6, 1731), n.p.

> *Spiritum Phoebus mihi, Phoebus Artem*
> *Carminis Nomenque dedit Poetae.*
>
>   Hor.[1]

'TWAS when a gloom my pensive Soul o're spread,
And every gay and chearful Thought was fled;
As o're the Expanded Fields I cast my Eye,
Two sportive, active Colts I chanc't to spy.

    A gamesome chace the Challenge first began,
And wanton Whinnies Eccho'd as they ran;
Then with a Wheel they Circled o're the Ground,
And meeting, strove to show the highest Bound;
When Breast to Breast Erect, They paw'd the Air,
And loving Raps, by turns, as freely Share;
Descending then, Each in the Pseudo Fight
Embrac'd so lovingly, and strove to bite;
But biteing hard, The weakest gave a Roar,
Turn'd Tail, Kickt up his Heels, and play'd no more.

    Bless Me, says I, so fares it with our *Witts!*
These Colts have only Acted o're their Tricks.
Strait at the Word, I felt my Bosome glow,
Nor could have Ease, till I those *Witts* should show.

    For choice of Diction, I would *B—ret—nl*[2] choose,
For just Conceptions, and a ready Muse;
Yet is that Muse too labour'd and prolix,
And seldom, on the Wing, knows where to fix.
So strictly regular is every Rise,

His Poems loose the Beauty's of Surprize,
In this, his Flame is like a Kitchen fire
We see the Billets cast, that mounts it higher:
Yet thro' the whole appear'd an Excellence,
And more of *Wit* would shine, but curb'd to much by Sense.

With Years opprest, and compass'd round with Woes,
A Muse with Fire fraught yet *T——y—lr*[3] shoes.
His fancy's bold, Harmonious are his Lays,
And were He more correct, He'd reach the Bays:
But Heedless of the Rein, He Ply's the Whip,
'And in's carreer make *Heavenly Mansions* speak;
'Avers, *America's* for this found Out,
'That *W—b*[4] might roar, and sing, and make a rout;
'Then tells us *Georgee* had been born at *Rome,*
'But that like other folks, He dropt at home.[5]
Yet such a Sweetness trills thro' all his Strains,
To have Our Ears so pleas'd, We could away with Brains.

Shew next, the Muse hath Rang'd the distent Spheres,
And when the Gods were speaking, cockt her Ears;
Heard the decrees of Thunder-flinging Jove,
And then came back, and told Us all for Love:
Twas *Georges* Muse rang'd this untrodden Track,
W—b! Who like *Bantoft's*[6] fam'd for the best Hack;
For thro' the Piece Poetick Genius shines,
Where, Thoughts sublime Meet in harmonious Lines:
Where, bounding *Pegasus* with loosen'd Rein,
Proud of the Course, shows a well order'd Flame.
Pleas'd with the Event, a second Heat he try'd,
And soar'd its true; but with a lessen'd Pride.
Some say he got a most confounded fall,
And snapt a Leg in two, against the Hall;
Which the *Chimeroans* seeing eas'd his Pain
By Paper Stampt, and sat all right again.

But see! A Poet of another Tribe,[7]
Stalks round *Parnasus* with a sullen Pride.
No Rhymer equal's him in false Sublime,
A Rumbling bombast loads the labouring Line:
Such in his Flights! But when his humbler Flame

Descends to common Sense, none write more plain;
With Sp—ws and Sh—tes he stuffs the savoury Song,
And Beatle like, seems mighty fond of Dung.

In *Br—ks*[8] Capacious Breast the Muses sit
Enrob'd with Sense polite, and poignant Wit;
His Lines run smoothly, tho' the Current strong;
He forms with Ease, with Judgment sings the Song.
As th'Awful Elm Supports the Purpling Vine,
So round his Sense his sprightly *Wit* Entwines:
Oh! would He oftner write, so should the Town
Or mend their Tasts, or lay the Muses down;
For after Manna, who would Garbage Eat!
That hath a Spark of Sense, or Grain of *Wit*.

William Smith

(1727-1803)

From "Copy of Verses,
Addressed to *The* Gentlemen *of the House of Representatives.*"

TEXT: *Some Thoughts on Education* (New York, 1752), pp. 19-36.

Ad Reipublicae formandas & *stabiliendas* Vires, & *ad sanandos Populos, omnis pertinet* Oratio.—Cic.[1]

"AND does the Glory and the Bliss of States
"Down thro' their whole Existence so much hang
"On planning early Laws for tutoring Youth?
"Is this the *Legislator's* noblest Task,
"The very Soul and Basis of his Work?"
    Oh! then, ye *Patriots!* whom this Infant-State
Selects to guard its *Liberties,* and plan
Its rising Grandeur, think how much the Fate
Of late *Posterity* depends on You;——
That on this long-neglected Work depends
No less, perhaps, than whether our *New-World*
(When by the sad Vicissitude of Things
The *Old* has sunk back to its pristin Sloth

And *Barbarism*) shall be the last Retreat
Of *Arts,* imperial *Liberty* and *Truth;*
The peaceful Refuge and the better Home
Of Worth distrest, and such as fly the Rage
Of Bigot-Zeal, or nobly scorn to bend
The Knee to sate a Tyrant's frantic Pride.
And let not little superficial Minds
Deem these wild Notions or Conjectures rash.
For turn impartial *Reason's* Eye abroad
To scan the State of Things;—what can we see,
But Fluctuation and abhorr'd Decay?
From Death and from Corruption (so first will'd
Th' all-forming SIRE) fresh *Generation* springs!
And the Production of One natural Mode,
Is but Destruction of Another.—Thus,
Eternal Change is *Nature's* State on Earth:
Some Hand behind for ever shifts the Scene,
From seeming *Jars* educing *Harmony,*
And ALL conducting to ONE gracious End.
Thus Life destroys itself; and from the Womb
Man's Body bears the Seeds of its own Death:
Thus *Empires* carry in them their own Bane,
And in a fatal Circle ever run
From virtuous *Industry* and *Valor,* first
To *Wealth* and *Conquest;* next to *Luxury;*
And then to foul *Corruption,* bloted *Morals,*
Faction and *Anarchy,* a horrid Train!
Till at the last they rush, by their own Weight,
A Prey to some brave, crafty, wicked MAN
Who feeds their *Wants,* their *Avarice,* and their *Vice,*
And sinks them in the Gulf of rotten *Sloth:*
Until again, weak-shooting here and there,
From their corrupted Ruins spring a Few
That, branch'd in separate petty States, afford
A sickly Image of their former Fame.

The Voice of Story speaks this Truth aloud,
With this sole Difference, that some have expir'd
In *Infancy;* while some of stabler Make,
By tumbling down the Superstructure oft,
Strengthening the *Basis,* and, on every Shock,

Still running back to their first Principles,
Have stood a Length of Years:—But all, at last,
(Fam'd *Lacedoemon, Athens, Carthage, Rome,*)
Have fall'n, and prove how frail are human Things.
And thus, since Death's th' inevitable Doom
Of every Body, th' Animal alike
And Politic; who does not, pensive, see
That even *Britannia's* self, the firmest State
That e'er was built, tho' founded on the Rock
Of *Freedom* and of *Right,* must moulder down;
And at the last (but O indulgent HEAVEN
Roll far that Day!) must sink into the Tomb
Where th' airy GHOSTS of mighty Empires stalk,
In melancholy Guise, with not one Mark
Of *Glory* left, their wither'd *Laurels* all
Dropt from their Brow to hiss the PRIDE OF MAN!

    Then whether we survive, (if *Time* survives,)
Or whether this our *State* shall meanly fall,
Before it reach its full *Maturity,*
Depends entirely on our Conduct now.
Our kindly MOTHER envies not our Bliss,
But in our Glory and Prosperity,
Her truest Honor, Strength and Safety finds.
Sure, then, it much imports US to exalt
Our drooping GENIUS, and rear up a Race
Of *Manners* polish'd, mild and just in *Peace;*
But nobly daring and untam'd in *War;*
That, when her *Fabric* once begins to slide,
We gratefully may prop her Fall, espouse
Her just Concerns; and rising dreadful, pour
Our Indignation on her every Foe:
And bid, in Ages hence, our generous Youth
Stream forth in ardent Bands (as at this Hour,
By thousand Insults rous'd, we greatly ought,
And, keen for *Vengeance,* only wait her Word)
To scourge the faithless *Spaniards,* when amid
The deep Tranquility of *Peace* they dare
Infest her watery Reign; and, beggar'd, send
The MERCHANT home a *Passenger* despoil'd
Of all that well-earn'd *Wealth,* for which he tore

Himself from the soft Bosom of his Wife,
And Children's dear Embrace, to beat the Surge
For many an anxious and unjoyous *Moon.*
Or when a Free-born BRITON (of more Worth
Than all *Iberia,* with her Realms of Gold,
Her King Himself and his whole *Host* of *Slaves*)
Is chain'd inglorious down to tug the *Oar,*
Or earth'd alive in the deep rayless Gloom
Of *Mines* inhuman;—O then big with Rage,
To pour our hostil Thousands glowing forth;
To roll our waken'd Thunders on their Head;
To drive them howling o'er the *Atlantic Foam,*
And make the *Dastards* shrink into their *Ports,*
(Alone in *Insult* bold, in *Murder* brave;)
Or whelm them in the Womb of watry Death
T' attone for guiltless *Millions,* in cold Blood,
Butcher'd unmanly, when, beneath the Mask
Of meek *Religion's* injur'd *Name,* they first,
With fell exterminating *Rage* disturb'd
PAN's peaceful Reign in this blest Hemisphere,
Peruvia's golden Glories laid in Dust,
With all the shining Pride of *Mexico,*
And robb'd them of their ancient Race of Kings,
Their YNCA's, and their MONTEZUMA's fam'd;
——Oh! thus, with Zeal indignant, to assert
Britannia's Honor, wreak our keenest *Wrath*
On polish'd *Ravagers,* and, duteously,
Thus stay a hoary *Parent's* failing Head,
Long hence, must be no vulgar *Luxury!*

And when at last, in Spite of human Skill,
In Spite of all her ancient Fame and Strength,
And our fond filial Struggles to protract
Her precious Period, by stern Fate's Decree,
She shall expire; and, on her joyless Shore,
Empire and *Liberty* their radiant Wings
Expand to quit the sluggish *eastern World;*
And cross the vast *Atlantic* meditate
Their Airy Passage to these western Climes,
In Quest of some Retreat to sojourn safe
Till Time shall end;—then may we fondly wait

To hail the glorious Guests on their Approach
To this *New World;* and woo them first to fix
Their Reign with us; until again (when we
Diseas'd and sunk, are ripe for Death) they're call'd
By Fate to bless a Race of more Desert.

   For as the SUN, refulgent GOD of Day,
Rejoycing Earth, diurnal, rides along,
Pompous, from East to farthest West; even so
Who knows but *Empire, Liberty* and *Arts.*
With their resplendant Train, are doom'd to move
From East still Westward; and, ere the long Day
Of Time shall end, in Soul-rejoycing Tour,
Surround the Globe and every People bless?
And thus, methinks, the *Universal* KING,
When first he spoke this *Earth* from *Chaos'* Gloom,
Gave them in Charge:—
                'Descend, ye heavenly Powers!
'And first illumin eastern Swains who tend
'Their feeding Flocks, and in the rural Cot
'With Innocence and simple *Nature* live:
'Then, gathering Glory still as you advance,
'Bend westward o'er *Hefestia, Persia, Greece;*
'Thence o'er *Hesperian* Realms; and as you move
'Sublime along, let your Heart-gladning Rays
'Far to the North, on *Scythia's* lonely Race
'And vast *Sarmatia,*[2] shine: Then, th' *Alpine*-Heights
'Ascend, there bidding Rocks and Mountains bare
'And Snow eternal, charm the SOUL even more
'Than *Arno's* teeming VALE, forsook by you:
'Then onward-coursing, o'er *Germania* bend;
'Reaching, the While, the farthest Polar Verge
'Of wintry *Scandinavia's* frozen Climes:
'Then westward still o'er fair *Britannia's* Isles,
'And utmost *Thule's* self, pursue your Course;
'There, on *Europe's* last, but noblest, Sons,
'Beam your full Blaze: and, fondly-lingring long,
'Forsake them not, till every virtuous Spark
'Forsakes their pulseless Breast; and the old World,
'Spurning all Cure, in broad *Corruption* lies.

'Then, steering o'er the western murmuring *Main,*
'Stretch o'er *America's* unknown Extent;
'Her every latent Nook explore; and pierce
'The awful central Depths of her wild Woods,
'Planted of old, where (blush ye Scenes of Art)
'Untutor'd *Nature* holds her bloodless Reign;
'Till all her sluggish and unthinking Sons,
'Of every Language and of every Hue,
'Rous'd and exalted by your genial Beam
'Boldly t'assert their native Rights as Men,
'Enjoy by turns, their Day of polish'd Bliss,
'And sink, by Turns, in *Slavery's* gloomy Night.
'Thus, when you have perform'd your destin'd Round,
'And shone, with setting Ray, on th' utmost Bourne
'Of **California,* which, far jetting out,
'Nearly embraces *Asia's* eastern Coast,
'Where in the Dawn of Time you first appear'd;
'Then will I, rising in my Might, stretch forth
'My strong right Arm, and *Renovation* give
'To *Nature;* will my Sceptre reassume;
'And bid you reascend to the bright Realms
'Of Day, for ever there, beneath my Sway,
'With stedfast *Peace* and *Order* join'd, to reign;
'Where Sloth, Corruption, Flux and sad Decay
'Can never come; where *Death* Himself must DIE.'

Thus has the MUSE assay'd to pierce the Gloom
Of DESTINY, to read our distant Lot,
And spread the goodly Prospect out to View;
Not th'idle Dream of *Fancy's* forgeful Brain,

---

* It is certain that the last-known Head-Land of *California,* (the most western Province of this Continent) is not many Degrees distant from *Japan* and the Peninsula of *Kamtschatka* towards the N.E. Parts of *Asia*: But as there has lately been discover'd by the *Russians,* an immense Tract to the East of *Kamtschatka* approaching to *North-America,* it is highly probable that this Continent is either immediately join'd, or, by Means of a Chain of Islands, has an easy Communication with that of *Asia*: And if this is denied, it will not be easy for all the Philosophy and Invention of the World, to account for the first Peopling of *America,* and the Variety of its Animals, if we allow the Deluge to have been universal. —*Vid. Dissert*: On Peopling *America,* annex'd to the 20th Vol. of *The Universal History,* &c. [Smith's note.]

But what sound Reason tells Us we may be;
What Parent-Heaven has plac'd full in our Sight
And whispers us to grasp; what on Ourselves
Depends entirely——and on this depends,——
    That we maintain our Constitution *sound,*
    Hardy and strong while now in Infancy.

    This we can only do by prudent Laws
T' inform young *Minds,* and mold the ductil Heart
To worthiest Thoughts of GOD and social Deeds.
For *Education* the great Fountain is
From whence Life's Stream, must clear or turbid flow.

    O then! no more delay this noble Work,
Nor let its Glory fall to others' Share!
'Tis yours but to begin; then all that claim
The *Patriot's* godlike Name will ardent join:
So shall its blissful Influence roll down
Your Names thro' Ages in a Tide of Praise;
So shall the Land for ever date its dawn
Of Happiness from noble CLINTON'S[3] Day!

....

Jacob Duché

(1738-1798)

"PENNSYLVANIA"

TEXT: *PENNSYLVANIA: A POEM. By a STUDENT of the College
of PHILADELPHIA.* (Philadelphia, 1756).

WHILE ruthless WAR strides o'er th'ensanguin'd Plain,
And lawless Rapine, Slavery, Death and Bonds,
Her direful Train, stalk horrible around;
While Home-bred *Faction* rends the sinking State,
And *Discord,* Hell-born Fiend, triumphant reigns;
O let the peaceful MUSE, whose tender Years
Ill brook this savage, rude, tumultuous Scene,

Retire awhile, and seek with anxious Eye
If haply she may find a calm Retreat,
Where in the Covert of some bowery Grove
Peace dwells with Shade and Silence, Sisters mild!
There vent her inward Grief in plaintive Strains,
And tell the listening Gloom her Country's Woe.

LED by my roving Thoughts full oft I stray
With measur'd Step along thy pebbled Shore,
O *Delaware!* whose silver-winding Wave,
Majestic rolling thro' a Length of Soil,
Visits the secret Haunts and deep Abodes
Of many a King and Queen of various Hue,
Whose artless Shoulders unadorn'd and plain
Groan not beneath the Load of regal State!
There lonely wandering on, I pensive court
Thy murm'ring Tide to sooth my Heart-felt Pain;
How sweet is Solitude, the secret Walk,
The gloomy, deepening Shade, and silent Hour,
To Him, whose Soul unruffled and serene
Can view with social Pity and Concern
The Feuds and Factions of a jarring World!

ONE Evening mild, as at my wonted Hour
I walk'd the Margin of my native Stream,
Musing of *Good* and *Just,* the sacred Themes
That thro' the Day, devolv'd from STREPHON'S Tongue,
Had charm'd my listening Ear——I chanc'd to stray
Where KENSINGTON her growing Honours spreads,
And views her Features in the chrystal Wave;
Strait with a Flood of Glory compass'd round
A Form celestial struck my dazled Sense;
In her majestic Mien, her Looks divine,
And graceful rich Attire, the Goddess shone;
And PENNSYLVANIA'S Genius stood confest.
But tho' surrounded with th'effulgent Blaze,
Her down-cast Eye and Tresses discompos'd
Some inward Discontent and Anguish spoke.
Torn from her Brow the peaceful Olive lay
All wither'd and neglected at her Feet.
Her Right Hand grasp'd the dreaded Spear of MARS,

And on her Left MINERVA'S Aegis hung.
Pensive and sad she fix'd her Eyes on thee,
Fair PHILADELPHIA! Offspring of her Toil;
And thus, with many a mingled Heart-fetch'd Sigh,
In Accent mild, she spoke, or seem'd to speak:

     AND is it thus my Cares are recompens'd?
Is this the Issue of my anxious Toils?——
To see this fertile Soil, this sacred Spot,
My fair Inheritance, the calm Abode
Of Peace and Virtue, Liberty and Law,
Laid waste and ravag'd by a cruel Foe!
To see my bleeding Sons, like blasted Plants,
Falling beneath the Ruffian Murderer's Hand!——
And not one Arm uplifted to assert
The pious Cause, avenge their guiltless Blood,
And hurl Destruction on an impious Race!——
Was it for *this* I left my native Soil,
Thee, great BRITANNIA! Mistress of the Main!
And sought these distant Shores then far remote
From the sweet Influence of thy temper'd Rule;
To spread thy Sway, and give this fruitful Land
A fair Accession to thy wide Domain?
Was it for *this* I plann'd the Scheme of State,
A Constitution just, impartial, free;
And gave my Sons to know the ruling Art,
To ballance fair the Legislative Pow'rs,
And teach the *Free-born* Subject *Freedom's* Laws?
Was it for *this* I bade the teeming Earth
Pour from its Bosom the luxuriant Crop,
To crown with smiling Plenty, Wealth and Ease,
The vig'rous Labour of my hardy Swains?
Was it for *this* I bade each useful *Art,*
Each Heav'n-born *Science* spread their Blessings round,
And taught my rising Sons bright *Wisdom's* Lore?
For *this* I toil'd with all a Mother's Care,
And rais'd by Patriot-Deeds my Infant State?——
To see at last the proud Usurper's Arm
Outstretch'd, in Act to seize by brutal Force,
And Rapine base my just and righteous Claim;
Myself, despairing yet of brighter Days,

Constrain'd to drink the bitter Cup of Woe!——
Great my Misfortunes now, as erst my Bliss!——

AVENGING Justice! whither art thou fled!
That thus the lawless Sons of Rapine act
In base Defiance of thy Sovereign Pow'r!
Oh come! and arm'd with thy vindictive Sword
Pour ample Ruin on their guilty Heads!
For their heap'd Crimes the Retribution just.

AH! what a Train of complicated Woes
In black Succession pass before my View,
Whene'er I turn my Eyes to yonder Plains?
Where in soft Murmurs thro' the verdant Soil
MONONGAHELA rolls his gentle Tide.
There doom'd to perish in a glorious Cause
Full many a gallant Youth and Veteran bold,
BRITANNIA'S hardy Sons, with BRADDOCK lie,
The hapless Partners of a Lot severe!
Great Chiefs, in Arms renown'd, in Suffering brave!

FLUSH'D with the Daring of their bold Emprize,
And fir'd with Thirst of Blood, and sordid Gain,
The Sons of FRANCE, in Council dark conven'd
Sternly resolve their Conquest to pursue.
And *now* send forth their gloomy painted Tribes,
Those human Monsters of the Desart wild!——
A dismal Prelude to their black Designs!

AND shall my Sons, a numerous Race robust,
With ill-tim'd, base Forbearance tamely brook
This savage Treatment from a treacherous Foe?——
And have you then forgot your high Descent,
The peerless Fame of your illustrious Line
Renown'd of old, from great BRITANNIA sprung?——
For sure I am, the Queen of Nations bore
Me, your presiding *Genius,* and uprear'd
Her PENNSYLVANIA with a Mother's Care;
Fair as the fairest of her beauteous Race,
And bless'd with equal Honour, Wealth and Strength.
And will you then my Sons, my much-lov'd Race!

For whom I toil'd so many a rolling Year,
At last degenerate from your pristine Worth,
And level all a Mother's tow'ring Hopes?
Why is the ruthless Sword of Vengeance sheath'd?
Why careless sleeps the *British* Lion bold,
Nor threats Destruction with his lifted Paw?
Ah say, what means this Lethargy supine,
Whose baleful influence lulls th'inactive Land?——
Is there no daring, martial Spirit here?
No dauntless Breast to rouze my slumbering Sons,
And guide their Strength combin'd against the Foe?——
O for some bold intrepid Son of MARS,
A God-like MARLBOROUGH, or a brave EUGENE![1]
To train my docile Race to Arms and War,
And lead them forth to Deeds of martial Fame.
Then should I see the haughty *Gallic* Troops,
With their confederate *Indians* black and fierce
All routed fly before my conquering Sword.
Then should I see well-pleas'd the *British* Flag
Triumphant rear'd on fair OHIO's Banks,
And proud DU QUESNE laid level with the Dust.

NOR blame, my Sons, these earnest Words sincere,
Nor call my Zeal ill-tim'd or idly warm!——
Ah should the base, insulting Foe presume
O'er yonder Hills to march their hostile Bands,
Lay waste the Labours of th' industrious Swain,
And whelm the Country in a general Blaze;
Tear from the bleeding Mother's fondling Arms
The wailing Babe, and in its guiltless Breast
With Hand inhuman plunge the reeking Blade;
Then, urg'd with Hope of Gain, in dread Array
Bear all their Terrors to your trembling Gates;——
Or should the gloomy *War-Ship,* arm'd and mann'd,
Full on your Front her thundering Cannon play,
And ceaseless hurl the fierce, destructive Bomb,
To raze my PHILADELPHIA'S towery Pride;
Ah then too late you may at last lament
Your blasted Laurels and your faded Fame;
Too late repent you of your long Neglect,
Your tame Forbearance, and ungenerous Ease;

And deem my Counsels wise, and just my Zeal,
Too late alas! when all is sunk and lost!
Then rouze at once, nor let th'impending Storm
That gathers fast, and frowns with boding Brow,
Burst unresisted on this prostrate Land.

    YET ere I close——one racking Thought disturbs
My anxious Bosom, and alarms me more
Than all the Terrors of a foreign War.
Still shall the *Gallic* Tyrant uncontroul'd
Spread wide his Conquests thro' my fair Domain,
And still persist in Violation base
Of perfect Rights, and Treaties sacred held;
While restless Party-Rage divides your Strength,
And Feuds intestine rend your infant State.
Where shall I find some generous healing Hand
Of dextrous Skill, and honest, friendly Views,
By calm, impartial Reason, and the Tongue
Of soft Perswasion, to close up the Breach
That Discord makes between my jarring Sons?
What means, ah say, what means this Phrenzy dire
That spreads and burns in every rankled Breast?
Rouze, rouze, my Sons, nor weigh in equal Scale
With Matters of high Import and Concern
Those of inferior Worth;——but *know* betimes,
And dearly prize, th'unconquerable Force
Of Arms united, and of Strength combin'd.

    THEN boldly march, assur'd of high Success,
And bid your Troops undaunted take the Field.
To guide your Infantry, with Conduct wise
In this brave Daring be ALPHONZO'S Care;
While fir'd with Thirst of Fame, and great Exploit
My bold CHAMONT[2] commands the flying Horse.
In all your Acts myself will still preside,
Unite your Counsels, and direct your Arms.

    BUT I must hence.——For lo! e'en now conven'd
Your thoughtful *Senate* calls my active Aid.
Thither I fly to warm the *Patriot-Breast*
With *British* Ardor in fair Freedom's Cause;

To wake each manly Purpose in the Soul,
And every generous Aim for public Weal.
That so my growing, well-supported State,
Spite of th'opposing Foe, may spread and rise.
And spread and rise it shall, while MORRIS[3] rules
Humane and just, and thro' the Country round
Sheds the mild Influence of a gentle Sway.

THUS spoke the ruling *Genius* of our Land,
Then sudden vanish'd from my wond'ring Gaze.
And now bright-issuing from her Eastern Dome,
In Silver Car the peerless Queen of Night
Triumphant rode thro' Heaven's illumin'd Vault.
Homeward I sped, and bade the *Muse* record
This awful Vision in her artless Strain.

Thomas Godfrey

(1736-1763)

"EPISTLE to a Friend; from Fort HENRY."

TEXT: *Juvenile Poems on Various Subjects. With the Prince of Parthia, A Tragedy* (Philadelphia, 1765), pp. 20-21.

Dated August 10, 1758.

FROM where his lofty head TALHEO rears,
And o'er the wild in majesty appears,
What shall I write that *——*[1] won't disdain,
Or worth, from Thee one moment's space to gain?
The Muse, in vain, I court the lovely maid,
Views with contempt the rude unpolish'd shade,
Nor only this, she flies fierce war's alarms,
And seeks where peace invites with softer charms;
Where the gay landscapes strike the travellers eyes,
And woods and lawns in beauteous order rise;
Where the glad Swain sings on th'enamel'd green,
And views unaw'd by fears the pleasing scene.
Here no enchanting prospects yield delight,

But darksome forests intercept the sight;
Here fill'd with dread the trembling peasants go,
And start with terror at each nodding bough,
Nor as they trace the gloomy way along
Dare ask the influence of a chearing song.

If in this wild a pleasing spot we meet,
In happier times some humble swain's retreat;
Where once with joy he saw the grateful soil
Yield a luxuriant harvest to his toil,
(Blest with content, enjoy'd his solitude,
And knew his pleasures, tho' of manners rude);
The lonely prospect strikes a secret dread,
While round the ravag'd Cott we silent tread,
Whose Owner fell beneath the savage hand,
Or roves a captive on some hostile land,
While the rich fields, with Ceres' blessings stor'd,
Grieve for their slaughter'd, or their absent lord.

Yet, Would I now attempt, some sprightly strain,
And strive to wake your breast to mirth again,
Yet, would I call you from your Delia's urn,
But *Britain's* Genius bids her sons to mourn;
She shews the fatal field, all drench'd in gore,
And in sad accents cries, my *Howe's* no more!
Then let again the briny torrents flow,
Oh! teach your breast a nobler kind of woe!
To mourn *her* faded beauties now forbear,
And give the gallant Chief a *British* tear.

"A CANTATA, on PEACE. 1763. To Mr. N. E."

TEXT: *Juvenile Poems,* pp. 73-74.

RECITATIVE.

WHERE *Schuylkil's* banks the shades adorn,
And roses op'ning to the morn,
Give odours to the breeze;
Thus *Corydon,* a tuneful Swain,
Tun'd his soft reed a soothing strain,

By Nature form'd to please.
While Wood-Nymphs list'ning round him stood,
The Naiads left the oozy flood,
    Caught by the heav'nly song.
Attention, to the Muse's aid,
Call'd *Silence* from her secret shade,
    And *Rapture* join'd the throng.

AIR.

Let Pleasure smile upon the plain,
    See *Peace,* with balmy wing,
Now hither bends her flight again,
    To crown the joyful spring.

Close by the fair One's side are seen,
    The *Arts,* with garlands drest,
Gay *Commerce,* with engaging mien,
    And *Wealth,* with gaudy vest.

Now may the *Muse* enjoy the shade,
    Now tune her pleasing song,
While wanton *Echo* thro' the glade
    Shall waft the strain along.

Then let all join the chearful sound,
    'Tis *Peace,* sweet *Peace* we sing!
And let the joyful groves around
    With the loud *Chorus* ring.

CHORUS.

Then let all join the chearful sound,
    'Tis *Peace,* sweet *Peace* we sing!
And let the joyful groves around
    With the loud *Chorus* ring.

"SONGS"

TEXT: *Juvenile Poems,* pp. 75-81.

I.

1.

THE day was clos'd beneath the shade,
    As pensive Celia sat,
For Damon mourn'd the lovely Maid,
    And rail'd at envious fate.
Thus to the night she gave her woe,
    While hush'd was all the wood,
Still were the winds, the streams ran slow,
    And *Silence* list'ning stood.

2.

Ah! but in vain are tears and sighs,
    In vain must Celia mourn,
From me the faithless Damon flies,
    And leaves me but his scorn.
Why do the flatt'ring Shepherds say,
    Who sees my beauty dies?
Why rob the Sovereign of the Day,
    To deck those dreaded eyes?

3.

Nor are those arts to man confin'd,
    The limpid streams deceive,
In the soft mirror charms I find,
    And what I wish believe.
But what are all these boasted charms;
    They cannot Damon move?
For glory now he leaves my arms,
    And slights my proffer'd love.

II.

1.

When in *Celia's* heav'nly Eye
Soft inviting Love I spy,
Tho' you say 'tis all a cheat,

I must clasp the dear deceit.

2.

Why should I more knowledge gain,
When it only gives me pain?
If deceiv'd I'm still at rest,
In the sweet Delusion blest.

III.

To SYLVIA.

1.

WHY seek you to know what your fond *Damon* feels,
Yet meet with derision what Passion reveals?
Thy bosom proud *Sylvia* distress ne'er could move,
Nor ever could feel the soft raptures of Love.

2.

When *Damon* would urge you with sighs, and with tears,
To pity his suff'rings, you laugh at his fears;
Thus cold, and thus cruel, those joys you'll ne'er find
Which virtue yields virtue in sympathy join'd.

3.

So some curious Image whose figure at most,
And beautiful outside is all it can boast,
By the Artist's kind hand all its beauties are drest,
And tho' mimicking Life is a Stone at the best.

4.

Then hear me, proud *Sylvia,* nor boast your bright charms,
Which ev'ry fond bosom so pow'rfully warms,
While thus like an image of life, but a show,
You're sway'd by no Passion, no Pleasure you'll know.

5.

Accept the advice which I friendly would give,
Drive hence Affectation e'er wrinkles arrive;
Or like some maim'd statue, disdainful thrown by,
With rubbish and lumber unheeded you'll lie.

IV.

1.

YOUNG *Thyrsis* with sighs often tells me his Tale,
And artfully strives o'er my heart to prevail,
He sings me love-songs as we trace thro' the Grove,
And on each fair Poplar hangs sonnets of love.
Tho' I often smile on him to soften his pain,
(For wit I would have to embellish my train)
I still put him off, for I have him so fast,
I know he with joy will accept me at last.

2.

Among the gay Tribe that still flatter my pride,
There's *Cloddy* is handsome, and wealthy beside;
With such a gay partner more joys I can prove
Than to live in a Cottage with *Thyrsis* on love.
Tho' the Shepherd is gentle, yet blame me who can,
Since wealth, and not manners, 'tis now makes the man.
But should I fail here, and my hopes be all past,
Fond *Thyrsis* I know will accept me at last.

3.

Thus *Delia* enliven'd the grove with her strain,
When *Thyrsis,* the Shepherd, came over the plain;
Bright *Chloris* he led, whom he'd just made his bride,
Joy shone in their eyes, as they walk'd side by side;
She scorn'd each low cunning, nor wish'd to deceive,
But all her delight was sweet pleasure to give.
In wedlock she chose to tye the Swain fast,
For Shepherds will change if put off to the last.

V.

1.

O Come to *Masonborough's* grove,[1]
   Ye Nymphs and Swains away,
Where blooming Innocence and Love,
   And Pleasure crown the day.

2.

Here dwells the Muse, here her bright Seat
   Erects the lovely Maid,
From Noise and Show, a blest retreat,
   She seeks the sylvan shade.

3.

Hence Myra, with that scornful air,
   Nor frown within this grove,
Fell hate shall find no resting here,
   'Tis sacred all to Love.

4.

And Chloe, on whose wanton breast
   Lascivious breezes play,
'Tis Innocence that makes us blest,
   And as the Season gay.

5.

Ye noisy Revellers retire,
   Bear your loud laughter hence,
'Tis Virtue shall our songs inspire,
   And Mirth without offence.

6.

The Queen of Beauty, all divine,
   Here spreads her gentle reign,

See, all around, the graces shine,
Like Cynthia's silver train.

Nathaniel Evans

(1742-1767)

"An ODE . . . To My Ingenious Friend, Mr. Thomas Godfrey."

TEXT: *Poems on Several Occasions* (Philadelphia, 1772), pp. 50-52.

I.

WHILE you, dear TOM, are forc'd to roam,[1]
In search of fortune, far from home,
  O'er bogs, o'er seas and mountains;
I too, debar'd the soft retreat
Of shady groves, and murmur sweet
  Of silver-prattling fountains,

II.

Must mingle with the bustling throng,
And bear my load of cares along,
  Like any other sinner:
For, where's the ecstasy in this,
To loiter in poetic bliss,
  And go without a dinner?

III.

FLACCUS, we know, immortal bard!
With mighty kings and statesmen far'd,
  And liv'd in chearful plenty:
But now, in those degenerate days,
The slight reward of empty praise,
  Scarce one receives in twenty.

IV.

Well might the Roman swan, along
The pleasing Tiber, pour his song,
  When blest with ease and quiet;
Oft did he grace Maecenas' board,
Who would for him throw by the lord,
  And in Falernian riot.

V.

But, dearest TOM! these days are past,
And we are in a climate cast
  Where few the muse can relish;
Where all the doctrine now that's told,
Is that a shining heap of gold
  Alone can man embellish.

VI.

Then since 'tis thus, my honest friend,
If you be wise, my strain attend,
  And counsel sage adhere to;
With me, henceforward, join the crowd,
And like the rest proclaim aloud,
  That MONEY is all VIRTUE!

VII.

Then may we both, in time, retreat
To some fair villa, sweetly neat,
  To entertain the muses;
And then life's noise and trouble leave—
Supremely blest, we'll never grieve
  At what the world refuses.

"To William Lauder, P.P."

TEXT: *Poems on Several Occasions,* pp. 92-95.

PEARS, apples, cheese, dear WILL, and wine,

If thou wilt grace my house, are thine;
    (For these are in my pow'r.
When the last ray of yon bright sun,
Shall round its whirling axle run,
    And hasten the sixth hour.

Thy wife delights in her neat home
And babes, but let her boldly come,
    Provided she's at leisure.
Thy beauteous boy shall also find,
Altho' unask'd, a welcome kind,
    And be receiv'd with pleasure.

And with thee haste the virgin Muse,
And jest that laughter shall diffuse,
    And mirth that cheers the soul:
Banish afar corroding care,
Severity with gloomy air,
    That might our joys control.

More wisely thou procrastinate
These evils to a wrinkled state,
    When life's no more inviting:
E'er age comes on, while yet thy blood
Flows in a sprightly vig'rous flood,
    Be cheerful and delighting.

Live! live, my WILL, for now's the day;
Time, like a current, glides away,
    On th'evanescent wind;
Unstaid by stout Herculean force,
Nought can protract its rapid course,
    And fleeting moments bind.

Shadows we are, or empty dust,
And vapour-like dissolve we must,
    Nor are we more secure;
Nought can escape the dreary pit
But virtue and immortal wit,
    Which endless shall endure.

"SONG."

TEXT: *Poems on Several Occasions*, pp. 48-49.

I.

OFT had I laugh'd at female pow'r,
    And slighted Venus' chain—
Then cheerful sped each fleeting hour,
    Unknown to eating pain;

II.

By Stoic rules, severely taught,
    To scorn bright beauty's charms,
Sage wisdom sway'd each rising thought,
    And woo'd me to her arms;

III.

Till Sylvia, heav'nly Sylvia, came,
    Sweet pleasure play'd her round;
Her lucid eyes shot forth a flame,
    That hardest hearts would wound.

IV.

Quick from my breast each bold resolve,
    In empty aether flew;
My limbs in trembling bliss dissolve,
    All wet with chilling dew.

V.

O charmer! cease that ardent gaze,
    Nor rob me of my rest;
Such light'ning from those eye-lids plays,
    It burns my tortur'd breast.

VI.

Deluded swains, who, vainly proud,
    Assume gay freedom's air,
And, boastful, scorn the prostrate crowd
    That sigh before the fair!

VII.

If once fair Sylvia you should meet,
    And view her heav'nly mien;
To *Love* converted, at her feet,
    You'll hug the pleasing chain.

"To BENJAMIN FRANKLIN, Esq; L.L.D.
Occasioned by hearing him play on the HARMONICA."

TEXT: *Poems on Several Occasions,* pp. 108-109.

IN grateful wonder lost, long had we view'd
Each gen'rous act thy patriot-soul pursu'd:
Our Little State resounds thy just applause,
And, pleas'd, from thee new fame and honour draws;
In thee those various virtues are combin'd,
That form the true pre-eminence of mind.

What wonder struck us when we did survey
The lambent lightnings innocently play,
And down thy rods beheld the dreaded fire
In a swift flame descend——and then expire;
While the red thunders, roaring loud around,
Burst the black clouds, and harmless smite the ground.

Blest use of art! apply'd to serve mankind,
The noble province of the sapient mind!
For this the soul's best faculties were giv'n,
To trace great nature's laws from earth to heav'n!

Yet not these themes alone thy thoughts command,
Each softer *science* owns thy fostering hand;
Aided by thee, Urania's heav'nly art,

With finer raptures charms the feeling heart;
Th' *Harmonica* shall join the sacred choir,
Fresh transports kindle, and new joys inspire——

Hark! the soft warblings, sounding smooth and clear
Strike with celestial ravishment the ear,
Conveying inward, as they sweetly roll,
A tide of melting music to the soul;
And sure if aught of mortal-moving strain,
Can touch with joy the high angelic train,
'Tis this enchanting instrument of thine,
Which speaks in accents more than half divine!

"ELEGY
To the Memory of My Beloved Friend,
Mr. THOMAS GODFREY,
Who died near *Wilmington, North-Carolina,*
August 3d, 1763."

TEXT: *Poems on Several Occasions,* pp. 104-107.

O DEATH! thou victor of the human frame!
The soul's poor fabric trembles at thy name!
How long shall man be urg'd to dread thy sway,
For those whom thou untimely tak'st away?
Life's blooming spring just opens to our eyes,
And strikes the senses with a sweet surprize,
When thy fierce arm uplifts the fatal blow
That hurls us breathless to the earth below.

Sudden, as darts the lightning thro' the sky,
Around the globe thy various weapons fly.
Here war's red engines heap the field with slain,
And pallid sickness there extends thy reign;
Here the soft virgin weeps her lover dead,
There maiden beauty sinks the graceful head;
Here infants grieve their parents are no more,
There rev'rend sires their childrens' deaths deplore
Here the sad friend—O! save the sacred name,
Yields half his soul to thy relentless claim;

O pardon, pardon the descending tear!
Friendship commands, and not the muses here.
O say, thou much lov'd dear departed shade,
To what celestial region hast thou stray'd?
Where is that vein of thought, that noble fire
Which fed thy soul, and bade the world admire?
That manly strife with fortune to be just,
That love of praise? an honourable thirst!
The Soul, alas! has fled to endless day,
And left its house a mould'ring mass of clay.

There, where no fears invade, nor ills molest,
Thy soul shall dwell immortal with the blest;
In that bright realm, where dearest friends no more
Shall from each other's throbbing breasts be tore,
Where all those glorious spirits sit enshrin'd,
The just, the good, the virtuous of mankind.
There shall fair angels in a radiant ring,
And the great SON of heav'n's eternal KING,
Proclaim thee welcome to the blissful skies,
And wipe the tears for ever from thy eyes.

How did we hope—alas! the hope how vain!
To hear thy future more enripen'd strain;
When fancy's fire with judgment had combin'd
To guide each effort of th'enraptur'd mind.
Yet are those youthful glowing lays of thine
The emanations of a soul divine;
Who heard thee sing but felt sweet music's dart
In thrilling transports pierce his captiv'd heart?
Whether soft melting airs attun'd thy song,
Or pleas'd to pour the thundring verse along,
Still nobly great, true offspring of the Nine,
Alas! how blasted in thy glorious prime!
So when first opes the eye-lids of the morn,
A radiant purple does the heav'ns adorn,
Fresh smiling glory streaks the skies around,
And gaily silvers each enamel'd mound,
Till some black storm o'erclouds the aether fair,
And all its beauties vanish into air.

Stranger, who e'er thou art, by fortune's hand
Tost on the baleful *Carolinian* strand,
Oh! if thou seest perchance the POET'S grave,
The sacred spot with tears of sorrow lave;
Oh! shade it, shade it with ne'er-fading bays.
Hallow'd's the place where gentle GODFREY lays.
(So may no sudden dart from death's dread bow
Far from the friends thou lov'st e'er lay thee low)
There may the weeping morn its tribute bring,
And angels shield it with their golden wing,
Till the last trump shall burst the womb of night,
And the purg'd atoms to their soul unite!
                    October 1, 1763.

Francis Hopkinson

(1737-1791)

"Science"

TEXT: *Science. A Poem* (Philadelphia, 1762).

THOU Goddess oft invok'd! who loves to stray
With light-wing'd FANCY thro' the Elysian Way:
Whether it chance to please the youthful Queen,
With airy Step to grace the rural Scene;
Or softly languish thro' the breezy Grove,
In all the dying tenderness of Love;
Or, Moon light wand'ring by the Surf-beat Shore,
Attend the Water's melancholy Roar—
Thou who canst bid the eager Spirit rise,
And dip her Plumage in the dewy Skies!
Once more propitious to my Pray'r attend!
Once more CELESTIAL MUSE! thy Influence lend.
   FAIR SCIENCE soft'ning, with reforming Hand,
The native Rudeness of a barb'rous Land;
Her radiant throne, uprais'd by pow'r divine;
Her num'rous Sons, low bending at her Shrine
I sing—Oh! could my artless Numbers seem
To flow inspir'd, and equal to my theme!

YE friends of LEARNING, patronize my Song,
To YOU the tributary Strains belong.
But chiefly *Thou,* beneath whose gentle sway
The Muse delights to swell the pleasing Lay;
Glad SCIENCE! *Thee* shall her MAECENAS hail,
WISDOM shall smile, and heav'nly TRUTH prevail.

IN yonder *DOME*[1]—it boasts no pompous Name,
Yet not the less shall swell the Page of FAME—
In yonder *DOME,* with modest Beauty crown'd,
Whose sober Walls its ample Area bound,
Bright SCIENCE dwells—how honour'd the Retreat
Where SCIENCE deigns to fix her fav'rite Seat?
High from her Throne she beams celestial Day,
And distant Lands confess th'enliv'ning Ray:
The GRACES ever in her Presence stand,
And VIRTUE blooms beneath her nursing Hand.

THERE first her youthful Vot'ry learns to please,
By just Expression, and becoming Ease—
Delightful Task! with early Care to teach
His lisping Tongue Propriety of Speech—
See! on the Stage the little Hero stands
With Eyes uplifted, and extended Hands:
Or from his Lips *Pope's* liquid Numbers flow
In Streams mellifluous—see the conscious Glow
Burns on his Cheek;—perhaps the Strains inspire
The infant Raptures of poetic Fire?—
Perhaps 'tis Modesty, with native Grace,
Bids rising Blushes tinge his youthful Face?
Or now the *Force* of Eloquence he tries,
And *Attic* Light'nings kindle in his Eyes;—
Methinks I see the deep-touch'd Senate glow,
Whilst mimic Thunders threaten from his Brow;
Or now his infant Tongue in borrow'd Lays,
Swells the *smooth* Tribute of his MAKER'S Praise;
See all the Ardor of the *Saint* exprest,
As if the Numbers fir'd his little Breast.
What Joy to hear, what Rapture to behold
The graceful Bard—so young, and yet so bold
In *Virtue's* Cause—bright *Truth* shall soon inspire
The lively Ardors of a *real* Fire.

BUT now glad SCIENCE to his riper Age

Unlocks the Treasures of the *Classic* Page.
Sweet *Heliconian* Draughts enrich his Soul;
From the pure Stream he drinks without Controul.
Virgil for him awakes the tuneful Lyre,
And lavish *Pindar* pours out all his Fire—
Pious Aeneas! who attends thy Woe
But deeply feels the sympathetic Glow?
Thro' ev'ry Page engaging Virtues shine,
And frequent Precepts grace each moral line.
Whilst *Horace* leads the *Lyric* Muse along,
With careless ease attunes the pleasing Song;
Th'unlabour'd Thought, harmoniously exprest,
Gives gayer Transports to the youthful Breast.
Homer more boldly strikes the *Epic* String—
Swift are we borne upon his rapid Wing,
Where bleeding Heroes stain th'empurpled Ground,
And angry Gods are heard in Thunder round.

NOW fearless grown, the Student loves t'engage
More arduous Heights—the *Mathematic* Page
Invites his riper Reason to explore
The mazy Windings of her subtle Lore;
The pleasing Toil delights th'enquiring Youth,
And *Science* guides him to th'entangled Truth.

AT length behold to his astonish'd Eye,
Nature' vast Volume all expanded lye.
From each *Effect,* he strives to know the *Cause,*
And deeply searches her mysterious Laws.
Earth, Air nor Sea, nor Heav'n's extended Space
Can bound the Search of Man's aspiring Race.
Upwards he lifts the *Astronomic* Eye,
Surveys those Worlds of Light that roll on High;
Mid Suns and blazing Stars he dares to rove,
And learns th'important Laws by which they move;
Sits in the Center, wrapt in Thought profound,
And views the radiant System rolling round.
To REASON'S Eye there shall the Cause appear
Why various Seasons form the changing Year.

SPRING first, in Mantle green, and Garlands gay,
Sweet-smelling as she passes, leads the Way;
With breezy Call awakes each rural Sound,
And fills with Music, Woods and Valleys round.

The SUMMER comes light-clad in glowing Red,
Whilst the thick Foliage nods around her Head;
With lavish Bounty from her lap she pours
Luxuriant Gifts of Herbage, Fruit and Flowers.
In yellow Garb, see AUTUMN next appear,
To crown with Plenty the rejoicing Year;
O'er new-reap'd Fields with airy Step she roves,
And paints with various Hue the fading Groves.
Then boist'rous WINTER howls along the Plain,
Affrighted Vegetation shrinks again
Back into Earth—Woods, Hills and Valleys stand
Stripp'd of their Pride by his relentless Hand;
In icy Bonds he holds the Water's Fall,
And in his snowy Mantle wraps them all.
    THUS shall his Eye important Truths pursue,
And in HIS Works the GREAT CREATOR view.
The painted Birds that wing the liquid Sky,
The varied Flowers that glow with grateful Dye;
The clustring Fruits that smile in Plenty round,
The Herbs medicinal that strew the Ground,
ALL must the *Philosophic* Bosom move
To Wonder, Gratitude and glowing Love.
    AND now the Pupil takes his boldest Flight;
See him adventrous scale the tow'ring Height
Of *Ethic* Learning—more extensive Fields,
More pleasing Views the boundless Prospect yields.
His Searches now pursue a nobler Plan;
Now comes that grand Enquiry—WHAT IS MAN?
How form'd? By whom?—Thence shall he learn to know
From his *Connections,* what great *Duties* flow!
What *Pow'rs* are giv'n those *Duties* to fulfil:
How form the *Judgment;* how direct the *Will.*
When *Passion* to indulge; when to restrain;
And how his HAPPINESS SUPREME obtain;
What is the Nature of his NOBLER PART;
Why with Ambition throbs his anxious Heart
To draw the Midnight-Curtains of the Tomb,
And look for Judgment, and a World to come.
    WHAT Joys from such important Knowledge flow;
See in his Visage conscious Virtue glow.
His Views enlarge; enlightned is his Mind;

More warm his *Heart;* his *Passions* more refin'd;
RELIGION kindles her celestial Ray;
And TRUTH breaks on him in a flood of Day.—
PIERIAN MUSE! thy Favour still prolong,
And let thy Presence animate my Song!—
    NOW SCIENCE joys to call the Youth her own,
And crowns with Laurel her adopted Son:
His *Alma Mater* now prepares to shed
Her rich Rewards on his distinguish'd Head.
The vaulted Roof, the rising Anthems rend,
And pressing Crowds the solemn Scene attend.
Prepar'd for Action now he takes the Field,
And *Speculation* must to *Practice* yield.
High on the Stage, and graceful to the View—
"Adieu! dear Seat of Bliss, he cries, adieu!"
Pathetic Sorrows in his Bosom swell,
And, with reluctant Voice, he sighs a last Farewell.
    WHAT means my trembling Pulse and throbbing Breast?
Why is the Scene to me so strong exprest?
Fancy again renews the awful Rite;
Th'encircling Audience swims before my Sight.
Once more my Heart beats quick with anxious Fear;
Once more methinks the solemn Charge I hear—
(a) "Go forth my Sons, our first, our early Pride!
"Thro' Life's dark Maze, be *Virtue* still your Guide:
"Without RELIGION *Learning* is but vain,
"And fruitless Toil, *Philosophy* to gain:
"'Tis not sufficient that the *Right* you know,
"Your *Conduct* ever must your *Knowledge* show.
"Should injur'd FREEDOM for Assistance cry,
"Nor *Eye,* nor *Ear,* nor *Hand* nor *Heart* deny;
"With pious Zeal upraise her drooping Head:
"There's nought but VICE and TYRANNY to dread."
    BLEST *Institution! Nurse of Liberty!*
My Heart, my grateful Heart shall burn for *thee.*
No common Pride I boast, no common Joy,
That *thy* Instructions did my Youth employ:

(a) *This Passage alludes to the Charge delivered by the Provost* [i.e., William
Smith] *to the Candidates for Degrees, at the first anniversary Commencement.*

Tho' not the *first* among thy Sons I prove,
Yet well I feel I'm not the *last in* Love.
Oh may'st thou still in Wealth and Power encrease,
And let thy sacred Influence never cease!
    IT must be so, prophetic Fancy cries,
See other *Popes,* and other *Shakespears* rise;
Each sage *Philosopher,* each learn'd *Divine,*
And *patriot Worthies,* an illustrious Line:
All *those,* who nobly fill FAME'S ample Page,
Again revive to grace a future Age—
Blest Institution hail! methinks I see
The shining Throng ascribe their Birth to THEE.
    THOU *Schuylkill,* from whose Clifts I love to view
Thy gurgling Stream its rocky Way pursue,
Shall own the Change—the savage Yell no more
With rougher Sounds shall rend thy rugged Shore.
Oh let thy Groves their richest Beauties wear,
And for approaching happier Times prepare.
    ALONG thy Banks the pensive Bard shall stray,
Sweep the sweet Lyre, and wake the tuneful Lay;
Echo shall love to catch the melting Sound,
And bid it soften all thy Rocks around.
Ev'n now thy flow'ry Paths I see him tread,
And pluck thy Laurels to adorn his Head:
How shall thy Waves elate flow proudly by,
And grow more turgid, but to catch his Eye.
Thy rural Scenes shall flourish in his Song,
And each romantic Height his Strains prolong.
    THERE, whilst his Breast with sacred Ardor burns,
RELIGION, JUSTICE, LIBERTY, by Turns,
And SCIENCE too, in more harmonious Strains,
Shall sweetly warble to the Woods and Plains.
    PERHAPS the Bard, when highest Noon prevails,
Beneath some Shade shall court refreshing Gales;
And, whilst his wand'ring Fancy roves more free,
May chance to think on earlier Times, and ME—
Presumptuous Thought! shall my unpractis'd Lay
Be borne in Safety down *Time's* rapid Way;
And still the Rocks of *Criticism* fly,
Or fearless pass *Oblivion's* Quick-sands by.
Enough for me, if, with the least Regard,

The FRIENDS OF SCIENCE shall my Song reward,
No speedy Death my artless Strains shall know,
Nor without Honour will my Numbers flow,
If thus indulgent THEY shall not refuse
To smile propitious on my humble Muse.

"Songs"

TEXT: *The Miscellaneous Essays and Occasional Writings of Francis
Hopkinson* (Philadelphia, 1792), III, 186-189.

SONG II.

I.

MY love is gone to sea,
    Whilst I his absence mourn,
No joy shall smile on me
    Until my love return.
He ask'd me for his bride,
    And many vows he swore;
I blush'd—and soon comply'd,
    My heart was his before.

II.

One little month was past,
    And who so blest as we?
The summons came at last,
    And Jemmy must to sea.
I saw his ship so gay
    Swift fly the wave-worn shore;
I wip'd my tears away—
    And saw his ship no more.

III.

When clouds shut in the sky
    And storms around me howl;

When livid lightnings fly,
    And threat'ning thunders roll;
All hopes of rest are lost,
    No slumbers visit me;
My anxious thoughts are tost
    With Jemmy on the sea.

SONG IV.

I.

ENRAPTUR'D I gaze when my Delia is by,
And drink the sweet poison of love from her eye;
I feel the soft passion pervade ev'ry part
And pleasure unusual plays round my fond heart.

II.

I hear her sweet voice, and am charm'd with her song—
I think I could hear her sweet voice all day long;
My senses enchanted, are lost in delight
When love and soft music their raptures unite.

III.

Beyond all expression my Delia I love,
My heart is so fix'd that it never can rove;
When I see her I think tis an angel I see,
And the charms of her mind are a heaven to me.

SONG V.

I.

SEE down Maria's blushing cheek
    The tears of soft compassion flow;
Those tears a yielding heart bespeak—
    A heart that feels for others' woe.
May not those drops, that frequent fall,
    To my fond hope propitious prove,

The heart that melts at Pity's call
   Will own the softer voice of love.

II.

Earth ne'er produced a gem so rare
   Nor wealthy ocean's ample space
So rich a pearl—as that bright tear
   That lingers on Maria's face.
So hangs upon the morning rose
   The chrystal drop of heav'n refin'd,
A while with trembling lustre glows—
   Is gone—and leaves no stain behind.

"The Battle of the Kegs"

TEXT: *Miscellaneous Essays,* III, 169-173.

N.B.   This ballad was occasioned by a real incident. Certain machines,
in the form of kegs, charg'd with gun powder, were sent down the river
to annoy the British shipping then at Philadelphia. The danger of these
machines being discovered, the British manned the wharfs and shipping,
and discharged their small arms and cannons at every thing they saw
floating in the river during the ebb tide. [Hopkinson's note.]

GALLANTS attend and hear a friend,
   Trill forth harmonious ditty,
Strange things I'll tell which late befel
   In Philadelphia city.

'Twas early day, as poets say,
   Just when the sun was rising,
A soldier stood on a log of wood,
   And saw a thing surprising.

As in amaze he stood to gaze,
   The truth can't be denied, sir,
He spied a score of kegs or more
   Come floating down the tide, sir.

A sailor too in jerkin blue,

This strange appearance viewing,
First damn'd his eyes, in great surprise,
Then said some mischief's brewing.

These kegs, I'm told, the rebels bold,
Pack'd up like pickling herring;
And they're come down t'attack the town,
In this new way of ferrying.

The soldier flew, the sailor too,
And scar'd almost to death, sir,
Wore out their shoes, to spread the news,
And ran till out of breath, sir.

Now up and down throughout the town,
Most frantic scenes were acted;
And some ran here, and others there,
Like men almost distracted.

Some fire cry'd, which some denied,
But said the earth had quaked;
And girls and boys, with hideous noise,
Ran thro' the streets half naked.

Sir William he, snug as a flea,
Lay all this time a snoring,
Nor dream'd of harm as he lay warm,
In bed with Mrs. L———g.[1]

Now in a fright, he starts upright,
Awak'd by such a clatter;
He rubs both eyes, and boldly cries,
For God's sake, what's the matter?

At his bed-side he then espy'd,
Sir Erskine[2] at command, sir,
Upon one foot, he had one boot,
And th'other in his hand, sir.

"Arise, arise, Sir Erskine cries,
"The rebels—more's the pity,

"Without a boat are all afloat,
   "And rang'd before the city.

"The motly crew, in vessels new,
   "With Satan for their guide, sir,
"Pack'd up in bags, or wooden kegs,
   "Come driving down the tide, sir.

"Therefore prepare for bloody war,
   "These kegs must all be routed,
"Or surely we despised shall be,
   "And British courage doubted."

The royal band, now ready stand
   All rang'd in dread array, sir,
With stomach stout to see it out,
   And make a bloody day, sir.

The cannons roar from shore to shore,
   The small arms make a rattle;
Since wars began I'm sure no man
   E'er saw so strange a battle.

The rebel dales, the rebel vales,
   Which rebel trees surrounded;
The distant wood, the hills and floods,
   With rebel echos sounded.

The fish below swam to and fro,
   Attack'd from ev'ry quarter;
Why sure, thought they, the devil's to pay,
   'Mongst folks above the water.

The kegs, 'tis said, tho' strongly made,
   Of rebel staves and hoops, sir,
Could not oppose their powerful foes,
   The conqu'ring British troops, sir.

From morn to night these men of might
   Display'd amazing courage;
And when the sun was fairly down,

Retir'd to sup their porrage.

An hundred men with each a pen,
 Or more upon my word, sir,
It is most true would be too few,
 Their valour to record, sir.

Such feats did they perform that day,
 Against these wick'd kegs, sir,
That years to come, if they get home,
 They'll make their boasts and brags, sir.

The Rising Empire

"... the last, the best / Of countries. ..."

Of the three ideal Americas prominent in colonial verse, two sprang from local aspirations. The Wilderness Zion was a New England ideal; the Athens of Mankind was to be Philadelphia or Boston, perhaps Charleston, not America. But around the middle of the eighteenth century, many writers began finding the local scene too limiting. One writer in Franklin's *Pennsylvania Gazette* asked in 1752 that colonial poets "study and compose, not only for a Province, or for all the Colonies, but for the whole *British Empire.*" Moreover, allegiance merely local was a handicap in the political debate with England, and a restraint on those expansionist cravings which by 1750 proposed an American Empire embracing the continent and ruling the seas.[1]

This is no place to follow in detail the drift from local to national thinking. It occurred with differing speed and unequal fervor in different colonies, even in different individuals, and grew out of a multitude of institutions and events: colleges in the middle colonies that gathered students from every part of the continent; the opening of the interior to trade after the Seven Year's War; intercolonial religious organizations, intercolonial plans for defense;[2] the spread from colony to colony of a uniform interpretation of the colonial past, which by emphasizing a shared heritage justified nationalistic strivings.[3] Whatever its origins, the sense of America as one large country differing from England to the point of conflict called fresh attention to every part of colonial life. Colonists travelling abroad wrote ever more critically of Britain and Europe, deemed them alien, bent for collapse because of indifference to social ideals, and called healthier America the society of the future. On the other hand, more and more British and continental travellers noted, always scoffingly, the existence of a distinct American speech.[4] To aid English readers of his poem on Maryland, Jonathan Boucher appended thirty-six footnotes glossing such barbarisms as "mad," "bug," and "humgh." As the colonies discovered mutual needs and interests, poets began to reach a wider audience, one sympathetic to local themes only as they touched on a mutual cause. Franklin published the verse of

Mather Byles in the *General Magazine;* the verse of Joseph Dumbleton appeared in the South-Carolina, Virginia and Maryland *Gazettes,* and in the Philadelphia *American Magazine.* A sense of the novelty of colonial life urged some writers to theorize about verse-forms uniquely suited to American conditions. In his letters to the wife of Governor James De Lancey, William Smith included an "Essay to Fix the Idea of an American Pastoral," and patriotic pastorals were regularly declaimed at colonial commencement exercises.[5]

One such pastoral is Freneau and Brackenridge's "The Rising Glory of America," delivered as a commencement exercise at Princeton in 1771. It is the first full sounding of the Imperial theme.[6] Deliberately the poets address all parts of the country, Georgia, Virginia and California as well as Pennsylvania, New York and Massachusetts, and prophesy a resplendent, single destiny. While their tone is far from bellicose, they renounce Britain as a subject ("No more of Britain, and her kings renown'd") and hail Boston patriots as "the firm supporters of our injur'd rights." They no longer see America as the Greek city-state nursing mankind's higher nature, but as the vast rising empire, the *Novus Ordo Saeclorum* where such key human ideals as freedom will for the first time be realized. That hope became the anthem of scores of later geopolitical fantasies. In Freneau's poem and its descendents, prophetical swoons, Biblical phrases, pastoral motifs and unlimited hyperbole create a fictive nation with a uniform heritage and a common mind, spanning a continent whose vastnesses poets seldom visited but always extolled.

Essentially the poem's vision of imperial America is an amplified version of the Translation, swollen to include all the riches of western history. America's fate is to be what great kingdoms expired in order that it might be. It is their fulfillment, the final stage of human history, a reconstruction of the vanished past and teeming crossroad of the present, a historiopolis:

> New states new empires and a line of kings,
> High rais'd in glory, cities, palaces
> Fair domes on each long bay, sea, shore or stream
> Circling the hills now rear their lofty heads.
> Far in the Arctic skies a Petersburgh,
> A Bergen, or Archangel lifts its spires
> Glitt'ring with Ice, far in the West appears
> A new Palmyra or an Ecbatan
> And sees the slow pac'd caravan return

> O'er many a realm from the Pacific shore,
> Where fleets shall then convey rich Persia's silks,
> Arabia's perfumes, and spices rare
> Of Philippine, Coelebe and Marian isles,
> Or from the Acapulco coast our India then,
> Laden with pearl and burning gems and gold.
> Far in the south I see a Babylon,
> As once by Tigris or Euphrates stream. . . .

The poets illustrate their ideal America by casting about into history at random, making promises both colossally optimistic and vague. So wanton and so much eclecticism betrays simple uncertainty about the definite forms America's greatness might take. And the poem's quite conventional diction tells how far the idea of a separate America was from being an emotional fact, how the national destiny had greater political than psychological reality.

The techniques of inflation by which a group of small provinces with a brief history becomes one state timeless and gigantic—the hails and hullabaloos, the sheer rhapsody and bluster—are licensed by the pastoral setting, where time is abolished and locale effaced. Ultimately the swains adopt a theatrical trance composite of the Old Testament prophets and of romantic 'flights' of imagination, transporting themselves to a past beyond record, and a future so distant that one may look back on the future. Annihilating time and space, the poem sacrifices itself to abstraction, and fails aesthetically. But its literary devices, especially when they lead to abstraction, make a political point. Its abstract, time-denying 'flights' from distant future to mythic beginnings derive from the new romanticism; they also imply that the heritage and destiny of America are non-British, and affirm resentment against Britain. Its abstract space-denying flights from the heavens to Mississippi derive from English visionary odes; they also imply the boundless growth through science, freedom and commerce, of America's domain, and affirm the vision of Imperial America.

By its encouragement to think of America as not British, more than British, by its national address, by its projection of the national past beyond the great migrations of the seventeenth century, "The Rising Glory of America" may be said to end the colonial period of verse.[7] Its destiny-filled optimism echoed the feeling in Europe that the American Revolution, coinciding with the climax of the Enlightenment, marked a new start in history,[8] when all humanity, at last, was preparing to realize the hitherto unfulfilled promise of a rich life.

NOTES

[1] R. W. Van Alstyne observes that "the early colonies were no sooner established in the seventeenth century than expansionist impulses began to register in each of them." *The Rising American Empire* (New York, 1960), p. vii.

[2] The influence of these institutions and events in unifying the colonies is stressed in Michael Kraus, *Intercolonial Aspects of American Culture on the Eve of the Revolution* (New York, 1928).

[3] Wesley Frank Craven, *The Legend of the Founding Fathers* (New York, 1956), *passim.* Craven's thesis is that the northern view of the emigration as a flight from tyranny grew acceptable to the colonies as a whole.

[4] William L. Sachse, *The Colonial American in Britain* (Madison, Wis., 1956), p. 206. Colonists travelling in England frequently complained that the country was too small to contain vast America. Franklin asked in 1762, "Why should that petty Island . . . enjoy in almost every Neighborhood, more sensible virtuous and elegant Minds, than we can collect in ranging 100 Leagues of our vast Forests?"

The new language itself accurately charts the shift to national allegiance. Edinburgh school records show that while before the Stamp Act students usually registered as from a particular colony, at the time of the tax a few began calling themselves Americans, and more and more, except Virginians, did. See Sachse, p. 203.

[5] According to Spence's *Anecdotes,* Pope himself had considered as a development of the pastoral form, "American pastorals, or rather pastorals adapted to the manners of several of the ruder nations, as well as the Americans."

[6] Actually, the first articulation of the theme in verse is John Trumbull's "Prospect of the Future Glory of America," which Trumbull recited at the conclusion of his commencement oration at Yale in 1770. I have chosen Freneau's poem because it treats the theme more elaborately and is rather more successful as verse. Some later examples of the type are Joel Barlow's "Poem Spoken at the Public Commencement" (1781), David Humphreys' "The Glory of America" (1783), and Part VII of Timothy Dwight's *Greenfield Hill* (1794).

[7] The significant fact about the appearance of epic poems after the Revolution is that they attempt to discover the national origins. They no longer assume those origins were British, although in form and style they are still English poems. Charles Brockden Brown, at sixteen, began three epics, one on the discovery of America.

[8] R. R. Palmer, *The Age of the Democratic Revolution* (Princeton, 1959), p. 257.

Philip Freneau and Hugh Henry Brackenridge
(1752-1832)   (1748-1816)

"A POEM,
ON THE RISING GLORY OF AMERICA;

Being an Exercise Delivered at the Public Commencement at Nassau-Hall, September 25, 1771."

TEXT: *A Poem, on the Rising Glory of America* (Philadelphia, 1772).

> ————*Venient annis*
> *Saecula seris, quibus oceannus*
> *Vincula rerum laxet et ingens*
> *Pateat tellus, Typhisque novos*
> *Detegat orbes; nec sit terris*
> *Ultima Thule*————[1]
> Seneca. MED. Act iii. v. 375.

ARGUMENT.

The subject proposed.—The discovery of America by Columbus and others.—A philosophical enquiry into the origin of the savages of America.—Their uncultivated state.—The first planters of America.—The cause of their migration from Europe.—The difficulties they encountred from the resentment of the natives and other circumstances.—The French war in North America—The most distinguished heroes who fell in it; Wolf, Braddock, &c.—General Johnson,—his character.—North America why superior to South.—On Agriculture.—On commerce.—On science.—Whitefield,—his character.—The present glory of America.—A prospect of its future glory, in science,—in liberty,—and the gospel.—The conclusion of the whole.

LEANDER.

NO more of Memphis and her mighty kings,
Or Alexandria, where the Ptolomies
Taught golden commerce to unfurl her sails,
And bid fair science smile: No more of Greece
Where learning next her early visit paid,

And spread her glories to illume the world,
No more of Athens, where she flourished,
And saw her sons of mighty genius rise
Smooth flowing Plato, Socrates and him
Who with resistless eloquence reviv'd
The Spir't of LIBERTY, and shook the thrones
Of Macedon and Persia's haughty king.
No more of Rome enlighten'd by her beams,
Fresh kindling there the fire of eloquence,
And poesy divine; imperial Rome!
Whose wide dominion reach'd o'er half the globe;
Whose eagle flew o'er Ganges to the East,
And in the West far to the British isles.
No more of Britain, and her kings renown'd,
Edward's and Henry's thunderbolts of war;
Her chiefs victorious o'er the Gallic foe;
Illustrious senators, immortal bards,
And wise philosophers, of these no more.
A Theme more new, tho' not less noble, claims
Our ev'ry thought on this auspicious day;
The rising glory of this western world,
Where now the dawning light of science spreads
Her orient ray, and wakes the muse's song;
Where freedom holds her sacred standard high,
And commerce rolls her golden tides profuse
Of elegance and ev'ry joy of life.

ACASTO.

Since then Leander you attempt a strain
So new, so noble and so full of fame;
And since a friendly concourse centers here
America's own sons, begin O muse!
Now thro' the veil of ancient days review
The period fam'd when first Columbus touch'd
The shore so long unknown, thro' various toils,
Famine and death, the hero made his way,
Thro' oceans bellowing with eternal storms.
But why, thus hap'ly found, should we resume
The tale of Cortez, furious chief, ordain'd
With Indian blood to dye the sands, and choak

Fam'd Amazonia's stream with dead! Or why,
Once more revive the story old in fame,
Of Atabilipa by thirst of gold
Depriv'd of life: which not Peru's rich ore,
Nor Mexico's vast mines cou'd then redeem.
Better these northern realms deserve our song,
Discover'd by Britannia for her sons;
Undeluged with seas of Indian blood,
Which cruel Spain on southern regions spilt;
To gain by terrors what the gen'rous breast
Wins by fair treaty, conquers without blood.

EUGENIO.

High in renown th' intrepid hero stands,
From Europes shores advent'ring first to try
New seas, new oceans, unexplor'd by man.
Fam'd Cabot too may claim our noblest song,
Who from th' Atlantic surge descry'd these shores,
As on he coasted from the Mexic bay
To Acady and piny Labradore.
Nor less than him the muse would celebrate
Bold Hudson stemming to the pole, thro' seas
Vex'd with continual storms, thro' the cold straits,
Where Europe and America oppose
Their shores contiguous, and the northern sea
Confin'd, indignant, swells and roars between.
With these be number'd in the list of fame
Illustrious Raleigh, hapless in his fate:
Forgive me Raleigh, if an infant muse
Borrows thy name to grace her humble strain;
By many nobler are thy virtues sung;
Envy no more shall throw them in the shade;
They pour new lustre on Britannia's isle.
Thou too, advent'rous on th' Atlantic main,
Burst thro' its storms and fair Virginia hail'd.
The simple natives saw thy canvas flow,
And gaz'd aloof upon the shady shore:
For in her woods America contain'd,
From times remote, a savage race of men.
How shall we know their origin, how tell,
From whence or where the Indian tribes arose?

ACASTO.

And long has this defy'd the sages skill
T' investigate: Tradition seems to hide
The mighty secret from each mortal eye,
How first these various nations South and North
Possest these shores, or from what countries came.
Whether they sprang from some premoeval head
In their own lands, like Adam in the East;
Yet this the sacred oracles deny,
And reason too reclaims against the thought.
For when the gen'ral deluge drown'd the world,
Where could their tribes have found security?
Where find their fate but in the ghastly deep?
Unless, as others dream, some chosen few
High on the Andes 'scap'd the gen'ral death,
High on the Andes wrapt in endless snow,
Where winter in his wildest fury reigns.
But here Philosophers oppose the scheme,
The earth, say they, nor hills nor mountains knew
E'er yet the universal flood prevail'd:
But when the mighty waters rose aloft
Rous'd by the winds, they shook their solid case
And in convulsions tore the drowned world!
'Till by the winds assuag'd they quickly fell
And all their ragged bed exposed to view.
Perhaps far wand'ring towards the northern pole,
The straits of Zembla and the Frozen Zone,
And where the eastern Greenland almost joins
America's north point, the hardy tribes
Of banish'd Jews, Siberians, Tartars wild
Came over icy mountains, or on floats
First reach'd these coasts hid from the world beside.
And yet another argument more strange
Reserv'd for men of deeper thought and late
Presents itself to view: In Peleg's days,
So says the Hebrew seer's inspired pen,
This mighty mass of earth, this solid globe
Was cleft in twain—cleft east and west apart
While strait between the deep Atlantic roll'd.
And traces indisputable remain

Of this unhappy land now sunk and lost;
The islands rising in the eastern main
Are but small fragments of this continent,
Whose two extremities were Newfoundland
And St. Helena.—One far in the north
Where British seamen now with strange surprise
Behold the pole star glitt'ring o'er their heads;
The other in the southern tropic rears
Its head above the waves; Bermudas and
Canary isles, Britannia and th' Azores,
With fam'd Hibernia are but broken parts
Of some prodigious waste which once sustain'd
Armies by lands, where now but ships can range.

LEANDER.

Your sophistry Acasto makes me smile;
The roving mind of man delights to dwell
On hidden things, merely because they're hid;
He thinks his knowledge ne'er can reach too high
And boldly pierces nature's inmost haunts
But for uncertainties; your broken isles,
Your northern Tartars, and your wand'ring Jews,
Hear what the voice of history proclaims.
The Carthaginians, e'er the Roman yoke
Broke their proud spirits and enslav'd them too,
For navigation were renown'd as much
As haughty Tyre with all her hundred fleets;
Full many a league their vent'rous seamen sail'd
Thro' strait Gibralter down the western shore
Of Africa, and to Canary isles
By them call'd fortunate, so Flaccus sings,
Because eternal spring there crowns the fields,
And fruits delicious bloom throughout the year.
From voyaging here this inference I draw,
Perhaps some barque with all her num'rous crew
Caught by the eastern trade wind hurry'd on
Before th' steady blast to Brazil's shore,
New Amazonia and the coasts more south.
Here standing and unable to return,
For ever from their native skies estrang'd,

Doubtless they made the unknown land their own,
And in the course of many rolling years
A num'rous progeny from these arose,
And spread throughout the coasts; those whom we call
Brazilians, Mexicans, Peruvians rich,
Th' tribes of Chili, Patagon and those
Who till the shores of Amazon's long stream.
When first the pow'rs of Europe here attain'd
Vast empires, kingdoms, cities, palaces
And polish'd nations stock'd the fertile land;
Who has not heard of Cusco, Lima and
The town of Mexico; huge cities form'd
From Europe's architecture, e'er the arms
Of haughty Spain disturb'd the peaceful soil.

EUGENIO.

Such disquisition leads the puzzled mind
From maze to maze by queries still perplex'd.
But this we know, if from the east they came
Where science first and revelation beam'd,
Long since they've lost all memory, all trace
Of this their origin: Tradition tells
Of some great forefather beyond the lakes
Oswego, Huron, Mechigan, Champlaine
Or by the stream of Amazon which rolls
Thro' many a clime; while others simply dream
That from the Andes or the mountains north,
Some hoary fabled ancestor came down
To people this their world.

LEANDER.

How fallen, Oh!
How much obscur'd is human nature here!
Shut from the light of science and of truth
They wander'd blindfold down the steep of time;
Dim superstition with her ghastly train
Of daemons, spectres and forboding signs
Still urging them to horrid rites and forms
Of human sacrifice, to sooth the pow'rs

Malignant, and the dark infernal king.
Once on this spot perhaps a wigwam stood
With all its rude inhabitants, or round
Some mighty fire an hundred savage sons
Gambol'd by day, and filled the night with cries;
In what superior to the brutal race
That fled before them thro' the howling wilds,
Were all those num'rous tawny tribes which swarm'd
From Baffin's bay to Del Fuego south,
From California to the Oronoque.
Far from the reach of fame they liv'd unknown
In listless slumber and inglorious ease;
To them fair science never op'd her stores,
Nor sacred truth sublim'd the soul to God;
No fix'd abode their wand'ring genius knew;
No golden harvest crown'd the fertile glebe;
No city then adorn'd the rivers bank,
Nor rising turret overlook'd the stream.

ACASTO.

Now view the prospect chang'd; far off at sea
The mariner descry's our spacious towns
He hails the prospect of the land and views
A new, a fair a fertile world arise;
Onward from India's isles far east, to us
Now fair-ey'd commerce stretches her white sails,
Learning exalts her head, the graces smile
And peace establish'd after horrid war
Improves the splendor of these early times.
But come my friends and let us trace the steps
By which this recent happy world arose,
To this fair eminence of high renown
This height of wealth, of liberty and fame.

LEANDER.

Speak then Eugenio, for I've heard you tell
The pleasing hist'ry, and the cause that brought
The first advent'rers to these happy shores;
The glorious cause that urg'd our fathers first

To visit climes unknown and wilder woods
Than e'er Tartarian or Norwegian saw,
And with fair culture to adorn that soil
Which never knew th' industrious swain before.

EUGENIO.

All this long story to rehearse would tire,
Besides the sun toward the west retreats,
Nor can the noblest tale retard his speed,
Nor loftiest verse; not that which sung the fall
Of Troy divine and smooth Scamander's stream.
Yet hear a part.—By persecution wrong'd
And popish cruelty, our fathers came
From Europe's shores to find this blest abode,
Secure from tyranny and hateful man.
For this they left their country and their friends
And plough'd th' Atlantic wave in quest of peace;
And found new shores and sylvan settlements
Form'd by the care of each advent'rous chief,
Who, warm in liberty and freedom's cause,
Sought out uncultivated tracts and wilds,
And fram'd new plans of cities, governments
And spacious provinces: Why should I name
Thee Penn, the Solon of our western lands;
Sagacious legislator, whom the world
Admires tho' dead: an infant colony
Nurs'd by thy care, now rises o'er the rest
Like that tall Pyramid on Memphis' stand
O'er all the lesser piles, they also great.
Why should I name those heroes so well known
Who peopled all the rest from Canada
To Georgia's farthest coasts, West Florida
Or Apalachian mountains, yet what streams
Of blood were shed! What Indian hosts were slain
Before the days of peace were quite restor'd.

LEANDER.

Yes, while they overturn'd the soil untill'd,
And swept the forests from the shaded plain

'Midst dangers, foes and death, fierce Indian tribes
With deadly malice arm'd and black design,
Oft murder'd half the hapless colonies.
Encourag'd too by that inglorious race
False Gallia's sons, who once their arms display'd
At Quebec, Montreal and farthest coasts
Of Labrador and Esquimaux where now
The British standard awes the coward host.
Here those brave chiefs, who lavish of their blood
Fought in Britannia's cause, most nobly fell.
What Heart but mourns the untimely fate of Wolf,
Who dying conquer'd, or what breast but beats
To share a fate like his, and die like him?

ACASTO.

And he demands our lay who bravely fell
By Monangahela and the Ohio's stream;
By wiles o'ercome the hapless hero fell,
His soul too gen'rous for that dastard crew
Who kill unseen and shun the face of day.
Ambush'd in wood, and swamp and thick grown hill,
The bellowing tribes brought on the savage war.
What could avail O Braddock then the flame,
The gen'rous flame which fir'd thy martial soul!
What could avail Britannia's warlike troops,
Choice spirits of her isle? What could avail
America's own sons? The skulking foe,
Hid in the forest lay and fought secure,
What could the brave Virginians do o'erpower'd
By such vast numbers and their leader dead?
'Midst fire and death they bore him from the field,
Where in his blood full many a hero lay.
'Twas there O Halkut![2] thou so nobly fell,
Thrice valiant Halkut early son of fame!
We still deplore a fate so immature,
Fair Albion mourns thy unsuccessful end,
And Caledonia sheds a tear for him
Who led the bravest of her sons to war.

EUGENIO.

But why alas commemorate the dead?
And pass those glorious heroes by, who yet
Breathe the same air and see the light with us?
The dead, Acasto are but empty names
And he who dy'd to day the same to us
As he who dy'd a thousand years ago.
A Johnson[3] lives, among the sons of fame
Well known, conspicuous as the morning star
Among the lesser lights: A patriot skill'd
In all the glorious arts of peace or war.
He for Britannia gains the savage race,
Unstable as the sea, wild as the winds,
Cruel as death, and treacherous as hell,
Whom none but he by kindness yet could win,
None by humanity could gain their souls,
Or bring from woods and subteranean dens
The skulking crew, before a Johnson rose,
Pitying their num'rous tribes: ah how unlike
The Cortez' and Acosta's, pride of Spain
Whom blood and murder only satisfy'd.
Behold their doleful regions overflow'd
With gore, and blacken'd with ten thousand deaths
From Mexico to Patagonia far,
Where howling winds sweep round the southern cape,
And other suns and other stars arise!

ACASTO.

Such is the curse Eugenio where the soul
Humane is wanting, but we boast no feats
Of cruelty like Spain's unfeeling sons.
The British Epithet is merciful:
And we the sons of Britain learn like them
To conquer and to spare; for coward souls
Seek their revenge but on a vanquish'd foe.
Gold, fatal gold was the alluring bait
To Spain's rapacious mind, hence rose the wars
From Chili to the Caribbean sea,
O'er Terra-Firma and La Plata wide.
Peru then sunk in ruins, great before

With pompous cities, monuments superb
Whose tops reach'd heav'n. But we more happy boast
No golden metals in our peaceful land,
No flaming diamond, precious emerald,
Or blushing saphire, ruby, chrysolite
Or jasper red; more noble riches flow
From agriculture and th' industrious swain,
Who tills the fertile vale or mountain's brow,
Content to lead a safe, a humble life
'Midst his own native hills; romantic scenes,
Such as the muse of Greece did feign so well,
Envying their lovely bow'rs to mortal race.

LEANDER.

Long has the rural life been justly fam'd;
And poets old their pleasing pictures drew
Of flow'ry meads, and groves and gliding streams.
Hence old Arcadia, woodnymphs, satyrs, fauns,
And hence Elysium, fancy'd heav'n below.
Fair agriculture, not unworthy kings,
Once exercis'd the royal hand, or those
Whose virtue rais'd them to the rank of gods.
See old Laertes in his shepherd weeds,
Far from his pompous throne at court august,
Digging the grateful soil, where peaceful blows
The west wind murm'ring thro' the aged trees
Loaded with apples red, sweet scented peach
And each luxurious fruit the world affords,
While o'er the fields the harmless oxen draw
Th' industrious plough. The Roman heroes too
Fabricius and Camillus lov'd a life
Of sweet simplicity and rustic joy;
And from the busy Forum hast'ning far,
'Midst woods and fields spent the remains of age.
How grateful to behold the harvests rise
And mighty crops adorn the golden plains?
Fair plenty smiles throughout, while lowing herds
Stalk o'er the grassy hill or level mead,
Or at some winding river slake their thirst.
Thus fares the rustic swain; and when the winds

Blow with a keener breath, and from the North
Pour all their tempests thro' a sunless sky,
Ice, sleet and rattling hail, secure he sits
In some thatch'd cottage fearless of the storm;
While on the hearth a fire still blazing high
Chears every mind, and nature sits serene
On ev'ry countenance, such the joys
And such the fate of those whom heav'n hath bless'd
With souls enamour'd of a country life.

EUGENIO.

Much wealth and pleasure agriculture brings;
Far in the woods she raises palaces,
Puisant states and crowded realms where late
A desart plain or frowning wilderness
Deform'd the view; or where with moving tents
The scatter'd nations seeking pasturage,
Wander'd from clime to clime incultivate;
Or where a race more savage yet than these,
In search of prey o'er hill and mountain rang'd,
Fierce as the tygers and the wolves they slew.
Thus lives th'Arabian and the Tartar wild
In woody wastes which never felt the plough;
But agriculture crowns our happy land,
And plants our colonies from north to south,
From Cape Breton far as the Mexic bay
From th' Eastern shores to Missisippi's stream.
Famine to us unknown, rich plenty reigns
And pours her blessings with a lavish hand.

LEANDER.

Nor less from golden commerce flow the streams
Of richest plenty on our smiling land.
Now fierce Bellona must'ring all her rage,
To other climes and other seas withdraws,
To rouse the Russian on the desp'rate Turk
There to conflict by Danube and the straits
Which join the Euxine to th' Egean Sea.
Britannia holds the empire of the waves,

And welcomes ev'ry bold adventurer
To view the wonders of old Ocean's reign.
Far to the east our fleets on traffic sail,
And to the west thro' boundless seas which not
Old Rome nor Tyre nor mightier Carthage knew.
Daughter of commerce, from the hoary deep
New-York emerging rears her lofty domes,
And hails from far her num'rous ships of trade,
Like shady forests rising on the waves.
From Europe's shores or from the Caribbees,
Homeward returning annually they bring
The richest produce of the various climes.
And Philadelphia mistress of our world,
The seat of arts, of science, and of fame
Derives her grandeur from the pow'r of trade.
Hail happy city where the muses stray,
Where deep philosophy convenes her sons
And opens all her secrets to their view!
Bids them ascend with Newton to the skies,
And trace the orbits of the rolling spheres,
Survey the glories of the universe,
Its suns and moons and ever blazing stars!
Hail city blest with liberty's fair beams,
And with the rays of mild religion blest!

ACASTO.

   Nor these alone, America, thy sons
In the short circle of a hundred years
Have rais'd with toil along thy shady shores.
On lake and bay and navigable stream,
From Cape Breton to Pensacola south,
Unnumber'd towns and villages arise.
By commerce nurs'd these embrio marts of trade
May yet awake the envy and obscure
The noblest cities of the eastern world;
For commerce is the mighty reservoir
From whence all nations draw the streams of gain.
'Tis commerce joins dissever'd worlds in one,
Confines old Ocean to more narrow bounds;
Outbraves his storms and peoples half his world.

EUGENIO.

And from the earliest times advent'rous man
On foreign traffic stretch'd the nimble sail;
Or sent the slow pac'd caravan afar
O'er barren wastes, eternal sands where not
The blissful haunt of human form is seen

Nor tree not ev'n funeral cypress sad
Nor bubbling fountain. Thus arriv'd of old
Golconda's golden ore, and thus the wealth
Of Ophir to the wisest of mankind.

LEANDER.

Great is the praise of commerce, and the men
Deserve our praise who spread from shore to shore
The flowing sail; great are their dangers too;
Death ever present to the fearless eye
And ev'ry billow but a gaping grave;
Yet all these mighty feats to science owe
Their rise and glory.—Hail fair science! thou
Transplanted from the eastern climes dost bloom
In these fair regions, Greece and Rome no more
Detain the muses on Cithaeron's brow,
Or old Olympus crown'd with waving woods;
Or Haemus' top where once was heard the harp,
Sweet Orpheus' harp that ravish'd hell below
And pierc'd the soul of Orcus and his bride.
That hush'd to silence by the song divine
Thy melancholy waters, and the gales
O Hebrus! which o'er thy sad surface blow.
No more the maids round Alpheus' waters stray
Where he with Arethusas' stream doth mix,
Or where swift Tiber disembogues his waves
Into th' Italian sea so long unsung.
Hither they've wing'd their way, the last, the best
Of countries where the arts shall rise and grow
Luxuriant, graceful; and ev'n now we boast
A Franklin skill'd in deep philosophy,
A genius piercing as th' electric fire,

Bright as the light'nings flash explain'd so well
By him the rival of Britannia's sage.
This is a land of ev'ry joyous sound
Of liberty and life; sweet liberty!
Without whose aid the noblest genius fails,
And science irretrievably must die.

ACASTO.

This is a land where the more noble light
Of holy revelation beams, the star
Which rose from Judah lights our skies, we feel
Its influence as once did Palestine
And Gentile lands, where now the ruthless Turk
Wrapt up in darkness sleeps dull life away.
Here many holy messengers of peace
As burning lamps have given light to men.
To thee, O Whitefield![4] favourite of Heav'n,
The muse would pay the tribute of a tear.
Laid in the dust thy eloquence no more
Shall charm the list'ning soul, no more
Thy bold imagination paint the scenes
Of woe and horror in the shades below;
Or glory radiant in the fields above;
No more thy charity relieve the poor;
Let Georgia mourn, let all her orphans weep.

LEANDER.

Yet tho' we wish'd him longer from the skies,
And wept to see the ev'ning of his days,
He long'd himself to reach his final hope,
The crown of glory for the just prepar'd.
From life's high verge he hail'd th' eternal shore
And, freed at last from his confinement, rose
An infant seraph to the worlds on high.

EUGENIO.

For him we sound the melancholy lyre,
The lyre responsive to each distant sigh;

No grief like that which mourns departing souls
Of holy, just and venerable men,
Whom pitying Heav'n sends from their native skies
To light our way and bring us nearer God.
But come Leander since we know the past
And present glory of this empire wide,
What hinders to pervade with searching eye
The mystic scenes of dark futurity?
Say shall we ask what empires yet must rise
What kingdoms pow'rs and states where now are seen
But dreary wastes and awful solitude,
Where melancholy sits with eye forlorn
And hopes the day when Britain's sons shall spread
Dominion to the north and south and west
Far from th' Atlantic to Pacific shores?
A glorious theme, but how shall mortals dare
To pierce the mysteries of future days,
And scenes unravel only known to fate.

ACASTO.

This might we do if warm'd by that bright coal
Snatch'd from the altar of seraphic fire,
Which touch'd Isaiah's lips, or if the spirit
Of Jeremy and Amos, prophets old,
Should fire the breast; but yet I call the muse
And what we can will do. I see, I see
A thousand kingdoms rais'd, cities and men
Num'rous as sand upon the ocean shore;
Th' Ohio then shall glide by many a town
Of note: and where the Missisippi stream
By forests shaded now runs weeping on
Nations shall grow and states not less in fame
Than Greece and Rome of old: we too shall boast
Our Alexanders, Pompeys, heroes, kings
That in the womb of time yet dormant lye
Waiting the joyful hour for life and light.
O snatch us hence, ye muses! to those days
When, through the veil of dark antiquity,
Our sons shall hear of us as things remote,
That blossom'd in the morn of days, alas!

How could I weep that we were born so soon,
In the beginning of more happy times!
But yet perhaps our fame shall last unhurt.
The sons of science nobly scorn to die
Immortal virtue this denies, the muse
Forbids the men to slumber in the grave
Who well deserve the praise that virtue gives.

EUGENIO.

'Tis true no human eye can penetrate
The veil obscure, and in fair light disclos'd
Behold the scenes of dark futurity;
Yet if we reason from the course of things,
And downward trace the vestiges of time,
The mind prophetic grows and pierces far
Thro' ages yet unborn. We saw the states
And mighty empires of the East arise
In swift succession from the Assyrian
To Macedon and Rome; to Britain thence
Dominion drove her car, she stretch'd her reign
Oer many isles, wide seas, and peopled lands.
Now in the West a continent appears;
A newer world now opens to her view;
She hastens onward to th' Americ shores
And bids a scene of recent wonders rise.
New states new empires and a line of kings,
High rais'd in glory, cities, palaces
Fair domes on each long bay, sea, shore or stream
Circling the hills now rear their lofty heads.
Far in the Arctic skies a Petersburgh,
A Bergen, or Archangel lifts its spires
Glitt'ring with Ice, far in the West appears
A new Palmyra or an Ecbatan
And sees the slow pac'd caravan return
O'er many a realm from the Pacific shore,
Where fleets shall then convey rich Persia's silks,
Arabia's perfumes, and spices rare
Of Philippine, Coelebe and Marian isles,
Or from the Acapulco coast our India then,
Laden with pearl and burning gems and gold.

Far in the South I see a Babylon,
As once by Tigris or Euphrates stream,
With blazing watch towr's and observatories
Rising to heav'n; from thence astronomers
With optic glass take nobler views of God
In golden suns and shining worlds display'd
Than the poor Chaldean with the naked eye.
A Niniveh where Oronoque descends
With waves discolour'd from the Andes high,
Winding himself around a hundred isles
Where golden buildings glitter o'er his tide.
To mighty nations shall the people grow
Which cultivate the banks of many a flood,
In chrystal currents poured from the hills
Apalachia nam'd, to lave the sands
Of Carolina, Georgia, and the plains
Stretch'd out from thence far to the burning Line,
St Johns or Clarendon or Albemarle.
And thou Patowmack navigable stream,
Rolling thy waters thro' Virginia's groves,
Shall vie with Thames, the Tiber or the Rhine,
For on thy banks I see an hundred towns
And the tall vessels wafted down thy tide.
Hoarse Niagara's stream now roaring on
Thro' woods and rocks and broken mountains torn,
In days remote far from their antient beds,
By some great monarch taught a better course,
Or cleared of cataracts shall flow beneath
Unnumbr'd boats and merchandize and men;
And from the coasts of piny Labradore,
A thousand navies crowd before the gale,
And spread their commerce to remotest lands,
Or bear their thunder round the conquered world.

LEANDER.

And here fair freedom shall forever reign.
I see a train, a glorious train appear,
Of Patriots plac'd in equal fame with those
Who nobly fell for Athens or for Rome.
The sons of Boston resolute and brave

The firm supporters of our injur'd rights,
Shall lose their splendours in the brighter beams
Of patriots fam'd and heroes yet unborn.

ACASTO.

'Tis but the morning of the world with us
And Science yet but sheds her orient rays.
I see the age the happy age roll on
Bright with the splendours of her mid-day beams,
I see a Homer and a Milton rise
In all the pomp and majesty of song,
Which gives immortal vigour to the deeds
Atchiev'd by Heroes in the fields of fame.
A second Pope, like that Arabian bird
Of which no age can boast but one, may yet
Awake the muse by Schuylkill's silent stream,
And bid new forests bloom along her tide.
And Susquehanna's rocky stream unsung,
In bright meanders winding round the hills,
Where first the mountain nymph sweet echo heard
The uncouth musick of my rural lay,
Shall yet remurmur to the magic sound
Of song heroic, when in future days
Some noble Hambden rises into fame.

LEANDER.

Or Roanoke's and James's limpid waves
The sound of musick murmurs in the gale;
Another Denham celebrates their flow,
In gliding numbers and harmonious lays.

EUGENIO.

Now in the bow'rs of Tuscororah hills,
As once on Pindus all the muses stray,
New Theban bards high soaring reach the skies
And swim along thro' azure deeps of air.

LEANDER.

From Alleghany in thick groves imbrown'd,
Sweet music breathing thro' the shades of night
Steals on my ear, they sing the origin
Of those fair lights which gild the firmament;
From whence the gale that murmurs in the pines;
Why flows the stream down from the mountains brow
And rolls the ocean lower than the land.
They sing the final destiny of things,
The great result of all our labours here,
The last day's glory, and the world renew'd.
Such are their themes for in these happier days
The bard enraptur'd scorns ignoble strains,
Fair science smiling and full truth revealed,
The world at peace, and all her tumults o'er,
The blissful prelude to Emanuel's reign.

EUGENIO.

And when a train of rolling years are past,
(So sang the exil'd seer in Patmos isle,)
A new Jerusalem sent down from heav'n
Shall grace our happy earth, perhaps this land,
Whose virgin bosom shall then receive, tho' late,
Myriads of saints with their almighty king,
To live and reign on earth a thousand years
Thence call'd Millennium. Paradise a new
Shall flourish, by no second Adam lost.
No dang'rous tree or deathful fruit shall grow,
No tempting serpent to allure the soul,
From native innocence; a Canaan here
Another Canaan shall excel the old
And from fairer Pisgah's top be seen,
No thistle here or briar or thorn shall spring
Earth's curse before: the lion and the lamb
In mutual friendship link'd shall browse the shrub,
And tim'rous deer with rabid tygers stray
O'er mead or lofty hill or grassy plain.
Another Jordan's stream shall glide along
And Siloah's brook in circling eddies flow,

Groves shall adorn their verdant banks, on which
The happy people free from second death
Shall find secure repose; no fierce disease
No fevers, slow consumption, direful plague
Death's ancient ministers, again renew
Perpetual war with man: Fair fruits shall bloom
Fair to the eye, sweet to the taste, if such
Divine inhabitants could need the taste
Of elemental food, amid the joys
Fit for a heav'nly nature. Music's charms
Shall swell the lofty soul and harmony
Triumphant reign; thro' ev'ry grove shall sound
The cymbal and the lyre, joys too divine
For fallen man to know. Such days the world
And such America thou first shall have
When ages yet to come have run their round
And future years of bliss alone remain.

ACASTO.

This is thy praise America thy pow'r
Thou best of climes by science visited
By freedom blest and richly stor'd with all
The luxuries of life. Hail happy land
The seat of empire the abode of kings,
The final stage where time shall introduce
Renowned characters, and glorious works
Of high invention and of wond'rous art,
Which not the ravages of time shall waste
Till he himself has run his long career;
Till all those glorious orbs of light on high
The rolling wonders that surround the ball,
Drop from their spheres extinguish'd and consum'd;
When final ruin with her fiery car
Rides o'er creation, and all nature's works
Are lost in chaos and the womb of night.

NOTES ON THE POEMS

Promotional Verse

"Newes from Virginia": 1. Sir Thomas Gates (fl. 1585-1621), colonial Governor of Virginia, and Christopher Newport (1565?-1617), commander of the voyage. 2. Bermuda.

"Spurring-Verses": 1. Lit. Here do you labor in service to elevate others to a throne;/ There will a generous soil reward your labor with usury. (John Mulder) 2. Lit. change its light. 3. River for which Amsterdam is named. 4. Lit. and give honor to the government for the wisdom of its rule. 5. Lit. whose members are deeply touched by the common welfare (as their own). 6. The mouth of the Amstel river.

Puritan Verse

"Of the wonder-working providences": 1. Glover, Green, Harver etc., New England ministers.

"From their Sleeping": 1. Of coarse grass.

Anne Bradstreet. "THE PROLOGUE": 1. Guillaume Salluste Du Bartas (1544-1590), French poet admired and often imitated by the Puritans. "To my Dear and loving Husband": 1. Anne Bradstreet's husband was Simon Bradstreet (1603-1697), Governor of the colony. "Another": 1. Launches. "The Author to her Book": 1. The first edition of Anne Bradstreet's poems was published in England, apparently by her friends and without her consent.

Nathaniel Ward, poem on Anne Bradstreet: 1. Out of weariness. 2. Shod.

Michael Wigglesworth. "GOD'S CONTROVERSY WITH NEW-ENGLAND": 1. The threats delivered by almighty God with royal voice,/ The announcements in which all the prophets concur,/ And my own tearful testimony on the divine anger,/ O reader and friend, do not take these as fancies. (John Mulder) 2. Archaic past of 'pitch.' 3. Cast down, dishearten. 4. Astonishment. 5. Burn. "Meditation": 1. Soap used for cleansing cloth. 2. Panacea.

"On the following Work": 1. Wigglesworth began writing verse when his long illness kept him from preaching. 2. Alluding to Wigglesworth's *Meat out of the Eater* (1670).

"New-Englands Crisis": 1. Pumpkin. 2. Buns made of fine flour. 3. Johnny cake or Journey cake; small loaves of corn bread. 4. Comets portending disaster. 5. Checked sharply. 6. ? The whole passage is a rendition of Indian speech. 7. Trips by horse and cart. 8. Wintry. 9. Crazy. 10. Official death tolls. 11. Dirty, unclarified fat. 12. Samuel Newman (1600-1663), first minister of Rehoboth.

"An Almanack for . . . 1647": 1. Obscure. The coal-white bird may be, as Kenneth Murdock suggests (*Handkerchiefs from Paul*), white men living among Indians, or God's grace, or a fever. If the last, the line "Only to shake you by your hands?" is a pun. Perhaps the black and white bird refers to the almanac itself. 2. A brook? The almanac? 3. Probably the factions on different sides of the May elections (White royalist.) 4. Murdock suggests that this stanza is a dialogue

between the orthodox (11. 1-2, 5-6) and their opponents. 5. Supply ships. 6. Meeting of the New England Confederacy. 7. Cf. *Judges* ix, 8-15. 8. Winter cold? 9. The cold freezes lakes and streams into "Great bridges."

"An Almanack for . . . 1657": 1. Vergil, Eclogue IV: See how all things rejoice in the coming of the new age. (John Mulder) 2. Causes them to be.

"An Almanack of Coelestiall Motions": 1. Stormy weather. 2. Cancer, fourth sign of the zodiac, announces summer.

The Puritan Elegy

"Thomas Dudley": 1. Anne Bradstreet's father (1576-1653); served as Governor of the colony for four terms.

"Upon the TOMB of . . . *John Cotton*": 1. John Norton (1606-1663), successor to John Cotton as pastor of the first church of Boston.

"A *Threnodia*": 1. See note 1 directly above. 2. The stone erected by Samuel to commemorate the victory over the Philistines. 3. An extract of the vital nature of something.

"Upon . . . William Tompson": 1. The elder Tompson, father of the poet, went insane.

"Gulielmi Tompsoni": 1. Name given by Christ to the two sons of Zebedee; a zealous preacher.

"Upon the setting of . . . John Winthrop": 1. Winthrop was known for his alchemical researches. 2. Pertaining to a chief physician, originally of the court of a Hellenistic king or Roman emperor.

"An Elegie upon . . . Thomas Shepard": 1. John Wilson (1588-1667) was for thirty-seven years minister of the Boston church. 2. John Leverett (1662-1724), president of Harvard from 1707-1724.

"LAMENTATIONS Upon . . . Sir WILLIAM PHIPS": 1. French and Indians. 2. On a treasure hunt, Phips recovered 300,000 £ of Spanish gold from the sunken galleon of Governor Boadilla. 3. Aboard the galleon was a table of gold weighing 3300 pounds.

"Of John Bunyans Life": 1. Freed of blemishes.

"Epitaph": 1. Shubael Dummer, pastor at York, was slain by some Indians in 1691.

"GRATITUDINIS ERGO": 1. Ezekiel Cheever (1616-1708) was master of the Boston Latin School for thirty-eight years. 2. In a reverend song I touch briefly on praiseworthy deeds, which no power of speech can justly celebrate. (John Mulder) 3. ? Perhaps Mather is thinking of Saint Sebastian. 4. Referring to the church in Loretto, Sicily, purported to have been the house of the Virgin Mary in Nazareth. 5. Elijah Corlet (c. 1610-1687) was master of the Grammar School at Cambridge for forty years. 6. Abraham's concubine; a servant or slave. 7. William Lilly (c. 1460-1522), author of a popular Latin grammar. 8. Angel of good. 9. A favorite Puritan description of prayer, borrowed from George Herbert. 10. John Davenport (1597-1670), founder of the New Haven colony. 11. I have omitted Mather's forty-line Latin epitaph on Cheever.

"A Mournful Lamentation": 1. The poem deals with the withdrawal from circulation of paper notes. The notes had been issued by Massachusetts to pay soldiers who served in the Canadian campaign.

Edward Taylor

N.B. Very full notes on Taylor's poems may be found in the glossary of Donald E. Stanford's *The Poems of Edward Taylor* (New Haven, 1960), pp. 523-543, from which some of the following notes are derived.

"The Reflexion": 1. Apparently a reference, one of many in Taylor's verse, to a mystical vision at Communion.

"6. Meditation": 1. Pun on the name of the seventeenth-century coin.

"10. Meditation": 1. Awning. 2. Small soup bowl.

"29. Meditation": 1. Woolgathering. 2. The musical scale.

"32. Meditation": 1. Knotty, twisted. 2. Tangles.

"40. Meditation": 1. Giants of Canaan who were slain by the Israelites. 2. A tub used for boiling yarn.

"Meditation 44": 1. The union of the divine and human in Christ. 2. Bows.

"56. Meditation": 1. On this and the following allusions see Stanford, p. 180. Taylor drew much of the imagery of the poem from Peter Heylyn's *Cosmographie* (1657). 2. An automaton built by Aquinas' teacher, Albertus Magnus. Aquinas destroyed the machine because it interfered with his studies. See Robert R. Hodges, "Edward Taylor's 'Artificiall Man'," *American Literature,* XXXI (1959), 76-77.

"66. Meditation": 1. Ornamental work. 2. Tumult.

"161A. Meditation": 1. Pustule. 2. A shrivelled apple. 3. Reference to a current story about a squirrel who warded off a rattlesnake by holding a snake egg up to it. See Stanford, p. 375, n. 23.

"Let by rain": 1. Hindered. 2. Sour.

"Huswifery": 1. Devices that twist thread and wind it around the bobbin. 2. Mills where cloth is pressed and cleansed.

Later New England Verse

"To John Saffin": 1. Saffin had presented a lawsuit to bring Adam, a Negro, back into slavery. 2. Text: bold/sworn.

"On C. Mr's Diploma": 1. Nathaniel Parkhurst, English divine who argued for cheerfulness in religious worship, publisher of Mather's *Magnalia*. The poem may have been written by Thomas Banister (1684-1716).

"A Prefatory Poem, on that Excellent Book": 1. The Quakers. 2. An unlocated Babylonian town. 3. A priestly family. 4. Brooches.

"A Brief Account of the Agency of . . . John Winthrop": 1. Probably Rev. John Warham, a minister aboard the *Mary and John,* one of the eleven ships in the 1630 migration. 2. Venomous serpents.

"Commencement": 1. Dupes, simpletons.

"The Times": 1. Plautus, *Capteivi*, I, 119: "Well of course, sir, we'd all rather be free than slaves" (Loeb) 2. Here and throughout the poem Church regrets his youthful panegyrics to the King, printed in *Pietas et Gratulatio*. 3. John Wilkes (1727-1797), who in his periodical *The North Briton* attacked the government's foreign policy. 4. A judge who declared illegal George III's warrant imprisoning Wilkes. 5. George. 6. Britons. 7. Scotch. 8. William Murray, Earl of Mansfield (1705-1793), attorney general of England, was accused of showing prejudice against Wilkes. 9. Richard Temple (1711-1779) defrayed the expenses for Wilkes' defense. 10. John Stuart, third earl of Bute (1713-1792), influential privy councilor and later prime minister. 11. George Grenville (1712-1770), who initiated the prosecution of Wilkes and proposed the Stamp Act of 1765. 12. In *North Briton* no. 36, Wilkes remarks that "the whole race of the *Nassaus* has been renowned for a love of liberty and their country. . . ." 13. Stampman.

Southern Verse

"Upon the Death of G. B.": 1. Rocket. On the possible authorship of Bacons Epitaph see Jay B. Hubbell, "John and Ann Cotton, of 'Queen's Creek,' Virginia," *American Literature*, X (May 1938), 179-201.

William Byrd. "Long has the Furious Priest": 1. The poem endorses the efforts of Governor Spotswood to convert the Indians to Christianity. "Upon a Sigh": Byrd's rendering of a poem by Anne, Countess of Winchelsea (1666-1720).

"TYPOGRAPHIA": 1. Sir William Gooch (1681-1751), popular colonial Governor of Virginia, argued the planters' interests before the London Board of Trade. 2. On Parks, see the Introduction to this section. In his introductory epistle to Gooch, Markland says that the poem was "occasion'd by the setting up a *Printing-Press* in *Williamsburg*," and he calls the poem "the first Essay of this Kind attempted here."

"The Sot-weed Factor": 1. sot-weed—tobacco, the weed that inebriates. 2. The gallows. 3. A dram that whets the appetite. 4. Liquor in an effervescent state. 5. A tobacco pipe. 6. Kidnapped. 7. Bag, pouch. 8. Sweetheart. 9. A delusion. 10. The jack of trumps, the highest card in the deck. 11. Woman (Dutch). 12. Prostitute. 13. A thistle valued for its healing powers. 14. Now Hampton Roads, Virginia.

Richard Lewis. "To . . . CALVERT": 1. Edward Holdsworth (1684-1746), English classicist and poet. His Latin poem *Muscipula* appeared first in 1709 and was translated into English ten times in the eighteenth century. "CARMEN SECULARE": 1. "I . . . joined in rendering the hymn welcome to the gods what time the cycle brought 'round again the festal days." (Loeb) 2. Cecilius Calvert, 2d Baron Baltimore (c. 1605-1675) received the province in 1632 in place of his father, who died as the charter was being issued. 3. By an act of 1640 allowing liberty of conscience to all believers in Christ, a fine was laid on any planted who reviled another with the name of a party or faction. 4. James Edward Oglethorpe (1696-1785), who founded Georgia as an asylum for debtor classes.

"ABSENCE": *The poem was written sometime before 1775. See Allen Walker Read, "Boucher's Linguistic Pastoral," *Dialect Notes,* VI (1933), 353-354. The footnote numbers in the text refer to line numbers, 1-97. I have put the footnotes in serial form, 1-36.

"Expeditio Ultramontana": 1. A letter to the editor, accompanying the poem, explains that "The *College of Williamsburgh* is obliged to pay Two Copies of Latin Verses to the Governour, every Fifth of *November,* as Quit-Rent for the Land. The *November* after Col. *Spotswood,* and his Train, return'd from their Progress amongst the Mountains . . . Mr. *Blair,* the President, chose for his Subject 'The Suppression of *the late Rebellion*': and Mr. *Blackamore,* the Humanity Professor, composed an excellent Poem on this *Mountain Expedition;* which the late Rev. *George Seagood* turn'd into *English.* . . . ." Alexander Spotswood (1676-1740), colonial Governor of Virginia, explored the frontier and encouraged settlement there.

"The PAPER-MILL": 1. The poem first appeared in the July 26th issue of *The Virginia Gazette,* of which no copy exists. 2. Met. 1. 2. "My mind is bent to tell of bodies changed into new forms." (Loeb) 3. Leap year.

"A RHAPSODY on *RUM*": 1. Possibly Meta. 4. 11-13 "they burn incense, calling on Bacchus, naming him also Bromius, Lyaeus, son of twice born, child of two mothers." (Loeb)

James Sterling. "A PASTORAL": 1. Ecl. V, 34-35 and IX, 40-43 "thou alone givest glory to thy people. Since the Fates bore thee off, even Pales has left our fields, and even Apollo." "Here is rosy spring; here, by the streams, Earth scatters her varied flowers; here the white poplar bends over the cave, and the clinging vines weave shady bowers. Come to me—" (Loeb) 2. "The name taken by *Pope* in his 2d pastoral" (Sterling's note). 3. A cape near Delaware bay. 4. "The same as loud huzzas among the *English*" (Sterling's note). 5. "The name given by the *Indians* to the governor of *Pennsylvania*" (Sterling's note). 6. "The great pains Mr. *Thomas* took last war in pressing home the argument for defence; and the happy success his extraordinary industry in cultivating a friendship with the *Indians* was attended with. . . ." (Sterling's note). "*The 22d Ode . . . imitated*": 1. Jeffrey Amherst (1717-1797), supreme commander of the British forces during the French and Indian War. 2. A bull-baiting pit.

"C. W. *in* Carolina *to* E. J.": 1. Cleland was minister of Prince Frederick Parish. Powel and Trapier were local gentlemen. 2. Gentlemen of St. John's Parish. 3. Minister of Dorchester Parish, "an eloquent gentleman; the Cicero of *Carolina*" (Woodmason's note). 4. Apparently a Gosport friend. 5. Michi, Taylor, Drayton—local gentlemen.

"VERSES *Occasioned by the SUCCESS*": 1. John Stanwix (1690?-1766), major general in the British army in America, builder of Fort Stanwix. 2. Horatio Sharpe (1718-1790), Governor of Maryland, whose efforts to determine Maryland's boundaries eventuated in Mason and Dixon's line. 3. Hochkirch: village in central Germany where in October 1758 the Austrians defeated the Prussians under Frederick the Great. 4. Edward Boscawen (1711-1761), British admiral who fought the French in the mouth of the St. Lawrence river. 5. Sir George Pocock (1706-1792), British admiral who sailed against the French and in 1762 reduced Havana.

"On LIBERTY-TREE": 1. This tree will also be revered, the oak sacred to liberty. (John Mulder) Charleston, like Boston, had a Liberty Tree. 2. John Pym (1583?-1643) and John Hampden (1594-1643), Puritan leaders of Parliament, influential in forcing Charles I to convene the Long Parliament. Their arrests helped precipitate the civil war. 3. See "The Times," n. 12.

Verse of the Middle Colonies

Henricus Selijns. "Bridal Torch": 1. Shell money. 2. Lit. And he who gives us happiness, has the power to bring happiness to her. For us this wight is neither child of Mars, nor son of Venus, nor yet the unchaste one; rather, it is the urge that leads us to wedlock and bars us from uncleanness. Therefore, we wish them increase etc. (John Mulder)

"The Junto": 1. The musician in Dryden's "Alexander's Feast." Apparently the members of the Junto identified themselves with prominent English writers. "Denham" is probably Franklin; "Waller" is probably Breintnal. 2. Jonathan Belcher (1681-1757) was sent by Massachusetts to England over a dispute with its Governor. While in England he was himself made Governor of Massachusetts and New Hampshire, and his sympathies changed.

"To . . . WILLIAM KEITH": 1. Sir William Keith (1680-1749), colonial Governor of Pennsylvania, visited the Six Nations in New York and was known for his fair dealing with the Indians.

"*The Wits* and *Poets* of Pennsylvania": 1. Odes IV. vi. 30. "Twas Phoebus lent me inspiration, Phoebus the art of song, and gave me the name of poet." (Loeb) 2. Joseph Breintnal. 3. Jacob Taylor. 4. George Webb. 5. See Taylor's prefatory poem to "Batchelors-Hall" in this section. 6. Apparently a local stable keeper. 7. Probably Samuel Keimer. 8. Henry Brooke, a local collector of customs, author of the lost poem "A Discourse of Jests" (1705).

"Copy of Verses": 1. *De Legibus.* I. 37. "our whole discourse is intended to promote the firm foundation of States, the strengthening of cities, and the curing of the ills of the people." (Loeb) 2. Now Russia and Poland. 3. Charles Clinton, who led a regiment against Fort Frontenac. His son was George Clinton (1739-1812), later Governor of New York.

"PENNSYLVANIA": 1. Eugene of Savoy (1663-1736), prince of Savoy, who with Marlborough won the Battle of Blenheim. 2. "Alphonzo" and "Chamont" apparently refer by anastomasia to leaders of the Pennsylvania militia. 3. Robert Hunter Morris (c. 1700-1764), Governor of Pennsylvania (1754-1756).

Thomas Godfrey. "EPISTLE": 1. Nathaniel Evans, the "Friend" of the title. "Song V.": 1. This song was set to music by Francis Hopkinson.

"An ODE . . . To My Ingenious Friend": 1. Godfrey was serving in the militia in Wilmington, North Carolina.

Francis Hopkinson. "Science": 1. The College of Philadelphia. "The Battle of the Kegs": 1. Sir William Howe (1729-1814), commander-in-chief of the British army in America. His troops settled in Philadelphia for the winter after defeating Washington at Germantown. "Mrs. L——g": Mrs. Loring, Howe's mistress in Philadelphia. 2. Sir William Erskine (1728-1795), brigadier general under Howe.

The Rising Empire

"ON THE RISING GLORY OF AMERICA": 1. "There will come an age in the far-off years when Ocean shall unloose the bonds of things, when the whole broad earth shall be revealed, when Tethys shall disclose new worlds and Thule not be the limit of the lands." (Loeb) 2. Probably Sir Peter Halket (d. 1755), commander of a regiment of Scots troops, killed on Braddock's expedition against Fort Du Quesne. 3. Sir William Johnson (1715-1774), superintendent of Indian affairs in America, who led the Indians in the conquest of Canada. 4. George Whitefield (1714-1770), English Methodist preacher who made seven spectacularly successful missions to America and raised funds for an orphanage in Georgia.

DF

I